12 - 9

Performance Appraisal

Human Resource Management Series

This text is part of the Allyn and Bacon Human Resource Management Series.

Richard Arvey, Consulting Editor

Performance

Appraisal

An Organizational Perspective

Kevin R. Murphy

Jeanette N. Cleveland

Colorado State University

Allyn and Bacon

Boston   London   Toronto   Sydney   Tokyo   Singapore

Series Editor: Jack Peters
Series Editorial Assistant: Carol Alper
Production Administrator: Annette Joseph
Production Coordinator: Susan Freese
Editorial-Production Service: TKM Productions
Cover Administrator: Linda K. Dickinson
Cover Designer: Susan Slovinsky
Manufacturing Buyer: Megan Cochran

Copyright © 1991 by Allyn and Bacon
A Division of Simon & Schuster, Inc.
160 Gould Street
Needham Heights, Massachusetts 02194

Library of Congress Cataloging-in-Publication Data

Murphy, Kevin R.
    Performance appraisal : an organizational perspective / Kevin R.
Murphy, Jeanette N. Cleveland.
      p.   cm.
    Includes bibliographical references and index.
    ISBN 0-205-12343-0
    1. Employees — Rating of. I. Cleveland, Jeanette. II. Title.
HF5549.5.R3M86   1990
658.3'125 — dc20   90-36287
                                               CIP

Printed in the United States of America

10 9 8 7 6 5 4 3 2 1   95   94   93   92   91   90

Contents

Preface

▶ This book began on the back of a cocktail napkin. At a conference, over drinks with Cris Banks and Janet Barnes-Farrell, we debated the state of the art of performance appraisal research, bemoaning the lack of progress in several areas. Jan Cleveland suggested that a simpler model of the appraisal process was needed and sketched it out on the napkin. That model, with several modifications and elaborations, became the four-component model of the appraisal process in organizations that is used to organize this book.

We used this model to organize a graduate seminar on performance appraisal and became convinced that it provided a useful framework for thinking about performance appraisal research and application. In particular, we believe that the model helps to bridge the gap between research and practice in performance appraisal (Banks & Murphy, 1985). We should stress that this model is not unique, nor is it comprehensive. Rather than include all of the possible variables that are likely to affect appraisal, this model focuses on four that we believe are most critical to researchers and practitioners.

Our model emphasizes context as the most important issue in appraisal and treats appraisal as a goal-directed process in which the goals are shaped primarily by the organizational context in which rating occurs. Our focus on context leads us to emphasize certain issues that have not received enough attention in other models of appraisal and to deemphasize some issues that have been the subject of a great deal of research. Two examples help to illustrate this. First, we discuss at some length the way in which the legal environment might affect the goals of various constituencies in the performance appraisal process (e.g., the rater, the organization) but devote little attention to the specific cases or legal principles that currently apply to litigation involving performance appraisal. Second, we discuss some of the psychological issues involved in rater training but do not cover the rather sizable literature comparing various rater-training strategies in terms of criteria such as rater errors or rating accuracy.

Chapter One introduces the four-component model. Chapters Two through Four examine ways in which the rating context affects performance appraisal processes and outcomes. Chapter Two deals with the external environment, whereas Chapters Three and Four deal with the internal environments of organizations. Several levels of context — ranging from the sociopolitical, economic, and technological environment to organization-specific norms for conducting and using performance appraisals — are examined in these chapters. Particular attention is given in Chapter Four to the ways in which the explicit and implicit purposes of performance appraisal in organizations help to define the overall context of appraisal, which in turn substantially affects the behavior of all individuals involved in the appraisal system.

Chapters Five through Seven deal with the judgments raters make about their subordinates' performance. Chapter Five examines the methods by which raters obtain the information needed to evaluate ratees' performance. Chapter Six examines an issue that has been largely ignored in research on performance appraisal — the formation and application of standards for evaluating performance. Chapter Seven reviews a topic that has dominated psychological research on performance appraisal over the last ten years — cognitive and affective processes involved in performance appraisal.

Chapters Eight and Nine examine a wide range of factors that lead raters to distort their ratings, usually by giving higher ratings than they think ratees truly deserve. Chapter Eight suggests that this distortion should not be dismissed as error but rather should be examined as a set of conscious decisions by raters that advance important and relevant goals. Chapter Nine research on forces in the organization that often motivate raters to distort and inflate their ratings.

Chapters Ten and Eleven examine the criteria that are used to evaluate appraisal systems. These chapters suggest frameworks for choosing criteria that are relevant and that provide clear indications of whether or not ratings are useful to the rater, the ratee, and/or the organization.

Chapters Twelve and Thirteen contain a number of specific suggestions about promising directions for future research and application in the area of performance appraisal. Chapter Twelve contains 73 specific suggestions about future research directions; Chapter Thirteen contains 55 suggestions for applying existing research in organizations. We believe that pursuit of these suggestions will advance our knowledge and will lead to better, more useful appraisals.

Acknowledgments

We thank the reviewers of this book for their helpful comments and suggestions: Richard D. Arvey, University of Minnesota; Raymond A. Noe, University of Minnesota; and Joyce E. A. Russell, University of Tennesse. We also express our gratitude to the many colleagues who generously shared preprints and ideas with us, including Bill Balzer, Cris Banks, Janet Barnes-Farrell, Bob Cardy, Angelo DeNisi, David Lane, Robert Morrison, Hank Sims, Dirk Steiner, Kevin Williams, and the graduate students who participated in our performance appraisal seminar.

Chapter One

Introduction

▶   Performance appraisal (PA) has traditionally been viewed by industrial/organizational psychologists as a measurement problem. Indeed, a quick review of its historical roots shows that early research on PA has focused on such issues as scale development, scale formats, reducing test and rater bias, and the like (Edwards, 1957; Guilford, 1954; Landy & Farr, 1980, 1983). To date, much of the research on performance appraisal can be described as a search for better, more accurate, and more cost-effective techniques for measuring job performance. In this book, we will depart from the traditional measurement orientation and, instead, approach PA from an applied social-psychological perspective. That is, we view PA primarily as a social and communication process rather than primarily as a measurement tool.

Viewing performance appraisal as a social-psychological process is not unique (Ilgen & Favero, 1982). However, we will argue strongly that the nearly exclusive treatment of PA by researchers as a measurement instrument is unrealistic. The assumption has led researchers to focus on questions that may not yield significant understanding or improvement in the practice of performance appraisals in organizations (Banks & Murphy, 1985). Currently, researchers know a great deal about the measurement problems involved in appraisals. The measurement perspective has enhanced our understanding of the mechanics of appraisal, however, with little consideration of the context of performance appraisal in organizations. Even the recent cognitive research on appraisal has attempted to improve appraisals as measurement tools with less application to their role as a communication or decision-making tool.

One advantage in considering appraisals from a social-psychological perspective is that the role of context receives greater attention. Further, this perspective provides psychologists with more opportunity to explore psy-

1

chological and social-psychological problems associated with the appraisal process. For example, it leads to questions about what role the social climate and norms of the organization play in the appraisal process or what role socialization processes play in the development of performance norms and standards.

Given our perspective, we have two general goals for this book. First, we hope that our treatment of performance appraisal, from a social-psychological perspective rather than the traditional measurement approach, will stimulate readers to think about performance appraisal in a different or a more macro way. Second, we hope that, given a different way of viewing PA, future research in this area will enhance the practice of performance appraisal in organizations.

This chapter presents a four-part conceptual model of performance appraisal in organizations. We will treat appraisal as a communication process, in which the rater attempts to convey information to the organization about subordinates' performance. The model is based on three assumptions: (1) rater behavior is goal directed, (2) performance appraisals are social interactions, and (3) performance appraisals in organizations function primarily as a decision aid rather than as a measurement instrument. The elements of the model include the rating context, the performance judgment, the performance rating, and the evaluation; these four components provide the general outline of the book. Before the model is introduced, however, we will review the history of PA research to identify the trends and events influencing our current research and practice.

Performance Appraisal: Early History

Although the interest in and use of performance appraisal has increased over the last 30 years, the practice of formally evaluating employees has existed for centuries. As early as the third century A.D., Sin Yu, an early Chinese philosopher, criticized a biased rater employed by the Wei dynasty on the grounds that "the Imperial Rater of Nine Grades seldom rates men according to their merits but always according to his likes and dislikes" (Patten, 1977, p. 352). In 1648, the *Dublin* (Ireland) *Evening Post* allegedly rated legislators using a rating scale based on personal qualities (Hackett, 1928). According to Heilbroner (1953), the first industrial application of merit rating was probably made by Robert Owen at his cotton mills in New Lanark, Scotland, in the early 1800s. Wood cubes of different colors indicating different degrees of merit were hung over each employee's work station. As employee performance changed, so did the appropriate wood cube. The merit rating or efficiency rating in the Federal Civil Service has been in place since at least 1887 (Petrie, 1950) and perhaps as early as 1842 (Lopez, 1968).

One impetus to the development of performance appraisal in U.S. industry (Patten, 1977) can be traced to the work of industrial psychologists at Carnegie-Mellon University and their early work in salesman selection and "man-to-man" rating forms based on trait psychology (Scott, Clothier, & Spriegel, 1941). The man-to-man rating form was later used by the army in World War I to assess the performance of officers (Scott et al., 1941), although formal PA probably began in the United States in 1813 (Bellows & Estep, 1954) when Army General Lewis Cass submitted to the War Department an evaluation of each of his men using such terms as "a good-natured man" or "knave despised by all."

Although the man-to-man ranking by department is not frequently used in industry or in appraising performance, it can be an effective method for determining the order of layoffs. In fact, in the late 1960s, it was used by many companies that experienced cutbacks in government contracts to make layoff and retention decisions (Patten, 1977). This technique was known as the "totem approach" to personnel cutbacks. After World War I, many of the individuals associated with the work of the man-to-man appraisal secured positions in industry, in part because business leaders were impressed by the contribution of industrial psychologists to army research. Despite early criticisms (Rudd, 1921), the graphic rating scale increased in popularity and remains predominant today. Just prior to and during World War II, the army again sought assistance from psychologists to improve its rating system. The outcome of these research efforts included the forced-choice technique and the critical-incident approach to merit rating (Flanagan, 1949; Sisson, 1948). Appraisal of industry employees became popular only after World War I, and appraisal of managers was not widely practiced until after World War II.

By the early 1950s, appraisal was an accepted practice in many organizations. In 1962, performance appraisal was conducted in 61% of the organizations surveyed (Spriegel, 1962) and typically top management was exempt from such ratings (Whisler & Harper, 1962). After the passage of the 1964 Civil Rights Act and the 1966 and 1970 Equal Employment Opportunity Commission (EEOC) guidelines for regulation of selection procedures, legal considerations exerted strong pressure on organizations to formalize their appraisal systems (DeVries, Morrison, Shullman, & Gerlach, 1986). Federal legislation and the civil rights and women's movements of the 1960s and 1970s created the need for rapid improvements in organizational appraisal practices.

DeVries and colleagues (1986) point out two particular trends in the *practice* of PA during the last 30 years. First, appraisal methods have evolved from traits and essay approaches to such behavioral and results-oriented methods as Behaviorally Anchored Rating Scales (BARS) and Management by Objectives (MBO). However, DeVries and colleagues note that although newer methods have evolved, the older trait-rating scales are still prevalent. A second trend is that the number of uses of PA in organizations has increased during the past 30 years (Cleveland, Murphy, & Williams, 1989; DeVries et al., 1986). As Figure 1–1 indicates, the earliest use of performance appraisal was as a basis for administrative decisions such as promotions, salary increases, and so on. However, throughout the 1960s and 1970s performance appraisals were increasingly used for employee development and feedback, corporate planning,

Figure 1–1.   Historical Trends in Performance Appraisal Research and Practice

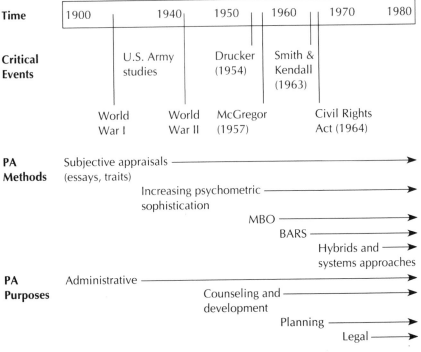

D. L. DeVries, A. M. Morrison, S. L. Shullman, & M. L. Gerlach, *Performance Appraisal on the Line* (Greensboro, NC: Center for Creative Leadership, 1986), p. 12.

legal documentation (DeVries et al., 1986), systems maintenance, and research (Cleveland et al., 1989).

Performance Appraisal Research: Historical Trends

The research on performance appraisal parallels the events and trends in industry and the military and can be categorized into a number of key content areas.

Objective versus Subjective Measures of Performance

There are many ways to measure performance. In general, performance data can be categorized into two groups: judgmental or subjective measures and nonjudgmental or objective measures (Landy & Farr, 1983). Although judgmental measures are more widely used, objective performance indices (e.g., production output, scrap rates, and time to complete a task) have been useful measures of performance for routine, manual jobs since the 1940s (Rothe, 1946a, 1946b, 1947, 1949, 1951; Rothe & Nye, 1958, 1959, 1961) and have received renewed attention more recently (Bass & Turner, 1973; Bassett, 1979; Goldstein & Mobley, 1971; Hackman & Porter, 1968; Kidd & Christy, 1961; Yukl & Latham, 1975). Further, other nonjudgmental measures that do not directly measure performance but would provide information on the general health of the organization (e.g., absenteeism, turnover, grievances, and accidents) have received renewed research attention (Chadwick-Jones, Nicholson, & Brown, 1982; Fitzgibbons & Moch, 1980; Mowday, Porter, & Steers, 1981; Muchinsky, 1977; Steers & Rhodes, 1978).

Specific objective measures are not without their unique problems, however. Although it is not possible here to discuss these measures exhaustively (see Landy & Farr, 1983, for a detailed discussion), each has specific limitations. For example, absence measures (1) do not apply to many jobs, (2) are frequently inaccurate, (3) have a variety of causes depending on the definition of absence, (4) vary in the length of observation, and most important (5) do not correlate with each other. A major drawback of using turnover as a criterion is that it is difficult to distinguish between voluntary and involuntary turnover. Grievances are limited in scope and generalizability because often they are not available for nonunion employees. The major problem with accidents is that there is confusion about whether they are the result of people or their environments, which calls into question the validity of such measures. Finally, rate of advancement or salary increases are poor criteria; the rate may be controlled by a quota, or salary adjustments may reflect organizational health (economic) but not individual performance.

Landy and Farr (1983) have identified several problems with objective measures and possible reasons why psychologists have pursued judgmental measures, especially for evaluating managerial behavior. First, objective indices tend to have low reliability. One reason for the low reliablity in absence measures, for example, is that the observation period may be not stable across measures. That is, assessing absence during a one-week period and then correlating it with another week may yield a low correlation because a longer period is required for a reliable measure (Chadwick-Jones, Brown, Nicholson, & Sheppard, 1971; Farr, O'Leary, & Bartlett, 1971; Ilgen & Hollenback, 1977; Latham & Pursell, 1975). Further, factors external to the individual such as the organization's sick-leave policies may influence the reliability of absence measures.

Second, objective measures tend to be available for only a limited number of jobs. For example, it would not be sensible to collect tardiness or absence measures from sales representatives or from corporate managers who may not have a predetermined or fixed eight-hour work day. Finally, Landy and Farr (1983) cite the changing nature of skilled and semi-skilled work as a final limitation to objective performance measures. For example, since operators are being replaced by machine tenders, productivity measures such as output are more dependent on machine functions than individual performance. The changing nature of work suggests that objective measures may be increasingly less appropriate for evaluating worker performance, and subjective measures may continue to experience popularity.

Rating Scale Formats

The most voluminous area of research on PA deals with the format of appraisal scales. These issues include between-person comparisons (norm-referenced criteria) versus comparison to a standard (criterion-referenced formats), use of trait versus behavioral anchors, the optimal number of anchors, identification of formats conducive to the fewest rater errors, scaling of anchors, and comparison of format validity. An example of each of the scale formats discussed below is provided in the Appendix.

Landy and Farr (1983) classify judgmental measures of performance into two general groups: norm-referenced criteria and criterion-referenced criteria. Examples of norm-referenced criteria include simple rankings and paired comparisons. Most research, however, has been devoted to the development of psychometrically sophisticated criterion-referenced scales. Since 1922, when Paterson introduced the *graphic rating scale,* an extensive amount of research has been conducted on scale format, with the goal of improving the measurement quality and the "numbers" that such scales yield (cited in Landy & Farr, 1983). As many psychologists indicate (Guion, 1965; Landy, 1987; Landy & Farr, 1983), early graphic rating scales consisted of trait labels and unbroken lines with varying types and numbers of adjectives below. Raters were asked to rate each employee on each trait or statement by circling a number or box that represented how much of that characteristic was present. Research on the graphic scale attempted to determine the meanings of the response categories (i.e., scaling) or anchors, the types of anchors (trait, behavior, adjective, number, etc.), and the number of anchors that resulted in discernible ratings and that raters found acceptable.

One systematic attempt to enhance the graphic scale was the result of work conducted by Smith and Kendall (1963), which led to the development of the *Behaviorally Anchored Rating Scales (BARS).* Smith and Kendall attempted to replace numerical or adjective anchors with behavioral examples of actual work behaviors. Using scaling procedures borrowed from psychophysics and attitude measurement, BARS were designed to have improved psychometric properties (Landy & Farr, 1983). Raters read a number of behavioral statements and then circle the number that corresponds to the statement that best describes the employee's behavior.

The *Behavioral Observation Scales (BOS)* were developed as an attempt to improve BARS (Latham & Wexley, 1977). Raters evaluate the frequency of specific employee behaviors or critical incidents that have been observed. A decade or so later, Blanz and Ghiselli (1972) designed the *Mixed Standard Rating Scale,* which disguised the nature of the performance dimension and the levels of performance described by the behavioral examples. This derived scale, where the employee's score is later calculated on the basis of the pattern of rater responses to three items comprising a particular dimension, was again intended to reduced rating errors. Raters respond to behavioral statements that reflect high, average, and low performance. For each statement, raters simply respond by indicating whether the employee's performance is better than (+), equal to (=), or worse than (−) the behavior reflected in each item. The *Forced-Choice Rating Scale,* similar to the mixed standard scale, also disguises the rating scale outcome (Zavala, 1965) with the intent to reduce rating errors.

Kane and Lawler (1979) introduced the *Distributional Measurement Model (DMM)* to performance measurement. In this approach, an attempt is made to obtain ratings in terms of the frequency or rate at which a person has exhibited a given performance dimension at a series of performance levels or benchmarks (Landy & Farr, 1983). Although the DMM is rather complicated and cumbersome, its proponents (Bernardin & Beatty, 1984; Kane, 1981; Kane & Lawler, 1979) indicate that it addresses three problems that beset all other appraisal methods:

1. DMM considers performance as the distribution of occurrence rates over the range of possible achievement levels (on each performance area/dimension).
2. DMM considers the extraneous factors such as machine failure or late delivery of supplies that may influence the performance of individuals.
3. DMM places a minimum of cognitive demands on the raters.

As Landy and Farr (1983) point out, however, more research is needed to determine the applicability of this model.

In parallel with the historical uses of PA, and consistent with Drucker's (1954) principle of management (to harmonize goals of the organization while allowing for full individual output), *Management by Objectives* (MBO) emerged as a technique intended to develop and motivate employees. MBO is an attempt to measure an individual's effectiveness or contribution to organizational goals (outcomes) rather than measure employee behavior (Odiorne, 1965). Although numerous MBO systems have been offered since Drucker, all have focused on (1) needing to quantify what must be accomplished, (2) specifying in some detail how the goal should be accomplished, (3) specifying the time when tasks should be accomplished, and (4) weighing the costs of the system versus the benefits (Bernardin & Beatty, 1984).

Much of the research on scale formats has attempted to determine what formats are superior measurement instruments (fewest rater errors) (Bernardin, 1977; Bernardin, Alvares, & Cranny, 1976; Borman & Dunnette, 1975; Borman &

Vallon, 1974; Burnaska & Hollman, 1974; Friedman & Cornelius, 1976; Jacobs, Kafry, & Zedeck, 1980). Extensive research has also been conducted on the characteristics of rating scales such as the number of response categories (Bendig, 1952a, 1952b, 1953, 1954a, 1954b; Bernardin, LaShells, Smith, & Alvares, 1976; Finn, 1972; Lissitz & Green, 1975), the advantages of the type of anchor (numerical, adjectival, or behavioral) (Barrett, Taylor, Parker, & Martens, 1958; Bendig, 1952a, 1952b, 1953; Shapiro & Shirom, 1980; Smith & Kendall, 1963), and the process of assigning scale values to the anchor (Bendig, 1952a, 1952b; Barnes & Landy, 1979).

Performance Appraisal and the Legal System

The single greatest influence on development and use of performance assessment in the United States has been the Uniform Guidelines on Employment Selection (1978) established by the EEOC. The guidelines apply to "tests and other procedures which are used as a basis for any employee decisions" (1978). In a key case, *Brito* v. *Zia* (1973), the Tenth Circuit Court of Appeals ruled that evaluations are, in fact, tests and are subject to guidelines enforced by the EEOC. Although recent cases (e.g., *Watson* v. *Fort Worth Bank*) may relax the application of these guidelines, it is probably best for employers to continue to regard performance evaluations as tests. Therefore, PA becomes an important legal issue when it is used in making any type of personnel decision. As we indicated earlier in the chapter, the oldest and most predominant purpose of appraisal is for making administrative decisions. More recently, it has been used as an employee development and feedback tool (DeVries et al., 1986).

In *Albemarle Paper Company* v. *Moody* (1975), the Court indicated that the accuracy or validity of PA could be examined in a validation study. In this decision, the Supreme Court discredited an empirical validation study because the criteria used were vague and open to many errors (Bernardin & Beatty, 1984). Therefore, performance appraisals are subject to court action or consideration on at least two grounds: (1) the accuracy or validity of ratings to predict future performance or promotability and (2) the validity or accuracy of ratings to assess past behavior. Additionally, as a result of EEOC guidelines and interpretation of the Age Discrimination in Employment Act in 1981, performance appraisal has emerged as particularly relevant for establishing a Bona Fide Occupation Qualification (BFOQ) such as a maximum age limit. In order to assert a BFOQ, the organization must demonstrate, usually through performance data, that an age limit is justified by business necessity or for public safety.

We do not intend here to review the legal cases concerning appraisal or issue of adverse impact. There are many excellent reviews of case law (see Arvey & Faley, 1988; Cascio, 1987; Cascio & Bernardin, 1980, 1981). Further, based on a review of 66 cases by Feild and Holley (1982), Bernardin and Beatty

(1984) outline a set of guidelines or standards for developing legally sound appraisals. These guidelines suggest that legally defensible appraisals must reflect standards that are based on job requirements, and the standards should reflect specific dimensions of job performance rather than an overall rating (Bernardin & Beatty, 1984; Cascio & Bernardin, 1981). The performance dimensions should be defined in behavioral terms and must be communicated to employees. A defensible appraisal system requires high-quality ratings. Whenever possible, there should be multiple raters rather than a single rater. Each individual rater should have the validity of his or her ratings assessed. Extreme ratings should be accompanied with documentation, including a critical incident, date, location, and so on. Finally, a sound performance appraisal system has a formal appeal process (Bernardin & Beatty, 1984).

With the Court's interpretations of the guidelines, the historical view of appraisal as a measurement device has been reinforced and given enhanced importance and visibility. This legal scrutiny may be one reason why appraisal research has focused on measurement issues, while largely ignoring (until recently) the social and organizational goals of the appraisal process. The heightened awareness that appraisals are subject to legal action highlights the importance of the measurement qualities of appraisal, but it also may have obscured the decision-making and communication roles of PA in organizations.

Criteria for Assessing Appraisal Effectiveness

Numerous criteria exist for assessing the effectiveness of performance appraisal outcomes. In the 1950s, representatives of the American Psychological Association defined a test as "nothing more than careful observation of actual performance under standard conditions" (Bernardin & Beatty, 1984; Mullins & Ratliff, 1979). Therefore, it is not surprising that the many criteria used to assess predictor effectiveness would also apply to appraisals. Frequently, the uses of PA as a criterion and as a predictor are interchangeable. One illustration of this was provided by the case of *Washington* v. *Davis* (1976). At one point in the court process, performance in a training program served as the criterion in an empirical validation study; at another point in the same case, evidence was presented to assess whether training performance predicted on-the-job performance (Bernardin & Beatty, 1984).

In addition to numerous criteria for evaluating appraisal effectiveness, there is an additional problem in that there has been little attempt to refine definitions or operational definitions of criteria. That is, it is often not clear or agreed upon as to what constitutes error in ratings. In Chapter Ten, the criteria for assessing appraisal effectiveness will be explored more fully. However, for the purposes of this chapter, research on rater errors can be categorized into three areas: (1) criteria for assessing appraisal effectiveness, including the utilization criteria of PA (i.e., utilization criteria, qualitative criteria, and quantitative criteria); (2) rating source (i.e., peer, supervisor, and subordinate) as it relates to appraisal errors and effectiveness; and (3) rater training.

Jacobs and colleagues (1980) provide a meaningful framework for describing the numerous types of appraisal criteria. They describe three categories against which any PA system should be evaluated; this framework nicely captures the type of research that has been conducted in appraisal effectiveness. The most basic are the *utilization criteria*, which address the purposes for which appraisal are conducted, including administrative decisions (i.e., promotion, disciplinary, selection, etc.) and employee development (i.e., feedback, training, diagnosis, etc.). The most frequent distinction is whether performance appraisal will serve individual or organizational goals and needs.

A related issue that has received much research attention is whether performance is best described by using multiple criterion measures or a composite criteria (Schmidt & Kaplan, 1971). Except for the issue of multiple and composite criteria, the utilization criteria have received less attention in the empirical literature than in trade or practitioner journals. One reason for this may be that practitioners are concerned more with quantitative criteria of appraisal effectiveness than qualitative criteria.

Qualitative criteria include the relevance of the appraisal to job performance, data availability, equivalence, interpretability, and practicality (Jacobs et al., 1980). Wexley (1986) has urged psychologists to use employee attitudes toward performance appraisal more frequently as a useful way of assessing appraisal effectiveness. Specifically, Wexley (1987) stated that the highly researched criterion of rating accuracy is an overused and less useful measure of effectiveness and instead suggested more practical qualitative measures.

The third criterion area, *quantitative measures of effectiveness,* has received extensive attention in the empirical literature. Definitions of rating errors have evolved throughout the history of performance appraisal. Kingsbury (1933) was perhaps first to list the three most frequently mentioned psychometric errors in the literature: halo, leniency, and central tendency. Halo refers to the tendency to rate the same on all dimensions, leniency to the tendency to give extreme ratings, and central tendency to the overreliance on the middle of the scale. Since then, many other criteria have been added, including reliability, interrater reliability, and validity (content, construct, predictive, concurrent; discriminant and convergent validity; etc.).

Bernardin and Beatty (1984) and others (Carroll & Schneier, 1982; Landy & Farr, 1983) describe in some detail the vast amount of research using these criteria to compare the effectiveness of various appraisal formats and systems. (We review this literature in Chapter Seven.) Given that appraisals have been viewed primarily as measurement tools, and considering the legal constraints imposed on appraisals, the extensive research devoted to the psychometric properties and accuracy of appraisal processes is understandable and warranted.

Another general consideration within the domain of appraisal concerns the appropriate source of ratings. Much research attention has compared peer, supervisory, and subordinate ratings (Mount, 1984a) using the criteria described by Jacobs and colleagues (1980). In general, the intent of this research is to determine what source or sources provide the most psychometrically sound and accurate ratings.

Rater training in PA — specifically Rater Error Training (RET), Rater Accuracy Training (RAT) (Bernardin & Pence, 1980), or frame of reference training (Bernardin & Beatty, 1984) — are all designed with similar objectives: to improve the psychometric properties of appraisals. The research literature on training is devoted to assessing the effectiveness of such training and the longevity of training effects.

Cognitive Research in Performance Appraisal

Reviews on performance appraisal have generated considerable research on the way in which raters mentally process information about ratees or the cognitive processes involved in evaluation. As we will discuss in Chapter Seven, the growth of research in cognitive process and appraisal can be traced to Wherry's seminal work (Wherry & Bartlett, 1982) as well as works by DeCotiis and Petit (1978) and Landy and Farr (1980). Other reviews by Feldman (1981), Ilgen and Feldman (1983), and DeNisi and Williams (1988) also have called attention to the importance considering the rater's capacity to evaluate. Current cognitive research draws on two models for hypotheses and for interpretations of experimental findings: one by Feldman and colleagues (Feldman, 1981; Ilgen & Feldman, 1983) and the second by DeNisi and colleagues (DeNisi, Cafferty, & Meglino, 1984; DeNisi & Williams, 1988).

The research in this area has focused on four major cognitive processes. The first process is *information acquisition,* which involves what behaviors and characteristics the rater selectively attends to and those ratee features and behaviors to which the rater devotes little attention. Research on information acquisition has focused on two influences: the context of observation (McArthur, 1980; Taylor & Fiske, 1978) and the purpose of observation (Balzer, 1986; Cafferty, DeNisi, & Williams, 1986; Murphy, Philbin, & Adams, 1989). The second process in the general cognitive model is *encoding and mental representation.* This research has focused on such issues as the categories, prototypes, and schema involved at this stage. Research on the *storage and retrieval* of information focuses on how memory works, how many types of memory exist (i.e., short-term versus long-term memory), and so on. Specifically, memory research in the area of social cognition and person perception has been primarily concerned with the effects of categorization on memory (Cantor & Mischel, 1977; Wyer & Srull, 1986). A fourth area of cognitive research on evaluation concerns the *integration of different pieces or types of information* (Cooper, 1981b; DeNisi & Williams, 1988; and Feldman, 1981).

Although the cognitive influence in PA research has enhanced understanding of the capabilities and limitation of raters as information processors and as evaluators, such research has not been without critics. These criticisms are reviewed in Chapter Seven.

Models of Performance Appraisals

Prior to 1975, few published or comprehensive models of performance appraisal were devoted to the identification of factors that influence rating outcomes. Instead, the literature reflected a concern with criterion measurement and understanding what (construct) is measured by criteria (James, 1973) in general and not with PA ratings specifically.

The debate on the usefulness of the *ultimate criterion model* (Blum & Naylor, 1968; Nagle, 1953; Thorndike, 1949) versus the *multiple criterion model* (Ghiselli, 1964; Guion, 1961, 1965) was waged during the 1960s and resolved more or less by Schmidt and Kaplan (1971). The major issue was whether criteria should be combined or interpreted separately. Little consideration was given to the various types of measures obtained or to other factors that may influence performance.

The model of managerial effectiveness proposed by Campbell, Dunnette, Lawler, and Weick (1970) and labeled the *general criterion model* by James (1973) progressed beyond the issue of one versus many indicators of performance by viewing managerial performance as a function of individual abilities, motivation, and organizational situation or opportunity. Although the Campbell and associates (1970) general criterion model is not a PA rating model per se, it is important because it (1) distinguishes motivation from ability and performance and (2) considers situational variables as they might influence job performance and organizational outcomes. The difference between the general criterion model and subsequent rating models (e.g., Landy & Farr, 1980) is that the unit of analysis is much broader; the model by Campbell and colleagues was concerned with understanding managerial performance and organizational effectiveness.

James (1973) proposed a fourth criterion model, called the *integrated criterion model,* which integrates the multiple and the general criterion model and construct-validation procedures. As with each of the other three models, the integrated model was intended to guide future criterion research by applying a rationale and a set of procedures to assess the underlying nature (construct) of criteria.

In the 1950s, Wherry developed a sophisticated psychometric model of rating (Wherry & Bartlett, 1982). Unfortunately, the model was described in unpublished technical reports and did not come to most researchers' or practitioners' attention until the 1980s. This model used the theory of reliability to derive a number of unique theorems about rating bias, the process, and so on.

In 1978, the first widely cited model of the PA process was published in the *Academy of Management Review* by DeCotiis and Petit. They proposed a model of the determinants of the accuracy of appraisal ratings and suggested several propositions and directions for future research. DeCotiis and Petit (1978) stated that rating accuracy was determined by rater motivation, rater ability, and the availability of appropriate judgmental norms. Although their work is similar to the subsequent Landy and Farr (1980) study (published in *Psychological Bulletin*), the DeCotiis and Petit model distinguishes itself in at least two ways: (1) there is an explicit distinction made between rater ability (i.e., rater skills in interpreting ratee behavior) and rater motivation (i.e., what energizes, directs, and sustains behavior) and (2) more emphasis is placed on organization or situational characteristics that may influence and shape rating outcomes.

The Landy and Farr (1980) model has reached a wider audience. Their process model of appraisal, although recognizing the influence of situational variables on ratings, most specifically addresses the rater's cognitive process. The model includes components such as rating process, observation and storage of performance information, retrieval of such information from memory, the actual judgment, and the performance description.

A Model for Research and Practice

Reviews, such as DeCotiis and Petit (1978) and Landy and Farr (1980), have stimulated a significant body of research on PA but, to date, this research has made few contributions to the practice of performance appraisal in organizations (Latham, 1986). We believe that the conceptual models that guide current research on PA (examples include process models developed by DeNisi et al., 1984; Ilgen & Feldman, 1983; and Landy & Farr, 1980) are partly to blame.

Although these models have helped to clarify research (especially cognitive research) in performance appraisal, they have (1) paid insufficient attention to the organizational context in which appraisals occur, (2) failed to identify issues of concern to both researchers and practitioners, and (3) failed to illustrate the links between the concerns of current performance researchers (e.g., research on the cognitive and affective bases of appraisal) and the practice of performance appraisal. A different type of conceptual model is needed in order to make progress in both research and application.

In this book, we present a conceptual model of PA in organizations (Cleveland, Murphy, Barnes-Farrell, & Banks, 1988). Performance appraisal research has traditionally treated appraisal as a measurement process and has treated context factors (to the extent that they are considered at all) as nuisance variables that interfere with accurate appraisal. We treat appraisal as a communication and social process. The rater is not a passive measurement instrument but rather an active agent pursuing specific goals. The central assumption is that appraisal outcomes are the result of a rater's goal-directed behavior, which is shaped by the organizational context in which rating occurs.

338-1960

This assumption, together with our analysis of the academic and applied literature dealing with PA leads to the four-component model illustrated in Figure 1-2.

Before introducing the four elements of the model, we will explain how this model is different from earlier models of the appraisal process (e.g., DeCotiis & Petit, 1978; Ilgen & Feldman, 1983; Landy & Farr, 1980). First, previous models tended to focus on a specific aspect of the appraisal process (e.g., judgment) without explicitly recognizing that the variables identified in the model operated in a larger, dynamic context. Our model identifies the context of performance appraisal, especially the organizational context, as the starting point from which other components should be examined. Second, previous models generated many "boxes and arrows." That is, they attempted to identify all possible variables or characteristics within a given box. As a result, the models provided detailed information about narrow portions of the question, yet many times lost sight of how the information fits into the larger understanding of performance. Further, it is difficult to determine from previous models what elements are and are not critical to understanding effective performance appraisal. The proposed model is intended to highlight a limited number of variables that we believe are critical in performance appraisal research and practice.

Our four-component model takes a more holistic approach than previous models. Therefore, we do not provide an exhaustive review of all of the variables that may play a part within each of our major components. Rather, our intent is to highlight the critical elements in this domain. We think that the critical questions in appraisal research have been confused or ignored among the myriad boxes and arrows of previous models. The proposed model is suggested as one approach for organizing PA research efforts. It may also provide a mechanism for posing research questions that will address PA problems that are encountered in organizations. The four-component performance appraisal model includes the following elements: the rating context,

Figure 1-2. Performance Appraisal in Context: A Four-Component Model

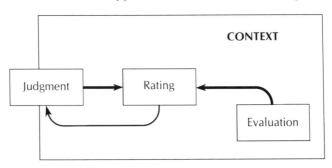

the performance judgment, the performance rating, and the evaluation of the appraisal system.

Rating Context

The organizational context in which ratings are collected influences the judgment process, the rating process, the evaluation process, and the eventual uses of the rating data. Performance appraisal research has traditionally followed a microanalytic approach, focusing on scale construction, scale format, rater biases, and so forth (Ilgen & Feldman, 1983). Research on the rating context can also profit from the consideration of two sets of macrolevel issues: (1) *intraorganizational factors,* such as organizational values, climate or culture within the organization, competition among departments or functions, status differences among functions, effect of downsizing on the PA system, and the like (Cleveland, Morrison, & Bjerke, 1986; Duncan, 1972; Duncan & Weiss, 1979); and (2) *organization-environment issues,* such as organizational performance within a specific industry, extent of competition within an industry, general economic/political conditions regarding the organization's products, and so on (Duncan & Weiss, 1979). For example, some departments of the organization are likely to contain fast-track employees, whereas others will not; the purpose, tone, and focus of appraisal may vary accordingly (Cleveland et al., 1989).

Consideration of the context within which performance appraisals are conducted, especially at the macroorganizational level, has been largely ignored by researchers (Ilgen & Feldman, 1983). However, an understanding of the context within which the appraisal system operates may enhance the implementation, utilization, or change of PA systems.

Cleveland and colleagues (1986) have categorized contextual variables into two groups: proximal and distal variables (Brunswick, 1955). According to these authors, *proximal variables* are those that directly impinge upon or influence the rater. They include the interaction between supervisor and employee, the nature of the rated task or job, consequences of ratings (Lawler, 1972), and rater time constraints (Wright, 1974). For example, the established interaction patterns between a supervisor and an employee are determined by the day-to-day interactions over time (Dansereau, Graen, & Haga, 1975). If a supervisor has a close, informal relationship as opposed to a more formal, distant relationship with his or her employee, it is reasonable to assume that this will have an impact on ratings used for salary increases or promotion recommendations.

Distal variables are those intra- and extraorganizational characteristics that influence judgments, ratings, and assessments indirectly. Distal contextual variables include organizational structure, organizational climate or culture, the value system within the organization, and so on. The status of the specific function or unit and external/legal entrance standards to a functional unit or job type (i.e., lawyer, nurse, engineer) are also examples of distal cues.

For example, Cleveland and associates (1989) found that organizational complexity and organizational coordination were correlated with ways in which organizations use performance appraisals in making decisions. Organizations high in complexity and coordination were more likely to use appraisal for within-person uses (i.e., feedback and identifying strengths and weaknesses in employees) and systems maintenance than other organizations. In addition, Cleveland and colleagues (1986) found anecdotal support for the influence of an organization's value system upon ratings. Specifically, employees whose jobs or activities were perceived as more closely linked with the organization's mission or purpose (i.e., what was valued) were rated systematically higher than employees in jobs that were perceived as less central to the organization's mission.

Cleveland and colleagues (1989) surveyed over 100 organizations on their uses of PA. Over 70% of those surveyed indicated that ratings had a moderate to substantial impact on two or more decisions or goals. The most frequently cited uses within an organization were administrative decisions (promotion, etc.) and employee feedback and development. There is research evidence (Meyer, Kay, & French, 1965; Sharon & Bartlett, 1969; Williams, DeNisi, Blencoe, & Cafferty, 1985) and anecdotal evidence from raters (Cleveland et al., 1986) suggesting that organizations may convey multiple and conflicting messages to raters when appraisal is used to achieve both individual goals (i.e., employee feedback) and organizational goals (i.e., administrative or between-person decisions) (DeCotiis & Petit, 1978). Furthermore, an appraisal system within such an organization may invoke different rater cognitive processes, yield different rating outcomes, and establish different criteria for evaluating the goodness of ratings than in an organization that conveys a unitary message to raters regarding the purpose of performance appraisal.

Context effects are not limited to those that determine the purpose of ratings. Additional evidence shows that contextual factors can affect effort or motivation and performance (Peters & O'Connor, 1980), differentially affect high- and low-ability individuals in organizations (Peters, Fisher, & O'Connor, 1982), influence organizational learning and intellectual flexibility (Kohn & Schooner, 1978; Medin & Schaffer, 1978), impact safety effectiveness (Zohar, 1980), and affect updating activities (Kozlowski & Hults, 1987).

Duncan (1972) and Schein (1971) suggest groupings of organizational characteristics that may be useful for defining the context of performance appraisal. Duncan (1972) suggests that contextual variables can be categorized into those that affect the internal environment or the external environment. The internal environment includes organizational personnel, organizational function and staff units, and organizational level. The external environment includes customers, suppliers, competitors, sociopolitical environment, and technological environment. Duncan and Weiss (1979) suggest that the components of the internal and the external organizational environments may be used by individuals through the process of enactment (Weick, 1977) to define or give meaning to the organizational situation.

Another way of looking at organizational context is through the three dimensions that Schein (1971) uses to describe an organization's defined role. The three dimensions in Schein's model of organizations are (1) functional — various tasks performed by members of the organization (i.e., finance, marketing, staff, etc.), (2) hierarchical — the distribution of rank within an organization (i.e., decentralized, centralized, etc.), and (3) the person's inclusion within the organization — an interactional dimension (i.e., newcomers versus a key or central figure).

In a report on performance appraisal practice in organizations, McCall and DeVries (1977) identify five contextual factors of organizations that appear to conflict directly with the requirements of an effective PA system. First, a manager's job includes activities short in duration, ad hoc contacts, tasks that are nonroutine, and a preference for current information (Mintzberg, 1980); whereas current PA systems require preparation, formal interviews, a focus on past behavior, and action as a result of the appraisal.

Second, organizations have limited resources, are hierarchical in structure, and decision making is subjective; whereas PA systems require administrative or development programs (with costs associated with them), require mutual problem solving, and there is an attempt for objective appraisals. Next, appraising individual performance assumes that performance varies, a person's performance is relatively independent of the performance of others, there is some consensus on what is good or bad, and performance can be changed via enhanced motivation and development; whereas the organizational reality may be that there is little variability in performance, performance is interdependent (on the group or the leader), there is a lack of agreement on what is good or poor performance, and performance is difficult to change.

Fourth, external environmental demands placed on the organization may clash with effective performance appraisals (DeVries et al., 1986). For example, unions favor the seniority system, whereas appraisals attempt to reward individual performance. Further, EEOC guidelines require appraisal validity, whereas the users of appraisal attempt to set mutual goals between the individual and the supervisor or the organization. Last, the day-to-day relationships that typify organizations is another source of potential problems (McCall & DeVries, 1977). For example, the authority relationship reflected in an organization may be inconsistent with the goal-setting interview of the appraisal; alternately, the goal of preserving the relationship may clash with the possibility of uncovering an insoluble performance problem in the appraisal interview.

Organizations send both formal and informal messages to raters about performance standards, norms for ratings, the immediate purpose of ratings, and the ways in which information regarding performance will be used. Much of the variance in ratings dismissed as rater error may be, in fact, an adaptive rater reaction to multiple, competing, and conflicting organizational forces. Rater behavior is an active, goal-directed process (Mohrman & Lawler, 1983). As such, goals may be a key concept in understanding how managers structure their performance appraisals.

Performance Judgment

Laboratory research on performance appraisal has focused primarily on judgments of raters who have observed or obtained information about the performance of workers. (See DeNisi & Williams, 1988, for a review of cognitive research in performance evaluation.) Judgments are part of the rating process, but judgments and ratings are not identical. *Judgments* represent private evaluations; *ratings* represent public statements about ratees' performance (Mohrman & Lawler, 1983).

Judgments are, in part, context free. Extensive research shows that global evaluative judgments are made in practically every context and that efforts to remove this component are likely to be fruitless (Hastie & Park, 1986; Murphy, 1982b; Osgood, 1962). Judgments are also context bound. The job context determines the specific judgments that must be made as well as the relative emphasis on discriminating between persons versus identifying individual strengths and weaknesses. Judgments are subject to a wide variety of biases, almost all of which are likely to be unconscious.

Context-free aspects of judgment consist of those that lie within the cognitive schema and evaluation criteria of the individual, regardless of job-specific context. These would include the appraiser's cognitive capacities, personal biases and decision heuristics, and prior experience with appraisal tasks. Clearly, appraisers differ along these attributes, and research is needed that delineates how each might be involved in generating accurate performance judgments.

Recent research suggests that the content of an appraiser's PA schema, independent of the data collected on a particular ratee or perhaps even independent of knowledge of the job in question, will influence how a ratee will be evaluated (Borman, 1987; Feldman, 1981, 1986). This means that appraisers will evaluate a ratee in part based on their own conceptualizations and implicit theories about people and only partially utilize the criteria supplied by researchers or by the organization. These internal evaluation criteria need to be acknowledged and explored in order to determine how accuracy of judgments may be increased.

Context-bound judgments consist of those aspects that rely on job- or organization-specific information to define performance levels. For example, performance evaluation cannot proceed without knowledge of the tasks, duties, and responsibilities involved in the job performed by the ratee. In addition, judgments must also include guidelines defining effective and ineffective performance (i.e., performance standards).

Judgments are also bound by the appraiser's opportunity to collect performance-related information and his or her ability to sort out to what extent job behavior is under the control of the ratee (Banks & Murphy, 1985). Finally, the structure of the appraisal system can affect how well appraisers can generate accurate judgments — for example, by the amount of structure in the appraisal, the amount of time that can be devoted to the judgment process, the comprehensiveness and representativeness of the performance dimensions included on the appraisal form, and the presence of mechanisms for recalling performance-related information accurately.

Much of the recent cognitive research in performance appraisal has focused on aspects of the judgment process. For the most part, this research has dealt with two issues: (1) how information about performance is acquired and (2) how this information is processed to form judgments. Research on information acquisition is consistent with our distinction between context-bound and context-free judgment. Some behaviors carry strong evaluative implications (e.g., yelling at a customer) and will be relevant in almost any context (Murphy, 1982b). Other behaviors become salient as a result of the observational goals of the rater (Murphy et al., 1989; Williams et al., 1985). These goals may be driven by the purpose of the appraisal task, organizational norms, individual theories of good or poor performance (Borman, 1983, 1987), and so on.

Judgments are not determined solely by the behaviors observed by raters. Several other forms of information about ratee performance influence judgments, such as previous impressions of the ratee (Murphy, Balzer, Lockhart, & Eisenman, 1985), observation of the results of behavior (Smith, 1976), and indirect reports concerning ratee behavior (e.g. complaints or praise from customers). A final source of information that will drive judgments is the rater's affective reaction to each ratee. Until recently, affect has not been included in PA models. There is evidence that performance evaluations are influenced by the degree to which the supervisor likes the subordinate (Cardy & Dobbins, 1986; Dobbins & Russell, 1986). There is also evidence that the rater's mood and temperament influence judgments (Clark & Isen, 1982; Isen & Daubman, 1984; Tsui & Barry, 1986).

Research on information processing in performance evaluation has focused on encoding and retrieval processes (DeNisi & Williams, 1988; Wyer & Srull, 1986). As is true in other areas of cognitive research, PA researchers have focused more on errors in information processing than on understanding what raters do well (Funder, 1987). Thus, it is apparent that biases in encoding and retrieval can lead to a variety of errors (Higgins & King, 1981; Ilgen & Feldman, 1983; Jeffrey & Mischel, 1979; Murphy et al., 1985; Murphy, Gannett, Herr, & Chen, 1986; Williams, DeNisi, Meglino, & Cafferty, 1986). What is not apparent is whether raters are capable of doing a reasonably good job of evaluating performance (Banks & Murphy, 1985).

It is commonly acknowledged that humans have a limited capacity for processing information. At present, there is no way to determine whether these limits hamper the accurate evaluation of performance. It may be that the task of evaluating subordinates' performance is a relatively easy one that most raters are perfectly capable of doing well. As we will discuss in the section that follows, the fact that *ratings* do not discriminate good from poor performers does not indicate that *raters* cannot tell good work from poor work.

Performance Rating

In our model, we make a distinction between judgment and rating behavior. That is, the numbers that are recorded on PA forms do not necessarily reflect the rater's judgments. More concretely, the fact that one subordinate receives a higher rating than another on a dimension such as "timeliness" does not necessarily imply that the rater truly believes that the individuals differ in this respect or even that the higher-rated subordinate is necessarily the better performer. The rating merely indicates that the rater wishes to convey something to the audience who will read the rating form. Exactly what the rater chooses to communicate will depend on the rater's goals and on contextual factors (discussed earlier).

The distinction between judgment and rating is not unique to this model; it is implied by a theory developed by Wherry in the 1950s (cf. Landy & Farr, 1983). Mohrman and Lawler (1983) distinguish between private and public evaluations and assume that they will not always correspond. Banks and Murphy (1985) distinguish between the rater's capacity to evaluate accurately ratee performance and his or her willingness to provide accurate ratings. What is unique to our model is the theoretical explanation for discrepancies between judgments and ratings.

Previous research has focused on leniency in rating, assuming that raters assign high ratings even when their private evaluation of ratees is not favorable (Landy & Farr, 1980, 1983; Murphy, Balzer, Kellam, & Armstrong, 1984). The assumption here is that raters hope to avoid the negative consequences (e.g., unpleasant confrontations) that are associated with harsh ratings (Bernardin & Buckley, 1981; Latham, 1986; Naiper & Latham, 1986). Other writers suggest that supervisors give high ratings because they do not know how to counsel workers who receive low ratings (Landy, 1985) or because they wish to avoid disapproval from others in the organization (Mohrman & Lawler, 1983).

The present model suggests that discrepancies between judgment and ratings cannot be explained solely in terms of a rater's attempts to avoid the consequences of low ratings. Rather, rating is a process of goal-directed communication. That is, the rater uses performance appraisal as a tool to achieve well-defined goals. Some of these goals may involve avoiding undesirable outcomes, but others involve positive end states. For example, if the rater believes that information from performance appraisal is used mainly as a basis for making promotion decisions, he or she may first decide who deserves a promotion and then fill out PA forms in a way that will maximize the likelihood that those promotions will occur (Cleveland et al., 1986).

Landy and Farr (1980) make explicit an assumption that appears to characterize most PA research — that ratings must contain some information about the ratee's performance. However, if performance rating is a goal-directed activity, there need not be any direct link between performance ratings and performance; in some settings, any correlation between true performance and rated performance might be spurious. In the example cited above, performance ratings will faithfully represent the rater's evaluations of each ratee's performance if and only if the rater decides who deserves a promotion solely on the basis of present performance. It would be entirely rational, however, for a supervisor largely to ignore present performance and to make promotion decisions on the basis of seniority, equity, past performance, or the perceived demands of the job that ratees might be promoted into. Under these conditions, ratings might bear little resemblance to the rater's private evaluations of each ratee's current job performance.

We assume that, under optimal conditions, raters are capable of forming accurate evaluations of important aspects of the performance of their subordinates (Borman, 1978). The question, then, is under what conditions the ratings that they record will also be accurate (i.e., will correspond with their judgment). Ratings are most likely to correspond with judgments if:

1. Organizational norms support distinctions between employees on the basis of their performance (Mohrman & Lawler, 1983).
2. Raters perceive a strong link between the ratings they give and specific outcomes (Landy & Farr, 1983; Thompson, 1967).
3. Raters believe that those outcomes should be based on present performance.
4. The valence of those outcomes is substantially larger than the valence of the negative outcomes that are associated with giving low ratings (Vroom, 1964).

The conditions listed above are most frequently encountered in research on the purpose of rating (Murphy et al., 1984). Here, ratings are collected for administrative purposes (e.g., salary, promotion) or for research or feedback purposes (i.e., they are not used to make decisions). It is likely that ratings collected for research purposes correspond closely with judgments; there are no adverse consequences for raters or ratees and probably no norms against giving truthful ratings. The same may be true for ratings collected in laboratory experiments (Latham, 1986; Wexley & Klimoski, 1984). There are several reasons to believe that the necessary conditions for strong links between judgments and ratings are not present in most other rating contexts.

First, ratings are typically used by organizations for a wide variety of purposes, ranging from salary administration to developmental feedback (Cleveland et al., 1989). It is unlikely that raters will believe that all of the decisions that might involve information about PA should be made on the basis of present performance. Even if they did believe so, different decisions emphasize different aspects of performance. For example, salary administration decisions reflect comparisons between individuals, in terms of their overall performance levels, whereas training needs assessments involve comparisons of strengths and weaknesses within individuals. There is evidence that information from performance appraisals is often used for both within- and between-individual comparisons (Cleveland et al., 1989) and that when this is done, raters tend to focus on one set of comparisons (usually between-individual) to the exclusion of the others (Cleveland et al., 1986). Thus, even when raters believe that decisions should be based on present performance, their ratings are likely to reflect only some aspects of their judgment (i.e., differences between individuals rather than individual strengths and weaknesses).

Second, the link between performance ratings and desired outcomes is often weak or uncertain. Factors other than present performance are, and should be, involved in making a variety of important decisions about ratees. Thus, the instrumentality link between ratings and desired outcomes may be weak (Mohrman & Lawler, 1983). In contrast, the link between low ratings and undesirable outcomes is likely to be strong; low ratings are almost certain to cause resentment and friction. This is the reason for our condition 4 that ratings will correspond with judgments only if the valence of desired outcomes is substantially greater than the valence of the undesirable outcomes associated with giving low ratings to some subordinates.

Evaluation

The question of whether ratings are meaningful as a communication tool cannot be sensibly answered without considering the way in which these ratings will be used in organizations. The ratings that are recorded by supervisors will also be driven by the uses to which these ratings are applied. For example, when ratings are used to make salary or promotion decisions, raters are likely to emphasize differences between individuals and deemphasize patterns of individual strengths and weaknesses (Cleveland et al., 1986; Cleveland et al., 1989). Consideration of the uses of PA information leads to alternate conceptions of the utility and accuracy of performance ratings.

Historically, performance ratings have been evaluated primarily in terms of their resistance to a variety of psychometric biases, or rater errors (Landy & Farr, 1980). The thrust of recent criterion research and development in the field of performance has centered around the importance of accuracy in performance ratings. We question whether this emphasis is always justified.

From the perspective of our model, it makes no sense to view rater errors, such as halo or leniency, as mistakes on the part of the rater. (For a related argument, see Funder, 1987.) For example, a high level of halo does not mean that the rater *cannot* discriminate among rating dimensions; it merely indicates that he or she *did not* discriminate. Saal, Downey, and Lahey (1980) note that many rater errors may in fact reflect desirable end states. For example, organizations do all they can to ensure that all subordinates perform at a high level, yet if everyone receives high ratings, psychologists suspect leniency rather than truly good performance. Our analysis suggests that many rater errors are consciously made and that failure to discriminate among persons or dimensions is often a highly adaptive behavior. Raters are not passive measurement instruments and should not be treated as such.

A number of serious questions may be raised about the practicality and adequacy of any particular method of operationalizing accuracy (Cronbach, 1955; Lord, 1985a; Sulsky & Balzer, 1988). A more general concern, however, is the extent to which accuracy is an appropriate criterion for PA ratings. Differences between actual and rated performance do not necessarily reflect measurement error; rather, they may simply reflect many forces in the organization that discourage accurate rating. Relatively context-free criteria, such as accuracy, may not make sense in the context-bound world of performance ratings. Consider why this is so.

A focus on accuracy is entirely appropriate when asking questions about the judgments that raters are able to make. However, performance ratings are not simply judgments. They are a means of communicating a message to the organization or to the worker. At times, the most useful message may differ somewhat from the message that would be conveyed if perfectly accurate judgments were recorded and transmitted as performance appraisals. The most useful message may be a simpler one or one that takes into account demand characteristics present in the organization. In other words, it may include motivated distortion intended to improve the usefulness of the performance appraisal.

This distinction between performance judgments and performance ratings has important implications for the criteria used to evaluate them. As noted above, it is probably not reasonable to assume that discrepancies between performance ratings and employee work performance represent inabilities to make accurate judgments about that performance. Likewise, it can be seen that accuracy does not ensure the usefulness of performance ratings that are applied in a particular organizational setting.

The parallel between this example and the judgment versus rating distinction is straightforward. The study of errors in performance judgments (i.e., accuracy indices) assists in clarifying the judgment process, but the evaluation of ratings is more appropriately cast in terms of the mistakes (e.g., incorrect decisions) that they produce (Feldman, 1986).

Another implication of distinguishing between the evaluation of performance judgments and performance ratings concerns the difficulty in identifying individual raters who are particularly adept at their task. There are very few ways to tell a good rater from a poor rater, as long as each worker is evaluated by only one rater. In order to assess accuracy, multiple raters may be needed (Murphy, 1982b). In order to increase the usefulness of ratings, however, it may be more feasible and efficient to utilize an organizational intervention or perhaps simply to identify a high-performing rater and utilize the skills of that individual.

Even if a reliable distinction between good and poor raters can be made, this may not be the critical point, since the accuracy of raters in field settings is probably driven more strongly by situational variables than by individual difference variables. Moving a good rater to a different context, with strong situational demands, might very well produce a "poor" rater (as judged in terms of accuracy). Therefore, time might be better spent focusing on the context of performance ratings as a central theme, rather than concentrating strictly on individual raters as the primary source of variation in the effectiveness of an appraisal system.

Summary

Previous psychological research on PA has focused on appraisal as a measurement process. The major concerns of this research have been whether performance ratings are accurate and valid measures and what technologies (e.g., scale formats) could be developed to increase accuracy and validity. This research has been characterized by models that do not facilitate the integration of science and practice in performance appraisal, because they do not identify the most important variables in appraisal and they fail to address concerns that are central to the practice of appraisal. Another approach to research and practice is needed.

The model we present in this chapter is intended to provide a guide both to research and practice. Ours is a social-psychological model rather than a psychometric model and it treats performance appraisal as a communication process that occurs in a well-defined organizational context. Our key concerns are identifying what the rater is trying to convey to the organization; what features of the rater, the ratee, and the context affect that message; and how organizations should evaluate the information that is communicated to them by raters. Our model points to a variety of issues that are treated in depth in Chapters Two through Eleven. Chapters Twelve and Thirteen discuss future directions for research and practice that are suggested by our model.

Chapter Two

Environmental Influences

▶   This chapter opens our discussion of the contextual factors that influence performance appraisal (PA) in organizations. One major theme of this book is that PA cannot be adequately understood outside of its organizational context — the same appraisal system, the same criteria for evaluating ratings, the same rater-training program, and so on are *not* the same if they exist in different contexts. We believe that the context is a major determinant of a rater's goal-oriented rating behavior, and that behaviors that seem to indicate rater error, or an inaccurate rating, when examined out of context, are often adaptive responses to the various contextual factors that surround performance appraisal. In this chapter, and in the two chapters that follow, we will discuss in depth the ways in which contextual factors affect PA processes and outcomes.

Context refers to a heterogeneous mix of factors, ranging from the social and legal system in which the organization exists to the climate and culture within the organization. One way to classify the various levels of context is to arrange them on a continuum from proximal to distal context factors. *Proximal* factors are those that impinge directly on the individual rater, whereas *distal* factors affect the rater indirectly (e.g., by determining norms for evaluating performance) (Cleveland, Morrison, & Bjerke, 1986). A model for distinguishing between proximal and distal effects is illustrated in Figure 2-1.

Proximal context factors include the purpose of rating, the organization's policies regarding feedback, the need to document good versus poor ratings,

Figure 2–1.   Effects of Proximal versus Distal Context Factors

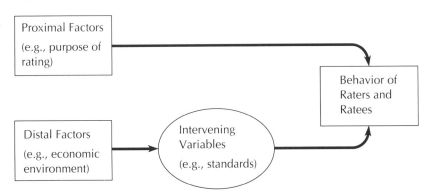

and whatever else the rater is doing at the time he or she fills out performance appraisals. Distal context factors represent the internal and external environments of organizations. Distal context factors range from the climate of the organization to the sociopolitical system of the society (e.g., capitalism versus socialism). This chapter is concerned with the more distal aspects of the context in which rating occurs and, in particular, with those factors that make up the external environment of an organization. We will examine the influence of these environmental factors as well as the mechanisms by which they might affect performance appraisals.

Defining the Organization's Environment

There is no single definition of the external environment of an organization nor is there any clear consensus among organizational researchers regarding the most useful ways to define and study an organization's environment. Table 2-1 vividly illustrates the range of terms and concepts that have been used to describe organizational environments. This table is not comprehensive nor does it include the alternative definitions of several of these terms that have been used by different authors in the literature on organizational environments. Nevertheless, Table 2-1 does provide an indication of the complexity of the term *organizational environment.*

Katz and Kahn (1978) noted five aspects of the environment that organizations must monitor and respond to in order to be effective: (1) societal values, (2) the political/legal environment, (3) the economic/labor environment, (4) the information/technological environment, and (5) the physical/geographical environment. Each of these aspects of the environment is likely to affect PA in some way. Some have a more direct impact on appraisal (e.g., legal environment), whereas others have an indirect, but nevertheless important, effect (e.g., societal values).

Table 2–1. Terms Used to Describe Organizational Environments

Term	Definition
Distant (Secondary Environment)	Everything beyond environment's domain
Domain	Organization's goals and the functions undertaken to meet them
Industry	Set of organizations producing substitutable products
Market	Set of customers who use organization's products
Niche	Environmental configuration that favors survival
Organization Set	Organizations whose roles interlock with subject organization
Organizational Role	Goals or tasks of an organization
Organizational Saga	Collective understanding within an organization
Role	Exchange relation with the environment
Strategy Set	Plan for future relationship with environment
Subenvironment	Environment of one department
Task Environment	Parts of environment that are relevant to goal accomplishment
Territory	Subset of domain organization seeks to dominate
Value Environment	Subset of distant environment that sets norms

W. H. Starbuck, in M. Dunnette (Ed.), *Handbook of Industrial and Organizational Psychology* (Chicago: Rand-McNally, 1976). Copyright © 1976, John Wiley & Sons, Inc.

Each of the characteristics of the environment listed in Table 2-1 are multidimensional. Two of the most frequently cited facets of environments are turbulence and munificence (Katz & Kahn, 1978; March & Simon, 1958; Thompson, 1967). *Turbulence* refers to the the extent to which the environment changes or remains stable. For example, Katz and Kahn (1978) note that the economic environment of Western nations was highly turbulent in the 1970s, with unpredictable swings between inflation and depression. Turbulent environments are thought to lead to uncertainty in organizations; this uncertainty could affect PA practices. *Munificence* refers to the degree of scarcity or abundance of critical resources in the environment. For example, when unemployment is high, the labor market is, from the organization's point of view, a munificent environment. Scarcity of critical resources is likely to lead to conflict within organizations (March & Simon, 1958). The implications of this conflict will depend largely on which environments are munificent and which are plagued by scarcity. For example, if the labor market is very tight, performance appraisals may be used quite differently than if the physical environment is characterized by scarcity.

Researchers have sometimes mentioned environmental variables as possible influences on performance appraisals; 12 of the environmental variables that have been discussed in the PA literature are (Carroll & Schneier, 1982; Landy & Farr, 1983):

- ► Technological development
- ► Competition
- ► Unionization
- ► Economic conditions
- ► Workforce composition
- ► Market share
- ► Profitability
- ► Market predictability
- ► Local unemployment
- ► National unemployment
- ► Demands for diversification
- ► Local, state, and federal legislation

Landy and Farr (1983) note, however, that there is virtually no empirical research on the effects of these environmental variables on PA processes or outcomes. In this chapter, we will draw on research from other areas of psychology and sociology to describe the potential effects of environmental variables on performance appraisal.

Objective and External Environments

Most discussions of environmental effects treat the environment as an objective variable that exists outside of the organization. It is typically assumed that there is some discernible boundary between the organization and its environment, and that the environment of an organization is discernible to an outside observer. Both of these assumptions are debatable. Research questioning these assumptions may have implications for the way environmental variables are linked to PA processes and outcomes.

Starbuck (1976) notes that the boundaries between an organization and its environment are often fuzzy. He uses a cloud or magnetic field as a metaphor for an organization and notes that when a person is either far enough inside or far enough outside of an organization, the organization appears to be a clear, distinct entity. However, if an individual is near the boundaries of an organization, the precise demarcation between the organization and its environment is not at all clear. A considerable amount of research literature has examined the roles of individuals who occupy positions near the boundaries of organizations (Adams, 1976). This literature suggests that occupants of boundary roles inhabit both the organization and the organization's environment. Although the literature is not completely clear on this point, we predict that the effects of environmental variables would be strongest for individuals near the boundary.

Yasai-Adekani (1986) notes that individuals and organizations do not react to objective aspects of the environment but rather to *perceived* aspects of the environment. In many cases, perceptions of organization members will correspond closely with objective reality but this is not always the case. For example, in the area of employment testing, many personnel managers appear to believe that employment discrimination laws discourage the use of ability tests but allow the use of more subjective methods (e.g., the interview) without the same level of scrutiny (Cascio, 1987; Wigdor & Garner, 1982). In fact, the opposite is probably true. Nevertheless, personnel managers have acted on their perceptions of the legal environment, and during the 1960s and 1970s, the use of ability tests appears to have declined (Hale, 1982).

If perceived environment is more important than the objective environment, one implication is that environmental effects might be highly variable within the same organization. For example, some managers might perceive the task environment as highly munificent, whereas others see scarcity. If all these managers were to rate the same subordinates, some differences in ratings would be expected solely as a function of the perceived environment. Thus, it may be that the organization is not the appropriate level of analysis for describing environmental effects. For some environmental variables, the effects on each department, or even on each rater in the organization, may need to be examined.

It is useful to examine the factors that lead some individuals to misperceive their environment. When these factors are present, wide individual differences in perceptions of the environment can be expected. These differences may also lead to significant variability in the extent to which the environment affects the rating behavior of various individuals. When these factors are absent, it may be predicted that all organizational members will develop similar perceptions of the environment, which may in turn lead to more homogeneous environmental effects.

Misperception of the environment is most likely when (1) environmental cues are ambiguous, (2) information about the environment is scarce, or (3) environmental cues are inconsistent. For example, if the economy is not clearly in a period of inflation, recession, or recovery, this may lead to wide individual differences in perceptions of the munificence of the economic environment. During periods of rapid technological advances, information about the technology that is likely to dominate one's market or niche is likely to be fragmentary, which could lead to considerable uncertainty in individual's perceptions of the technological environment. It might be difficult to develop a consistent perception of the legal environment (especially in areas related to personnel administration), because of conflicting court decisions or because of conflicts between the executive and the judicial branches.

How the Environment Affects Appraisal

As discussed earlier, there is very little empirical research on the links between environmental variables and appraisal. Consequently, very little is known about the mechanisms by which environments affect appraisal processes and outcomes. By definition, these effects will be at least partially indirect (i.e., external environments represent distal cues), which means that some variable or set of variables will intervene between the environment and the behavior of individual raters and ratees. We can suggest several possible intervening variables, including:

1. Performance standards
2. Performance dimensions
3. Frequency of appraisal
4. Supervisor-subordinate relationship
5. Consequences of high versus low ratings
6. Legitimacy of appraisal.

These six variables do not exhaust the list of possible mediating variables, but they do provide a basis for describing the different ways in which the environment might indirectly affect performance appraisal.

Environments are complex, and different aspects of the environment could have different effects on each of the intervening variables listed above. To help structure our discussion of environmental effects, we will restrict our attention to the effects of the munificence of the five aspects of the environment identified by Katz and Kahn (1978). Munificence can be defined in the following ways for each aspect of the environment:

1. Societal — the extent to which sociopolitical norms and values support the concept of performance appraisal, as typically practiced in organizations
2. Legal — the extent to which the legal system facilitates and allows typical performance appraisal practices
3. Economic — the extent to which general economic conditions are favorable for the organization
4. Technical — the extent to which an organization possesses or controls the technology and work methods needed to carry out the organization's functions
5. Physical — the extent to which necessary physical resources are available.

Our predictions regarding the effects of munificence are summarized in Table 2-2. The rationale for these predictions is discussed below.

Performance Standards _____

We predict that the standards that define good and poor performance on the job will be strongly affected by four of the five aspects of the environment. For example, the question of whether one should expect all workers to perform well, or should set standards that allow some workers to succeed and others to

Table 2–2.   Effects of Environmental Munificence on Six Aspects of Appraisal Systems

Aspects of Appraisal	Aspects of Environment				
	Societal	Legal	Economic	Technical	Physical
Standard	Strong	Moderate	Strong	Strong	Strong
Dimensions	Moderate	Moderate	Strong	Strong	Strong
Frequency	Weak	Moderate	Moderate	Weak	Moderate
Relationship	Moderate	Weak	Strong	Strong	Moderate
Consequences	Moderate	Strong	Strong	Weak	Moderate
Legitimacy	Strong	Strong	Moderate	Strong	Weak

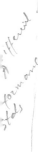

fail, is in part a philosophical one, whose solution might depend on the values of society as a whole. A society that emphasizes competition and achievement might lead to different (probably higher) performance standards than one that emphasizes satisfaction with work.

The legal system probably also affects performance standards, although to a lesser degree. That is, the legal system may not have a main effect on standards (i.e., raising or lowering standards) but it is likely to affect the degree to which standards are made explicit, as well as the degree to which they are enforced. A legal system that is basically antagonistic to performance appraisal will probably lead to the formulation of explicit, concrete standards that are communicated directly to employees.

We would expect different (higher) performance standards during a business recession than during a period of economic growth or stability. We would also expect the technological position of a company to affect standards. A company that is behind the times technologically might try to compensate by setting high standards; a company that is technologically sophisticated might not see strong links between the performance standards enforced for individual workers and the output of the organization. Companies that employ assembly-line technologies might have different performance standards than companies that rely on semi-autonomous work teams to produce their product.

Finally, the effects of physical munificence are likely to be very similar in strength to those of economic munificence, but perhaps in a different direction. When the physical resources needed for production are not available, it may be necessary to adjust performance standards downward (Peters, O'Connor, & Eulberg, 1985).

Performance Dimensions

The definition of what constitutes performance and the relative importance of different parts of the performance domain are likely to be affected by the environment. A comparison of U.S. versus Japanese management styles provides an example of societal influences. A U.S. manager is likely to emphasize individual task performance, whereas a Japanese manager is likely to emphasize ability to work with the group when evaluating the performance of the same subordinate (Pascale & Athos, 1981).

The legal system will probably also have a moderate influence. As the legal system becomes less munificent (i.e., less favorable to current appraisal practices), we predict that organizations will emphasize dimensions that involve clear, concrete, objective outcomes, and will deemphasize interpersonally oriented performance dimensions.

The munificence of the economic environment will strongly affect the choice of performance dimensions. In an unfavorable economic environment, we expect that organizations will define performance in terms of short-term, bottom-line goals. Thus, a supervisor who is not good at producing products but who is good at developing subordinates might receive different evaluations, depending on the economic environment. The technical environment will also have a strong impact on the choice of performance dimensions. The importance of technically oriented dimensions will probably vary across industries (and companies) with varying levels of technical sophistication.

The munificience of the physical environment will strongly affect the extent to which performance is defined in terms of efficiency versus output. When resources are scarce, the worker who produces less but conserves materials and resources might receive a more favorable evaluation than a worker who produces a great deal but is wasteful. The reverse might be the case when resources are cheap and plentiful.

Frequency of Appraisal

Societal values will probably have a weak impact on the frequency with which an organization conducts appraisals. However, the practice of annual appraisals is a strong norm, and these values could affect an organization that tries to conduct appraisals less or more frequently than once a year. The legal system is likely to have a moderate, albeit indirect, effect on the frequency of appraisals. Many organizations make major administrative decisions (particularly salary decisions) on a roughly annual schedule. If the legal system encourages strong links between appraisals and administrative decisions, this might lead to a strong preference for annual or semi-annual appraisals that coincide with the organization's schedule for making administrative decisions.

Both the economic environment and the physical environment are likely to have a moderate effect on the frequency of appraisals. As the economic and physical environments become more unfavorable, there will be stronger incentives for frequent performance appraisals, coupled with programs to increase the output of poor performers. When the economic and physical environments are highly munificent, there will probably be less interest in performance appraisal.

We do not expect the technical environment to have a strong effect on the frequency of appraisals. Perhaps the one exception is the situation where the supervisor is not familiar with the technology of production. We might expect this supervisor to avoid doing performance appraisals, if at all possible, and to turn in appraisals that are not informative when they are demanded by the organization.

Supervisor-Subordinate Relationship

Societal values will have some impact on the nature of the relationship between supervisors and subordinates, particularly with regard to the extent to which this relationship is autocratic versus participative. Agervold (1975) notes that the decline of authoritarian methods of supervision in some Swedish industries is a direct result of a cultural value system that emphasizes workplace democracy. We do not think that the legal system will have a strong impact on supervisor-subordinate relationships, although an adverse legal climate might lead supervisors to try to avoid litigation by being more formal, and retaining better documentation of the interaction with subordinates.

Both the economic and technical environments, and to a lesser extent the physical environment, are likely to affect supervisor-subordinate relationships significantly. Economic or physical environments that are unfavorable, or technical environments that are complex, are likely to increase the degree to which the supervisor is dependent on subordinates. When the economic or physical environment is unfavorable, there is likely to be pressure on the supervisor to produce; he or she must in turn depend on obtaining good performance from subordinates. As the technology becomes increasingly complex, the supervisor might also become increasingly irrelevant, especially if the supervisor cannot operate the computers, instruments, or machines that his or her subordinates use.

Consequences of High versus Low Ratings

As discussed in the last chapter, one of the key determinants of whether a supervisor gives high or low ratings is the consequences that are attached to the ratings. Rating inflation is quite likely when ratings have a strong influence on salaries or promotions, and is least likely if ratings are not used to make administrative decisions (see Chapter Nine). Four of the five aspects of the environment will have at least a moderate effect on the consequences of giving high versus low ratings; for two of the five aspects, this influence may be substantial.

Societal norms and values will have some influence on the consequences of high versus low ratings. The extent of this influence will be determined by the degree to which societal values support or discourage treating good and poor workers differently. For example, the question of whether individuals should be rewarded in proportion to their level of performance would probably be answered differently in the United States than in Japan. In socialist and communist states, the answer might be different from that in either the United States or Japan.

The legal system will strongly affect the degree to which performance appraisals are likely to be connected to administrative decisions. A legal system that is hostile to PA, as it is typically practiced, will also be hostile to the use of performance ratings as a primary basis for allocating organizational rewards. A legal system that strongly acknowledges management's rights to evaluate the performance of workers will also probably support linking rewards directly to performance ratings.

The lower the munificence of the economic environment (and, to a lesser extent, the physical environment), the greater the incentive to tie rewards to performance levels. We predict that organizations will be more likely to use performance appraisals to make administrative decisions, ranging from salary and promotions to layoffs, when the economic environment is unfavorable than when it is favorable. In part this is because organizations have less slack (i.e., less ability to survive given substandard performance) in an unfavorable economic environment than in a favorable one.

We do not predict that the munificence of the technological environment will affect the organization's decision of whether or not to link rewards to one's performance ratings. However, the technological environment might still have an effect on rating, especially if the supervisor is not capable of using the technology that workers employ. In this case, one might find range restriction. Our rationale here is that supervisors who do not understand or have never performed major portions of the job may be less willing (or able) to distinguish between good and poor performers.

Legitimacy of Appraisal

The question of legitimacy can be thought of in two ways. First, at the broadest level, it is likely that some people regard the evaluation of individual job performance as a perfectly legitimate managerial function, whereas others do not accept the idea of performance evaluation at all. Second, it is likely that some people will regard any particular performance appraisal *system* as acceptable, whereas others will not. The organization's environment might affect both aspects of the legitimacy question.

Societal values will be a strong determinant of perceptions of the legitimacy of performance appraisal per se, as well as perceptions of any particular appraisal system. Although we know of no empirical research on this topic, we predict that if different countries were rank-ordered in terms of the degree to which the dominant culture viewed individual performance appraisal as a reasonable and acceptable activity, the United States would be at or near the top of the list. Countries in which the primary orientation was toward the performance of groups or classes of workers (e.g., Japan and some countries with socialist or communist systems) would probably be ranked lower. The acceptability of any particular appraisal system would also depend on the degree to which the system was consonant with the society's values.

One function of the legal system, in this case, is to codify the societal values that are relevant to PA practice. For example, the U.S. legal system accepts the principal of performance appraisal, but also demands certain safeguards be in place to protect workers from arbitrary and capricious supervisory judgments. The technological environment also has a strong effect on determining the legitimacy of performance appraisal, but the direction of this effect is not as easy to predict. If the technology is complex *and* the supervisor is not familiar with the technology, the idea of the supervisor evaluating subordinates' performance might not be acceptable. On the other hand, if the supervisor is familiar with or expert in the technology used by subordinates, there may be little resistance to using the supervisor as the primary or sole source of performance appraisals.

The economic environment might affect supervisors' and subordinates' assessments of the legitimacy of different PA methods. There is evidence that economic hardship contributes to conflict and suspicion in organizations (Whetten, 1987). Subordinates may most strongly resist supervisors' attempts to separate good from poor performers in situations where resources are tight and poor performance ratings may result in adverse outcomes.

Finally, we do not predict a strong effect for the munificence of the physical environment of the perceived legitimacy of performance appraisal. However, there is one circumstance in which the effects of the physical environment could be strong. If there are strong situational constraints that prevent individuals from performing well, workers might not accept an appraisal system that tries to separate good from poor performers.

Research on Environmental Effects

As noted earlier, empirical research that *directly* examines the role of environmental variables in performance is virtually nonexistent. Nevertheless, we can draw on research outside of the area of performance appraisal and from nonempirical papers in the PA literature to document some of the likely effects of environmental variables on performance appraisal processes and outcomes. As with the preceding section, our discussion is arranged around the five aspects of an organization's environment that are critical in determining the organization's health and survival.

Societal Environment

Research on the effects of societal norms and values on behavior in organizations has concentrated primarily on political issues, particularly the extent to which the sociopolitical system encourages democratic versus authoritarian systems of control, and capitalistic versus socialistic systems of ownership. Some studies have also examined the internal political environment of organizations (e.g., Longenecker, Sims, & Gioia, 1987); this research will be discussed more fully in Chapters Three and Four.

Locke (1983) examined the practice of PA under capitalism, socialism, and a mixed economy. First, he concluded that, under capitalism, the market would help guarantee effective performance appraisals. His reasoning, similar to that often employed by classical economists, is that any personnel practice that survives for long periods in an organization must be an effective one; otherwise, organizations that used more effective methods would soon overtake the organization that was doing a poor job in evaluating its employees. (A similar line of reasoning is employed by sociobiologists, who argue that the long-term survival of any species-specific characteristic is an indication of its evolutionary value.) Second, he concluded that there was very little incentive for PA under socialism, noting that "socialism eliminates at the outset the foundation on which objective performance evaluation is based — namely the price system and its free market corollary, the profit system" (p. 317). Third, Locke concluded that in a mixed economy (a category that would include the United States, Europe, and much of the Third World), performance appraisal would be very difficult. (For an opposing point of view, see Lerner, 1983.)

We would be more willing to accept Locke's (1983) conclusions if there were more data available to support them. His arguments appear to rest on many of the assumptions of classical economics (e.g., that a completely free market can exist, and that decision makers possess the information necessary to make optimal decisions) that have been shown to be untenable (March & Simon, 1958). Relatively few studies have examined Locke's hypotheses to date. Thus, we regard the question of whether PA is easier under capitalism, socialism, or a mixed economy as unsettled.

Goldman (1983) examines performance appraisal from the Marxist perspective. Goldman does not address the question of whether it is possible to evaluate performance accurately, but rather asks whether performance *should* be evaluated, regardless of the technical capacity to do so. He argues that the practice of distinguishing among workers on *any* basis, such as their level of performance, is in the interest of management but is not in the interest of workers. According to Marxist thought, the primary basis for workers' power is their solidarity. Any procedure that singles out workers and separates them from their colleagues dilutes the workers' power, and therefore increases the power of management to exploit workers. Implicit in this argument is the assumption that the gains associated with performance appraisal for individual workers who *are* good performers are smaller than the losses that workers as a group will have to endure if distinctions are made between good and poor workers.

Our discomfort with Goldman's (1983) conclusions closely mirrors our objections to those of Locke (1983). The argument would be more convincing if it were accompanied by more data. Unfortunately, empirical research has not, in general, supported key aspects of the Marxist position. For example, Form (1987) notes that Marxist theory assumes that capitalists will attempt to simplify jobs in order to increase efficiency, control, and profits. A careful review of the literature led Form (1987) to conclude that skill levels of jobs have not declined in modern history. The proportion of skilled to unskilled jobs in the economy has not changed substantially since the Industrial Revolution.

In his survey of the history of organizational theory, Perrow (1973) noted that the decline of scientific management was not due to the fact that this method did not work but rather occurred because of social, political, and cultural changes that created dissatisfaction with the highly directive and paternalistic aspects of this approach.

Similarly, Agervold (1975) noted that the growth of movements for industrial democracy in Europe (particularly Scandinavia) was a reflection of a broader social and cultural norm that rejected authoritarian styles of leadership. If social norms are moving away from top-down (from authoritarian power structures toward more democratic structures), PA practices could change substantially. For example, under a more strongly democratic culture we might see more emphasis on self-appraisal, peer appraisal, and the use of appraisals for counseling and development, and less emphasis on using appraisal to rank-order workers.

Both historical and cross-cultural research is needed to assess the effects of the sociopolitical environment on performance appraisal. We have noted earlier that the sociopolitical environment of the United States is highly favorable to performance appraisal. A good deal could be learned about the ways in which such an environment affects PA by studying appraisal methods in other times or cultures. This topic is likely to become increasingly relevant with the growth of multinational organizations whose corporate appraisal policies are different from those typically encountered in the United States. Historically, our nation has been able to impose its sociopolitical values on workers in U.S. multinational corporations. With the rise in foreign-owned multinational corporations in this country, however, the situation is starting to reverse itself (i.e., values and practices from other cultures are being employed with U.S. workers). Cultural differences revolving around PA could become a significant problem for U.S. employees of foreign multinationals.

Legal Environment

Passage of the Civil Rights Act of 1964 dramatically changed the legal environment of performance appraisals. Prior to 1964, it was difficult for any employee to contest legally his or her performance evaluation, no matter how subjective, capricious, or inaccurate the appraisal. (One exception would be where a performance appraisal was used to carry out some unfair labor practice, such as giving all union organizers poor ratings.) The reason for this is that there was no legal requirement that private organizations accurately evaluate workers' performance. The same is true today, except in the case where a test or measure has adverse impact on some protected group (typically minorities or women). Adverse impact occurs when a test, measurement device, or procedure has markedly different outcomes for different groups. For example, if most men passed a strength test but most women failed, the test would have adverse impact on women if it was used to make decisions about hiring, firing, promotion, and the like. Any measure that has, or might have, adverse impact is potentially vulnerable to legal scrutiny. If adverse impact is demonstrated, the employer must establish the validity or business necessity of the PA system.

Legal issues connected with PA are reviewed by Barrett and Kernan (1987), Bernardin and Beatty (1984), Cascio (1987), Cascio and Bernardin (1981), and Latham (1986). Some general guidelines (Bernardin & Beatty, 1984; Feild & Holley, 1982) for complying with federal antidiscrimination laws in carrying out performance appraisals are:

> ► Performance appraisals should be based on specific dimensions whose relevance has been established through job analysis.
> ► Raters should receive training or instruction.
> ► Performance dimensions should be defined in terms of behaviors.
> ► Feedback should be given to the ratee, and there should be an appeal process for ratings that the individual feels are inaccurate.
> ► Raters should have adequate opportunities to observe the performance they will be asked to evaluate.
> ► Extreme ratings should be documented.
> ► If possible, there should be multiple raters.
> ► Appraisals should be frequent — at least annual.

All of these guidelines can be thought of as safeguards designed to protect employees from arbitrary or subjective evaluations that may more closely reflect the rater's biases than they reflect the ratee's performance.

There is clear evidence that the legal environment affects the way in which performance appraisals are done. Cleveland, Murphy, and Williams (1989) surveyed over 100 corporations to determine the degree to which performance appraisals were used for various purposes in organizations. In their confirmatory factor analysis of 20 potential uses, one of the four factors was labeled "Documentation" and referred to the uses of performance appraisals to meet federal, state, and local requirements, in particular to justify adverse personnel actions (e.g., firing a worker for poor performance).

The surveys showed that documentation represented one of the most frequent uses of performance appraisal. Although Cleveland and colleagues (1989) did not investigate the issue, we suspect that the use of PA to document personnel decisions is highest in organizations that are willing to fire poor performers and is lowest in situations where it is not possible to take action in the face of performance that is at least marginally acceptable (e.g., where a strong union prevails). Only the most foolish employer will now dismiss a worker for poor performance without first collecting clear and convincing documentation.

As we will discuss in Chapter Five, most PA systems rely on the direct supervisor as the sole judge of his or her subordinates' performance. Although the appraisal form might also require the signature of the supervisor's superior, the direct supervisor has the ultimate responsibility for assessing workers' performance. The legal system, although not hostile to this practice, nevertheless discourages it. The issue is not that the supervisor is less qualified than someone else to evaluate subordinates' performance but rather that it is impossible to rule out rater biases if only one person evaluates each worker's performance (see Chapter Ten). No matter how explicit the rating form or how detailed the training program, there is no safeguard against conscious or unconscious distortion by any single rater. Although using multiple raters does not completely solve the problem of rater bias (e.g., if all raters are white males with similar backgrounds, they may share similar biases), it seems to be the only reasonable procedure if the problem of rater bias is serious. We do not know of any case that has been decided on the basis of whether the plaintiff used one rater or several but we would not be surprised to see this issue raised in lawsuits in the near future.

The current legal environment for performance appraisal clearly reflects the broader sociopolitical environment. At one time in our history, the right of the employer to use *any* personnel practice, except perhaps for those that placed employees at great physical risk, was basically unchallenged. This is no longer true. The current legal environment is one where the outcome of conflicts between the rights of the employer and the rights of employees cannot be easily predicted. However, even if the outcome of lawsuits challenging personnel practices is highly uncertain, it is likely that the legal environment will continue to have a strong influence on PA practice. Organizations are likely to take steps to prevent lawsuits from ever arising (even if an organization wins a lawsuit, the expense of defending the suit can be ruinous). Thus, we expect that the guidelines outlined on the previous page will continue to strongly affect performance appraisal.

Economic Environment

Organizational researchers have paid relatively little attention to the effects of the economic environment on behavior in organizations. It has long been known that the munificence of the environment affects the frequency and intensity of conflict within the organization (March & Simon, 1958). Low munificence is associated with heightened conflict. It is also known that economic conditions strongly affect strategic goals (Starbuck, 1976). However, the literature on economic environments has had little to say about the influence of those environments on performance appraisal.

Although research on the growth and decline of organizations is not concerned solely with the economic environment, this literature is nevertheless the source for several hypotheses about the relationship between the state of the economy and the methods used to evaluate workers' performance. Early in their life cycles, organizations are often characterized by liberal goals and flexible structures. However, as organizations prosper and grow, they tend to become inflexible and autocratic (Whetten, 1987). As organizations decline, relationships within the organization become increasingly politicized (Pfeffer & Salancik, 1978). Decline leads to higher levels of conflict, secrecy, and scapegoating, and to lower levels of morale, satisfaction, and participation (Whetten, 1987). We might expect similar phenomena to occur during either highly prosperous (growth) or economically unfavorable (decline) times.

As organizations grow and prosper, we would expect that PA will become increasingly formalized. In part, this is a product of the size of the organization; as the organization gets larger, informal relations between workers at different levels become less likely. As organizations decline, documentation of poor performance is emphasized more, especially if the organization is forced to lay off a significant portion of its workforce. We might also expect less emphasis on feedback and development (as a result of the increasing emphasis on secrecy) and more interest in using PA as an instrument to increase production.

Negative economic trends probably have a greater impact on behavior in organizations than do positive ones. In particular, personnel practices that are adopted during hard times are likely to be retained when the economy rebounds. This is precisely the pattern with union-management relations in the early and mid-1980s. The recession in the early 1980s created conditions where unions were forced to make substantial concessions to management, often in the form of decreases in pay. When the recession ended, few organizations restored their earlier contracts; requests for pay cuts and other major concessions are still common in union-management negotiations.

Technical Environment

Changes in technology can have a substantial impact on PA processes and outcomes. In part, this is due to incidental changes in the organization of work that accompany new technology. For example, Woodward (1965) noted that as technology becomes increasingly complex, the span of control of first-line supervisors tends to increase. Thus, the addition of new technology may increase the number of persons a supervisor is asked to evaluate. An increasing span of control also implies that the supervisor (1) has less time to observe each worker's performance, (2) must spend more time doing performance appraisals, and (3) has a larger comparison group available for evaluating each worker's performance. The first two factors may lead to lower levels of accuracy; the last factor may lead to increased levels of accuracy.

Another example of the indirect effects of technology on performance appraisal involves changes in supervisor-subordinate relations (Barley, 1986). Fry (1982) notes that when the technology becomes complex, the workers who use that technology may become more expert in their jobs than their supervisors. In the extreme case, the supervisor who cannot operate the current technology could become completely dependent on his or her subordinates. This change in relationship is likely to have several effects on performance appraisal.

First, as noted earlier, the frequency of appraisals may go down if the supervisor does not feel able to sensibly evaluate subordinates' performance. (In this case, we would also expect severe range restriction in whatever ratings were collected.) Second, workers may not accept appraisals from a supervisor who does not understand precisely what they do. One basis for the supervisor's power is usually his or her presumed expertise (French & Raven, 1959). The supervisor who does not understand the technology no longer has expert power. Third, in a related point, the supervisor may lose position power (French & Raven, 1959) as a result of the introduction of new technologies. Particularly in areas such as communications or computers, new technologies may change the nature of work in such a way that the supervisor becomes superfluous. A loss in position power will probably also lead to lower levels of acceptance of performance appraisals by subordinates.

Shamir and Salomon (1985) note that advances in telecommunications and microelectronics have made it progressively easier for a number of workers to work at home, rather than going to the workplace. It is possible that a supervisor will never see or even meet some of his or her subordinates. The performance of an individual who works at home can hardly be assessed in behavioral terms. In this case, PA might depend solely on a count of products, reports, or other results achieved. Furthermore, in evaluating the performance of a worker who is off-site, the supervisor (if there even is one) might be bypassed entirely, and performance counts may be recorded through the same medium (e.g., a personal computer) that the worker uses to submit the results of his or her work.

Advances in technology have made it possible to automate some aspects of the PA process. Landy (1985) described the use of computers to measure the performance of claims processors at a health insurance office. The computers that these workers used not only recorded the results of their work but also monitored their performance. The computer recorded performance on a minute-by-minute basis, constantly comparing productivity to company production standards, and provided weekly reports on each worker's performance. Workers' pay was adjusted up or down, according to their performance levels. As might be expected, the workers reacted very negatively to this system, and complained of fatigue, stress, and an assembly-line atmosphere at work.

The use of computers or other technological means to monitor workers' performance will inevitably lead to a debate over the employer's right to get full-time work for full-time pay, versus the workers' rights to protection against invasions of privacy. Regardless of one's position in this debate, this application of technology is not one we recommend. Although the use of automatic monitoring of performance may be legally permissible (this issue has not yet, to our knowledge, been ruled on in court), the practice is likely to be a public-relations disaster. Personnel policies that are regarded as invasive or unjustified are likely to lead both members of the organization and outsiders to develop a negative image of the organization, which may in turn affect the organization's ability to recruit, hire, and keep good employees (Cascio, 1987; Murphy & Reynolds, 1988b; Schwab, Rynes, & Aldag, 1987).

Even if the public-relations problem could be solved, we are not sure that there is anything one could or should *do* with minute-by-minute reports about each worker. First, suppose that it was found that an individual took frequent breaks. Wouldn't the evaluation of that individual still depend on what he or she accomplished between breaks? The minute-by-minute report might say more about an individual's style of work than his or her level of performance. Second, reports that cover a short period, such as a week, are probably not reliable indicators of an individual's overall performance. It is known in test theory that reliability increases with the number of opportunities to observe the subject's behavior (i.e., with the number of test items). This same principle also applies to performance appraisal. If reports are produced only for blocks of time that allow for reliable measurement (this might require several weeks or months, depending on the nature of the work), minute-by-minute reports will be so voluminous as to be useless.

There have been proposals for partially or fully automating performance appraisal by recording ratee behavior on checklists and then using algorithms that apply Kane's (1986, 1987) performance distribution model to derive performance indices from the behavioral data. This strategy is a variation of one that is often recommended in research on clinical versus statistical procedures for integrating multiple pieces of data. (See Wiggins, 1973, for a review.) That is, human judges have the responsibility for collecting the data, and a statistical or mechanical procedure is used for integrating the data. We are somewhat skeptical about the practicality of this approach.

Although the use of some objective, automatic means to integrate data is appealing, the strategy is only as good as the data that are recorded. We doubt that checklists that include most or all of the important behaviors could be assembled for many jobs (e.g., personnel manager). Even if they were, it is not clear whether supervisors are capable of objectively recording the behaviors they have observed. Cognitive research suggests that supervisors' perceptions of subordinates' behaviors are far from objective records of what has happened. (See DeNisi & Williams, 1988, for a review.) Rather, the behaviors that are checked are strongly influenced by subjective overall impressions about each ratee (Murphy, Martin, & Garcia, 1982).

A more modest proposal for partially automating performance appraisals would involve: (1) obtaining ratings on specific dimensions from raters; (2) assessing, via job analysis, the importance of each dimension; and (3) computing a composite measure of overall performance that weighted the dimensions in proportion to their importance. This would preserve the primary advantage of using an objective method to integrate information about performance (i.e., the absolute reliability of an objective function) without the need for a comprehensive checklist that contained all important work behaviors.

One final aspect of the technological environment is the increasing emphasis on workgroups. Many manufacturing technologies, for example, have moved away from a reliance on individual workers in the assembly line, and now use teams of workers to perform complex tasks. Performance appraisal has traditionally been concerned with the performance of individuals. An increasing reliance on work teams may force organizations to develop methods of evaluating both individual and team performance.

Physical Environment

Although the physical environment is rarely considered by PA researchers, there is a body of literature on situational constraints on job performance that examines the effects of munificence of the physical environment on performance and performance measurement. This literature has been reviewed by Peters and O'Connor (1980) and, more recently, by Peters and associates (1985). Of the 11 categories of situational constraints reviewed, 3 represent aspects of the physical environment that might constrain an individual's ability to perform well: (1) shortages of tools and equipment, (2) lack of materials and supplies, and (3) an unfavorable work environment (e.g., poor lighting).

Researchers have identified a number of consequences of situational constraints. First, there is evidence that situational constraints lead to lower levels of performance (Peters & O'Connor, 1980). This should not be surprising since situational constraints are defined as variables that constrain one's ability to perform well. Second, it has been hypothesized that the presence of situational constraints will lead to decreased variability in performance, in part because of a ceiling effect. Empirical research, however, has not consistently supported this hypothesis (Peters et al., 1985; Peters, O'Connor, & Rudolph, 1980). As we will note below, the failure to find range restriction effects may say more about the extent to which situational constraints exist than about their effects. Third, situational constraints appear to lead to negative affective reactions and to lower motivation, although research results here are somewhat mixed (Phillips & Freedman, 1982; Peters et al., 1985).

In their review, Peters and colleagues (1985) note that serious situational constraints are rare. It may be that the small effect sizes found in situational constraint research reflect the fact that work environments are generally munificent and that the situational constraints that do exist are too minor to have much of an impact. This is another area in which cross-cultural and historical research methods may be worthwhile. Researchers may be under-estimating the effects of situational constraints as a result of doing research in a time and place where these constraints are rare. We predict that there would be stronger effects in settings where the seriousness of situational constraints was variable rather than being uniformly low.

In situations where situational constraints cannot be removed, it is necessary to develop methods of measuring performance that take these constraints into account. It is hardly fair to compare the performance of someone who has all of the tools, equipment, and supplies necessary to complete the task to someone else who does not. Peters and associates (1985) review the results of several studies that have attempted to develop PA methods that take situational constraints into account. Unfortunately, the results of these studies have not been encouraging. It is unclear if any method will be developed that leads raters to adjust adequately for the presence or absence of situational constraints.

Some of the effects of the physical environment tend to mirror those of the economic environment. In both cases, we expect that shortages and scarcity will lead to growing levels of conflict and to increasing politicization of the organization. Scarcity also leads to an emphasis on conservation and efficiency, which may lead to a change in the performance dimensions that are viewed as most important by an organization. However, the physical environment may have a more immediate and vivid impact. If the tools, resources, information, and so on that are necessary to do the job are not available, the consequences are felt immediately, whereas poor economic conditions may take a significant period to lead to changes on the shop floor.

External Environments and Rater Goals

At the beginning of this chapter, we noted that context is a major determinant of the goals that the rater forms. Some raters may use performance appraisal to reward or secure promotions for particular employees. Others will use appraisal as a tool for punishing least-favored subordinates. Still others will use PA as a method of shifting their problem employees to some other supervisor. (It is not unheard of to give high ratings to a particularly obnoxious employee to assure that he or she is promoted out of your workgroup or department [Longenecker et al., 1987].) Although the internal environment of an organization is likely to have a stronger impact on rater goals than will the external environment, there are some areas in which the effects of external environments will be substantial. This is particularly true of the societal, legal, and economic environments.

A societal value that will directly affect the rater's goals is the extent to which the society emphasizes individual advancement. In a culture where promotions are highly valued and/or rapid, raters are likely to use performance appraisal as an instrument for promoting employees who they regard as deserving. In this same culture, raters might be very reluctant to give low ratings because such ratings could jeopardize the worker's future success in the organization. The legal system might also strongly shape goals. Our current legal environment is one in which most organizations will go to great lengths to avoid litigation. The rater who supervises a marginal performer may give high ratings to avoid any possible challenge. The other possibility is that the rater will carefully collect evidence to document the low ratings he or she wishes to give to the poor performer.

The state of the economy may also shape the rater's goals, and the direction of this effect might be the opposite from the effect of the economy on the *organization's* goals. When the economy is bad, organizations might become highly motivated to weed out poor performers. However, the rater might be very unwilling to take steps that will eventually cost a subordinate his or her job if the prospects for getting another job are dim. When the economy is bad, raters might become more lenient, whereas organizations become more severe.

The technological environment will sometimes affect a rater's goals. As the technology becomes more complex, the supervisor will be more interested in retaining and motivating workers who are skilled in the technology. As a result, the rater may give higher ratings. The physical environment could also sometimes have an effect. If situational constraints are present, raters may be reluctant to distinguish among ratees and may use performance ratings as a device to encourage workers who are presently constrained from performing well.

Summary

This chapter examined the influence of the external environment on performance appraisals in organizations. Although the research literature dealing with the relationships between organizations and environments is large, few definite conclusions can be drawn about how environments affect behavior in organizations, or about what facets of the environment are or are not important. However, it is possible to speculate about the ways in which environmental variables might affect PA processes and outcomes.

We identified several aspects of performance appraisal that are likely to be affected by environmental variables, including the standards used to evaluate performance, the definition of exactly what constitutes performance (i.e., the performance dimensions chosen), the frequency of appraisals, supervisor-subordinate relationships, the consequences of high or low ratings, and the perceived legitimacy of performance appraisal. All of these may be affected in varying ways by events and conditions in the sociopolitical, legal, economic, technical, and physical environment in which work is carried out.

It is very reasonable to assume that the external environment affects a number of practices in organizations, including performance appraisal. However, we still know very little about *how* environmental variables affect organizations, or *which* environmental variables are most or least important.

The challenge to researchers concerned with environmental effects is that the concept of environment is both broad and fuzzy. That is, everyone knows what it means, but nobody can provide a clear definition of precisely what the environment is or how it affects individuals, groups, or organizations. Better articulation of the links between environmental variables and performance appraisal processes and outcomes might be one small step in understanding the ways in which environmental variables affect organizations.

Chapter Three

Organizational
Influences

▶   This chapter continues our discussion of the contextual factors that influence performance appraisal (PA) in organizations. In Chapter Two, the influence of factors in the environment external to the organization were discussed. In this chapter, we discuss the contextual factors internal to or within the organization that may influence the process and outcomes of performance appraisal. Before the literature on organizational context and appraisal is reviewed, we will describe what we mean by context, drawing from the social and personality psychology literature. In addition, we will identify the range of methods and approaches used to analyze and describe situations.

Although the meaning of a situation is important when discussing the environment external to an organization, we have placed this discussion within the current chapter for two reasons. First, we believe that the internal organizational context is a more salient set of variables that has greater impact on the rater and appraisal than distal, external environmental variables. Because they have more impact, a more extensive discussion of the terms *context* or *situation* is warranted in this chapter. Second, there is an extensive literature on the psychology of situations that is more appropriately applied to the organization as the general context.

This chapter also presents a range of context variables that are likely to influence performance appraisal. Further, we will identify relevant context factors that have not been extensively investigated in the context of PA and discuss how they might affect appraisal in organizations. Interactional psychology is then introduced as an approach to investigating the interaction between a pattern of organizational characteristics and a pattern of person (rater or ratee) characteristics as they affect the PA system.

Within-Organization Context

There is little research on organizational differences in appraisal process and outcomes (Davis & Dickinson, 1987; Landy & Farr, 1983). Most appraisal research has focused on the actual measurement and process of rating; few researchers have investigated the influence of the surrounding organizational context within which appraisals are conducted and utilized. (For exceptions, see Davis & Dickinson, 1987; Eulberg, O'Connor, Peters, & Watson, 1984; Lawler, 1967.) Before describing situational influences on behavior, it is important to understand what is meant by *situation* or *context.*

Brunswick (1952) and others (Magnusson, 1981) have urged psychologists to develop a better understanding of the dynamics underlying and defining situations. In order to understand more fully and predict the perceptions and behavior of individuals, psychologists should systematically investigate the relevant features of the context within which people behave. Brunswick and more recent theorists have urged psychologists to develop a "psychology of situations." There are a number of considerations in the process of defining situations.

Magnusson (1981) notes that the description and classification of situations raises many problems. He describes three major considerations: (1) units of analysis, (2) time and space measures, and (3) characteristics that can be used for description and classification of situations. We believe that research on PA can benefit from increased knowledge about the context of the appraisal. In order to conduct such research adequately, each of these issues warrants more discussion.

Units of Analysis

When managers refer to the context of appraisal, they can be referring to very different aspects of the appraisal situation, including the pattern of ratee's past performance, the composition of workgroup performance, the nature of the job and/or department, the values of the organization, and so on. Therefore, it is critical to articulate clearly the unit of context under consideration.

The unit of context for situational analysis can range from microlevel (e.g., the type of task performed) to macrolevel (e.g., organzational climate) variables (Magnusson, 1981). Context variables can also be conceptualized as proximal, having a direct impact on an individual's behavior or perceptions, to distal variables, having a less direct influence on the perceptions or behavior of people (Cleveland & Hollmann, in press; See Figure 2-1 in Chapter Two of this book). According to Magnusson (1981), in research on situation variables there is a need to identify the appropriate unit of analysis along these dimensions (micro to macro) for each specific question or problem. However, since there do not appear to be definite boundaries between one unit of analysis to another, the distinction among units of context may be somewhat arbitrary.

The concept of context or situation can also vary along two other dimensions: (1) from physical to perceived characteristics of the situation and (2) from molecular to molar units. For example, Magnusson (1981) described four uses of the term *situation* that vary along these two dimensions: the actual situation, the perceived situation, the situation type, and the life situation.

The *actual situation* refers to the physical and biological variables of a part of a total environment that are available to the individual for a certain amount of time. Further, attached to the biological and physical characteristics of context, there are sociocultural factors (e.g., norms, rules, roles, etc.) that contribute to the definition of the situation. Two subunits of the actual situation can be identified: situation stimuli and situation events. *Stimuli* refer to a sound or the presence of a supervisor on the shop floor, and function as signals in themselves. *Situation* events are specific parts of a total situation that can be classified in cause/effect terms. Studies of organization structure and design, and environmental psychology use the actual situation as the unit of analysis.

More important to our discussion of appraisal is the *perceived situation* as the unit of analysis, especially from the rater's perspective. The perceived situation is generally the actual situation as it is perceived, interpreted, and assigned meaning or as it is construed in the mind of the perceiver (Magnusson, 1981). This implies that the same actual situation leads to many different perceived situations, depending on the rater's interpretation. Magnusson (1976) identifies two units of analysis in perceived situations: within situation and overall or general situation. The former refers to the flow of stimuli and events as they are perceived and interpreted by the perceiver, whereas the latter refers to the factors that contribute to our interpretation of a total situation. As frames of reference, the overall situation factors may guide our selection and interpretation of specific stimuli and events, as well as our expectations and predictions regarding options and courses of action (Magnusson, 1981).

Both the situation type and the life situation reflect more molar units of analysis of the environment. The *situation type* refers to the general kind of actual or perceived situation without specification of time and space. Bem's (1981) and Cantor's (1981) work on situation prototypes employ concepts similar to the analysis of situation types. An example of a situation type might be "an appraisal assessment and feedback session," as opposed to a momentary situation such as "an appraisal of John's performance by his supervisor, Mary, on June 29 at 8:30, covering the performance period from January to June."

Life situation refers to those parts of the total world that an individual can experience and also does perceive and interpret as having relevance to self and behavior. The life situation includes actual conditions under which a person finds himself or herself, including type of professional and work organization, family relations, geographic area, socioeconomic conditions, and so on, and the individual's own experiences and evaluations of the actual conditions.

Time and Space

A second consideration in the discussion of situation and relevant to the appraisal context involves the time and space considerations. Situations change continuously; some circumstances, such as a 20-minute appraisal feedback session, have a clear beginning and end. Many events, however, are not so clearly defined. For example, "observing an employee's performance on the job" refers to an event without clear time or space boundaries.

The focus in appraisal research is usually on a momentary situation, which includes both a time dimension and a distal-proximal dimension. The physical information available on this situation includes (1) what is in the focus of attention; (2) what is considered, but peripheral and not attended to; and (3) what is not considered at all. The focus of attention and the peripheral considerations change continuously. The temporal or time dimension determines what is attended to and what is peripheral. That is, both are dependent at a specific moment on what happened before and to some extent what will happen next in the process. Later in this chapter, we describe appraisal research that has demonstrated that a person's performance at a given time can influence the rater's perceptions of his or her past and subsequent performance (Murphy, Balzer, Lockhart, Eisenman, 1985). This research is using past or subsequent ratee performance as part of the definition of rating context.

Situation Characteristics

No taxonomy of situation characteristics defined in terms of outcome variables is available. Further, there is no set of characteristics available that can be used to analyze all situations. The situation characteristics that might be used to analyze a situation may be, in part, determined by what features are most relevant to the specific context. However, two general categories have emerged: actual situation properties and person-bound properties.

The *actual situation properties* include situation complexity (Schroeder, Driver, & Streufert, 1967), clarity, strength, promotion versus restriction, tasks, rules, roles, physical settings, and other persons (Magnusson, 1981). The most common among these is the analysis of situations in terms of their restrictive versus promotive effects on behavior. The nature of restrictions and promotion, the types of behaviors that are restricted versus promoted, and strengths of the reinforcements and punishments are assumed to be important for individuals in forming perceptions, interpretation, and methods of dealing within a situation.

Situations can also be described using *person-bound properties,* including goals, perceived control, expectancies, needs and motivation, and affective tones or emotions. Goals or intentions are a key situation variable. They are important in guiding or directing an individual toward situations. Goals also influence what cues the individual attends to, what alternatives he or she has, and what strategies are applied. Long-term goals may be appropriate when the situation unit of analysis is the 10-year career pattern of an employee (factors important to the life pattern in a broad sense). Short-term goals may be bound to specific types of situations and may differ depending on different stages of development.

Both actual situation properties and person-bound properties are important to understanding the context of ratings. For example, organizations may inadvertently promote inaccurate performance ratings by rewarding raters on the rated performance levels of their subordinates, or the organization may restrict the accuracy of ratings by punishing the rater for being too harsh. Person-bound properties are also critical considerations in appraisal. For example, the goals of the raters must be considered in order to understand what the performance ratings are intended to convey. We believe that these person-bound properties, especially rater goals, are so important that we devote a more detailed discussion of them in Chapter Eight.

Describing the Rating Context

Many of the studies that suggest typologies of situations identify specific aspects of an organization's context. These features may also affect rating processes and outcomes. The typologies listed in Table 3-1 can be grouped into two general categories: environmental and organizational.

In the class of environmental classification schemes, Moos (1973) discusses both the physical and social aspects of environments. He also conceptualizes three basic dimensions that characterize and discriminate among work environments. These include a relationship dimension (e.g., support, involvement, etc.), a personal development dimension (e.g., self-enhancement), and a system maintenance and system change dimension (e.g., control, order) (Moos, 1973). In Chapter Four, each of these three dimensions is discussed in more detail and reflects some of the purposes or uses of appraisals in organizations.

Krause (1970) categorizes social behaviors into seven groups that reflect different ways of personal interaction (e.g., joint working, sponsored teaching). The intended use of the classification was for research purposes. However, the categories can be applied to assess the nature of interactions in the appraisal exchange. Ekehammar (1974) utilizes five dimensions to describe a situation. Similar to other researchers (Endler, 1982; Endler & Magnusson, 1976), Ekehammar distinguishes between the subjective-psychological aspect and

Table 3–1.   Characteristics Used in Classification of Context

Environmental

Moos (1973)
Ecological dimensions
Behavioral settings
Parameters of organizational structure
Personal and behavior parameters of
  environment
Climate, organizational, and
  psychosocial variables

Argyle (1981)
Goal structure
Environmental setting
Roles
Skills and difficulties
Concepts
Repertoire of elements
Rules
Sequence of behaviors

Krause (1970)
Social situations:
  — joint working
  — trading
  — fighting
  — sponsored teaching
  — serving
  — self-disclosure
  — playing

Rotter (1955); Fredericksen (1972)
Taxonomy based on similarity of
  behavior evoked by situation

Fuller (1950)
Incentive value:
  — field incentives, field impedance
Complexity

Ekehammar (1974)
Physical and social characteristics
Need concepts
Single reaction elicited by situation
Individual's reaction pattern elicited
  by the situation
Individual perceptions of situation

Mischel (1977)
Strong, powerful situations:
  — lead everyone to perceive the
    situation in the same way
Weak situations:
  — not uniformly encoded

Organizational

Forehand (1968)
Environmental variables
Personal variables
Outcome variables

Etzioni (1975)
Coercive organizations
Utilitarian organizations
Normative organizations

Duncan & Weiss (1979)
Internal organizational environment:
  — personnel component
  — functional and staff units
  — organizational-level component

VanMaanen & Schein (1979)
Functional
Hierarchical
Person's inclusion

the objective aspects of the environment. The physical and social environment in which a person interacts is called *ecology*. Actual behavior occurs in a situation or a part of ecology that a person perceives and reacts to immediately (Endler & Magnusson, 1976).

Argyle (1981) uses another classification scheme to study the basic features of situations. His approach maintains that people continuously renegotiate their shared definition of a situation. Further, he states that individuals can alter the nature of the situation entirely. Both Frederiksen (1972) and Rotter (1955) suggest that understanding behavior would be enhanced if a taxonomy of situations was developed based on the similarity of the behaviors they elicited. Fuller (1950) describes three types of interactions that a person may display in order to reach a goal (directive, cybernetic, and effective interactions). Finally, Mischel (1977) classifies context into strong, powerful situations and weak situations. Strong situations differ from weak in a number of ways:

1. Strong situations induce uniform expectancies regarding appropriate behavior, whereas weak situations do not.
2. Strong situations provide adequate incentive for the performance of the behavior, whereas weak situations do not.
3. Strong situations require skills that everyone has, whereas weak situations fail to provide the learning conditions necessary for successful emergence of behavior.

The remaining authors listed in Table 3-1 attempt to describe situations by drawing from the organizational literature. In discussing the dimensions of organizational climate, Forehand (1968) states that three sets of variables are involved: (1) environmental variables external to the individual (e.g., size, structure, etc.); (2) personal variables, including abilities, aptitudes, and motives of organizational members; and (3) outcome variables, including employee satisfaction, motivation, and performance. He states that climate is the configuration of environmental variables as perceived by individuals.

Similar to Forehand (1968), Duncan and Weiss (1979) classify organizations as having internal and external components. The internal environment includes the personnel component (e.g., skills and education of employees), the functional and staff component (e.g., interdependence), and the organization-level component (e.g., goals, products, etc). The external environment includes such components as customers, suppliers, and competitors.

Another model of the organization is to describe the environment in terms of organizationally defined roles. VanMaanen and Schein (1979) use three dimensions to define roles: functional (e.g., tasks performed by the organization, such as finance and marketing), hierarchical (e.g., centralized or decentralized), and the person's inclusion within the organization (e.g., newcomer or employee "on the edge"). Finally, Etzioni (1975) classifies organizations on the basis of how they exert control over their members.

Specifically, an organization may exert control primarily through coersion (coercive organization), remuneration (utilitarian organization), or normative power (normative organization). Etzioni (1975) also identifies a fourth category, dual compliance structures, where two patterns of control occur with similar frequency.

Methods of Situation Analysis

In addition to knowing what is meant by the rating context, it is also important to develop methods for assessing the features of the rating situation. There are a number of techniques already developed by situational researchers and personality psychologists that may be usefully applied to the organizational context. Among the first to classify situations empirically in terms of situation perception are Pervin (1968), who used a semantic differential technique, and Magnusson (1971), who used multidimensional scaling for analyzing similarity of information. Frederiksen (1972) suggested using cluster analysis and factor analysis as methods for categorizing situations.

Most studies that attempt to analyze situations do so in terms of how people perceive and interpret them. For example, Cantor (Cantor, 1981; Cantor & Mischel, 1979; Cantor, Mischel, & Schwartz, 1982) has investigated the lay perceiver's categorical knowledge about everyday situations. This knowledge is called a *prototype* and captures the meaning of the category. Using prototypes, Cantor's strategy for investigating perceptions of situations includes:

1. Establish taxonomies of commonly used situation categories and obtain agreement that taxonomies reflect hierarchies.
2. Ask subjects to generate prototypes for each category in each taxonomy, and then identify the characteristics subjects listed to describe the same category to obtain a consensual prototype for each situation category.
3. Assess the consensus to determine the depth and complexity of situation prototypes, the structure of situation taxonomies, and the content of the descriptions of everyday situations (Cantor, 1981).

Similar to Cantor's approach, Bem (1981) uses a template-matching technique. A *template* is a description of how one would expect a specific type of person to behave or what outcomes one would expect for a specific type of person in a given situation. Situations are similar to the extent that similar persons receive similar outcomes (Bem, 1981). Drawing from and extending the research by Block and Block (1981) on the Q-sort techique, Bem and Funder (1978) modified the Q-sort procedure to obtain information about a situation and perhaps identify sources of behavior inconsistencies across seemingly similar situations. They proposed that situations be characterized as sets of template-behavior pairs, with each template being a Q-sort description of an idealized type of person (Bem, 1981, p. 250). This person is expected to behave in a specified way in that particular situation or setting. The behavior of actual individuals in the setting is predicted by comparing one's own Q-sort with each template. It is predicted that individuals will display a behavior that is associated with the template of closest match. The actual method for constructing a template is described in Bem and Funder (1978) and Green (1980).

The previous techniques are examples of *idiographic* approaches in assessing situation similarities. In addition to the Cantor and Bem methods, situations can be assessed through direct similarity ratings (Magnusson, 1971; Magnusson & Endler, 1977) in which subjects are asked to assess how similar various pairs of situations are, or by goal satisfaction similarities in which situations are grouped by how instrumental they are in satisfying goals (Lord, 1982). On the other hand, the *nomethetic* approach relies on consensus across individuals on situation similarity. There is evidence that the idiographic approaches are superior to the nomethetic approaches in predicting cross-situational consistency (Lord, 1982). Further, there are substantial individual differences in what people pay attention to as they move from one situation to the next (Magnusson, 1981).

Microlevel Context Variables and Performance Appraisal

Major reviews and subsequent models of appraisal (Bernardin & Beatty, 1984; Carroll & Schneier, 1982; DeCotiis & Petit, 1978; Landy & Farr, 1980) have consistently acknowledged the importance of the situation or context within which appraisals are conducted. Although the organizational context is viewed as important by these authors, their books and reviews have given less attention to these variables than, for example, scale format or psychometric properties of formats. One reason for this may be that there has been little empirical research on situational factors and their impact on behavior in organzations, specifically on appraisals. A more plausible reason is that PA traditionally is viewed as a research and applied topic within industrial or personnel psychology rather than as a topic within organizational psychology or organizational development.

As we noted in Chapter One, appraisal scales have usually been treated as tests or instruments. Consequently, past research has emphasized instrument development and assessment in terms of accuracy, psychometric properties, and, to a lesser degree, utility of the instrument. In our model, we view appraisals in organizations as a social-communication-decision instrument. There is a need to develop and refine the measurement qualities of appraisals as scale instruments as well as acknowledge appraisals as a decision tool in organzations. Recognizing these needs, PA is clearly a topic that rests at the intersection of industrial and organizational psychology and would be best approached from both perspectives. The research literature reviewed here reflects a movement by researchers to apply knowledge about organzational behavior to the traditionally industrial topic of performance appraisal.

Recently, a few researchers have investigated the influence of numerous contextual factors on appraisal outcomes (Cleveland, Morrison, & Bjerke, 1986; Davis & Dickinson, 1987; Dobbins, Cardy, & Platz, 1988). For example, Davis and Dickinson (1987) examined the influence of individual-level context variables and unit-level context factors on the utility of performance appraisals in organizations. They found that individual-level variables, such as role ambiguity, leader trust and support, and leader interaction and facilitation, accounted for systematic variance in performance ratings. On the other hand, ratings of the extent to which appraisals are used for salary and promotions was predictable from unit-level variables, such as participation in decision making, organizational communication, organizational goals and planning, and climate for innovation (i.e., encouragement of risk taking and creativity). Employee ratings of the administration, fairness, and accuracy of PA were predicted by a combination of individual and unit-level variables. We believe that more research like that conducted by Davis and Dickinson (1987) is needed. Further, we agree, in part, with these authors that it may be very fruitful to view the PA process as an organizational development intervention.

The literature on the psychology of situations is somewhat unclear as to what variables to include in a discussion of microlevel context variables. However, Cummings and Schwab (1973) suggested that three sets of factors comprise the performance environment: task design, leadership, and the reward systems. We believe that this taxonomy represents a useful starting point. Our review of the literature includes group, task and leadership characteristics, and reward and punishment or threat considerations. We also believe that more recent research suggests other important situation considerations.

Focusing on the rater perspective and perceptions of context, recent research has examined the influence of past or previous performance and the performance level of the ratee on rating outcomes (Murphy, Balzer, Lockhart, & Eisenman, 1985; Murphy, Herr, Lockhart, & Maguire, 1986). In addition, rater and ratee acquaintance (interpersonal relations) and affect have been found to influence the effectiveness of appraisals. The work by Dobbins and associates (1988) and others have highlighted the specific features of the appraisal systems as important in the quality of rating outcomes and in acceptance of the appraisal process. Finally, the goals and purpose of the appraisal (both organizational and rater goals) will be discussed as an important context factor.

In summary, the influence of microlevel context factors on appraisal quality, accuracy, and acceptance will focus on the following six sets of contextual factors: (1) group, leader, and task characteristics; (2) rewards, trust, threats, and punishment; (3) ratee past performance and level of performance; (4) appraisal system features; (5) rater acquaintance, commitment, and affect; and (6) goals and purpose of appraisal.

Group, Leader, and Task Characteristics

According to Hackman (1976), groups have a number of ways in which they can influence individuals. Groups can influence a person's knowledge and skills of individuals, the level of psychological arousal while working, and a person's effort and performance strategies. Further, norms or expectations develop within groups regarding acceptable levels of performance. These norms become stronger as the group increases in cohesiveness.

Not only do norms develop concerning productivity but also concerning the levels of acceptable performance ratings. For some groups, a norm develops that leads raters to believe that high or inflated ratings are the only acceptable ratings. It may be unacceptable for a rater to record ratings that depict average or below-average performance even when such ratings are accurate. Based on information from rater interviews, Cleveland and colleagues (1986) found that when there were high entrance or educational standards for admission into a group or job community, raters were reluctant to evaluate employees as average or below. The rater's rationale was that these individuals passed through numerous performance hurdles in order to gain access to the group, and therefore were all "superior."

The characteristics of a group, such as the performance variability of its members (Ilgen & Feldman, 1983; Liden & Mitchell, 1983) and the salience of specific group members (Brewer, 1979; Linville & Jones, 1980; Quattrone & Jones, 1980), also influence the accuracy and the leniency of ratings. Raters do not evaluate one person on a single occasion; rather, evaluation occurs for many people over an extended time or covering many tasks. Therefore, there is opportunity for other group members to influence specific ratings by providing raters with information for comparative rather than absolute judgments (Ilgen & Feldman, 1983).

Mitchell and Liden (1982) found that in a workgroup with one poor performer and two good ones, the evaluation of the poor performer was higher than it should have been and the evaluations of good performers were lower. This was especially true when the poor performer was portrayed as high in popularity and leadership skills. Also, the degree of task interdependence among group members was related to rating outcome and performance variability. Specifically, Liden and Mitchell (1983) found that good performers were rated higher and poor perfomers lower when group members were portrayed as working independently. On the other hand, when group members were interdependent, good performers were rated lower and poor performers were rated higher.

Liden and Mitchell (1983) suggest that in highly interdependent groups, it may be difficult for the rater or supervisor to evaluate the contribution of the individual group members even when the performance of one member is poor in comparison to other members. Grey and Kipnis (1976) found that performance ratings of a compliant group member were higher when the others were inept and possessed a bad work attitude than when other group members were also compliant. This suggests that if an individual is, in some important way, different than the other members of a group, he or she may be evaluated differently than in a relatively homogeneous group. That is, the individual who is different may be more salient to the rater and may be characterized in a stereotypic way (Kanter, 1977).

Related to the hetereogeneity of group members is the existence of in-group and out-group members of a workgroup (Graen, 1976) and leader perceptions and evaluation of these individuals. Supervisors do not treat all subordinates in the same way, nor should they. One theory of leadership, Vertical Dyadic Linkage (VDL) theory, suggests that each supervisor-subordinate dyad may involve a somewhat different style of interaction (Dansereau, Cashman, & Graen, 1973). However, the theory suggests that dyads can be classified into those involving members of the in-group and those involving members of the out-group. In-group members receive more information and trust from supervisors, and perform more complex and interesting tasks. Mundane and routine tasks are relegated to members of the out-group (Dansereau & Graen, 1975; see also Chapter Eight in this book).

According to Brewer (1979), factors such as intergroup competition, similarity, and status differentials of individuals affect in-group bias indirectly, by influencing the salience or distinctions between the in- and out-groups. Linville and Jones (1980) proposed and tested a model that assumes that people have more complex schema regarding in-group members than out-group members. As a result, appraisals of out-group members will tend to be more polarized. They found that when application credentials were positive, the out-group member was evaluated more positively than the in-group member. When the credentials were weak, out-group members were evaluated more negatively than were in-group members. They also found support for the complexity-extremity hypothesis. That is, white subjects demonstrated greater schema complexity for whites than for blacks and greater complexity resulted in more moderate ratings. Brewer (1979) suggests that bias reflects increased favoritism toward in-group members rather than increased hostility toward the out-group.

Related to group features, task characteristics appear to influence both the consideration of what scale or evaluation approach to take and the accuracy of ratings. Lee (1985) suggests that matching the task with the appraisal format will increase appraisal effectiveness. Bernardin and Beatty (1984) also suggest that different types or purposes of decisions (i.e., promotion to the next level versus individual feedback) may require different scale formats (i.e., trait versus behavioral) in order to maximize appraisal utility.

Balzer (1986) found that the cognitive processes in ratings were influenced by the interaction of the centrality of the task to the rater and the rater's initial impression of the ratee. That is, when raters were told to observe a lecturer and learn the content of the lecture (low centrality), subjects with a positive initial impression recorded fewer behavioral incidents than subjects with a negative initial impression. When raters were told that the behavioral diary or the recording of behaviors was their sole task (high centrality), subjects with positive initial impressions recorded more incidents than those with a negative initial impression. This interaction affected raters' observation and coding of positive critical incidents and not negative incidents.

Rewards, Trust, Threats, and Punishments

Jones, Tait, and Butler (1983) found that actions that are perceived as rewarding by employees were characterized by public visibility, tangibility, implied esteem, and long-term implications. Actions perceived as punishment had similar qualities (although scaled in opposite directions), with visibility most closely related to perceived severity. Few empirical studies have investigated directly the influence of organizational rewards or punishments on appraisal ratings. Mohrman and Lawler (1983) and others have described how rater motivation contributes to accurate ratings. One factor that they say influences motivation is rewards. Longenecker, Sims, and Gioia (1987) interviewed executives concerning the politics of appraisal and found that raters inflated appraisal outcomes in order to avoid negative or uncomfortable feedback sessions and to avoid negative consequences or actions for the ratees (e.g., a poor appraisal in the employees' permanent files). Further, Longenecker and colleagues (1987) found that the most frequently cited reason for rating inflation was to obtain rewards for the subordinate (e.g., maximize merit increases).

Bjerke, Cleveland, Morrison, and Wilson (1987) found similar results from interviews with Navy officers (raters) and a small sample of industry personnel managers. In much of the military, there are few negative consequences for raters who give inaccurate, inflated ratings (i.e., raters are not penalized for inaccuracy); however, there are incentives for raters to inflate ratings, primarily to secure promotions for their junior officers. From managers interviewed, Bjerke and associates (1987) found that at times managers were punished for ratings that were seen as inaccurately favorable or unfavorable by their own superior.

Most of the research on the influence of rewards and punishments has involved field interviews or the manipulation of other variables (i.e., appraisal purpose) and explaining the outcomes by implied consequences of accurate ratings. More research is needed to address how organizational rewards and punishments influence appraisal processes and outcomes.

Related to the consequences of appraisals is the trust and or threat perceived by the rater (and ratee) in the appraisal process (Bernardin, Orban, & Carlyle, 1981; Bernardin & Villanova, 1986; Kay, Meyer, & French, 1965;

Longenecker & Gioia, 1988). Trust and threat appear to influence both the psychometric quality of rating outcomes (i.e., leniency) and the acceptance of the appraisal system. Organizational climates characterized by low trust, either between raters or across organizational levels, can lower the effectiveness of an appraisal system (Lawler, 1971).

Trust in the appraisal context reflects the extent to which raters believe that fair and accurate appraisals will be or have been made in the organization. Lawler (1971) notes that trust may be more important when appraisals are used for promotion or administrative decisions than when used as a basis for individual feedback (e.g., the interaction of two context variables such as trust and purpose of rating; see Chapter Four). Bernardin and associates (1981) found that trust in the appraisal process accounted for 32% of the variance in ratings. Regardless of appraisal purpose (i.e., promotion versus feedback), raters with high trust provided ratings with less leniency, whereas raters low in trust provided more lenient ratings.

Perceptions of threat by subordinates are also related to attitudes toward the appraisal (Kay et al., 1965). A manager who attempts to assist employees by pointing out improvement needs is likely to be perceived by subordinates as threatening to their self-esteem, which can result in defensive behavior. Also, the more threats perceived by the subordinates, the less favorable their attitudes toward appraisal and the smaller the subsequent improvement in performance.

Longenecker and Gioia (1988) reported five sources of appraisal apprehension as identified by executives:

1. The quality of working relationship with one's supervisor (i.e., trust)
2. The extent to which the subordinate manager's job responsibilities, authority, and goals are ill-defined
3. Whether or not the individual had been receiving specific feedback throughout the year
4. The appraisers' level of honesty or perceptions of a "hidden agenda"
5. The political nature of appraisals (discussed in Chapter Four)

In general, trust was highest when there was a good working relationship, well-defined roles, specific feedback, honesty, and a low tolerance for political manipulation.

Ratee Past Performance and Current Level of Performance

According to Magnusson (1981), one key consideration in situation analysis is time. Practitioners concerned with appraisal in organizations are also concerned with a time factor and have criticized laboratory research on appraisals for not taking into consideration the fact that the supervisor interacts with, observes, and assesses employees over a period of time.

Evaluation does not occur after one performance episode. Rather, an employee performs a given task at a certain level for a period of time and this task or time period may be preceded or followed by performance at the same or at a different level of efficiency. Therefore, a case could be made that the employee's performance on a given task or on a given day is embedded in a context or pattern of employee performance over time. The rater observes the employee's performance over time; performance probably varies in level from one time to another.

Murphy and colleagues (Murphy et al., 1985; Murphy et al., 1986) investigated the effects of previous and subsequent performance on the evaluation of present performance. They (1985) conducted two studies to examine the influence of previous employee performance on ratings of current performance. In study 1, subjects looked at videotapes of positive or negative performance followed by a video of an average performance by the same person. They found that exposing raters to positive or negative performance of a ratee had significant effects on subsequent ratings. Specifically, contrast effects were found, indicating that an employee who performed well initially was rated lower in current performance than if the same person had performed poorly in the first tape. In study 2, Murphy and colleagues (1985) included a one-day delay condition. Results suggested that contrast effects did not occur when ratings were provided from memory. Rather than strengthening the contrast, increased demands on memory appeared to lead to a decay in contrast effects.

In a study examining the effects of subsequent performance on evaluations of previous performance, Murphy and associates (1986) asked subjects first to view an average performance videotape and then either a good or poor performance video. The researchers also had an immediate performance rating condition and a delay condition. They found an assimilation effect in the delay condition but not in the immediate rating condition. Subsequent performance (i.e., the second performance episode) influenced memory-based behavior ratings (e.g., the frequency a behavior occurred) but did not influence ratings on performance evaluation dimensions. Further, they found that under conditions posing minimal demands on memory, subsequent performance had a relatively weak effect. However, when demands on memory through delay were increased, subsequent performance exerted a stronger influence on ratings of previous performance. One implication of this finding is that supervisors may be biased in the direction of their current impression of the employee rather than correctly assessing past performance.

It has been suggested that the level of employee performance may contribute to the type of ratings that are given (DeNisi & Stevens, 1981). In particular, managers avoid evaluating low performers. Cummings and Schwab (1973) suggested that employees at different performance levels should be appraised differently. That is, different appraisal systems should be structured for low, average, and high performers. Distinguishing features of these systems would include type of information collected, frequency of performance reviews, and role of the employee in the appraisal process.

Appraisal System Features ⎯⎯⎯⎯⎯⎯⎯⎯⎯⎯⎯⎯⎯⎯⎯⎯⎯⎯

The specific features of appraisal systems referred to here include type of scale, instructions and item content or anchors, purpose of rating, participation in the appraisal process, presence of a training program, frequency of evaluation, secrecy of appraisal process, and opportunity to develop action plans to correct performance weaknesses. Bernardin and Beatty (1984) suggest that if the purpose of rating is to predict future performance or potential, a trait scale may make more sense than a scale that asks for ratings of specific behaviors (based on the assumption that traits at one level predict performance in another job). Bernardin and Beatty suggest, however, that behavioral definitions may help to decrease the subjectivity of trait ratings.

Wexley and Klimoski (1984) also suggest that the format of the scale (traits versus behaviors) might be matched with the purpose of rating. Appraisals can reflect behavioral (process) or result (outcomes) measures. Result measures tell employees little about their relative strengths or weaknesses and why they did not meet an objective. Behaviorally oriented scales seem appropriate for development. Wexley and Klimoski (1984) suggest that the use of trait scales may heighten employee defensiveness in feedback sessions.

The scales used in the appraisal process can influence important appraisal outcomes in two other ways. First, Murphy and Constans (1987) found that the specific behavioral anchors in BARS scales can affect the cognitive processes of the rater. When the scales had anchors that were actually observed by the rater, but not representative of the ratee's overall performance, ratings were biased in the direction of the unrepresentative anchor. Murphy and Constans (1987, 1988) recommend that the representativeness of anchors be considered as well as whether the items reflect poor, average, or good performance.

Second, participation in scale development also has multiple, positive effects. Silverman and Wexley (1984) found that ratees who participated in the development of scales on which they were rated believed that:

1. The appraisal interview was more useful.
2. The supervisor was more supportive.
3. They were given more opportunity to participate.
4. Goals and objectives were set to a great extent.
5. They made a greater impact or contribution to the appraisal interview.

Those who participated in scale development were also more satisfied with the appraisal interview and more motivated to improve performance.

Dobbins and associates (1988) examined the relationship between five appraisal characteristics (secrecy, opportunity to participate, opportunity to develop action plans, presence of a rater training program, and frequency of evaluation) and employee satisfaction with the appraisal process. They hypothesized that these five characteristics would be moderated by uncertainty, role ambiguity, and role conflict. In general, they found that ratees were more satisfied with the appraisal process when they were able to provide input into the process, assisted in the development of action plans, and were knowledgeable about dimensions and procedures of evalution.

Dobbins and colleagues (1988) also found that the three organizational characteristics moderated the relationship between appraisal characteristics and appraisal satisfaction. The relation between the development of action plans and satisfaction was moderated by role ambiguity and closeness of supervision. When there was high ambiguity and low closeness in supervision, this relationship was stronger. The relation between frequency of evaluation and satisfaction was moderated by role conflict and quality of leader-member exchange. More frequent evaluation was more important for ratees who experienced more conflict and when ratees had a low-quality relationship with their supervisor. Rater training was more positively related to satisfaction when the employee experienced high levels of role conflict or when employees could not be closely monitored by their supervisor. Finally, the relation between secrecy and satisfaction was most negative when employees were closely monitored or when employees experienced little role conflict. Dobbins and colleagues (1985) suggest that high secrecy paired with role clarity or close supervision may send mixed messages to ratees.

Comparing managerial and employee satisfaction with a PA system, Mount (1983) determined that managers' attitudes reflected seven factors and employees' attitudes reflected five factors.

Managers' Attitudes	**Employees' Attitudes**
Content of appraisal forms	Content and ratings on appraisal forms
Ratings on appraisal forms	
Company policy regarding appraisal	Company policy and appraisal procedures
Appraisal procedures	Physical characteristics of appraisal forms
Physical characteristics of appraisal forms	
Communication of the program	Communication of the program
General appraisal satisfaction	General appraisal satisfaction

Managers appeared to have more complex, fine-grained perceptions of the appraisal system. Mount (1983) suggests that this may result from the different roles that managers and employees have. For example, managers perceive company policy and appraisal procedures as distinct, whereas employees tend to put them together.

Through the factor analysis, Mount (1983) found that appraisal satisfaction for employees is due to a general satisfaction factor, including such
items as overall experience with the appraisal system, quality of the appraisal
discussion, how the forms aid discussion of performance, and how the forms
help to formulate development plans (common variance 42.7%). On the other
hand, the same factor accounted for only 4% of the variance in managerial
ratings. Instead, the largest percentage of variance was accounted for by the
type of ratings on the forms. That is, the extent to which performance ratings
help communicate employee's performance seemed to predict a significant
portion of the manager's satisfaction with appraisal.

Rater Acquaintance, Commitment, and Affect _____

Kingstrom and Mainstone (1985) investigated the influence of rater-ratee
acquaintance on rating bias. They distinguished between task and personal
acquaintance to examine how each relates to rating favorablity (i.e., leniency
and halo). No relationship was found between task and personal acquaintance
and halo. Personal acquaintance and task acquaintance were related to
leniency although the latter was less strongly related. Ratees who were
assessed high in personal and task acquaintance received more favorable
ratings. Using multiple regression, Kingstrom and Mainstone found that
personal and task acquaintance accounted for variance in ratings not
accounted for by actual sales productivity. However, actual productivity was
related to supervisory perceptions of personal and task acquaintance.
Therefore, more favorable ratings may be due, in part, to true performance
differences, and personal and task acquaintance are correlates.

Freeberg (1969) found that appraisal ratings were more accurate when
the raters possessed task-relevant acquaintance (e.g., relevant knowledge or
contact) with the ratee than when raters possessed irrelevant acquaintance
(e.g., socializing). Using interview data, Kallejian, Brown, and Weschler (1953)
found a similar relationship between the supervisor and the subordinate's
interpersonal relationship and appraisal ratings.

Related to rater acquaintance with the ratee is the commitment of the
rater to the ratee and the proximity between the rater and ratee. Bazerman,
Beekum, and Schoorman (1982) assessed the influence of prior commitment
of the rater to the ratee on performance evaluations. They predicted that raters
who made an initial commitment (e.g., promotion) to the employee would be
biased (i.e., more lenient) in their subsequent evaluations of that employee in
order to justify the initial support of the employee. That is, a rater will evaluate
a poorly performing person higher if the rater previously promoted this person
than when another rater made the initial promotion decision, because they feel
higher responsibility. Bazerman and colleagues (1982) found that high-
responsibility raters gave higher performance evaluations, greater pay increases, more vacation days, and so on. These raters were also less likely to
demote or lay off the employee.

Imada and Hakel (1977) did not find that rater proximity (i.e., whether the rater was the actual interviewer or an observer) influenced hiring judgment. However, they did find that nonverbal cues, especially eye contact, smiling, attentive posture, gestures, and smaller interpersonal distance, were related to an interviewer's recommendation for hire. If the interviewee demonstrated the above behaviors, he or she was more likely to be recommended for hire. Imada and Hakel (1977) indicated that raters had very different affective responses to interviewees who demonstrated greater contact, smiling, and the like, suggesting that the interviewer may be more involved in an affective dimension of the interview then previously believed.

Tsui and Barry (1986) directly assessed the influence of interpersonal affect on rating errors. They found that the level of ratings given by raters with positive affect toward ratees was highest, followed by ratings from raters with neutral affect, and lowest for raters with negative affect. The average intercorrelation among ratings were highest for raters with negative affect and lowest for raters with neutral affect. This finding was similar across sources of ratings (e.g., supervisory, subordinate, and peers). Raters with neutral affect had the most range restriction.

Goals and Purpose of Appraisal

There is a good deal of research that indicates that appraisal goals and purpose influence the psychometric properties of ratings (e.g., halo, leniency, etc.), accuracy of ratings, and judgment processes. They also interact with other appraisal features (e.g., format, scale anchors, etc.) (Bernardin & Beatty, 1984; Cleveland et al., 1989; DeNisi et al., 1984; Landy & Farr, 1980). The stated purpose of performance appraisals (either organizational or individual purposes) could very well be the single most important contextual factor in understanding appraisal process and outcomes. Therefore, we devote a full chapter (Chapter Four) to a discussion of this issue. Further, the perceptions or interpretations of raters and the translation of these purposes into his or her own goals is discussed extensively in Chapter Eight.

Macrolevel Context Variables and Performance Appraisal

Macrolevel situational variables describe the more general, within-organizational context. In Chapter Two, macrolevel variables outside of the organization were described. In this section, we will discuss three macroorganizational variables and how they may influence the process and outcomes of appraisal. The set of variables includes (1) organizational life cycle and structure, (2) organizational goals, and (3) organizational culture, climate, and values.

We assume that macrolevel variables, both internal and external to the organization, are largely distal to the rater and the ratee. That is, they do not immediately impinge on the individual participants of appraisal. Further, employees may not be aware initially that these variables play a role in the judgments and decisions that they make. We believe that macroorganizational variables most often influence appraisal outcomes indirectly through more proximal, microlevel, situational variables (e.g., organization climate for cooperation may be reflected by tasks performed in teams, which in turn has direct implications for appraisal outcomes). However, we recognize the possiblity that macrolevel situational variables could have a direct impact on appraisal decisions. For example, if organzational goals or values are very strong, focused, or unidimensional (e.g., in the military, the main goal of appraisal is the development and promotion of future commanding officers), then a rater would likely be very aware of the influence such variables have on his or her own judgments and decisions.

Organizational Life Cycle and Structure

Whetten (1987) suggests that the structure and process within an organization are shaped to some degree by the stage a company is in its organizational life cycle. Borrowing from life-cycle models, Whetten and Cameron (1983) described four growth stages: (1) entrepreneurial — reflecting early innovation, niche formulation, and high creativity; (2) collectivity — including high cohesion and commitment; (3) formalization and control — emphasizing stability and institutionalization; and (4) elaboration and structure — reflecting domain expansion and decentralization. These stages cover the growth of an organization and may reflect groups of problems or issues that are specific to each stage.

Whetten (1987) suggests that we also examine possible stages in the decline of organizations. He notes that both growth and decline stages have four important applications in organizations. First, they serve as reasonable diagnostic tools. Awareness of the organization's current stage can convey information about problems and experiences that are likely to be encountered by organizational members. Second, it serves as a reminder that organizational goals, priorities, and criteria for effectiveness shift over the life span of the organization. Third, it is an important source of contextual information that must be factored into our analyses of organizational research results. For example, rapidly growing versus rapidly declining organizations may have different structural properties and internal processes. Fourth, an understanding of the clusters of problems that an organization is likely to encounter at different stages of development, as well as insights for effectively managing transitions between stages, represent important aids for organizational leaders and researchers (Whetten, 1987).

The life-cycle approach to organizational growth and decline suggests that appraisal systems in organizations are not static systems nor should they be assumed to be equally effective (if not altered in some important way) across different stages. The goals of organizations evolve and change; as a result, the purpose and format of the appraisal may be expected to change as well. The view that this book takes — that performance appraisals are a social and decision-making tool and, secondarily, a measurement instrument — is consistent with the notion that the context of appraisal is not static and the appraisal itself is a dynamic process. Typically, as a measurement tool, appraisals are assumed to measure stable characteristics of ratees. However, they may also measure or be influenced by the constantly changing environment of which it is a part.

As Whetten (1987) suggests, the life stage of an organization may influence its actual structure. Further, the structure (i.e., the organization level that employees occupy) has been found to influence job attitudes and performance (Berger & Cummings, 1979). Specifically, Berger and Cummings (1979) found that there is a relatively stable pattern of relationships between organizational level and attitudes, such as job satisfaction and satisfaction with appraisal.

Schneier and Beatty (1978) found differences in performance expectations at different levels of the organizational hierarchy. Raters rated the same behavior lower than did subordinates. Davis and Dickinson (1987) found that appraisal utility decreased in organizational units where employees could take little action without permission from their supervisor. Berger and Cummings (1979) found little relationship between line versus staff positions in job attitudes. However, McCall and DeVries (1977) suggest that appraisals may be caught in a staff versus line conflict. That is, appraisals are designed by staff employees for personnel uses or for larger organizational concerns, yet they are completed by line managers. There is potential here for the appraisal not to meet the needs or goals of the line manager. In addition, there appears to be a small to moderate relation between span of contol and job attitudes and performance. Finally, absenteeism increased with the size of the total organization (Berger & Cummings, 1979).

Although more research is needed to address the relationship between organizational structure and appraisal, there is sufficient evidence using other dependent measures to suggest that organizational structure probably does influence appraisal.

Organizational Goals

Organizations are systems that are activated and directed by goals (Katz & Kahn, 1978). These goals are not necessarily actively chosen or consciously established; they may emerge initially from the types of persons who established the organization (Schein, 1985). Cartwright and Zander (1968) draw a distinction between goals of an individual for a group and goals of a group or an organization. The first refers to individual attainment and the others to group or organizational attainment. Also, the first type of goal is held individually, whereas the last two are held collectively. Although there is research suggesting that organizational goals influence behavior and that conflict occurs when there are mixed goals (Zald, 1962), other researchers have criticized the concept of organizational goals. Etzioni (1975) suggests that goals be replaced with a systems model. That is, the criterion of effectiveness should reflect a balanced or optimum allocation of resources rather than when organizational goals are met or not met.

According to Mohr (1973), oganizational goals have two aspects: intent and outcomes. The former could be viewed as the process that makes goal attainment possible, including appraisal and reward systems. It is reasonable to suggest that an appraisal system may be structured and administered differently depending on the goals of the organization. Davis and Dickinson (1987) found that appraisals were viewed more positively in units that possessed lateral and vertical communication. Further, employees in units having more complete and formal goals and planning practices viewed appraisals more positively. The second aspect, outcomes, refers to a criterion for organizational effectiveness (i.e., has the organization attained or accomplished goals?). The activation and guiding processes (i.e., goals) within an organization and the role of appraisal in this process needs to be addressed more directly through research.

One contempory theory of organizational effectiveness that might be usefully applied to evaluating performance appraisal is the constituency theory of effectiveness. A *constituency* is any group within or outside of the organization that has a stake in organizational performance (Connolly, Conlon, & Deutsch, 1980; Daft, 1986; Friedlander & Pickle, 1968). Each constituency may have different criteria for evaluating effectiveness, because each has a different interest in the organization. The various constituencies involved in PA include the rater, the personnel decision makers (e.g., persons involved in making salary or promotion decisions), and the courts, to name a few. It is likely that an organization finds it difficult to fulfill simultaneously the demands or goals of all groups.

Research on performance appraisal using the constituency approach as a general framework may yield some interesting theoretical insights, as well as practical recommendations. For example, if it is impossible to fulfill the expectations of all constituencies, the design of a PA system must include procedures for identifying the most important goals and constituencies for different parts of the appraisal system.

Organizational Culture, Climate, and Values

Schein (1985) distinguishes three levels of culture: basic assumptions, values, and artifacts (special jargon, rituals, dress, etc.). Martin and Siehl (1983) add a fourth level, management practices. These practices include training, allocation of rewards, and performance appraisal. Research suggests that culture offers an interpretation of an institution's history that members can use to decipher how well they will be expected to behave in the future.

Culture can also generate commitment to corporate values or management philosophy, so that employees feel that they are working for something they believe in. Finally, culture serves as an organizational control mechanism that informally approves or prohibits some patterns of behavior (Martin & Siehl, 1983).

Culture is a more amorphous concept than organizational climate (Schneider, 1985). Culture refers to assumptions and values attributed to why certain behaviors and activities are rewarded and expected. Climate focuses on how the organization functions (i.e., *what* is rewarded, supported, and expected). Culture is transmitted through myths and stories, particularly when large groups of people share the interpretation of the myths (Schein, 1985; Schneider, 1985, 1987; Tagiuri & Litwin, 1968). For example, through interviews with Naval commanding officers, Cleveland and colleagues (1986) found that the Navy's values concerning the importance of warfare readiness influenced what raters thought about when completing evaluations of subordinate officers. That is, raters appeared to assess subordinates solely in terms of warfare readiness and the ability to be a good commanding officer rather than assessing their performance in specific assignments.

According to Schneider (1975, 1987) much of the climate research makes two assumptions: (1) people try to attain order in their environment and to create order through thought and (2) people attempt to create order in their environment so they can effectively adapt their behavior to the work environment. Fredericksen, Jensen, and Beatrin (1972) found that the intercorrelations among dimensions of an in-basket varied as a function of the climate under which people worked. That is, the pattern of what was important and what covaried depended on the climate. Further, Fredericksen (1962, 1972) found that performance on the in-basket was higher when climates provided consistent cues to performance than in climates that reflected inconsistent information. Russell, Terborg, and Powers (1985) attempted to determine whether organizations that valued and emphasized training are more effective. A favorable training climate was found to have a positive relationship with organizational performance.

Schneider (1985) addressed the issue of the content or dimensions of the climate construct. He stated that the key question for determining the content of the perceptual climate is, Climate for what? Research that has defined climate globally has not found a strong relationship between climate and job performance (Pritchard & Karasick, 1973). On the other hand, specific domains of climate, including safety climate or a technical updating climate, are related to measures of performance (i.e., accident prevention, safety effectiveness, etc.) (Kozlowski & Hults, 1987; Zohar, 1980). To date, little research has been conducted on the influence of various climates on performance appraisals in organizations. However, we believe that research on culture and climate will contribute to the understanding of performance appraisals.

Appraisal Research and an Interactionist Perspective

Interactional psychology may be usefully applied to appraisals in organizations; indeed, some appraisal research currently reflects the interactionist approach (e.g., Cleveland & Landy, 1983; Dobbins et al., 1988). One major advantage of the interactional approach is that the assumptions and questions posed can help in identifying future research needs in performance appraisal. We will describe the interactionist approach briefly and then relate it to the appraisal process specifically by identifying current research knowledge as well as research needs for the future.

Interactional psychology emphasizes continuous interactions between person and situation characteristics as the major determinants of behavior. That is, situations are as much a function of the person's behavior as the person's behavior is a function of the situation (Bowers, 1973). Interactionists recognize that situations vary in terms of cues, rewards, and opportunities and that people vary in their cognitions, abilities, and motivations (Terborg, 1981).

Endler and Magnusson (1976) describe four propositions of interactional psychology:

1. Actual behavior is a function of a continuous, multidirectional process of interaction or feedback between the individual and the situation encountered.
2. The individual is an intentional, active agent in this interaction process; the person is both changed by situations and changes situations.
3. On the person side, cognitive, affective, and motivation factors and ability are essential determinants of behavior.
4. On the situation side, the psychological meaning of situation for the individual and the behavior potential of the situation for the individual are essential determinants of behavior (Terborg, 1981).

Thus, the situation is in some way a function of the observer. The observer's cognitive schema filter and organize the environment in a way that makes it impossible to completely separate the environment from the person (Bowers, 1973). Further, a great deal of a person's social environment is generated by his or her own behavior. For example, there is a fair amount of consistency in the kind of environments that people create for themselves (Bowers, 1973; Schneider, 1978, 1983a; 1985, 1987; Wachtel, 1973). Schneider (1983b; 1985) has applied the interactionist perspective to the notion of organizational effectiveness. He notes that organizations are defined by the kinds of people attracted, selected, and remaining in them. As a result of this cycle (attraction-selection-attrition), organizations can become too homogeneous, which may result in a decrease in capacity to adapt or change.

There are at least two major concerns in interactional psychology. The first is the attribution of cause either to internal or external factors. That is, causes of behavior could reside in the person, the situation, or both. The second issue involves the notion of coherence of behavior. It concerns whether behavior is inherently stable and predictable without necessarily being stable in absolute or relative terms. That is, interactional psychology asks whether the individual's pattern of stable and changing behavior across situations of various kinds is characteristic of that person. Interactionists say that coherence of behavior results from information processing. People are viewed as proactive perceivers who, through perceptions and cognitions, *actively* structure the external world. Further, the situation is not construed in research as the physical situation. The central notion is that active involvement (i.e., experience) in a situation through perception and other behaviors is the way that people come to understand situations. The interactionists' notion of active involvement has similar philosophical grounds as does the approach of action scientists (Argyris, 1980).

The application of interactional psychology to appraisals in organizations suggests that we need to understand fully the characteristics of individuals that affect rating processes and outcomes as well as the features of the situation that are instrumental in determining appraisal outcomes. Unfortunately, interactional psychology also informs us that it may be difficult to distinguish fully between the effects of the individual and the situation. The research on appraisals to date reflects an emphasis on the identification of person variables, including demograhic variables (e.g., age, sex, etc.) and cognitive processes of raters. Currently, a good deal is known about how the rater observes, recalls, and makes judgments that lead to various appraisal outcomes. Therefore, the largest portion of this book is devoted to issues concerning the individual rater. Less is known about the context within which appraisals are conducted.

Summary

Little is known about what context factors raters perceive or consider in determining what course of action to pursue through appraisal (e.g., type of ratings to give in a specific appraisal situation). In this chapter, we have identified some contextual variables that may be relevant to understanding the appraisal process. For example, it is clear that the composition of the workgroup influences a rater's evaluation of an employee's individual performance. However, there are a number of other organizational and contextual variables that are relevant to the appraisal process and effectiveness. These factors include organizational values, climate (cooperative, competitive etc), trust in the appraisal system, the centrality or status of the job or department in which the appraisal is conducted, entrance standards in the job community (Cleveland et al., 1986), and so on. There has been some research concerning these factors, but more research is needed to assess how each influences appraisal effectiveness. Each variable can be considered relevant to appraisals, although little is known about the influence of them on appraisal process and outcomes.

The literature of the psychology of situations and interactional psychology suggests that some context factors may be more important than others in their interaction with key person variables in the appraisal process. We believe that the purposes or uses of appraisal in an organization represent a critical contextual consideration and mediates the relationship between rater characteristics and appraisal effectiveness. Therefore, Chapter Four is devoted exclusively to the discussion of the purpose of rating.

Related to the purpose of rating, a second key variable in appraisal is the rater's goals. Although rater goals might be classified as a person variable, we believe that it may be difficult to distinguish between the person and situation features of rater goals. That is, we can draw on the goal-setting literature that informs us how individuals set goals and how these goals guide subsequent judgments and behavior. However, we also must consider how the rater perceives and integrates information from the appraisal situation, what information the rater uses as cues, and how the rater integrates and interprets this contextual information to formulate his or her own goals in the rating process. Chapter Eight is devoted to a discussion of rater goals in performance appraisal.

Chapter Four

Purposes of
Performance Appraisals

▶ In the last two chapters, we discussed a variety of environmental and organizational context factors that may affect the outcomes and effectiveness of an organization's performance appraisal (PA) system. In this chapter, one context factor has been selected for more detailed attention — the purposes of performance appraisal. Discussion of these purposes is important for at least three reasons:

1. Performance appraisal is used for a wide variety of purposes within and across organizations.
2. The purpose of appraisal influences the ratings and the effectiveness of the system.
3. Purposes provide the key mechanism by which the context of rating interacts with the capabilities and cognitive and judgmental processes of the rater (Cleveland, Murphy, & Williams, 1989).

Understanding the effects of the purposes of PA on appraisal processes and outcomes will help advance the knowledge of contextual factors in appraisal.

A key concern of this chapter is that information from performance appraisals is used by raters, ratees, and organizations for many purposes. The goals pursued by the rater and ratee are not necessarily the same as those pursued by the organization (see Chapter Eight). Therefore, the material presented in this chapter can be viewed as a transition from a discussion of external context factors and ratings to a discussion of the rater or decision maker's goals and his or her "survival" techniques in the organization.

First, we will survey the use of performance appraisal in organizations. Next, we will examine ways in which the purpose of rating influences the outcomes of PA. That is, we will identify and discuss what outcomes to expect as a function of the purpose of appraisal, and how purpose influences various rater variables (e.g., judgment strategy). Third, because the purpose of an organizational appraisal often reflects the constituents it serves (the organization, the rater, the ratee), political and power issues are an integral part of the use of the PA system, and we will discuss these issues. Further, conflict may emerge among organizational and individual uses of performance appraisal; we will explore the potential conflict among incompatible purposes.

Uses of Performance Appraisals

Several surveys of business organizations indicate that between 74 and 89% of those surveyed have a formal PA system (Feild & Holly, 1982; Lacho, Stearns, & Villere, 1979; Lazer & Wikstrom, 1977). Further, surveys concerning the prevalence of formal appraisal systems indicated that approximately 76% of the city governments (Lacho et al., 1979), and 100% of the state governments sampled (Feild & Holly, 1975) had appraisal systems. Large organizations were more likely to have performance appraisal than smaller organizations (95 to 84% respectively), and lower (74%) to middle (71%) management levels were more likely to have formal appraisals than top management (55%) (Lazer & Wikstrom, 1977). Finally, in a recent study, approximately 96% of the organizations surveyed that had an industrial/organizational psychologist on staff also had at least one formal PA system (Cleveland et al., 1989). In general, then, performance appraisal appears to be widespread (DeVries, Morrison, Shullman, & Gerlach, 1986).

Historically, information from performance appraisals has been used as a basis for administrative decisions (Whisler & Harper, 1962). More recently, the purposes of appraisal have expanded considerably. In 1957, McGregor proposed that performance appraisal be used for feedback and developing employees (DeVries et al., 1986). Proponents of Management by Objectives (MBO) suggested using appraisals for organizational planning (Drucker, 1954; Odiorne, 1965). PA experts (Bernardin & Beatty, 1984; DeVries et al., 1986) predict that appraisal will continue to be used in the 1990s for human resource planning and replacement. Since the passage of the 1964 Civil Rights Act and the Age Discrimination in Employment Act, performance appraisal has also been used increasingly to safeguard organizations against discrimination lawsuits.

Performance appraisal is not only a United States phenomenon but is also widespread in Great Britain. Approximately 82% of organizations in Great Britain have some type of formal appraisal system, with a substantial increase in appraisals for nonmanagement employees during the last 10 years (DeVries et al., 1986). The most frequently cited uses of PA in Great Britain are to (1) improve current performance, (2) set objectives, and (3) identify training and development needs. Further, there is a recognition and trend toward the separation of performance review from potential review.

Tables 4-1 and 4-2 present the results of surveys, conducted since 1970, of uses of performance appraisal in the United States. Administrative uses of performance information continued to be the most frequent application of performance appraisal in the 1970s and 1980s. In the 1970s, 50 to 85% of the organizations surveyed used appraisal for administrative decisions such as salary administration, promotion, and retention and dismissal. Cleveland and associates (1989) found that when asked to identify the most frequent use of information from performance appraisals, respondents (this study surveyed industrial/organizational psychologists) ranked salary administration and developmental feedback as the top two uses. As Table 4-2 indicates, the purposes for which appraisals are *infrequently* used include (1) criteria for validation studies, (2) determining organizational training needs, (3) reinforcing the authority structure, and (4) manpower planning.

In surveys from the 1970s, PA was used for validating selection procedures in only 12 to 23% of the organizations surveyed. More recent surveys suggest a greater emphasis on validation and, more generally, on the documentation and justification of personnel decisions. Cleveland and colleagues (1989) found that when 20 uses for PA were factor analyzed, a documentation factor clearly emerged as one of four major uses of information from performance appraisal. The specific items within the documentation factor included (1) criteria for validation research, (2) document personnel decisions, and (3) meet legal requirements.

The results of Cleveland and colleagues' (1989) analysis, which are summarized in Table 4-2, provide a useful classification of the purposes of performance appraisal. In addition to the documentation factor described above, this study suggests that organizational uses of PA can be grouped into three categories:

1. Between-person uses, including salary administration, promotion, retention/termination, recognition of individual performance, layoffs, and identification of poor performers
2. Within-person uses, including identification of individual training needs, performance feedback, determining transfers and assignments, and identifying individual strengths and weaknesses
3. Systems maintenance uses, including use of appraisal for workforce planning, determining organizational training needs, evaluating goal achievement, assisting in goal identification, evaluating personnel system, reinforcing authority structure, and identifying organization developmental needs

Table 4–1. Results of Surveys from 1970s

Use	Lazer & Wikstrom (1977) (%)	Bureau of Nat'l Affairs (1974) (%)	Lacho, Stearns, & Villere (1979) (%)
Individual Performance Planning	73–82 (performance feedback)	57 (setting goals)	—
Salary Administration	63–70	85	80
Promotion	50–66	64	74
Training & Development	54–60	55	62 — Development 44 — Assessing training needs
Retention & Discharge	—	—	69 — Dismissal 64 — Demotion
Manpower Planning	23–34	37	—
Validation of Selection Techniques	12–13	23	23

D. L. DeVries, A. M. Morrison, S. L. Shullman, & M. L. Gerlach, *Performance Appraisal on the Line* (Greensboro, NC: Center for Creative Leadership, 1986), p. 22.

Table 4–2. Means, Standard Deviations, and Factor Loadings for Twenty Uses of Performance Appraisal

Factors/Uses	Mean	Standard Deviations
Between-Person Decisions		
Salary Administration (.79)[a]	5.58[b]	1.16
Promotion (.68)	4.80	1.18
Retention/Termination (.78)	4.75	1.40
Recognition of Individual Performance (.62)	5.02	1.52
Layoffs (.58)	3.51	1.68
Identify Poor Performance (.74)	4.96	1.54
Within-Person Decisions		
Identify Individual Training Needs (.77)	3.42	1.40
Performance Feedback (.77)	5.67	1.35
Determine Transfers & Assignments (.76)	3.66	1.53
Identify Individual Strengths & Weaknesses (.75)	5.41	1.44
Systems Maintenance		
Manpower Planning (.82)	2.72	1.58
Determine Organizational Training Needs (1.0)	2.74	1.49
Evaluation Goal Achievement (.74)	4.72	1.59
Assist in Goal Identification (.73)	4.90	1.62
Evaluate Personnel Systems (.82)	2.04	1.18
Reinforce Authority Structure (.16)	2.65	1.69
Identify Organizational Development Needs (.98)	2.63	1.52
Documentation		
Criteria for Validation Research (.45)	2.30	1.35
Document Personnel Decisions (.91)	5.15	1.27
Meet Legal Requirements (.48)	4.58	1.80

Adapted from J. N. Cleveland, K. R. Murphy, & R. E. Williams, Multiple uses of performance appraisal: Prevalence and correlates, *Journal of Applied Psychology, 74* (1989).

[a] Maximum likelihood estimates of loading are in parentheses.

[b] Ratings were based on a 7-point rating scale measuring the impact of appraisal on a variety of organizational decisions and actions, where 1 = no impact, 4 = moderate impact, and 7 = primary determinant. Factors are boldfaced.

In general, both between-person (e.g., salary administration) and within-person decisions (e.g., feedback regarding strengths and weaknesses) were more frequently cited as purposes of appraisal systems. Systems maintenance (e.g., workforce planning) and documentation (e.g., documenting personnel decisions) were less frequently cited as important uses of appraisal information.

Performance appraisal researchers (Cleveland et al., 1989; DeCotiis & Petit, 1978; Jacobs, Kafry, & Zedeck, 1980; Mohrman & Lawler, 1983; Tiffin & McCormick, 1958; Wexley & Klimoski, 1984) and practitioners (Burchett & DeMeuse, 1985; Cocheu, 1986; Friedman, 1986; Haynes, 1986; Martin, 1986; Massey, 1975; Olsen & Bennett, 1975) have promoted the idea that there are many uses or goals to which a PA system can contribute. Cleveland and associates (1989) identified at least 20 different uses in both the scientific and practitioner journals. Further, the surveys indicate that organizations are in fact using performance appraisals for a large number of purposes. Recently, however, there has been an increasing awareness among researchers and practitioners that although appraisal can be used effectively for many purposes, one PA system may not effectively address all of these purposes equally well (Cleveland et al., 1989; DeVries et al., 1986).

Jacobs and colleagues (1980) suggested that a critical decision in using information from performance appraisals is whether to focus on satisfying individual needs (e.g., employee development and feedback) or organizational needs (e.g., administrations decisions such as promotion, salary increases, etc.). Others distinguish between administrative decisions and the identification of employee strengths and weaknesses (Wexley & Klimoski, 1984) or between person decisions and within-person decisions (Cleveland et al., 1989). In addition, uses of performance appraisal have been categorized according to their impact on various organizational constituents (Balzer & Sulsky, in press; Mohrman & Lawler, 1983). Thus, when discussing the uses of PA, it is important to distinguish among organizational goals, rater goals, ratee, goals, and the performance appraisal researcher goals.

Further, Mohrman and Lawler (1983) discussed both private and public PA behaviors; the public-private distinction is similar to the rating-judgment distinction discussed in Chapter One. Mohrman and Lawler indicate that rating behavior is an outcome of the rater's perception of the situation. There are two determinants of those perceptions: the appraisal system itself (format, frequency, etc.), and the context of performance. As noted earlier, the purpose of performance appraisal is one critical aspect of the rating context. Thus, it is reasonable to conclude that the purpose of appraisal will affect the rater's behavior.

With the proliferation of the organizational and individual uses of information from performance appraisals, researchers and practitioners have begun to observe that an appraisal system that is used for one purpose may not (under similar circumstances) yield the same outcome when the purpose is different. Also, information about performance collected under one set of conditions (purpose) may not be useful for other purposes. As we will discuss later in this chapter, the use of PA for a wide range of individual and organizational uses is not always effective or efficient. When several uses are incompatible or in conflict, attempts to use performance appraisal as an all-purpose tool may fail.

Purposes of Appraisal and Rating Outcomes and Processes

In the previous section we discussed the many purposes or goals associated with performance in organizations (Jacobs et al., 1980; Landy & Farr, 1980;

Murphy, Balzer, Kellam, & Armstrong, 1984; Zedeck & Cascio, 1982). According to both the DeCotiis and Petit (1978) and Landy and Farr (1980) PA models, the intended use of information from performance appraisals is thought to have a significant impact on appraisal outcomes, such as the properties of ratings (e.g., reliability, leniency, accuracy), and on the rating process. The research on the impact of purpose on rating can be divided into several areas, including: (1) impact on psychometric quality of ratings, (2) impact on the accuracy of judgments, (3) impact on rating and judgment processes, and (4) impact on the structure and administrative practices of performance appraisal. The first two areas are tied to outcomes; the latter two are tied to the rating process.

Rating Outcomes

Research that evaluates the effect of purpose on the measurement qualities of ratings (e.g., psychometric properties, accuracy) has covered a fairly wide range of topics. However, there is a substantial body of literature dealing with the effects of purpose of rating on one specific psychometric property of ratings — leniency.

Leniency   Starting in the 1950s, several studies documented the impact of purpose of rating on leniency, or the level of ratings. Field research, in particular, has consistently documented the impact of purpose. For example, Taylor and Wherry (1951), using ratings from army personnel, found that average ratings of officers were significantly higher for administrative purposes than when ratings were collected for research purposes. Using ratings of 400 job applicants, Heron (1956) obtained results similar to Taylor and Wherry's, with a negatively skewed distribution of ratings for administrative purposes. Sharon and Bartlett (1969) found that ratings used in making real administrative decisions were more lenient than ratings obtained for research purposes. Bernardin, Orban, and Carlyle (1981) found that probationary officers were rated significantly higher by police sergeants when ratings were used to make personnel decisions than when they were used to provide feedback. However, other studies have found no mean difference in ratings when comparing administrative and research purpose conditions (Berkshire & Highland, 1953; Borreson, 1967; Sharon, 1970) or comparing administrative and feedback purposes (McIntyre, Smith, & Hassett, 1984; Meier & Feldhusen, 1979).

It is important to note that field studies usually find greater leniency for ratings that are used for promotion or other administrative decisions than do laboratory studies that use students as subjects and use ratees that are not known to the student raters (Bernardin & Villanova, 1986; McIntyre et al., 1984; Murphy et al., 1984). Some of the inconsistency in findings regarding leniency may be an artifact of the different methods employed in research on the purpose of rating.

Purpose and Accuracy   During the last decade, PA researchers have used a number of accuracy measures to assess the effectiveness of ratings (see

Chapter Ten). Unlike much of the research on the psychometric properties of ratings, research on the accuracy of ratings has been largely conducted in laboratory settings using students as raters, rather than using real ratings collected in organizations. Results of these studies are mixed. Murphy, Philbin, and Adams (1989) found that subjects were more accurate in evaluating teachers when performance evaluation was the primary purpose for observing teaching behavior than when the evaluation was the secondary goal (with the primary goal to "learn the lecture"). However, accuracy in the evaluation condition did not hold up over time. When there was a delay between observation (of the lecture) and the actual rating task, subjects for whom performance appraisal was a secondary task showed higher levels of accuracy. It is important to note that in this study, the researchers varied the purpose of *observation.* In most other studies, the purpose of rating has been manipulated.

In a study of faculty ratings, Dobbins, Cardy, and Truxillo (1986) investigated both the accuracy and level of ratings collected for three purposes: (1) feedback, (2) scale validation or merit, and (3) promotion decisions. They found that male professors were rated more favorably than females only when the evaluations were made by men and used for administrative decisions. The accuracy measures indicated that men were rated higher than their true performance levels, whereas women were rated lower than their true performance levels.

More recently, Dobbins, Cardy, and Truxillo (1988) investigated the effects of two purposes: research versus merit pay and promotion, and individual differences in stereotypes of women (traditional versus non-traditional) on the accuracy of appraisals. Here, female ratees were evaluated less accurately and less favorably by raters with traditional female stereotypes than by raters with nontraditional stereotypes of women. However, this difference in accuracy occurred only when ratings were used to make administrative decisions. Finally, McIntyre and colleagues (1984) assessed accuracy under three purpose conditions: hiring, feedback, and research. They found that ratings in the research condition were marginally more accurate than in the hiring condition.

Bernardin, Abbott, and Cooper (cited in McIntrye et al., 1984) suggested that the effect of purpose on ratings might be due to confounding the format of rating with the purpose of rating. When these researchers looked at purpose and held format constant, they found no influence of purpose on rating accuracy. Similarly, Murphy and associates (1984) found that purpose did not affect the accuracy of ratings collected using two different rating formats.

Summary   The purpose of rating appears to influence the psychometric quality of ratings. This especially holds in research conducted in the field using actual raters and ratees; this effect is less consistently found in laboratory research. The pattern of significant results in field research and the non-significant results in the laboratory is the reverse of what occurs in many other research areas. Because of the more highly controlled conditions and the demand characteristics that are present in laboratory studies, lab research will usually yield larger effect sizes than those found in field settings (Murphy, Herr, Lockhart, & Maguire, 1986). This is clearly not the case in research on the influence of rating purpose on rating outcomes.

Although more research is required to understand fully why purpose affects the outcomes of ratings, several hypotheses have been made. DeCotiis and Petit (1978) suggest that raters may inflate their ratings of subordinates so they (the raters) can receive a high rating or evaluation from their own supervisor. Ilgen and Feldman (1983) suggest that leniency is likely to occur when the appraisal has important consequences for the ratee (i.e., administrative decisions). Mohrman and Lawler (1983) suggest that leniency will occur when the rating has positive or negative oucomes for the rater as well. Waldman and Thornton (1988) and others indicate that when the rating is made public (and would likely have negative consequences for either rater or ratee), more lenient ratings are likely to occur.

Murphy and associates (1984) describe three ways in which appraisal purpose could affect ratings. First, purpose may directly affect ratings. Raters or decision makers may use one standard when rating for administrative decisions and another standard when rating for research purposes. Similar to Ilgen and Feldman (1983) and Mohrman and Lawler (1983), Murphy and colleagues (1984) suggest that raters will hesitate to give poor ratings because they are likely to lead to negative outcomes. Second, purpose may affect ratings indirectly, through basic cognitive processes including observation, encoding, and recall. This is also implied by Landy and Farr (1980) and DeNisi, Cafferty, and Meglino (1984), the latter emphasizing information acquisition. Finally, Murphy, and colleagues (1984) suggest that purpose may affect the way in which a rater integrates behavioral information when forming judgments about performance (see also Crowder, 1976). Decision strategies may differ in tasks that require high memory demands, and strategies are apt to change as the complexity of the task increases (Payne, 1976) or when time pressures or distractions are present (Wright, 1974). Different purposes may pose different constraints or demands on the rater.

Rating Processes

There are two different ways in which purpose might affect the rating process. First, as noted above, purpose might affect the judgment process (we will expand on this notion below). Second, the purpose of rating might dictate a number of administrative features of rating, ranging from the frequency of ratings to the type of scales employed.

Purpose and the Judgment Process   Another area of research on the influence of purpose assesses its impact on the observation, attention, storage, memory, and retrieval processes involved in ratings (DeNisi & Williams, 1988; Henemen & Wexley, 1983; Waldman & Thornton, 1988; Williams, DeNisi,

Blencoe, & Cafferty, 1985; Zedeck & Cascio, 1982). DeNisi and colleagues have conducted a number of studies that indicate that the purpose of appraisal affects the way in which the rater acquires information. Williams and associates (1985) found that raters used information from appraisals differently when ratings were used to make decisions regarding pay (as opposed to promotion or remedial training). More lenient ratings were found for promotion than for the other two purposes. In a second experiment, Williams and colleagues (1985) found that raters searched for different types of information under the various purpose conditions.

Zedeck and Cascio (1982) investigated the effects of appraisal purpose on rating strategies and rating oucome. They used policy-capturing techniques to identify which performance dimensions contributed to students' ratings. Their analyses indicated that rater strategies varied with the purpose of rating. The researchers concluded that individual dimensions of performance were weighted, combined, and integrated differently depending on rating purpose. Specifically, raters differentially attended to positive and negative information reflected in the job dimensions as a function of perceived purpose. Zedeck and Cascio also found that accuracy of ratings varied by purpose, with accuracy highest for ratings of retention of a probationary employee, and decreasing for employee development and merit pay. Heneman, Wexley, and Moore (1987) noted that in this study the accuracy in ratings decreased when the magnitude of the decision increased.

Reilly and Balzer (1988) asked subjects to rate their teaching assistants and found that purpose influenced the psychometric quality of ratings and the recording of positive and negative behaviors. Ratings were more lenient in the administration condition than in the feedback condition. Further, in both the administrative and the administrative-plus-feedback condition, subjects rated positive behaviors as occurring more frequently than in the feedback-only condition. The authors suggest that this may be a way that subjects justify more lenient ratings.

Purpose and Characteristics of the Appraisal System   Few empirical studies have addressed the question of whether the purpose of rating determines the effectiveness of certain structural and administrative features of a PA system. At least four aspects of the rating process might be influenced by purpose.

The first issue is *who* should be evaluated. Cummings and Schwab (1973) suggest that employees at different overall levels of performance should be appraised differently. They suggest that separate appraisal systems should be structured for low, average, and high performers. It may also be that as one progresses higher in the organizational hierarchy, the purpose or use of performance appraisal changes. For middle managers, appraisal may be used as a control mechanism to identify and distinguish among employee per-formance levels, and may possess a strong administrative component. On the other hand, for upper-level managers, PA may be used to assign executives to specific and challenging activities that develop targeted skills.

The second issue concerns the *source(s)* of the ratings. Although raters are most often the ratee's immediate supervisor, it may be more effective to use peers as raters when the purpose is to provide developmental feedback to the employee. Here, a clear separation could be made between the administrative and feedback purposes by obtaining ratings from different sources. Third, the purpose of rating might influence the *frequency* with which the appraisal is conducted. For administrative decisions, information may need to be updated yearly in order to correspond with budgetary cycles. On the other hand, if the purpose of rating is to provide developmental feedback, employees may want this information more often (and perhaps less formally) than on an annual basis. Furthermore, if an employee's performance is to improve, feedback may be neccessary every three to six months, or even more often, depending on the task.

Finally, Bernardin and colleagues (Bernardin & Beatty, 1984; Bernardin & Villanova, 1986) note that the *purpose* of rating has usually been ignored when comparing rating scale formats. If the purpose of performance appraisal is to predict future performance or potential, traits or more general skill ratings may make more sense than somewhat specific behavioral ratings. On the other hand, behavior-based scales may be more meaningful, appropriate, and effective when used to provide developmental performance feedback to employees.

Power, Politics, and the Use of Appraisal

Few performance appraisal researchers or practitioners would deny that power and politics are important determinants of appraisal processes and outcomes. However, other than a few recent empirical articles (e.g., Longenecker, Sims, & Gioia, 1987) and brief mention of the topics in books and chapters on performance appraisal (e.g., Bernardin & Beatty, 1984; Carroll & Schneier, 1982; DeVries et al., 1986), power and politics (as associated with appraisal practices, generally, and with rating purpose, specifically) have received inadequate attention. In this section, we will attempt to specify the role of power and politics in performance appraisal, and explore the possiblity that the influence of political considerations may depend on the purpose of appraisal.

Power and Appraisal

The notion that performance appraisal serves as a control system in organizations is not new (Lawler, 1976). In fact, a PA system, when operating as the organization designed and intended it, has inherent power. In such a system, raters evaluate employees accurately, identifying each employee's strengths and weaknesses and distinguishing among the good and poor employees, and ratings are followed by important organizational consequences. These consequences can be formal, including monetary rewards to good performers and dismissal or punishments to poor performers. Informal consequences might include a humiliating, demoralizing feedback session for a ratee or an uncomfortable awkward feedback session for the supervisor (Whisler, 1958). If raters were willing to provide accurate ratings and accurate feedback, the PA system would become a very powerful tool.

In addition to being linked with salient rewards or consequences, the performance appraisal system derives power from the organization when it serves to clarify lines of authority. In most appraisals, the organization assigns the responsiblity for performance evaluation to managers. Further, these managers rate only the employees they manage (as opposed to peer evaluation or subordinate evaluation). That is, employees with more power in the organization provide ratings for employees occupying lower and less powerful positions (Pfeffer, 1981).

Power implies the ability to influence one's environment. Performance appraisal provides one means for the organization to influence its internal and external environments. When using an appraisal system for documenting the validity of selection and promotion practices used by the organization, the influence that the organization may have over its environment, especially the legal environment, is enhanced. If ratings provide thorough documentation of personnel decisions, employees may be less likely to perceive the system as unfair, and less willing to bring a lawsuit against the company.

The organization's top management can influence employees by establishing the type, format, frequency and purpose of its PA system. It can communicate to employees what it values in work activities and what it rewards and it can set a climate for performance (Zand, 1981). A supervisor may attempt to exert power on the organization when ratings are used to make salary recommendations or promotion decisions. Additionally, a supervisor may use the performance ratings of his or her subordinates as a means of competing for a valued project for the department or unit.

Performance appraisal has obvious implications when it is tied to the supervisor's attempts to influence his or her subordinates. In particular, when the purpose of appraisal is to make salary or promotion decisions, a supervisor possesses significant reward or coercive power to influence valued outcomes. When there is no apparent link between ratings and administrative outcomes (French & Raven, 1959), the supervisor will have less power over the subordinate. Finally, there are opportunities for upward influence from subordinate to supervisor in feedback sessions. Here, the employee is likely to have some opportunity to explain his or her performance and behavior. There also is an opportunity for the ratee to influence the supervisor by providing additional information that the rater may not have access to (Backburn, 1981; Mechanic, 1962; Porter, Allen, & Angle, 1981).

Although in theory the appraisal system provides a way to exercise power, in fact the many constituents of a performance system are likely to *obtain* power through their use of the appraisal system. Further, there may be power conflicts among constituents. The emergence of political behavior in the PA process is likely to occur. One consequence of such behavior may be that the appraisal system may not yield the information that was intended.

Politics and Appraisal

There are multiple constituents for any PA system; these include the organization, the rater, the ratee, and the researcher (Balzer & Sulsky, in press; Mohrman & Lawler, 1983). Each of these constituents has its own set of needs and goals to achieve through performance appraisal. Although there may be overlap among these goals and constituencies, inconsistencies and conflict are not uncommon.

Longenecker and associates (1987) refer to politics of appraisal as the "deliberate attempts by individuals to enhance or protect their self-interests when conflicting courses of action are possible" (p. 184). Therefore, the authors state, political action is typically a source of bias or inaccuracy in employee appraisal. From interviews with 60 upper-level executives, Longenecker and colleagues (1987) found evidence of deliberate manipulation of formal ratings by executives. Much recent research on performance appraisal has been devoted to understanding and improving the accuracy of ratings — ways to perfect an instrument's measurement qualities. However, Longenecker and colleagues and others (Bernardin & Beatty, 1984) point out that appraisal takes place in an environment that may not be completely rational, straightforward, or objective.

Managers often do not care about accuracy but rather about the extent to which they have discretion needed to balance effectiveness and survival. If accurate performance appraisals can hurt the manager (e.g., by negatively influencing interpersonal relationships), it may be irrational to give accurate ratings. Therefore, managers have their own motives and may manipulate ratings in order to accomplish their own goals or agenda. Longenecker and associates (1987) found that executives adjust or manipulate employee ratings in two directions — both higher and lower than the actual employee performance level. Inflated ratings occur frequently (most often on overall performance ratings rather than on specific performance items) and, not surprisingly, there are many reasons for inflation. Longenecker and associates and Cleveland, Morrison, and Bjerke (1986) suggest that raters first determine the overall rating they want to give an employee and then go back and complete the specific items. Why? The most frequently cited reason from the Longenecker and colleagues' (1987) interviews was to maximize a subordinate's merit increases. Nearly all other reasons reflect the intense social nature of performance appraisal that, although not completely ignored, have apparently not been included in much current PA research.

Although executives hestitate to manipulate employee ratings down-ward, deflated ratings do occur. The reasons for deflating ratings cited by managers include (1) to shock the subordinate back into increasing his or her performance, (2) to teach rebellious subordinates a lesson regarding who is in charge, (3) to send a message to a subordinate that he or she should consider leaving the organization, and (4) to build a strongly documented record of poor performance that could expediate the termination process (Longenecker et al., 1987).

Although politics may always be a part of appraisal, the extent to which politics is operating in ratings may vary considerably, depending on political culture of the organization — in particular, whether the performance appraisal is taken seriously. There are a number of influences on the political culture of the organization (Longenecker et al., 1987), including the following:

- ► The economic health and growth potential of the organization
- ► The extent to which top management supports or does not practice political tactics when appraising its own subordinates
- ► The extent to which executives believe appraisal is necessary
- ► The extent to which executives believe they would be scrutinized by superiors on their appraisal of subordinates
- ► The extent to which organizations will train managers in performance appraisal
- ► The degree of open discussion of the appraisal process among executive and subordinates (i.e., trust)
- ► The extent of which executives believe that the appraisal becomes more political at higher levels of the organzational hierarchy

In general, when top management believes strongly in the necessity of performance appraisal, the influence of political factors on ratings is not likely to be substantial (Longenecker et al., 1987). When appraisal is not strongly and visibly supported by top management, political factors are more likely to emerge.

Conflicts among Organizational and Individual Uses of Appraisal

Throughout this chapter, we have identified a number of organizational uses for performance appraisal information. Further, we have discussed how appraisal purposes can influence the processes and outcomes of appraisals. Until now, we have discussed the impact of purpose as if only one purpose is operating at a time in a given organization. This is the implicit assumption of much of the laboratory research on the effects of purpose. However, appraisal experts recognize that information from any one performance appraisal system is likely to be used for multiple purposes. Cleveland and associates'

(1989) survey specifically asked organizations to indicate the extent to which their PA system was used for various purposes. They found that over 71% of the respondents indicated that information from appraisals was used "moderately to extensively" for both between-person decisions (i.e., pay, promotion, etc.) and within-person decisions (i.e., feedback). They noted that these two purposes are often in conflict.

Whether or not performance appraisal should be used simultaneously for personnel decisions, on the one hand, and for employee feedback, on the other hand, was questioned by Meyer, Kay, and French (1965). More recently, DeVries (1983) suggested that a performance appraisal system designed to improve employee performance may not be the most effective for salary administration. Further, DeVries and associates (1986) found that the uses of appraisal have expanded considerably within the last 25 years. The purposes that human resource managers have in mind and those that employees have may not always be the same. They warn that the several uses may conflict, giving way to less useful ratings and ultimately to dissatisfaction with the system.

It is important to understand what is meant by conflicting purposes in performance appraisal. Two types of conflict have been noted: (1) the conflicts between the multiple constituents of appraisal (i.e., the organization, the rater, the ratee, etc.) and (2) the conflicts that occur when appraisal is used to satisfy multiple organizational and individual purposes (e.g., using appraisal for both promotion decisions and employee feedback) (Cleveland et al., 1986; Cleveland et al., 1989).

Mohrman (1986) and others (Balzer & Sulsky, in press) indicate that conflicts may arise among the constituents of an appraisal system. Specifically, raters may use appraisal to achieve different objectives or purposes than the ratee. Further, the ratee may think that appraisal is used for purposes quite different from those envisioned by the organization. Especially with a new PA system, there is a danger that the system will create a discrepancy between the espoused purposes and actual purposes of appraisal (Mohrman, 1986).

Mohrman (1986) found that although managers and subordinates sometimes agreed on the extent to which different purposes *should* be achieved through the performance appraisal system, subordinates rarely perceived that the actual goal of appraisal *was* achieved to the extent that managers did. Further, subordinates and managers differed in terms of the extent to which they believed that some purposes should be stressed. For example, Mohrman (1986) found that subordinates wanted an explanation of pay during appraisal, whereas managers did not think it was necessary. Neither constituent views pay as being discussed to any great extent; subordinates often feel that this need remains unmet after leaving the appraisal session (Mohrman, 1986).

Although conflicts are possible, they are not universal. Both the needs of the organization and the employee can be met in the appraisal session. Prince and Lawler (1981) found that salary discussion can have a positive impact on the usefulness of the appraisal meeting, even when the message delivered is a negative one. One reason for this is that the discussion can be effective in meeting the purposes of the subordinate as well as those of the supervisor and the organization. Mohrman (1986) suggests that there is a need to determine ways to balance the multiple purposes of performance appraisal rather than rely on systems that are designed to control purposes of appraisals.

Closely related to the conflict that emerges among the various constituents is the conflict that may emerge for the rater when the appraisal he or she completes is used for multiple organizational and individual purposes. That is, given that the organization uses information from appraisals (e.g., to make promotion decisions, to terminate employees, to provide developmental feedback to employees), the rater must somehow weigh each of these purposes, incorporate his or her own agenda (Longenecker et al., 1987), and then decide what appraisal ratings to provide. There are a number of issues of concern here.

First, there is a need to understand what uses of PA are compatible and what uses are incompatible. For example, it is likely that a supervisor experiences little conflict when information from performance appraisals is used for providing feedback to employees regarding their strengths and weaknesses and to recommend employees for training programs. Both of these purposes reflect within-person decisions. These decisions require the rater to compare the strengths and weaknesses of different skills and behaviors for a given individual. On the other hand, raters may experience conflict when the organization uses the appraisal information for both developmental feedback and promotion decisions. The latter purpose reflects a between-person use (Cleveland et al., 1989), which requires the rater to make comparisons of good and poor performance among all of his or her subordinates.

Second, as suggested elsewhere (Cleveland et al., 1986), when operating in an organizational context that requests appraisal information as a basis for multiple and possibly conflicting uses, the rater may attempt to balance these purposes, frequently resulting in ratings that reflect political judgments rather than judgments about performance. There is also evidence that in some settings the rater will select one purpose or goal and then complete the appraisal with that purpose in mind (Bjerke, Cleveland, Morrison, & Wilson, 1987).

A third issue involved when appraisal is used for multiple purposes is how the rater decides what to do (e.g., how to balance incompatible purposes) and, in particular, how limitations of the rater may affect this decision. Cognitive research suggests that the purpose of rating affects the way in which information about performance is acquired, categorized, stored, and retrieved. (See DeNisi & Williams, 1988, for a review.) A particularly important finding in this research is that when the purpose of rating changes, raters might find it difficult to provide ratings that are useful for the new purpose. That is, when raters initially have one purpose in mind, this purpose interferes with the purpose in the subsequent task. The rater is less able to process information appropriately when completing ratings whose purpose differs from the purpose the rater had in mind when he or she observed the ratee's performance. These studies suggest that under multiple purpose conditions, the organization may sometimes ask raters to perform an activity that is beyond their capabilities.

Finally, results from the laboratory and from interviews with raters in the field suggest that when a rater faces multiple and possibly conflicting purposes, the organization may be sacrificing not only accuracy but also the usefulness of the ratings (i.e., ratings are so inflated that they provide no meaningful information). It is conceivable that the rater selects one salient or consequential purpose and ignores the rest. The information provided by the rater may have some utility for that particular decision but may have little utility for other purposes. It is also conceivable that organizations are not obtaining useful information for *any* organization or individual purpose when the ratings are collected for multiple purposes. That is, if performance appraisal is attempted for a large number of incompatible purposes, there is a risk of putting the rater in an impossible situation, and the ratings he or she finally gives may be affected by so many confounds that the ratings are not useful for any of the system's purposes.

Summary

Performance appraisals are used for many purposes in organizations. Different organizations might emphasize different purposes, and any given organization might pursue several different purposes with the same appraisal system. The variety of appraisal purposes often reflect the variety of goals different constituencies want to pursue when participating in performance appraisals. The goals of different constituencies are often in conflict; one result of these conflicts may be the use of power and politics in the appraisal process and outcomes. We suggest that organizations assess the compatibility of the various intended uses of performance appraisals. We strongly believe that appraisals cannot be used for all of the purposes they often appear to serve in organizations, and that attempts to use appraisals for a wide range of purposes may doom the system. PA systems will work best when the formal goals and organizational uses of performance appraisal are consistent with the goals of other appraisal constituents, including the rater and ratee.

Chapter Five

Obtaining Information about Performance

► The focus of this chapter is on understanding how supervisors evaluate the work of their subordinates and how those evaluations change as the work behaviors of subordinates change. As we discussed in Chapter One, the supervisor's evaluation of a particular worker is not necessarily identical to his or her formal appraisal of that worker (i.e., the numbers that are recorded on a performance appraisal form). Supervisors are often motivated to give high ratings (or avoid low ones) even when they know that the worker is not performing well. Therefore, understanding the judgment process is not sufficient for understanding the ratings a supervisor will record. However, it does provide a first step toward understanding the complex process of performance appraisal (PA) in organizations.

Figure 5-1 presents a simple model that will be used in the discussion about the performance judgment process. First, the supervisor must obtain information about the subordinate's performance. This information might include direct observation of work behaviors; reports from clients, customers, or other members of the organization; or inspection of the results of job performance (e.g., products, reports). Other sources of information include the supervisor's prior evaluation of the subordinate (Balzer, 1986; Murphy, Balzer, Lockhart, & Eisenman, 1985) as well as the subordinate's general reputation as a good or bad performer (March & March, 1978). The supervisor must then apply judgment strategy to combine, integrate, and make sense of this information. The term *strategy* should not be taken to indicate a conscious

Figure 5–1. The Performance Judgment Process

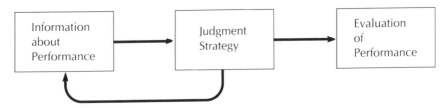

plan or well-formulated policy; judgment strategies are often nothing more than simple heuristics and rules of thumb (Hogarth, 1980; Naylor, Pritchard, & Ilgen, 1980; Tversky & Kahneman, 1974), and judges are not completely consistent in using even the simplest of strategies (Dawes & Corrigan, 1974). The judgment strategy will, in turn, influence the type of information needed when evaluating others. Thus, the sales supervisor who believes that the sign of a good salesperson is a firm handshake will base performance appraisals on information different from one who takes into account the salesperson's timeliness, accuracy of records, sales volume, and so on. Finally, the product of the information and judgment strategy is an evaluative judgment — an assessment of whether the subordinate is a good, poor, or average worker.

This chapter is concerned with the first box in the model depicted in Figure 5-1 — the acquisition of information about performance. We will deal with the question of how and under what circumstances supervisors obtain information about the performance of different subordinates. This chapter concentrates on "new" information about performance; Chapter Six will discuss the impact of information that is already in the supervisor's head (e.g., reputation of individual as good or poor performer, prior impressions and previous evaluations of the individual). We will also discuss the types of information that might be available to persons other than the supervisor, such as peers or subordinates of the individual being evaluated. The use of multiple sources of evaluation provides an opportunity to consider information that is typically not available to the supervisor. However, as we will note in this and subsequent chapters, using a variety of sources for evaluating workers may lead to problems, ranging from low levels of agreement among different sources to political difficulties that arise when the power hierarchy of an organization is violated (e.g., when a subordinate evaluates his or her supervisor).

What Should Supervisors Observe?

Before determining how supervisors obtain information about job performance, it is necessary to define what is meant by *job performance*. In other words, it is useful to define the thing that supervisors obtain information about before discussing how they obtain that information.

The fundamental question in determining the content of the job performance domain is whether performance should be defined in terms of behavior or in terms of the results of behavior (James, 1973; Smith, 1976). From the organization's point of view, there is a strong temptation to define performance in terms of results. After all, results are what count (at least in the short run). However, there are several reasons for defining performance in terms of behavior rather than in terms of results. First, an exclusive emphasis on results is likely to lead to behaviors that are dysfunctional for the organization. Landy and Farr (1983) note that if performance is defined exclusively in terms of countable outcomes (i.e., results), incumbents will be strongly motivated to maximize those outcomes at the expense of other activities (e.g., maintenance, planning conservation) that are vital to the organization. Second, results are more complexly determined than behaviors, in that results are a joint function of what the person does and the situation in which he or she does it. Defining performance solely in terms of results makes it difficult to determine what is being measured — the person or the situation in which he or she performs. Consider the case of sales clerks who work on different days or different shifts. Their sales volume may be a better measure of the number of customers in the store at different times than of their individual effectiveness in selling the product. A final point is that results-oriented criteria can lead supervisors and subordinates to ignore a wide range of behaviors (e.g., maintaining good interpersonal relations) that are critical to the survival and effectiveness of the organization but are not uniquely tied to any given product or result.

Our conclusion is that performance must ultimately be defined in terms of behaviors. The results of behaviors are, to be sure, extremely important in evaluating those behaviors. Nevertheless, we believe that the domain of performance is best defined as a domain of behaviors rather than as a set of outcomes.

The next question that must be answered is what kinds of behaviors define performance on the job? In other words, what sorts of behavior does the supervisor need to know about in order to sensibly evaluate a subordinate's job performance? It seems reasonable to assume that the definition of job performance should not include *all* behaviors that occur on the job but rather only some subset of relevant behaviors. One way to define *relevant* is in terms of those behaviors that are clearly linked to accomplishing the specific tasks that are included in a person's job. Carroll and Schneier (1982) take this perspective and define performance as the quality of task-oriented behavior. From this perspective, the growing body of research dealing with the determinants and the nature of task performance (cf. Fleishman & Quantance, 1984; Salvendy & Seymour, 1973) provides the key to understanding job performance. If job performance is equated with task performance, research priorities in this field should be directed at developing better job descriptions and at aggregating measures of performance on several separate tasks into an overall measure of job performance.

There are several reasons to believe that job performance *cannot* be equated with task performance. First, most observations of work behavior confirm the common perception that workers spend relatively little time performing what would be regarded as tasks. For example, Bialek, Zapf, and McGuire (1977) reported that enlisted infantrymen spent less than half of their work time performing the technical tasks for which they had been trained; in many cases, only a small proportion of a soldier's time was in any way devoted to accomplishing the tasks specified in his or her job description. Campbell, Dunnette, Lawler, and Weick (1970) noted similar patterns for managers. A substantial part of the manager's day is spent doing things that cannot be unambiguously linked to the accomplishment of specific tasks.

The fact that most people's work time is not devoted solely to tasks has serious implications for several aspects of criterion development. For example, many methods of job analysis are based explicitly on the assumption that most, if not all, of a worker's time is spent working on identifiable tasks. (This is true of the Air Force's task analysis system; see Christal, 1974.) Since much of the work day is spent doing something outside of the typical domain of tasks, indices of the percentage of time spent on different tasks present a warped view of the activities actually carried out by workers. Unless one is willing to ignore much of what a person does at work, it is difficult to equate job performance with task performance.

Second, many of the PA systems currently in use in the civilian and military sectors include specific measures or indices that are only tangentially related to task performance. Examples include measures of absenteeism and turnover, as well as supervisory ratings of broad traits such as dependability or motivation. Admittedly, the use of such measures does not prove that the job performance domain is broader than the task performance domain; it is possible that these measures, although widely used, are invalid. Nevertheless, the widespread use of measures that do not relate directly or solely to the accomplishment of tasks does suggest that the job performance domain is *perceived* to be broader than the domain of task performance.

A third argument for assuming that job performance cannot be defined solely in terms of task performance is that job performance must be defined over longer time periods and in relation to more organizational units than is true for task performance. This can be seen most clearly by considering the case of a machinist who successfully accomplishes his or her tasks by depleting all available reserves of material and by diverting resources from other work units. Although the individual successfully achieves the main task, the long-term implications of such task performance are clearly not favorable. In many jobs, it would not be difficult to provide examples of individuals who successfully complete most tasks, but whose performance was judged to be poor.

An alternative approach to defining the set of relevant behaviors can be derived from Astin's (1964) definition of *conceptual criterion.* Astin (1964) noted that in developing criteria, the relevant goals of the sponsor or the measurer must be identified. In the context of work, the relevant goals of the organization would include both short-term goals, such as the successful completion of specific tasks, as well as long-term goals, such as the maintenance of effective relations between workgroups, departments, and so on. According to Astin (1964), the conceptual criterion is nothing more than a verbal abstraction of the relevant goals or the outcomes desired; the set of possible criterion measures would include any observable index or state that is judged relevant to the conceptual criterion. If we substitute "performance construct" for "conceptual criterion" and "performance dimensions" for "criterion measures," it becomes possible to define the domain of performance and to indicate the set of behaviors that are included in that domain. *Performance domain* is defined as the set of behaviors that are relevant to the goals of the organization or the organizational unit in which a person works.

In order to specify the range of behaviors that define performance, one would have to know the relevant goals of the organization. Note here that the global set of goals that define the overall effectiveness of the organization (e.g., maximize after-tax profits) are not as relevant as the set of goals that are defined for an incumbent in a specific position within the organization. The organization defines a set of goals to be met by an incumbent in each job, and the relevant goals may vary considerably from job to job or across different levels in the organization. This is particularly true when specific task goals are considered but will also be true for several nontask goals. For example, one goal that is likely to be broadly relevant, but not tied to any specific task, is that incumbents must maintain effective interpersonal relations with their co-workers and with other organizational members with whom they interact. The type and extent of these interpersonal contacts will vary across departments and across levels of management. One might infer that the skills and behaviors that contribute to successful maintenance of interpersonal relations will vary from job to job. Nevertheless, within the great majority of jobs, this general class of behaviors is likely to represent one aspect of effective performance.

Dimensions of Job Performance

The preceding section suggests that to evaluate subordinates' performance, supervisors must observe a wide range of behaviors that are relevant to the goals of the job. One way to impose structure on this task is to define the dimensions of job performance that can be used to classify behaviors into homogeneous clusters.

The traditional approach to defining the dimension of job performance is through a careful job analysis (McCormick, 1976, 1979). A variety of analytic methods have been used to define performance dimensions, ranging from the Job Element Method (Clark & Primoff, 1979) to critical incident methods (Flanagan, 1954; Latham, Fay, & Saari, 1979) to those that relay on structured questionnaires, such as the Position Analysis Questionnaire (Cornelius, Hakel, & Sackett, 1979; McCormick, Jeanneret, & Mecham, 1972).

Although formal job analysis provides an empirical basis for determining the dimensions of job performance, it may not provide a total solution. Cognitive research suggests that the dimensions raters use to organize their observations are a product of implicit theories about the job (Borman, 1983, 1987). Although implicit theories often contain a great deal of accurate information (Lay & Jackson, 1969; Stricker, Jacobs, & Kogan, 1974), the dimensions used by raters are not necessarily the same as those that are derived through a formal job analysis.

In one of the few studies of supervisors' "folk theories" of job performance, Borman (1987) found that the dimensions that defined supervisors' conceptions of performance included the following:

- ▶ Initiative and hard work
- ▶ Maturity and responsibility
- ▶ Organization
- ▶ Technical proficiency
- ▶ Assertive leadership
- ▶ Supportive leadership

These dimensions are notable in two ways. First, several of them refer to global traits rather than to specific behaviors. The position that performance appraisal *should be* based on traits is accepted by only a few researchers (e.g., Kavanaugh, 1971). Borman's (1987) results suggest that, regardless of what should be done, performance appraisals *are* done in terms of global traits rather than specific behaviors. This position is also implicit in several of the recent cognitive models of performance appraisal (DeNisi, Cafferty, & Meglino, 1984; Feldman, 1981; Ilgen & Feldman, 1983; Nathan & Lord, 1983). Second, they range from those that are tightly focused on carrying out specific tasks (e.g., technical proficiency) to those that are more diffuse and more concerned with effective interpersonal relations (e.g., supportive leadership).

There is a clear need for more research on supervisors' theories of the job. At present we know very little about which dimensions of performance supervisors typically emphasize, about variation from supervisor to supervisor in the dimensions that are attended to, or about the circumstances that will lead to either widespread consensus regarding the dimensions of performance or widespread disagreement. Yet it seems likely that:

1. Supervisors hold implicit theories of the job that define, for them, the meaning of job performance.
2. The dimensions emphasized by supervisors will not always be the same as those that are derived through formal job analysis.
3. It is the implicit theory, not the job analysis, that guides the supervisor's observation, interpretation, and recollection of subordinates' job performance.

A better understanding of supervisors' theories of the job would help considerably in understanding judgments regarding job performance.

How Is Information Obtained?

Accurate observation is assumed to be the cornerstone of accuracy in evaluating performance (Iglen, 1983; Spool, 1978). This assumption has received empirical support (Murphy, Garcia, Kerkar, Martin, & Balzer, 1982), but the mediating variables (i.e., judgment strategies) that link behavior observation with accurate evaluations of job performance are poorly understood (Lord, 1985a). It is useful in this context to consider *observation* as an umbrella term that covers the many methods that supervisors might use to obtain information about subordinates. These include direct observation of the subordinate's behavior, observation of the results of that behavior, or a variety of secondhand methods of obtaining relevant information, such as customers' reports, reports from co-workers, or reports from members of other organizational units.

Direct Observation

It is an open question whether the direct observation of subordinates' behavior is feasible, even under the best of circumstances. Research on the perception of ongoing behavior suggests that individuals chunk behaviors into meaningful units, and the units employed by one supervisor may not be identical to those employed by another (Newtson, 1976; Sandlands & Calder, 1987). Consider the situation illustrated in Figure 5-2. Behavioral reports from these three observers are likely to vary in many ways. First, the observers may

Figure 5–2. Consequences of Individual Differences in "Chunking" Ongoing Behavior

Time Over Which Behavior Occurs

| Observer 1 | Beh 1 | Beh 2 | Beh 3 | Beh 4 | Beh 5 |

| Observer 2 | Beh 1 | Beh 2 | Beh 3 |

| Observer 3 | Beh 1 | Beh 2 | Beh 3 | Beh 4 | Beh 5 |

Note: Each rectangle represents a chunk, or discrete behavior perceived by the observer.

not report the same number of discrete behaviors. Some reports might refer to similar incidents (e.g., Behavior 1 for observers 1 and 3), but others will report the same incident in fundamentally different terms (e.g., Behavior 1 + Behavior 2 for observer 3 is the same as Behavior 1 for observer 2).

In our judgment, individual differences in chunking of behaviors are not likely to pose a serious threat to the accurate observation of work behaviors. There are two reasons for believing this. First, work is a formally structured activity. Thus, discrete chunks are already built into much of what people do at work (e.g., specific tasks might define chunks). Extensive individual differences in the perception of behavior at work are not as likely as in other settings, where formal demands and preexisting structure are not so readily apparent. Second, several studies (e.g., Foster & Cone, 1980; Komaki, Collins, & Thoene, 1980; Martinko & Gardner, 1985) have demonstrated that accurate behavioral observation in a work setting is possible. However, it may be very costly to obtain an accurate behavioral record (a point we will return to later).

Although technically feasible, extensive direct observation of behavior is relatively rare. It is known that the accuracy of performance judgments increases as a function of the rater's opportunity to observe the ratee's behavior (Heneman & Wexley, 1983) and of the time actually spent observing behavior (Heneman, Wexley, & Moore, 1987), but apparently few organizations are willing to devote the resources necessary to ensure accurate observation. Indeed, several models of the appraisal process are based on the assumption that appraisals incorporate only limited samples of behavior. Although not phrased in these terms, this argument is essentially similar to the argument put forth by proponents of validity generalization (e.g., Schmidt & Hunter, 1981) — that small samples produce unreliable results. Some of the consequences of relying on insufficient samples of behavior in making performance-related decisions (i.e., promotion) include the following (March & March, 1978):

1. *False Record Effect:* Differences in career outcomes will be larger than true differences in ability or performance. This is because sampling error determines many promotions.
2. *Hero Effect:* The faster the rate of promotion, the less likely it is justified. A fast promotion rate implies *very* small samples of performance, and thus extensive opportunities to capitalize on chance.
3. *Disappointment Effect:* Newly promoted employees are, on average, a disappointment. The best performers are promoted, but regression to the mean suggests that people who score best on a measure (especially an unreliable one) will not do so well on a subsequent measure of the same construct.

In addition to the problems associated with the limited reliability of small samples of behavior, insufficient sampling of behavior could be an issue if the validity of performance measures is challenged in a legal action (e.g., a suit charging violations of equal employment opportunity laws; see Barrett & Kernan, 1987; *Brito* v. *Zia,* 1973). Given the potential importance of accurately observing subordinates' behavior, it is useful to ask why direct observation of subordinates' behavior is not more frequently carried out.

Barriers to Direct Observation   The most obvious barriers to extensive observations of subordinates' behavior are the numerous demands on the supervisor's time. Simply put, supervisors typically have better things to do than to stand around watching their subordinates work. (Unfortunately, research on performance evaluation is often carried out in settings in which raters do *not* have anything to do but observe and evaluate ratees [Murphy, Philbin, & Adams, 1989]. Conflicting task demands or the lack of conflicting task demands almost certainly affect the accuracy of observation [Balzer, 1986].) This lack of time affects not only the frequency of observation but also the style of observation. That is, supervisors who can devote only limited periods to the direct observation of subordinates are unlikely to spend that time in passive observation. Rather, they are likely to have definite goals when observing subordinates' performance and are likely to use observation as a means of answering specific questions about subordinates (e.g., Is this worker having problems scheduling activities?).

It is well known that observational goals affect the way in which observers attend to, encode, store, and retrieve information (Murphy et al., in press; Williams, DeNisi, Blencoe, & Cafferty, 1985). Thus, the behaviors that are observed and remembered by a busy supervisor may not be the same as those that would be noticed and recorded by someone whose sole task was behavioral observation.

Time pressures are not the only obstacle to accuracy in behavioral observation. First, the proximity of supervisors to subordinates varies greatly within and across organizations (Kaufman, 1960). Wherry's work on a psychometric model of performance rating suggests that evaluations are most accurate when supervisors and subordinates work in close proximity (Wherry & Bartlett, 1982); supervisors who do not work directly with employees may find it very difficult to observe subordinates' work behavior. Second, the information that is available to supervisors may interfere with their ability or inclination to observe subordinates' behavior. Supervisors often observe or are informed of the *results* of behavior, and knowledge of results may lead them to infer behaviors (Bernardin & Beatty, 1984). (See Murphy, Martin, & Garcia, 1982, for a similar argument regarding inferring behaviors from global evaluations.) If results are acceptable, the supervisor may give little thought to behaviors and may concentrate on observing subordinates whose results are not so impressive.

There is evidence that the *relevance* rather than the frequency of observation is the most important determinant of the accuracy of evaluations

(Freeberg, 1969; Kleiger & Mosel, 1953; Landy & Guion, 1970). Traditionally, it has been thought that increasing familiarity with the person and the job being observed would increase the accuracy of observations and judgments. This may not be so. Kingstrom and Mainstone (1985) note that frequency of observation is likely to be critical only when the subordinate is new to the job. Supervisors quickly develop impressions and global evaluations of each subordinate, and these are likely to affect all subsequent observations and assessments of work performance (Murphy et al., 1985). Thus, the supervisor who is familiar with a particular subordinate's work may spend little time in the future observing that subordinate, and any behavior that *is* observed is likely to be interpreted according to the supervisor's general impressions.

Features of the job, organization, and environment can directly affect supervisors' opportunities, strategies, and inclinations toward observing the performance of their subordinates. Some jobs consist mainly of observable behaviors, whereas others consist of unobservable mental ability. Task environments can be highly stable or highly turbulent (Kane & Lawler, 1979; Thompson, 1967). Turbulent task environments (e.g., those in which technology, procedures, workgroup composition, etc., change frequently) are characterized by a high degree of uncertainty; more extensive observations may be needed to assess performance accurately in a turbulent environment than in a static one. Rambo, Chomiak, and Price (1983) suggest that performance in some jobs can be highly stable over time, but also note that stability of behavior and performance may depend as much on characteristics of the situation (e.g., design of the reward system) as of the person. Since the stability of performance directly affects the likelihood that limited samples of behavior will provide accurate assessments, the question of whether performance is stable is a highly relevant one (Murphy, 1989).

Does Observation Affect Behavior? Supervisors must not only contend with barriers to direct observation but must also consider the possibility that the act of observing subordinates' behavior changes that very behavior. In fact, subordinates' belief that they are being observed may lead to changes in behavior. There are several explanations for this link. First, the presence of an observer can interfere with work activities (e.g., by distracting workers or by getting in the way) (Dornsbusch & Scott, 1975). Second, it has long been known that workers resent and resist the routine observation of their activities (Kahn & Katz, 1953; Merton, 1957); this issue has received renewed attention since the introduction of computerized monitoring systems. They may adopt a variety of strategies to deal with this problem, ranging from strict enforcement of work norms, to filing a grievance, to removing the unwanted observer, and may not revert to their usual work habits until the observer is gone.

In psychological testing, a distinction is made between a test of typical performance and a test of maximal performance (Cronbach, 1970). The former measures day-to-day performance; the latter measures performance under circumstances where the individual is motivated to perform at the highest level possible. This distinction is clearly relevant in comparing the behavior of subordinates who believe they are not being observed by their superiors to that of subordinates who believe they are being observed. It is likely that the maximal performance that is exhibited for the benefit of the observer (i.e., the supervisor) is different from more typical, day-to-day performance.

Several authors have noted that performance on standardized, closely observed work samples is not highly correlated with global ratings of performance (Campbell, Crooks, Mahoney & Rock, 1973; Murphy, 1986; Schmidt, Hunter, & Outerbridge, 1986). This low correlation is usually taken as an indication of the dismal validity of ratings, but the present analysis suggests a different conclusion. Work samples are clearly tests of maximal performance (Murphy, 1986); measures based on work samples may not provide appropriate criteria for evaluating ratings. One piece of evidence in favor of this interpretation is the finding that objective measures of typical and maximal performance are not highly correlated (Sackett, Zedeck, & Fogli, 1988). In a more general sense, it may be difficult, under conditions where observation itself affects behavior, to obtain via direct observation the information needed for valid assessments of an individual's performance level.

Observation Aids Three strategies have been suggested to help increase the accuracy of behavior observation. The first revolves around training and experience. It is known that behavior observation skills training can be effective (Boice, 1983; Spool, 1978; Thornton & Zorich, 1980). In the 1950s, Wherry suggested that raters should be trained on what and how to observe (cited in Wherry & Bartlett, 1982); this suggestion is still a good one. There is also evidence that experience in activities that involve detailed observations of behavior (e.g., serving as an assessor in a managerial assessment center) leads to higher levels of accuracy in other observation tasks (Lorenzo, 1984).

A second strategy for increasing the accuracy of ratings is based on the use of Behaviorally Anchored Rating Scales (BARS). Although this point has not been emphasized in most applications of BARS, these scales were originally designed to aid raters in observing and categorizing the behavior of ratees (Bernardin & Smith, 1981; Smith & Kendall, 1963). The idea here is that by carefully defining scale dimensions and providing specific behavioral examples, BARS will provide raters with a standard frame of reference. The strategy of using BARS to improve observation might be especially helpful if it is combined with observation skill training. Here, BARS help tell the rater what to look for, while training will increase the rater's skills in observing and recording those behaviors.

Martinko and Gardner (1985) suggest the most comprehensive strategy for increasing observational accuracy. They describe the use of multiple methods, some of which are listed here, that can be applied in observation:

- ► Time sampling
- ► Behavior diaries
- ► Self-observation
- ► Use of multiple raters
- ► Use of large behavior samples

They suggest that it *is* technically feasible to obtain accurate behavioral records, but the authors also note a dilemma. A high level of accuracy in behavioral measurement at work may require the use of several methods, some of which are both cumbersome and expensive. It is not clear whether the results will always justify the cost.

Indirect Observation

Much of what supervisors know about subordinates' performance is probably the result of indirect rather than direct observation. As noted earlier, indirect observation encompasses many areas, such as viewing videotapes, reading descriptions of subordinates' behavior, receiving complaints or letters of praise, and hearing wholly unfounded rumors about the subordinate. Unfortunately, our understanding of these indirect methods of obtaining information about subordinates' performance is not commensurate with the scope or the importance of the problem. For example, communication specialists have long known that the same message has different meaning when conveyed via two different media (Shannon & Weaver, 1948). Thus, observing a subordinate insult a customer is a different thing than hearing about it. Hearing about it may mean different things, depending on the source (e.g., the customer versus a rival worker) or the context.

Studies comparing the impact of direct versus indirect observation on performance appraisals and other evaluations in organizations are rare. Two studies from the interviewing literature help to illustrate issues that might arise in performance appraisal. Maier and Thurber (1968) showed that judgments are more accurate when based on audio or written records of interviews than on direct observation. There are several possible explanations for this effect. First, written and audio records contain less information than is obtained through direct observation, and much of the missing information is largely irrelevant (e.g., physical attractiveness, nonverbal interaction styles) (Banks & Murphy, 1985). Second, information that is presented in written or audio form may be encoded, stored, and retrieved differently than information that is obtained through direct observation (Murphy, Herr, Lockhart, & Maguire, 1986). This is particularly true for written stimuli; a different memory system (semantic versus episodic) might be involved when reading a description of what a person does, as opposed to observing him or her do it (Tulving & Thompson, 1973).

Imada and Hakel (1977) showed systematic differences between the perceptions of subjects who interacted with candidates in an interview and subjects who observed those interactions. Their results can be best understood in terms of the actor-observer distinction that has long been drawn in both social psychology and cultural anthropology. That is, persons who are actively involved in an event will observe different things than will be observed by uninvolved spectators. The supervisor's status as actor versus observer may be uncertain or unstable, particularly if he or she has input into the activities of the subordinate. Actor-observer status may even vary across subordinates, tasks, or time. Thus, the information obtained about different subordinates may vary as a function of the supervisor's perspective.

Although there has been little research on the effects of indirect observations on performance judgments, research from other fields provides a basis for speculating about the variables that are most likely to moderate the impact of indirect observations. Eight such variables are presented in Table 5-1. The first consideration is the source of the message, which affects both its credibility and the weight that is attached to the message. Thus, the observation that employee A did a particularly good job with a specific assignment will probably have a different impact, depending on whether it is received from a good friend and co-worker of the person being evaluated, a customer or client, or the CEO of the organization. The same comment from a customer might be received quite differently if it comes from a customer who frequently praises your employees' work, frequently criticizes your employees' work, or has never before commented on your employees' work.

The question of whether indirect observations are solicited by the supervisor, are volunteered by others, or are encountered by chance (e.g., accidentally overhearing a comment about one of your subordinates) is an important one. Information that is acquired incidentally is processed and stored differently from information that is consciously sought out (Balzer, 1986; Murphy et al., 1989). The supervisor who requests a report from some indirect source is probably pursuing a specific question and is likely to attend most closely to the information that is relevant to that question. Therefore, the

Table 5–1. Variables That Might Determine Impact of Indirect Observations of Performance

1. Source of the Report	Colleague, customer, supervisor, etc.
2. Initiator of the Report	Is report requested by supervisor?
3. Form of the Report	Descriptive versus evaluative; detailed report versus summary
4. Medium	Letter, memo, conversation, etc.
5. Referent	Behavior versus results
6. Timing	Time elapsed since episode
7. Motive for the Report	Why is information provided?
8. Consistency of Report Observations	With other reports and with supervisor's report

same report may be perceived differently when received on request than when it is encountered unexpectedly. The effect of unsolicited reports may be quite different when they are delivered directly to the supervisor than when they are encountered by chance. In the former case, the supervisor may interpret the report differently, depending on his or her interpretation of the sender's motives for delivering the report (see point 7, Table 5-1).

The form of secondhand reports about a subordinate's performance can vary on many dimensions. One relevant dimension is whether the report is primarily descriptive or evaluative (Ilgen, Fisher, & Taylor, 1979; Jacobs, Jacobs, Feldman, & Cavior, 1973). Descriptive reports consist primarily of recitations of what occurred, whereas evaluative reports consist primarily of an individual's subjective assessment of the quality or the effectiveness of what was done. Admittedly, the distinction between description and evaluation is not completely clear; most descriptions imply a positive or negative evaluation (Hoxworth, 1988). Nevertheless, a supervisor is likely to get different information from a descriptive report than from a report that takes the form of "Bill did a good job on our project." The implication of both source and motive variables (see points 1 and 7, Table 5-1) may be different for descriptive versus evaluative reports. That is, description from many sources might be credible and might affect the supervisor's judgments. The same supervisor may ignore some evaluative judgments and give great weight to others (e.g., those that come from credible sources).

Another related dimension for classifying the form of secondhand reports is the extent to which they provide detailed information as opposed to short summaries. Several methods of judgment research involve the use of short written vignettes, in which subjects are asked to make judgments based on the information they read. The use of those methods in studying evaluation in organizations has been criticized (Gorman, Clover, & Doherty, 1978; Ilgen, 1983; Wendelken & Inn, 1981; c.f. Dipboye, Stramler, & Fontenelle, 1984), at least in part because these vignettes contain too little information and are more neatly packaged than the observations that are typical of real decision makers. This criticism may apply when generalizing from judgment studies to direct observation but probably does *not* apply as strongly to indirect observation. In fact, it is likely that many of the reports received by raters are short ones that contain only a small amount of information. These reports probably contain little of the irrelevant information (e.g., physical attractiveness of the person being observed) that is present in direct observation (Banks & Murphy, 1985). The ratio of relevant to irrelevant information may be even higher for short summaries than for longer reports.

The medium by which a report is delivered could markedly affect the information conveyed. The same message presented verbally versus in written form will not convey the same information, especially if one medium allows for more interaction than the other (e.g., does the supervisor have a chance to ask questions?). The medium will probably also affect the form of the message (e.g., short versus long; point 3, Table 5-1), may be a function of who initiates the message (point 2, Table 5-1), and may be affected by the timing of the message (e.g., a short verbal report is more likely than a long written one immediately after the event; point 6, Table 5-1). Informal memos will probably contain different information than formal reports and are likely to be produced under different circumstances. A detailed, formal report is unlikely except when it is formally required or an unusual event (e.g., very good or very poor performance) occurs; a brief memo might be produced at the spur of the moment.

Earlier in this chapter, information was presented about the controversy over whether performance should be defined in terms of behavior or results. The same question arises when considering secondhand reports concerning performance. In general, short evaluative reports will probably refer to results; it is only the long formal reports that are likely to include extensive descriptions of behavior. Again, as noted earlier, results-oriented reports may require supervisors to infer behaviors. Since results are not perfectly correlated with behavior, these inferences will not always be accurate, even when the results report itself is entirely accurate.

The timing of reports about subordinates' performance will affect both the credibility and the use of those reports. Reports that occur shortly after the event may be more credible, particularly if a great deal of behavioral detail is required. Behavioral reports that are received shortly before a PA is to be completed might exert more influence than reports that were received long before the PA was due. The timing of reports may also vary as a function of the source of the report (e.g., the CEO might not rush to tell you about a particular subordinate's performance), the form of the report (e.g., short memos might come sooner and more often than long formal reports), and even the referent of the report (e.g., results may take a long time to determine).

The principal concern of attribution theory (Jones, Kanhouse, Kelley, Nisbett, Valins, & Weiner, 1972) is the way in which an individual explains the behavior of others. Depending on the supervisor's attributions, he or she may do anything from taking reports at face value to discounting them altogether. When receiving a report, the first question a supervisor must ask is *why* the report was given; the interpretation of the report may vary depending on the answer to that question. For example, if the report is seen as an attempt to harm a rival or as an exercise to impress management, the report may receive little weight. There are multiple motives for most behaviors in organizations, and a report that is perceived as a means of furthering an ulterior motive will receive less weight than a similar report from a disinterested source.

The final issue noted in Table 5-1 is the consistency of the report with other reports and with the supervisor's own evaluation. Agreement among secondhand reports should increase credibility. If one report disagrees with all of the others, only that report will be affected. However, widespread and general disagreement among external sources may lower the credibility of *all* reports.

Inconsistency between a secondhand report and the supervisor's own observations and evaluations is a more complex matter. On the one hand, there is evidence of a pervasive confirmatory bias in human judgment. People tend to seek out information that confirms their initial impressions and discount information that does not (Darley & Fazio, 1980). Thus, it is possible that supervisors will ignore or explain away inconsistent reports. On the other hand, some reports come from sources that have a great deal of power and/or credibility. It is possible that these reports will lead the supervisor to change his or her evaluation, at least in situations where the supervisor is not strongly committed. (See Bazerman, Beekum, & Schoorman, 1982, for a discussion of what happens when a person is committed to an evaluation.) However, the extent of this change (i.e., the impact of the report on the supervisor's judgment) may be complexly determined.

Research on attitude change and opinion revision (Freedman, Sears, & Carlsmith, 1981; Slovic & Lichtenstein, 1971) suggests that even when people do pay attention to information that is inconsistent with their prior observations or beliefs, they often do not give the information sufficient weight. To complicate matters further, the impact of reports that are inconsistent with the supervisor's prior observations might depend on the timing of those reports. There is evidence that inconsistent information is more easily remembered than information that is either neutral or consistent (the evidence is more equivocal for the latter than the former) with prior observations (Hastie, 1980; Murphy et al., 1985). Thus, inconsistent information may have a greater impact on memory-based evaluations than on those that are formed immediately after the event or that are based on careful examination of records of the event.

The issues presented in Table 5-1 suggest (but certainly do not exhaust) a set of research questions that to date have been largely ignored. Supervisors cannot possibly obtain all of the information needed for accurate appraisals solely through direct observation. Time pressures and their physical separation from subordinates force supervisors to rely in part on secondhand reports when evaluating subordinates. There is a clear need for both descriptive research and process-oriented research. First, it is important to know more about what actually happens in organizations. What sort of information do supervisors receive through secondhand reports and how do they use this information? The eight points listed in Table 5-1 suggest several points of departure for process-oriented research. We look forward to progress in these areas.

The assumption throughout this chapter has been that supervisors use *some* information about a subordinate's behavior when evaluating his or her performance. This is not necessarily the case. A supervisor who has no information about a subordinate's behavior during a given period is unlikely to return a blank performance appraisal. It is well known that appraisals are heavily influenced by general impressions and that early evaluations exhibit a powerful influence on subsequent ones (Balzer, 1986; Kingstrom & Mainstone, 1985; Murphy et al., 1985). We are not sure that evaluations conducted in the absence of any relevant information would be much different from evaluations carried out by a well-informed supervisor. Unfortunately, if this is true, it might be hard to demonstrate that information that is obtained through direct or indirect observation makes much of a difference, at least after the supervisor has formed an initial evaluation.

We are not as pessimistic as the preceding paragraph might imply. Research on human judgment has focused on errors, inconsistencies, suboptimal strategies, and poor choices, in part because errors often more clearly illustrate underlying processes than do correct decisions (Funder, 1987). It is important not to lose sight of the fact that people generally do better in real-life judgment than in research studies designed to assess their errors. Thus, the knowledge that initial evaluations can cloud later judgments or that appropriate weight is not always given to new information should not lead to the conclusion that supervisors are impervious to what is going on around them. Although there are many sources of error in performance evaluations, there is also some "true score" in a typical PA (Landy & Farr, 1983). We think that in most cases the subordinate's behavior *does* have an impact on the supervisor's evaluation. Thus, it is worthwhile to continue to pursue research on the ways in which supervisors obtain information about subordinates' performance.

Who Should Obtain Information?

The preceding section was built around the assumption that supervisors should be the people responsible for obtaining information about their subordinates' performance and that information from other sources should be filtered through the supervisor. This is certainly a common practice in organizations (Cleveland, Murphy & Williams, 1989; Long, 1986) but it is not clear that this is the optimal practice (Kane & Lawler, 1979). People other than the supervisor may be better qualified to evaluate. Even when the supervisor is the best evaluator, it is not necessarily advantageous for the supervisor to be the *only* evaluator. Peers, subordinates, customers, or colleagues of the supervisor might provide additional information or fresh perspectives on information that is available to the supervisor.

Kingstrom and Mainstone (1985) discuss the importance of *task acquaintance,* which they define as the amount and type of work contact the evaluator has with the person being evaluated. The quantity and quality of task acquaintance vary considerably as a function of level in the organization; peers and subordinates see different facets of an individual's task behavior than is seen by supervisors (Borman, 1974). This difference is even more pronounced for the behaviors that define interpersonal relations at work, which are critical in task performance (Murphy, in press). The frequency and style of interpersonal interactions will greatly reflect the power hierarchy of organizations. Thus, one's boss, peers, subordinates, and so on will all experience different social interactions with an individual and may evaluate interpersonal relations quite differently.

Table 5-2 lists five different potential sources of information about a person's work behavior and indicates whether or not each source is likely to have access to information about both behaviors and results of behaviors as they relate to task accomplishment and interpersonal relations at work. Some of the entries in Table 5-2 will probably vary across organizations. For example, subordinates have more opportunity to observe their supervisors' task behaviors in organizations where supervisors and subordinates work together than in organizations where they work apart. Nevertheless, the table provides a useful starting point for our discussion.

The frequency with which individuals at different levels in the organization encounter information about behaviors and results will vary, both as a function of the job itself (e.g., proximity between workers at different levels) and as a function of the roles of the observer and the person being observed. Individuals who are far removed from the target employee will only rarely have access to relevant information, and will more frequently know about results than about behaviors. However, no one (not even the individual himself or herself) has frequent access to all of the relevant information. Thus, a worker may know what he or she has done but may not be fully aware of the results of those behaviors. A manager who is several levels above the target employee may receive only occasional information about the results of tasks performed.

The research we review, which deals with the use of sources other than or in addition to the supervisor, is concerned with *rating* rather than with the behavioral reports that serve as data in forming evaluations of performance. As discussed in Chapter One, rating, judgment, and the collection of information about performance are all separate activities. Nevertheless, research on ratings obtained from different sources does shed some light on those sources' access to relevant information. Unfortunately, this research raises some complex issues, since it deals with evaluation as well as with the collection of behavioral information. The recurring them of much of this research is the

Table 5–2. Access to Information about Task and Interpersonal Behaviors and Results

	Source				
	Subordinates	Self	Peers	Next Level (Supervisor)	Higher Level (Upper Management)
Task					
Behaviors	Rare	Always	Frequent	Occasional	Rare
Results	Occasional	Frequent	Frequent	Frequent	Occasional
Interpersonal					
Behaviors	Frequent	Always	Frequent	Occasional	Rare
Results	Frequent	Frequent	Frequent	Occasional	Rare

impact of the power hierarchy of an organization on evaluations obtained from a variety of sources. Supervisory evaluations follow the natural flow of power and authority, in which the immediate supervisor is responsible for evaluations. Evaluations obtained from other sources will either bypass the natural lines of authority (evaluations from upper management), circumvent them (evaluations from peers, self), or reverse the usual authority structure of an organization (evaluations from subordinates).

Mahew (1983) surveyed societies and organizations ranging in time from the sixth century B.C. to the present, and in scope from the Achaemenid Empire of ancient Mesopotamia and Persia to the Columbus (Ohio) Police Department. He concluded that hierarchical differentiation with a unity of the flow of authority and power from the top down is essentially universal. That is, organizations are structured so that decisions, orders, and control flow from the top levels down, with very few instances of egalitarian or bottom-up rule. Dornbusch and Scott (1975) noted, "Evaluation is required if power is to be employed to control behavior" (p. 134).

One substantial barrier to the involvement of sources other than the supervisor (especially sources at or below the level of the person being evaluated) in performance appraisal is that it does not fit an apparently universal principle of hierarchical organization. Thus, performance appraisals that incorporate input from peers or subordinates are rare and often not well received where they are applied. Nevertheless, Table 5-2 suggests there are potential benefits in involving multiple sources in PA, since no single source is likely to have access to all of the information needed for accentual appraisal.

We have chosen to classify alternative sources of information about individuals' performance in terms of their relative standing in the power hierarchy of the organization. This is not the only method that might be used; Carroll and Schneier (1982) classify alternative sources in terms of the roles they occupy. Thus, the same individual might have access to different information about a person when interacting with him or her in different roles (e.g., assistant, mentor, friend). Although this role-based analysis has some merit, we find it more helpful to describe sources in terms of the one universal characteristic of all organizations — the power hierarchy.

One thing that must be kept in mind when examining research of rating sources is that different sources often give similar ratings. For example, in a meta-analysis of research on rating sources, Harris and Schaubroeck (1988) found an average correlation of .62 between peer and supervisory ratings (self-supervisor and self-peer correlations were .35 and .36, respectively). Although there are many reasons why different sources *might* give very different ratings, this does not always happen.

Subordinates as Sources

Involving subordinates in evaluation is a potentially serious violation of the status hierarchy (Dornbusch & Scott, 1975; Thompson, 1967). There is evidence that both subordinates and superiors are uncomfortable with subordinate evaluations of performance (Carroll & Schneier, 1982). Superiors' discomfort with subordinate ratings can probably be explained in terms of reversals of power; subordinates' discomfort may reflect concern that superiors will retaliate for low ratings.

The use of subordinate ratings in evaluation is quite rare; empirical assessments of subordinate ratings are therefore also rare. Mount (1984a) reports some evidence for the reliability and validity of rating obtained from subordinates, and notes that when supervisors, subordinates, and the target individual all provide ratings (the last source is a self-rating), supervisors and subordinates agree more closely with one another than either source agrees with self-ratings. It is not clear whether this latter result explains more about the validity of the ratings (and if so, which ratings are more valid) or the actor-observer differences.

Data in Table 5-2 suggest that subordinates only rarely have access to information about task performance, and when they do, they are likely to know more about results than about behaviors. However, they do have frequent access to information about interpersonal behaviors and the results of these behaviors; direct subordinates will directly experience these behaviors and can testify firsthand about their results. Other subordinates (i.e., those who are at lower levels but do not work directly for the target individual) are also likely to be well informed about the interpersonal style of people higher in the organization, both through direct and indirect observation. It is axiomatic that power flows downward in organizations. It is equally axiomatic that gossip flows both sideways and down. We know of no empirical test but it is a common observation that workers frequently compare and discuss their bosses, especially if the boss has particularly bad or particularly good relations with his or her subordinates.

One of the keys to effective performance as a manager is the ability to get good work from one's subordinate (Mintzberg, 1980). That is, the manager who wishes to have a positive effect on his or her subordinates must communicate well with them and must earn their trust. There are, of course, some technical skills involved in managing. However, interpersonal relations are an integral part of management, and the accurate evaluation of a supervisor or manager's performance may not be possible without information about interpersonal relations between the supervisor and the subordinate. Subordinates may be the optimal source for this information.

It is interesting to note that there is one setting in which subordinate ratings are widely used — teacher evaluation. Student evaluations of teachers are conducted under special circumstances where the rater is anonymous and does not have to be concerned about the future consequences of giving high or low ratings. Teacher ratings are not always held in high regard as criteria but the fact that they are widely used suggests that, in at least some situations, persons in a subordinate position will be willing and (some skeptics will dispute this) able to evaluate their superiors.

Workers' resistance to subordinate rating systems might not be so extreme if they could feel the same sense of anonymity and freedom from reprisal that is present in most teacher rating systems. Unfortunately, this would require a large number (N) of participants as well as a high level of trust. Subordinates who are qualified to rate a supervisor may often be too small in number to assure anonymity. The supervisor whose average rating is low is in a better position to guess who gave low ratings when $N = 2$ than when $N = 15$. Trust may be an even more difficult problem (Bernardin & Beatty, 1984). In order to have a successful subordinate evaluation system, subordinates must believe that their ratings will not somehow become known to the supervisor being rated. Such a level of trust is probably not the norm.

Self as a Source

Although the use of self-ratings as the sole method of evaluating performance is rare (Bernardin & Klatt, 1985; Long, 1986), self-ratings are more likely than subordinate ratings to be included as a component of a PA system. Table 5-2 suggests an obvious advantage to the use of the target individual as a source of information — being reasonably certain that this source will be well informed. The outstanding barrier to using self-ratings is the nagging suspicion that people tend to overrate their own performance.

There is evidence that self-ratings are typically more lenient (i.e., higher) than ratings obtained from supervisors (Meyer, 1980; Thornton, 1980). This by itself is not necessarily evidence of the invalidity of self-ratings, since it is possible that self-ratings are accurate and supervisory ratings are unduly harsh. Similarly, evidence that self-ratings are not highly correlated with supervisory ratings (Landy & Farr, 1983; Steel & Ovalle, 1984; Thornton, 1980) is difficult to evaluate, since supervisory ratings are not the optimal criteria for evaluating self-assessments. However, there are two lines of evidence that would seem to point unambiguously to deficiencies in self-ratings.

First, self-ratings tend to move closer to supervisory ratings if extensive performance feedback is given (Steel & Ovalle, 1984). Although this finding may represent nothing more than criterion contamination (e.g., workers distort their self-assessments to correspond more closely with their supervisor's assessment), it may also indicate that feedback causes self-raters to adopt a frame of reference more similar to that of the supervisor. We would argue that this change would not occur if individuals were confident of the accuracy of their self-assessments. Thus, the instability of self-assessments may be an indirect indication of their inaccuracy.

Second, there is at least one study showing clear evidence of distortion (i.e., leniency) in self-assessment. Farh and Werbel (1986) present evidence that self-ratings are less lenient if raters know that the ratings will be checked against some objective criterion. This may in part reflect a conservative bias among raters who do not trust the system (i.e., negative consequences are more likely if performance is overrated than if underrated), but the finding described above seems to point toward deliberate and conscious distortion in self-appraisal.

One interpretation of the inflation of self-ratings is in terms of a self-serving bias (Mitchell, Green, & Wood, 1981), which might occur in situations where the rater has a direct interest in receiving high ratings (e.g., where ratings are used to make promotion decisions). Attribution theory presents another explanation. At one time attribution researchers believed that people tend to explain the behavior of others in terms of internal causes (e.g., ability or effort), but tend to explain their own behavior in terms of external causes (e.g., luck or situational constraints). This phenomenon was referred to as the "fundamental attribution error" (Jones & Nisbett, 1971). Although no longer regarded as universal or fundamental, this tendency may still explain the leniency of self-ratings. Individuals tend to be aware of and make allowance for the external factors that cause them to perform poorly. Thus, a person might explain away his or her own poor performance (i.e., give lenient ratings) much more readily than when evaluating the performance of others.

Although self-ratings may not be entirely trustworthy, there is still an argument for including the target individual as one source of information about the individual's behavior at work. The target individual clearly has access to information about his or her behavior and is probably well informed about the results of those behaviors. However, concerns regarding the leniency of self-ratings might also apply to self-generated descriptions of behavior. Research has clearly shown that the evaluation of the person being observed affects the behaviors that are attended to and recorded in diaries (c.f. Balzer, 1986). Although this research has been conducted in settings where one individual evaluates another, this effect may also be present in self-evaluations. That is, self-generated descriptions of behavior might represent biased samples that contain too many positive and too few negative behaviors. This bias may exist even where there are no conscious efforts on the part of the target individual to bias or pad the record.

The considerations outlined above lead us to believe that self-generated descriptions of behavior are not generally a useful and practical source of information in evaluating performance. Even when the ratee intends to provide an unbiased record, his or her observations and recollections regarding performance are quite likely to be biased. Although we know of no data linking bias in self-generated behavior records, it stands to reason that the extent of this bias is negatively correlated with performance levels. That is, we would expect the behavior reports of poor workers to be least credible, since they have the most to explain away. A final practical objection to self-generated behavior reports is that, regardless of their accuracy, supervisors will be inclined to disbelieve them. We foresee the potential of a vicious cycle, in which supervisors interpret the behavioral records they read in an unfavorable fashion, which leads ratees to inflate their records of good behavior, which causes supervisors to further discount these behavioral records, and so on.

Peers as Sources

Peer rating systems are frequently encountered in the military (Landy & Farr, 1983) but are rarely used in other settings (Bernardin & Klatt, 1985; McEvoy & Buller, 1987). When they are used in nonmilitary settings, peer ratings are not well accepted by raters or ratees. (In a true peer rating system, everyone is *both* a rater and ratee. Evidence suggests that peers are uncomfortable in both roles.) However, peer ratings that are used for developmental purposes are more widely accepted than those that are used to make administrative decisions (McEvoy & Buller, 1987).

The resistance to peer ratings does not seem to be connected to concerns over their psychometric shortcomings. There is ample evidence that peer ratings show levels of reliability and validity comparable to supervisory ratings (Kane & Lawler, 1978, 1980; Landy & Farr, 1983; Wexley & Klimoski, 1984). An advantage of peer ratings is that they can be pooled — a procedure that can substantially increase reliability and partially remove idiosyncratic biases of any particular rater (Kenny & Berman, 1980; Murphy, 1982b). Rather, it appears that the resistance to peer ratings can be traced to two causes: concerns over role reversals and concerns over distortion. The first issue, role reversals, has been noted earlier. Incorporation of peer ratings changes the power structure of an organization in such a way that people who are at the same level in the formal power hierarchy neverthless have power over one another.

There are two reasons that lead many managers to conclude that peer ratings will be unduly lenient. First, it is widely believed that the friendship between peers will lead to inflated ratings (Landy & Farr, 1983). In fact, there is little evidence that friendship bias is an important factor, although bias might be a problem if the ratee is aware of individual raters' scores. A second problem, and a potentially more serious one, is range restriction. It is plausible that peers will be unwilling to differentiate good from poor performers in the workgroup, for fear of rocking the boat. This problem is no doubt present in some settings, but there is little evidence to suggest that peers are any more susceptible to range restriction than are supervisors.

The theoretical argument in *favor* of peer rating is suggested by Table 5-2. Because peers often work in close proximity, they have ample opportunity to observe each others' behavior. Wherry's theory of rating cites rater-ratee proximity as one key to accuracy in rating (Wherry & Bartlett, 1982). Thus, peers' frequent opportunity to observe task behaviors, interpersonal behaviors, and results may make them a uniquely valuable source. However, Imada (1982) cautions that there is little data to support the assumption that peers' opportunity to observe behavior is related to the accuracy of their judgments. Considerations of the work roles of peers might even suggest that their observations will *not* be the best source of information about a particular individual's performance. We alluded earlier to actor-observer differences and to research showing that people involved in an event will report it differently than people who passively observe the same event (Imada & Hakel, 1977). Peers will often work directly with one another. Thus, a co-worker who is at an individual's side all day has an excellent opportunity to observe that individual's behavior, but is likely to record different observations than would be obtained from a disinterested passive observer. Note that we said that the behavior records would be *different;* the empirical evidence does not allow us to say which record would be more accurate or more useful.

The behavior observed by peers is both quantitatively and qualitatively different from that observed by supervisors and subordinates because peers see more and different behaviors than do other sources. This is particularly true in the domain of interpersonal relations. An individual may be on his or her guard when interacting with superiors or subordinates but is more likely to behave naturally (whatever the person's natural style of interaction) among peers. Peers are also likely to encounter secondhand information about interpersonal behaviors. Colleagues tend to talk about colleagues, and interpersonal issues are likely to be a frequent topic of conversation.

Upper Management as Sources

It is common practice to involve the supervisor's supervisor (and perhaps higher-level superiors) in the performance appraisal process, at least to the extent that they "sign off" on the supervisor's evaluation (Long, 1986). As Table 5-2 suggests, higher-level supervisors and managers are likely to be informed about only a narrow range of behaviors; they may know the results of some tasks but are unlikely to know much about behaviors except in those rare circumstances that behavior is either so effective or so ineffective that it is brought specifically to their attention. However, higher-level supervisors may have a crucial yet indirect role in the behavior-observation process. That is, they are not well equipped to observe behavior but they can have a significant impact in deciding what to observe.

At the beginning of this chapter, performance was defined as the total set of behaviors that are relevant to the goals of the position. One of the crucial functions of management is to set these goals. Another is to communicate those goals (House, 1971). Upper management can communicate these goals and the set of behaviors that define good performance directly, but this is rare. More frequently, goals and desired behaviors are communicated via the climate and culture of the organization (Koprowski, 1983; Schneider, 1985). Effective managers and executives will communicate the goals of the organization, the company, and the work unit to organization members. Thus, one indirect indicator of effective upper management might be the extent to which supervisors understand the goals associated with the positions they oversee, and the extent to which they agree in their "theories of the job." If goals are made clear, one might expect that supervisors will look for similar behaviors when evaluating individuals in similar jobs. In an organization where goals are unclear or contradictory, every supervisor might look for different behaviors, and when two supervisors observe the same behavior, they might evaluate it differently.

Disagreement among Sources

Subordinates, peers, the target individual, and supervisors at all levels will have different perspectives when observing the behavior of an individual. The implication is that different sources should be expected to disagree. We do not regard this disagreement as a problem to be resolved but rather as an indication of the benefit of multiple sources. If all sources agreed, there would be no reason to collect information from multiple sources (Campbell, 1982).

The potential for disagreement among sources need not be a serious problem. First, the disagreements that are noted in the research literature (e.g., Borman, 1974) are more likely to involve *evaluation* than description. That is, disagreements about whether a behavior was effective or ineffective are more likely than disagreements over what behaviors occurred. Second, and more important, the assumption that disagreements must be reconciled is not necessarily correct. As discussed in Chapter One, performance appraisals are used for a wide variety of purposes (c.f. Cleveland et al., 1989), and information from different sources may not be equally useful for every purpose. Thus, information from peers and subordinates may be most useful in evaluating a person's interpersonal interactions, whereas input from upper management might be useful in deciding whether the individual is contributing to the goals of the organization.

Cleveland and colleagues (1989) note that two of the major purposes for performance appraisal are to make distinctions between individuals and to discriminate an individual's strengths from his or her weaknesses. The immediate supervisor is probably best qualified to evaluate overall performance levels; input from higher levels in the organization may be useful in determining which dimensions of performance should be emphasized and which behaviors are or are not valued. *All* sources may have insights regarding an individual's strengths and weaknesses but peers may represent the single best-informed source.

Disagreement among sources may depend on the structure of the organization. For example, some organizations have very flat structures with minimal distinctions between levels in the hierarchy, whereas others have very sharply defined authority structures. In comparing there two types of organizations, two conclusions seem sensible: (1) use of sources at multiple levels will be easier in organizations with a very loose, informal structure than in an organization with a rigid power structure; and (2) disagreement among sources is more likely when there is a rigid, hierarchical structure than when the power structure is flat and loosely defined. These two conclusions lead to a third: (3) sharp disagreement between levels will be most often found in organizations whose structure is not amenable to the use of multiple sources. In other words, the higher the chance that multiple sources will be used, the lower the likelihood that they will seriously disagree.

Summary

Throughout this chapter, we have noted that information from several sources might be necessary for accurate performance appraisals. However, accuracy is not always the ultimate criterion in organizations (see Chapters One and Eleven) and even if it is, it may not be worthwhile for the supervisor to devote the time and attention needed to do accurate appraisals.

If performance appraisal is approached from the perspective of a cost-benefit analysis, the supervisor might be well advised *not* to bother with accurate performance appraisals. Mohrman & Lawler (1983) note that there are typically few rewards and many penalties for doing accurate appraisals. Workers are likely to regard a less-than-glowing PA as a punishment (even if it is richly deserved) and honest appraisals are likely to lead to ill-will between supervisors and subordinates. This suggests to us that the organization that is truly interested in accurate performance appraisals must do two things.

First, the organization must create conditions that allow for adequate direct observation and a plan for collecting information from other sources that is sensibly related to the purpose(s) of the appraisal. Second, the organization must create conditions in which raters are motivated to seek out and use the information that is needed to form accurate appraisals. The extent to which an organization allows PA to be conducted in a haphazard fashion is a concrete indicator of the importance of accurate performance appraisals.

In creating conditions that allow for adequate observation, organizations might find it useful to ask who *can* do appraisals rather than asking who *should.* The almost universal reliance on the supervisor as the sole source of evaluations may make sense when considered from the perspective of the organizational power hierarchy, but it will not always make sense from the perspective of obtaining accurate evaluations. Thus, the first question that should be asked in evaluating the use of alternative sources in performance appraisal is who has the best opportunity to observe and obtain information about each individual's performance. If the supervisor does not have sufficient opportunities to observe, formal and regular channels should be opened up for obtaining relevant information from other sources.

In creating conditions that motivate raters, more formidable problems may be faced. First, raters must be buffered from the negative consequences that are likely to occur if low ratings are given (e.g., deterioration of interpersonal relationship). Second, some means of assessing the accuracy of ratings must be established so that accurate raters can be rewarded. This may be very difficult to do in most organizations because ratings are usually collected from only one individual (the supervisor) and there is no readily available standard for evaluating those ratings (Murphy & Balzer, 1989). Chapters Ten and Eleven will examine the problem of evaluating ratings in some depth. It is sufficient to note here that there are no easy solutions to the problem of evaluating the accuracy of ratings obtained in organizations. Our present inability to discriminate inaccurate from accurate raters (and to reward the latter) may be the most significant barrier to achieving accuracy in observation, judgment, and rating.

Chapter Six

Standards for Judging Performance

► *Evaluation* is a useful term because it makes it clear that judgments about performance (e.g., Is this individual a good, bad, or average worker?) involve *values* as well as objective information. That is, the same behavior may be judged to be very good, and very bad, or neutral, depending on the values and standards of the judge. This chapter is concerned with the values and standards that are used in judging performance. In particular, we will discuss how the values that determine performance judgments (i.e., performance standards) are defined, developed, and used, and whether different judges (e.g., peers, supervisors) are likely to have different values. As we noted in the preceding chapter, disagreements over the evaluation of what has occurred could result from either disagreements over facts (i.e., different perceptions of what actually happened) or disagreements over values (i.e., different opinions regarding what behaviors are acceptable, good, unacceptable, etc.). This chapter examines the latter perspective.

The term *value* is rarely encountered in research on performance appraisal (PA). (However, this topic is receiving increasing attention in related areas. The *Journal of Value-Based Management* was recently established to provide an outlet for this research.) There are two related terms that have very similar meanings in this context: *performance standard* and *performance norm*. The term *norm* has a relatively longer history and refers to a somewhat broader range of phenomena. For example, the normative regulation of behavior at work is a research topic that dates back to the Hawthorne studies

(Roethlisberger & Dickson, 1939; Sonnenfeld, 1982) and was pursued actively by social psychologists in the 1950s (Dalton, 1955; Zaleznik, Christensen, & Roethlisberger, 1958). Hackman and colleagues have integrated research in several areas to present models of normative regulation that consider features of both workgroups and the work environment (Hackman, 1976; Hackman & Morris, 1975; Hackman & Oldham, 1980). Finally, Keller (1983) has explored normative regulation of a specific (and poorly understood) behavior — absenteeism.

Sherif and Sherif (1969) define a norm as "an evaluative scale (e.g., yardstick) designating an acceptable latitude and an objectionable latitude for behavior, activity, events, beliefs, or any other object of concern to members of a social unit" (p. 141). That is, norms represent beliefs about which behaviors are good or bad. Norms have typically been studied as properties of groups; in this context, norms refer to widely shared beliefs about acceptable and unacceptable behaviors (Sherif & Sherif, 1969). However, the concept applies equally well to an individual who is asked to evaluate others' performance (e.g., the supervisor). Thus, understanding an individual's norms regarding good, poor, and average performance is one key to understanding evaluative judgments.

The term *performance standard* has essentially the same meaning as *performance norm* (as the latter term is used above). We prefer *standard* for two reasons. First, the term carries less excess meaning than *norm* and thus can be used more precisely to refer to an individual's beliefs about the effectiveness (or goodness, or acceptability) of specific behaviors at work. Second, the term *standard* allows us to establish links to several literatures in which terms such as *norms* would not necessarily be used. For example, cybernetic control theory incorporates the concept of "standard" in describing the feedback loops that control many complex systems (Miller, Galanter, & Pribram, 1960; Taylor, Fisher, & Ilgen, 1984). One such control mechanism is the TOTE (test-operate-test-exit) loop, illustrated in Figure 6-1. A TOTE loop

Figure 6–1.   A TOTE Loop

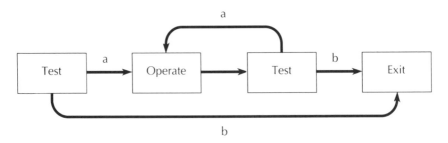

a — system does not match standard

b — system matches standard

begins with information about the state of the system, tests that information against a standard, and either adjusts the system or exits the control loop. A thermostat is an example of a mechanism that is built around the TOTE loop.

Control theory has been applied to a variety of behavorial phenomena, including reactions to feedback and self-regulation of behavior (Carver & Scheier, 1981; Taylor et al., 1984). It is directly relevant to several phenomena in performance appraisal, particularly the problem of understanding how raters revise their evaluations of their subordinates (Murphy, Balzer, Lockhart, & Eisenman, 1985). Control theory suggests that this revision occurs only when the difference between previous and present performance is sufficiently large to trigger a reevaluation process.

Several models of judgment and evaluation include the assumption that evaluative judgments are made with reference to either implicit or explicit standards (DeCotiis & Petit, 1978; Higgins & Stangor, 1988; Ilgen, 1983; Sherif & Sherif, 1969). The process that is assumed to underlie evaluative judgment is illustrated in Figure 6-2. This figure suggests that evaluation involves (1) the judge's perception of what has occurred (behaviors), (2) the judge's standard(s) for evaluating that domain of behaviors, and (3) a comparison process. Depending on the nature of the standard(s), this comparison could range from a simple matching process, in which the judge scans a set of behaviors to determine whether one or more critical behaviors has occurred, to a complex integration process, in which the judge assigns values to all behaviors and combines those values to reach an evaluation. The result of this process, the evaluation itself, is a classification of what has occurred (or what the judge perceives to have occurred) on a positive-negative or good-bad continuum.

Evaluations vary in their direction (good versus bad) and their intensity (indifferent versus extreme) but nevertheless are fundamentally the same regardless of what or who is being evaluated. That is, all evaluations fall along the same continuum, allowing for meaningful comparisons across persons,

Figure 6–2. The Evaluation Process

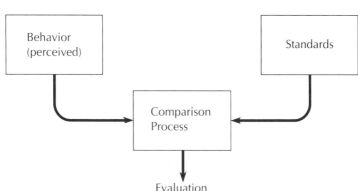

Evaluation

tasks, situations, and the like. The universal nature of this general evaluative dimension has been noted in several separate research literatures (Kim & Rosenberg, 1980; Osgood, 1962; Wegner & Vallecher, 1977). In the context of PA, the existence of a single and universal evaluative dimension implies that the consistent scaling of performance is at least theoretically possible. Even though the behavior of different workers may be qualitatively different (in the extreme case, there may be no overlap in actual behaviors), workers can still be meaningfully compared on a common good-bad dimension.

Figure 6-2 suggests two questions that must be answered in order to understand evaluative judgment. First, what do standards look like? In other words, what is the content of a performance standard? To answer this question adequately, we must first discuss types of standards and then discuss the process by which standards develop and change. Second, what is the nature of the comparison process? Are standards simply lined up side-by-side with behaviors to check for a match, with a negative evaluation resulting when they don't match, or is there a more complex process? Is the product (the evaluation) a function of the type of comparison process followed? These issues are explored in the two sections that follow.

Standards

The specific types of standards that might be used in evaluating performance will vary depending on the job, the work environment, the judge (e.g., self, peer, supervisor), and so on. One useful way of categorizing and describing standards is to separate standards that are explicit and external to the judge from those that are implicit and internal. Thus, standards might range from production goals that are posted in the workplace (e.g., a furniture manufacturer might post the number of chairs a workgroup is expected to assemble each day) to a specific supervisor's definition of what constitutes good, average, and poor performance on a task. These two types of standards are not (or should not be) completely independent. Posted goals may help to define the supervisor's own implicit standards; these standards may be derived in part from the individual standards of the parties who decided on the posted standard. Nevertheless, it is useful to discuss these two types of standards separately. They may involve different behaviors or tasks, may lead to different comparison processes, and may result in very different evaluations of both behaviors and results.

External Standards

External standards for judging performance are those that are explicitly imposed by the organization. These may range from posted production goals to those that are passed on to new supervisors from more experienced members of the organization. These external standards are public rather than private and they exist independently of any particular decision maker.

External standards will often refer to results of performance. Thus, a standard may exist that defines the minimum number of units that a worker or a workgroup is required to produce each day. External standards may also refer to behaviors, especially when these standards take the form of *rules*. Rules may exist that define sets of behaviors that are required at work (e.g., dress codes, standard practices) as well as sets of behaviors that are forbidden (e.g., substance abuse policies). In both cases, external standards may allow for simple and straightforward comparison processes. Thus, if a standard defines daily production quotas, evaluation may be a simple matter of comparing actual production to the quota. If standards define behaviors that are either required or forbidden, evaluation may be a simple matter of comparing the actual behaviors to the behaviors that are cited in the rules. It is important to note, however, that external standards do not guarantee that the comparison process that leads to an evaluation will be a simple one.

External standards are most likely to lead to simple comparison processes when the standards are concrete and specific and when the work environment is sufficiently stable to allow the consistent application of those standards. For example, standards may identify broad categories of acceptable behaviors (e.g., "appropriate attire will be worn at all times") or may specify the exact behaviors that are expected (e.g., "all employees will report to work by 8:30"). Standards that leave room for interpretation will necessarily also require more complex comparison processes. To apply a standard such as "appropriate attire will be worn at all times," the judge must first decide what constitutes appropriate attire. Depending on the latitude of the individual judge's definition of appropriate attire, the same behavior could be evaluated positively or negatively.

Even when standards are highly concrete and specific, the work environment may complicate their application. Environmental constraints may make it impossible to meet a specific standard. On the other hand, environmental opportunities may make it necessary or useful to adjust a previously defined standard. Thus, standards may be set that determine sales quotas for a particular product. If the product suddenly becomes part of a consumer trend, demand may skyrocket and new standards will be needed to define good, poor, and adequate sales. The issue of adjusting standards to take into account environmental constraints and opportunities will be examined in the section of this chapter that deals with the comparison processes.

Standards need not refer to specific behaviors or results but could refer to *distributions* of behaviors and results (Kane & Lawler, 1979). That is, standards could define tolerances, in the sense that they refer to ideal outcomes, but also specify the extent to which deviations from the ideal are tolerated. Thus, a standard might define a specific level of output as "normal" and might also define a range of output levels that are treated as equivalent to normal. Performance that exceeds or falls below this range could possibly trigger rewards or sanctions.

There are several processes that might be used in defining external performance standards. Specific standards are often defined in applications of human factors psychology and industrial engineering (Alluisi & Morgan, 1976; Campbell, 1983). Here, performance standards define optimal levels of functioning for the system for which standards are derived or defined. One industrial engineering concept that is broadly relevant to PA is that optimal standards are not necessarily the highest standards. The industrial engineering perspective suggests that one criterion for evaluating performance ratings may involve determining the degree to which the implicit and explicit standards that are used for evaluating performance are appropriate for a work situation in which they are applied.

Time-and-motion studies are often used to determine both work standards and the optimal procedures for achieving those standards. This method simultaneously defines standards for results (i.e., output levels) and behaviors (i.e., standard procedures to be followed). Although Taylor's system of scientific management (which relied heavily on time-and-motion studies) was regarded by many as a method that dehumanized work and exploited workers, it is useful to remember that Taylor's system was designed primarily to aid the worker. By carefully following the procedures that resulted from a time-and-motion study, workers could increase their output without increasing levels of exertion or effort. This increase in output would presumably lead to higher pay (especially where piece-rate systems are employed) and thus would maximize the benefit to both employers and employees.

The notion of standard operating procedures permeates the armed services, especially when applied to tasks that are carried out by enlisted personnel. Detailed manuals exist that describe standard methods for performing a wide variety of tasks (e.g., engine maintenance), and the evaluation of performance can depend on the extent to which standard procedures were followed, irrespective of the results actually obtained. Research is currently underway in several of the services on methods of evaluating the job performance of enlisted men (Hakel, 1986). In some services, checklists for comparing actual work methods to standard methods are being developed.

In the private sector, manuals that define standard procedures are common in a wide variety of repair occupations. Although deviations from standard procedures are not often used in assessing performance in the private sector, the question of whether standard procedures were followed is likely to be highly salient if a repair fails or if attempts to repair a problem only make things worse.

Standards are often set through negotiation, particularly when unions or other bargaining units are involved. Some of the issues that are likely to be negotiated as part of a union contract include the following (Saal & Knight, 1988).

- ▶ Determining disciplinary procedures
- ▶ Scheduling of work and overtime
- ▶ Determining work methods
- ▶ Determining production rates

Each of these defines a particular standard. Negotiations over disciplinary procedures determine what types and levels of behavior can be the focus for official sanctions, what time frames apply in applying discipline (e.g., maximum time that can elapse between the infraction and the response), and what procedures will be followed to determine whether discipline is required or allowed for specific incidents. Negotiations regarding schedules and overtime might determine both actual working hours and the degree of latitude in determining whether schedules are met (e.g., how late an employee has to be to be classified as late). Negotiations over work methods might determine the standard procedures that are followed.

In general, it is in management's interest to devise procedures that are labor efficient, whereas it is in the union's interest to devise procedures that are labor intensive. Here, the optimal set of work procedures may be those that achieve the best working compromise between these incompatible goals. Finally, production rates may be determined by negotiation and may be set in a way that maximizes benefits for both management and the union.

The processes of goal setting and Management by Objectives (MBO) involve creating explicit standards through negotiation, albeit not in the formal, adverserial mode that is typical of negotiations between management and unions. MBO often involves a process in which the employee proposes a set of standards or goals that will define performance on his or her job, the supervisor reviews the goals and suggests revisions (if needed), and the two parties negotiate to reach a set of mutually agreeable goals (Szilagyi & Wallace, 1983).

Research on goal setting suggests that participating in determining goals is critical to success (Locke, Shaw, Saari, & Latham, 1981). That is, goals have a greater impact on performance when the employee helps to determine the goals than when goals are imposed from above. Since goals represent one type of external performance standard, the question of how goals are set might be a critical one for evaluating a goal-oriented performance appraisal system, at least with regard to the acceptability of the system to those who are being evaluated. (See Chapter Ten for a further discussion of this point.)

Although research on this point is lacking, it seems likely that external performance standards will deal with minimally acceptable levels of results and performance-related behaviors (Carroll & Schneier, 1982). For example, rules are likely to spell out in great detail the behaviors that are not acceptable, yet define the set of acceptable behaviors vaguely, if at all. Similarly, rules regarding production rates are more likely to specify the minimum acceptable level of production than they are to specify a maximum beyond which further production is not allowed. Manuals that describe standard procedures are perhaps an exception, in that they concentrate explicitly on what behaviors *are* required, but with this exception it seems reasonable to conclude that external standards will concentrate only on the breakpoint that separates acceptable from unacceptable performance.

The inference that can be drawn from this assumption is that external standards may often result in binary evaluation, in which workers are classified as either unacceptable or acceptable. This last category might better be labelled "not unacceptable." The point is, if external standards concentrate mainly on minimum performance levels, they may not be useful for the large number of workers who are not unacceptable. We will return to this point in our discussion of comparison processes.

Internal Standards

External standards may represent valuable information for determining performance evaluations, but they are generally not sufficient to account for judgments. As discussed earlier, the process of performance evaluation is one in which behavior is compared to some set of values. Some of these values are likely to be implicit and particular to the individual who is judging another's performance.

Figure 6-3 illustrates three factors that will influence the implicit, internal standards that are used to evaluate performance. First, the figure suggests that the effect of explicit external standards on individual judgments is indirect. That is, it is assumed that judgment occurs when behavior is compared to internal standards, which are in turn affected by the external standards defined by the organization. The influence of external standards on judgment may depend to a large extent on the degree to which the supervisor identifies with and internalizes the values of the organization (Mowday, Porter, & Steers, 1982). Supervisors who are highly committed to the organization may form internal standards that conform to and build upon the external standards of the organization. Supervisors who are not committed or who do not view their

Figure 6–3. Factors That Influence Internal Standards

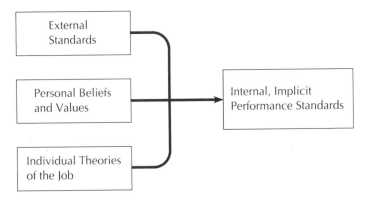

superiors as credible sources for standards may form standards of their own that do not correspond at all to external standards that are defined by the organization.

Personal values and beliefs are likely to influence implicit performance norms and standards. Most workers and supervisors have well-developed ideas of what constitutes a "fair day's work" (Dalton, 1955; Zaleznik, Christensen, & Roethlisberger, 1958). These ideas reflect the individuals' opinions about the amount of effort and production that should be exchanged for the pay and benefits associated with the job. General beliefs about human nature are likely to affect both the standards themselves and their application (Wexley & Youtz, 1985). For example, popular theories of management describe two sets of assumptions about human behavior that are likely to affect the choice of a leadership style (McGregor, 1960). Managers who ascribe to *Theory X* believe that workers are inherently lazy and that they must be motivated by external rewards and closely supervised in order to achieve acceptable levels of performance. Managers who ascribe to *Theory Y* believe that workers are intrinsically motivated and that they will respond most readily to challenges and opportunities for growth at work. A Theory X manager is likely to have a detailed, strict set of standards and is likely to give very low evaluations to behaviors that deviate from those standards. A Theory Y manager is likely to have standards that allow for greater latitude in behavior and that are less punitive with regard to behaviors that deviate from those standards.

Borman's (1987) research on "folk theories" of the job suggests a third influence on internal standards. Each judge may have a unique theory of what is and is not important on the job. Since norms and standards are generally developed only for important behaviors and results (Hackman, 1976; Sherif & Sherif, 1969), the judge's theory of the job may have a profound impact on implicit performance standards. Individual theories of the job will influence the levels of performance standards as well as their content. Thus, the level of performance in some specific area that is viewed as acceptable may depend on the judge's implicit theory of how the job is structured and how it is performed.

In discussing the cognitive requirements for accurate evaluations of performance, Feldman (1986) uses the concept of "performance model" to describe the standards that are used in evaluating performance on different tasks. This performance model defines reference points for evaluation; the nature of the task, in turn, defines the nature of the model. In Feldman's (1986) taxonomy, the methods appropriate for appraising tasks are classified as analytic, intuitive, and quasi-rational.

In analytic performance appraisal, standards are defined in terms of a small number of concrete behaviors or outcomes, and performance can be judged in terms of deviations from that concrete standard. In intuitive appraisal, standards are part of the rater's abstract task schema or their implicit theory of the task. Tasks in which several different procedures might lead to the same outcome or in which outcomes cannot be clearly ranked on a common evaluative scale are likely to be evaluated in an intuitive fashion. Feldman (1986) notes that the implicit theories that define the standards used in intuitive appraisal may vary considerably from judge to judge, and that measures of interrater agreement may say more about the extent to which judges share common task schema than about the extent to which they agree in their perceptions of ratees' behavior.

Quasi-rational PA represents a middle ground between analytic and intuitive methods of appraisal. Quasi-rational appraisal characterizes tasks in which performance cannot be fully described using a simple, objective model, but where objective standards partially define performance. Feldman (1986) suggests that most performance appraisals are examples of quasi-rational judgment tasks. One implication is that the standards that drive most performance appraisals are likely to include a mix of objective and highly subjective standards. Although the behavioral components of these standards may be defined objectively, it is likely that there will be no well-defined performance model for integrating that behavioral information in most PA applications.

One result of the quasi-rational nature of most performance appraisals is that there is room for honest disagreement. That is, all quasi-rational appraisal tasks incorporate at least some standards that represent the subjective values of individual raters. Chapter Five stated that different sources (e.g., peers versus supervisors) might observe different behaviors. Later in this chapter, we will take up the question of whether these sources are also likely to have different standards. One implication of potentially different standards is that a subordinate may view your performance as good, you might view it as average, your superior might view it as poor, and you all might be right. Since evaluation is ultimately a value judgment, differences in evaluation are not necessarily a sign of inaccuracy.

The preceding discussion suggests that the organization has a legitimate interest in trying to develop consistent standards among those who will evaluate other workers' performance. In part this can be accomplished if (1) supervisors identify closely with the organization and (2) the organization is able to articulate clear and consistent objective standards and work procedures. Another possible strategy for inducing common standards have been suggested in research on rater training. Frame-of-reference training is designed to provide all raters with a common set of standards regarding (1) which behaviors are most and least relevant for defining performance and (2) the effectiveness of each of these behaviors (Borman, 1979). Feldman's (1986) analysis suggests that frame-of-reference training will represent only a partial solution to the problem of developing common standards. The problem with frame-of-reference training is that it applies most readily to analytic tasks. Knowing the relevant behaviors and their respective values will not be enough to assure consistency in a quasi-rational task, since a model to integrate those behaviors cannot be specified a priori.

Yet another approach to developing consistent standards can be derived from research conducted at McGill University in the 1950s (Webster, 1964). Researchers noted that interviewers made their decisions by comparing each applicant to their stereotype of an ideal applicant (i.e., their standard). Rather than trying to teach interviewers not to rely on stereotypes, the researchers suggested training interviewers to adopt a common, valid stereotype. In the parlance of social cognition, this suggestion boils down to providing a prototype that all interviewers can use to represent the category "good applicant." In performance appraisal, specific workers (or perhaps a hypothetical composite of several specific workers) might be held up as a common standard. The practicality of this strategy will depend on an organization's ability to locate individuals who clearly are good workers and whose behavior is well known to many raters, which may represent a tall order. Nevertheless, we think that this strategy has sufficient theoretical and empirical support to warrant further research.

Development of Standards

The process by which internal, implicit standards for evaluating performance are developed is poorly understood. For example, it is well known that some judges have unusually high standards and that others have unusually low standards (this disparity in standards may explain rater errors such as leniency/severity), but very little is known about *why* some judges are harsh and others are lenient (Vroom, 1969). Similarly, it is well known that standards can vary over time, but little is known about the circumstances under which they are likely to vary or to remain constant.

Standards refer to a wide range of phenomena; they may be tied to tasks, goals, behaviors, or results (Dornbusch & Scott, 1975; Lee, 1985). It is likely that different processes are responsible for the development of different types of standards. Objective methods such as time-and-motion studies or work sampling may provide information that affects analytic (versus intuitive) standards (Carroll & Schneier, 1982), but many standards will refer to tasks in which objective definitions of "good" are effectively impossible. There is a need, then, to study the psychological processes by which these standards are formed.

There is little empirical work dealing directly with performance standards. However, there is a substantial body of research dealing with a closely related topic — the development of norms — that can be used to identify processes that are likely to be involved in the development of performance standards. For example, we know that norms usually develop gradually (Hackman, 1976), although unusual events can trigger the quick development of a new norm (Sherif & Sherif, 1969). The same probably applies to performance standards. We also know that norms are highly resistant to change; research in both the lab and the field has shown that norms can be transmitted across generations, in the sense that a group norm may continue to influence behavior even after all of the group members who originally generated the norm have left the group (Jacobs & Campbell, 1961; Sherif & Sherif, 1969). If performance standards are somehow communicated from rater to rater, the same phenomenon may occur. That is, the organization's current standard for defining adequate performance may reflect the dead hand of history, in that it may be the result of standards that were set and articulated by supervisors who are no longer part of the organization.

Research on the development of norms suggest four mechanisms through which performance standards might be developed: (1) direct communication, (2) observation of reference groups, (3) direct experience, and (4) extension of values, attitudes, and beliefs from other domains.

Direct Communication   If taken literally, the implicit-explicit distinction would suggest that implicit standards cannot be communicated directly from one person to another. Although it may be impossible to communicate implicit standards in all of their details, the essence of these standards can probably be communicated quite clearly (Taylor et al., 1984). The popular literature on corporate culture suggests one medium for communicating performance standards — through corporate myths and stories. Thus, a widely told story about an especially effective (or ineffective) worker might serve to establish a prototype, and future workers may be evaluated in comparison to that prototype. Although the prototype may be widely shared, each judge will fill in whatever missing information is needed to flesh out the performance standard in a potentially unique manner. The same myth or story will not necessarily lead to the same standard for all judges.

Taylor and colleagues (1984) suggest that performance feedback can change the evaluation standards of the *recipient.* This is particularly likely when (1) the recipient has not formed a well-developed standard for evaluating that aspect of performance, (2) the feedback comes from a credible source, and (3) the feedback is repeated. Under these conditions, the performance feedback will define a standard for both self-evaluations and for evaluations of the performance of the recipient's performance.

Direct, explicit communication of performance standards (i.e., one person directly telling another what the standards are) is most likely when the recipient of this information is new to the organization. Experienced members of the organization may take on the formal or informal role of mentor and trainer; part of their job in socializing new members of the organization will be to communicate performance standards (VanMaanan, 1976). New employees are also the most likely to inquire directly about performance standards. Research on group norms suggests that allowances are typically made for newcomers' lack of knowledge of relevant norms (Sherif & Sherif, 1969). Thus, although it would be inappropriate for an established member of the group to inquire about important norms, this behavior would be tolerated and even encouraged for newcomers.

A variant on direct communication of standards is the situation in which organization members directly observe the *application* of those standards.

Thus, if a rater publicly communicates his or her evaluation of a set of behaviors, this also communicates information about performance standards. If a highly credible judge publicly expresses approval or disapproval of certain behaviors (or allows his or her evaluations to become known), this may influence the performance standards of other judges. This is part of the rationale that is often cited when the organization (or some individual) decides to make an example of a particular employee. For instance, many organizations have programs for formally and publicly recognizing the "employee of the month" (or week or year). The main purpose of these programs is to motivate and reward employees, but they may serve the subsidiary purpose of establishing and clarifying performance standards. The supervisor who knows that the chosen employee is always an individual who shows initiative in dealing with customers is likely to incorporate "initiative in dealing with customers" as a dimension of his or her performance standard.

Informal communication among supervisors represents another channel for exchanging information about standards. Even if conversations among supervisors never directly address theories of the job or the values attached to different behaviors, results, or performance, they are likely to convey information about evaluation. This is conjecture, but we think it is likely that supervisors will occasionally talk about their best and worst employees. These conversations will certainly convey information about supervisors' standards and may help to establish some consensus regarding performance standards.

Finally, ratees are likely to seek information about performance standards (Ashford & Cummings, 1983). Therefore, one should not think of communication about standards as unidirectional (i.e., from supervisor to subordinate), but rather must also consider the subordinate's role in eliciting feedback about performance standards.

Reference Groups   Research on social norms suggests that these norms are often formed by incorporating some features of a particular reference group. In this context, a reference group is a group or person with which an individual identifies (Sherif & Sherif, 1969). Individuals adopt and internalize the norms of their reference groups, particularly when these groups are highly attractive. An individual typically belongs or aspires to belong to the reference group.

In the context of performance appraisal, the reference group is likely to represent individuals who are at the same or higher organizational level as the judge; the hierarchical nature of organizations implies that judges will not aspire to belong to groups at subordinate levels. Reference group research suggests that a judge will adopt standards that are similar to those he or she believes are held by the appropriate reference groups. For example, a supervisor may believe that managers higher in the organization have higher, more demanding standards. If that supervisor aspires to move up in the organization, reference group theory predicts that he or she will give harsh evaluations. This analysis suggests that some instances of inappropriate standards (e.g., leniency error in rating) may represent a combination of faulty diagnoses of the reference group's standards and ambition. The more ambitious the judge (i.e., the more he or she aspires to move up in the organization), the more critical the judge's accuracy in diagnosing the standards that are held by higher management.

The concept of comparison groups is related to that of reference groups, which suggests another mechanism by which performance standards may be formed. A comparison group is a group that is seen by the judge to be similar to the person being evaluated. This comparison group may be co-workers or contemporaries of the person being evaluated or may be comprised of workers who the supervisor has observed in the past. This comparison group may even be idealized, in the sense that it is made up of the judge's prototypes of different categories of workers. Regardless of its nature, the comparison group may define a performance standard, and the target individual's standing relative to that group may determine his or her evaluation. In particular, Haberstroh (1965) suggested that evaluations might be done by comparing an individual to the best performer in a comparison group. Thus, the difference between a target individual's performance and the performance of the best worker in the comparison group may define how far the target individual is from the top end of the judge's evaluative scale.

Both reference and comparison groups have their greatest influence on the development of standards for evaluating performance on novel tasks (Lewin, Dembo, Festinger, & Sears, 1944). One reason for this is that judges are unlikely to establish firm standards for tasks they have never or rarely encountered, and thus may have to rely on external sources for standards. Observation of comparison groups provides information about the range of performance that might be encountered in a novel task. There may even be reference groups in the organization for whom a particular task is *not* a novel one, and the judge may adopt that group's standards for evaluating the performance of his or her subordinates.

The choice of reference groups seems to depend more on characteristics of the judge (e.g., personality, motivational variables, etc.) than on character-istics of the situation (Oldham, Kulik, Stepina, & Ambrose, 1986). This suggests that the study of reference and comparison groups could provde an indirect method of studying supervisor's "theory of the job" (Borman, 1987). For example, the composition of a comparison group chosen by a supervisor provides a concrete illustration of the jobs that are regarded by the supervisor as similar to that of the target individual.

Consider the case illustrated in Figure 6-4, in which two college deans are asked to nominate a comparison group for evaluating the performance of an associate professor of biology. Dean A chooses all associate professors from the natural sciences. Dean B chooses all biology faculty. Neither dean chooses faculty from the History Department. These choices would suggest that Dean A's theory of the job emphasizes rank and general area (e.g., natural science versus humanities and social science) as relevant dimensions for defining the

Figure 6–4.   Comparison Groups for Evaluating an Associate Professor of Biology

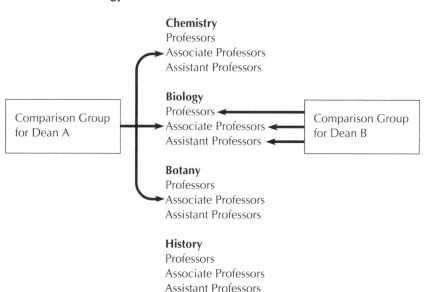

job. Dean B has a theory of the job in which the discipline or department (i.e., biology) is the most salient defining feature. Sociometric methods have long been used to describe structural characteristics of groups (Cartwright & Zander, 1968). These same methods might be useful for inquiring into the theory of the jobs that leads to the formation of these groups.

Studying comparison groups may provide valuable information about the supervisor's theory of the jobs he or she is evaluating. Studying the reference group whose norms and standards the supervisor adopts may provide information about the supervisor's theory of his or her *own* job. Does the supervisor identify with line or with staff? Does the supervisor identify with his or her own level or with higher levels of the organization? Answering questions like these may provide information about their supervisors' career aspirations as well as their visions of where their current jobs fit in the grand scheme of things.

Direct Experience   Supervisors' standards for evaluating performance may arise as a result of their own experience with the job or tasks they are evaluating (Ilgen, 1983). It is not uncommon for supervisors to rise through the ranks and to supervise workers in jobs they once held. This is probably more common for first-level supervisors than for middle- and upper-level managers, but, in general, it is likely that a supervisor will have some experience in the tasks he or she is asked to evaluate.

There are several reasons to believe that direct experience in carrying out the tasks one is asked to evaluate will lead to the development of somewhat inflated standards and expectations. First, supervisors are probably not chosen at random; individuals who are chosen to supervise are more likely to be superior performers than to be inferior or average performers. The supervisor who uses his or her own performance as the standard and who expects the same level of performance from all subordinates is likely to be disappointed.

Second, research on self-ratings (see Chapter Five) suggests that these ratings are inflated. One possibility is that to maintain positive self-images, individuals attend more carefully to their own positive behaviors, remember those behaviors more readily, and give those behaviors more weight when integrating them to form self-evaluations. (Research on the cognitive principles involved in evaluation is reviewed at length in DeNisi and Williams, 1988, and in Ilgen and Feldman, 1983.) Attribution research suggests that people will explain away the negative instances they *do* remember and will overestimate the frequency and importance of the positive ones (Jones & Nisbett, 1971). The net effect of this cognitive distortion is that supervisors are likely to view their own experience through rose-colored glasses and are likely to overestimate how well they actually *did* perform. When a subordinate shows exactly the same behaviors as were previously shown by the supervisor himself or herself, the supervisor is likely to perceive that behavior as worse than the standard set by the supervisor's past performance.

When the supervisor has no direct experience with the task itself, indirect or vicarious experience may still play a role in establishing standards. First, standards may be set on the basis of precedent (Dornbusch & Scott, 1975), which may be viewed as the accumulated experience of previous supervisors. As noted earlier, standards can be acquired from reference groups. It is possible that a supervisor chooses reference groups on the basis of their experience and thus indirectly inherits the results of their experience.

Vicarious experience may be obtained by forming a mental image of how the task is performed (Kosslyn, 1980). This image may be the product of the rater's theory of the job or performance schemata (Borman, 1987; Foti, 1988), his or her training (e.g., through viewing training films), his or her implicit theories of human behavior (Krystofiak, Cardy, & Newman, 1988), or job descriptions, procedure manuals, or observations of others performing the task. Once an image of how the task should be performed is created, that image may serve as a standard for evaluating the performance of others.

Experience in evaluation (as opposed to experience with the task) may itself lead to the development and crystallization of standards. Lorenzo (1984) noted that participation as an assessor in an assessment center increased managers' ability to record and evaluate behavioral information accurately, and increased their effectiveness in communicating that information. One possibility is that having to judge others and to defend those judgments forces managers to develop specific, well-articulated standards. Extending a bit on this line of reasoning suggests that highly experienced supervisors may have more detailed and more realistic standards than new supervisors. As we will discuss later (see Chapter Nine), this tendency may be strongest in organizations that attempt to reward accurate appraisals. Supervisors who receive feedback about the accuracy of their appraisals will have a chance to test the adequacy of their standards. By receiving feedback from other parts of the organization about the performance of their subordinates, raters have a potentially unique chance to determine whether their standards are similar to the standards of others.

Values, Attitudes, and Beliefs   The values, attitudes, and beliefs of supervisors represent yet another source for performance standards. At the most basic level, different standards might be expected from a supervisor who ascribes strongly to the *Protestant Work Ethic (PWE)* than from one who does not. This value system emphasizes (among other things) hard work and dedication. A subordinate who achieves very good results through what appears to be a lackadaisical approach might be evaluated harshly by a strong proponent of the PWE.

Dickson and Buchholz (1977) describe five different sets of general beliefs about work that characterized the values of managers in the United States and Scotland. These belief systems are described in Table 6-1. Subsequent research by Buchholz (1978) and by Mora (1985) suggests that these beliefs generalize to other occupational groups (e.g., blue-collar workers) and cultures (i.e., Venezuela).

As noted above, belief in the PWE is likely to lead to performance standards that emphasize activity and effort. The *organizational* belief system, on the other hand, might lead to performance standards that emphasize the interpersonal dimensions of job performance (see Chapter Five). A worker who does not fit in well with the workgroup may be evaluated harshly by a supervisor who ascribes to the organizational belief system.

Table 6-1.   Five Work Belief Systems

Belief	Description
Protestant Work Ethic	Hard work is good in itself and bestows dignity on the person. Success is linked to one's own effects.
Organizational	Work derives its meaning from the workgroup and organization. Work is a source of fulfillment through belongingness.
Humanistic	Work is meaningful if it is designed to fulfill higher-order needs.
Marxist	Workers are alienated from their activity and exploited by the ownership class. Workers should strive for more control.
Leisure	Work has no meaning itself, but provides money and resources for leisure. The less work, the better.

A *humanistic* belief system may lead the supervisor to develop performance standards that emphasize the tendency to seek challenge and growth through work. A worker who does his or her job, but shows little or no intrinsic interest in the work itself or in the challenges posed by solving problems at work, might be evaluated harshly by a supervisor whose work beliefs are humanistic; this same worker might be favorably evaluated by a supervisor who accepts the PWE. The *Marxist* belief system might lead supervisors to emphasize the political dimensions of work. A worker who shows little interest in the class struggle might be evaluated more negatively than one who is actively involved in efforts to redistribute power to the workers. The *leisure* belief system might lead supervisors to give low ratings to workers who show too much interest in and enthusiasm for their jobs. (The Marxist and leisure belief systems are less common among U.S. managers than among other groups [e.g., other countries, labor, etc.] [see Mora, 1985].)

We noted earlier that most workers have a very specific idea of what represents a "fair day's work." The determination of what is fair probably depends on a combination of highly stable values and attitudes toward the organization. Equity theory (Adams, 1965) predicts that the determination of what is fair will depend in part on a person's perceptions of how he or she is treated by the organization. The organization distributes or controls a wide range of rewards (e.g., pay, promotion, opportunities to interact with co-workers), some of which are highly valued and some of which are not. An individual's own standard for what represents a fair exchange will depend on the perceived value of the rewards, his or her perception of the organization's policy for distributing those rewards, and the perceived value of the effort that he or she expends to achieve these rewards. A supervisor who places a high value on wages may develop an increasingly strict standard for evaluating performance as wages increase. A supervisor who believes that workers' efforts are not closely connected to the rewards they receive may develop more lenient and more flexible standards.

Values are often widely shared among organization members. In fact, it can be argued that the primary purpose of organizational socialization is to instill a common set of values in new members of the organization (VanMaanen, 1976). These shared values can directly affect PA, in that raters may use appraisals to attain valued outcomes (Bjerke, Cleveland, Morrison, & Wilson, 1987). These shared values probably also affect appraisals indirectly, via their influence on performance standards. For example, in the navy, operational (i.e., warfare) skills and activities are most highly valued, and officers are evaluated according to those skills, even if the job is predominantly administrative (Bjerke et al., 1987). Not only are certain skills and performance areas emphasized over others (regardless of their relevance to the current job), it is also likely that the standards for evaluating performance in these areas are both stricter and less flexible. We noted earlier that norms are likely to be developed only for behaviors and tasks that are important. Values tell you what is and is not important.

Precision of Standards

Organizational researchers have noted that performance standards are often ambiguous and poorly defined (French & Caplan, 1973; Kahn & Quinn, 1970). Ambiguity of standards has been cited as a leading source of job stress (Kahn, Wolf, Quinn, Snoeck, & Rosenthal, 1964). The typical explanations for ambiguity in performance standards suggest that (1) supervisors have well-developed standards but do not communicate them effectively or (2) several persons evaluate an individual's work and they do not all share the same standard. Stress could result from not knowing what the standard is or not knowing which standard to apply.

Feldman's (1986) analysis suggests a third possibility. For tasks in which evaluation is wholly or partially intuitive, standards may be inherently unstable and imprecise. That is, there may be no fixed standard for evaluating performance on certain tasks. It is useful to make a distinction between shifting standards and shifting evaluations. The same behavior might be evaluated differently if exhibited by different persons, at different times, or in different environments without necessarily indicating shifting standards. It is possible that the standard stays constant but that the comparison process changes over ratees, tasks, environments, and so on. However, the subjective, intuitive nature of many performance standards suggests that they may not always be fixed, stable quantities.

We know little about precisely how standards develop, and even less about why some standards might be invariant and others may shift. An analogy from psychometric theory helps in understanding the conditions under which standards might be highly stable and precise versus those in which standards are inherently unstable and imprecise. The classic theory of psychometrics suggests that observed scores can be broken down into true scores and random errors of measurement. More modern theories (e.g., generalizability theory, theories for imperfectly parallel tests; see Cronbach, Gleser, Nanda, & Rajaratnam, 1972; Lord & Novick, 1968) suggest a breakdown similar to this:

$$X = T + S + e$$

where:

X = observed score
T = true component
S = systematic error variance
e = random measurement error

In the context of standards,

X = standard that is actually applied
T = the part of the standard that is stable
S = systematic variation in the standard over time, occasions, ratees, and so on
e = random variation in the standard

The first and most obvious issue is the relative size of T, S, and e for standards of different types. Standards that are inherently stable will have small values for both S and e. Second, it is not clear whether e is always a relevant concept when applied to standards. Are the standards a person carries around in his or her head subject to some degree of random variation? If so, what is the explanation for that variation. If e exists at all in this context, is it a facet of the standard (e.g., some standards are unreliable), the person (e.g., some persons are unstable), or both? Does S exist in this context? If so, what are the facets over which one would expect systematic variation? Some possibilities have already been cited (ratees, occasions, tasks, environments). Are there others?

The precision of standards is an important topic for the simple reason that it places an upper bound on the precision of judgments, which in turn may affect the accuracy of performance ratings (although ratings do not always directly reflect judgments). In diagnosing inaccurate judgments, it is important to assess the potential role of (1) inaccurate perceptions of behavior, (2) unstable standards, and (3) improper comparison procedures. The first topic has been examined extensively but the other two topics have received little attention. We think there is a clear need for more research on the precision and stability of performance standards.

The final issue we wish to pursue in this section is the question of whether subordinates and supervisors are likely to have different standards. In general, the answer seems to be yes (Long, 1986). Supervisors and subordinates clearly disagree in their assessments of subordinate performance (see Chapter Five). Although this may in part be due to different perceptions of behavior, it is probably also due to differing standards.

Socialization processes can explain some of the differences in standards between supervisors and subordinates. It is well known that the norms and standards of new members of the organization differ from those of more established members (Schein & Ott, 1962; VanMaanen, 1975) and that socialization processes are designed to reduce these differences. The same phenomena no doubt occur at different *strata* in the organization. That is, new members of the upper strata (e.g., supervisors) are likely to take on the norms and standards of that strata. Thus, if the general performance norms differ across strata, individual supervisors and subordinates are likely to adopt the standards of their own strata, leading to predictable differences in evaluation.

The socialization process presents only a partial explanation for differences in the norms of supervisors and subordinates. This explanation is based on the assumption that, in general, the norms of these two strata will differ, but provides little explanation for *why* they might differ. For example, why do supervisors and subordinates identify different dimensions of performance as important (Borman, 1974)? Why do supervisors have higher standards of performance than do subordinates (Beatty, Schneier, & Beatty, 1978; Schneier & Beatty, 1978)? The concept of egocentric bias may help to answer these questions.

We noted earlier that norms are developed only for behaviors that are considered important. Egocentric bias suggests that each group (i.e., supervisors, subordinates) will develop norms and standards for the behaviors that are relevant and important *to them* (Carroll & Schneier, 1982). For example, subordinates may develop elaborate standards for evaluating interpersonal and group-maintenance behaviors; these same behaviors may have little impact on supervisors' evaluation. Both behaviors and results probably differ in their relevance for supervisors and subordinates. The simplest explanation for supervisors' higher expectations and the tendency for self and peer ratings to be lenient when compared to supervisory ratings is that supervisors consider high levels of output very important, even if little attention is paid to interpersonal relations. However, subordinates consider interpersonal relations to be very important, and care less about output levels.

Although some progress has been made in research on implicit theories of the job (e.g., Borman, 1987), little attention has been given to comparisons between the theories of supervisors and subordinates. Radical disagreements over the importance and centrality of different tasks, behaviors, and results are likely to lead to radical disagreements concerning standards. On the other hand, if supervisors and subordinates have similar implicit theories of the job (i.e., theories of the subordinate's job), more consistent evaluations, higher satisfaction with PA, feelings of equity, and so on can be expected. Our analysis suggests that some supervisor-subordinate conflicts stem from the fact that the two strata are likely to emphasize different criteria and develop different standards for evaluating job performance.

The Comparison Process

Research on cognition and judgment provides some useful insights into the processes that may be involved when comparing behavior to standards. Studies suggest that this process is complex rather than simple, depends on characteristics of the standards, and may not result in the same evaluation for a given behavior exhibited by different persons or in different situations.

One generalization that can be drawn from cognitive-perceptual research is that the complexity of the comparison process is a function of the complexity of the stimulus. With simple stimuli that can be characterized along a single dimension (e.g., comparing the loudness of two tones, the weight of two objects, etc.), comparison processes are simple, although the psychophysical functions describing these comparisons may look complex (Brown & Herrnstein, 1975). In evaluating performance, the stimuli are never simple. Even if evaluation is tied to a single concrete behavior, elaborate preprocessing of stimuli is needed to segregate the ongoing stream of behavior into discrete chunks (Newtson, 1976). To better understand the complex comparisons that are involved when evaluating job performance, some of the structural characteristics of standards must be described.

Characteristics of Standards

Sherif & Sherif's (1969) description of norms provides a starting point for a discussion of the structural characteristics of standards. They noted that norms could be categorized as ways of defining (1) the latitude of rejection — the set of behaviors that meet with disapproval, (2) the latitude of acceptance — the set of behaviors that are approved, and (3) the latitude of noncommitment — the set of behaviors that engage in neither approval nor disapproval. Much of their research from the 1940s to 1960s dealt with features of the individual and the social situation that led to large or small latitudes of acceptance or rejection.

In PA, the latitude of acceptance spans the set of behaviors that are positively evaluated. Within this set, behaviors can be scaled from those that meet with mild approval to those that are highly valued. The latitude of rejection spans the set of ineffective behaviors (from slightly to very ineffective behaviors), whereas the latitude of noncommitment spans the set of behaviors that would not lead to any evaluation, positive or negative.

Jackson (1965) presented the Return Potential Model (RPM), which is a structural model of norms closely related to Sherif and Sherif's (1969) formulation. (Hackman, 1976, describes several applications of this model.) Several features of the model, which is depicted in Figure 6-5, are of interest. First, the latitudes of acceptance (behaviors d and e), rejection (behaviors a, b, g, h, i, and j), and noncommitment (behaviors c and f) are clearly illustrated. The model allows one to compute (1) point of maximum return — the behavior that meets with the most approval (i.e., behavior e); (2) potential return difference — the overall mean amount of approval, minus disapproval,

Figure 6–5. The Return Potential Model

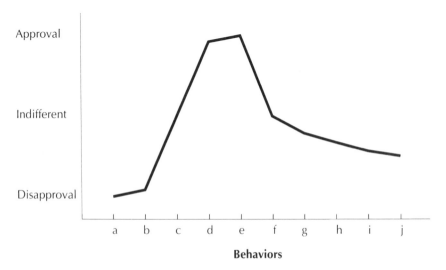

over the whole range of behaviors; (3) intensity — the overall strength of the norm, defined as the amount of approval *or* disapproval assigned to the set of behaviors; and (4) crystallization — the degree of consensus regarding the amount of approval and disapproval assigned to specific behaviors.

Several phenomena in performance appraisal could be studied using the analytic procedures developed by Jackson (1965). For example, potential return difference is likely to be related to leniency and severity of judgment. A rater who assigns poor evaluations to most behaviors will tend to give harsh judgments. Second, intensity is likely to be related to central tendency or range restriction error. A rater who assigns little approval or disapproval to most behaviors is likely to evaluate most workers as "average." Finally, measures of crystallization might be used in investigating interrater agreement. Raters whose RPM graphs are very different might perceive behavior similarly but assign very different evaluations.

Research on cognitive categorization is also related to Sherif and Sherif's (1969) formulation for describing norms. (Lord and colleagues have, in several studies, examined categorization processes in perceptions of leadership. See, for example, Lord, Foti, and DeVader, 1984). There are stable individual differences in individuals' tendency to employ very broad versus very narrow categories for classifying specific behaviors, objects, or events (Garber & Miller, 1986). The category of "good worker" or "good performance" may be very broad for some raters and very narrow for others.

Category breadth is a concept that is closely related to latitudes of acceptance and rejection, especially in contexts such as PA, where categories are by their very nature evaluative. One useful contribution of more recent research is evidence that category breadth is domain-specific (Garber & Miller, 1986); it may also be level-specific. Thus, the same rater might have a broad category to represent good performance in some parts of the job and a narrow category to represent good performance in some others. The "good" category might be broader or narrower than the "poor" category.

Fox and Thornton (1987) present a model of evaluative judgment that incorporates another concept that is closely related to latitudes of acceptance, rejection, and noncommitment. They note that people have implicit theories about the *distribution* of behavior across both individuals and traits; these theories may even include assumptions about person-by-trait interactions. Implicit distribution theories may define boundary conditions for establishing norms and standards. That is, the latitudes of acceptance, rejection, and noncommitment are likely to be defined only over the range of behaviors that are seen as likely to occur. Thus, a supervisor whose theory leads him or her to expect only a narrow range of behaviors relevant to the trait "speaking style" is likely to have narrow latitudes of acceptance, rejection, and noncommitment. All other things being equal, the range of behaviors that are target for approval or disapproval will be directly related to the level of variability that categorizes a person's implicit distribution theory.

Higgins and Stangor (1988) draw a useful distinction between standards that are based on the distribution (or the mean of the distribution) of an attribute for members of a category and standards that are based on exemplars of different levels of that attribute (e.g., specific images of what constitutes good, average, and poor performance). At present, not enough information is known about performance standards to determine whether norm-based or exemplar-based standards predominate. However, these two types of standards may evoke slightly different comparison processes, especially if there are only a few exemplars. More research is needed to determine the implications of this distinction between types of standards for performance appraisal.

Assuming that standards are defined in terms of categories or *ranges* of acceptable and unacceptable behaviors, the comparison process is one in which the rater must sort the behavior he or she observes into the appropriate category. The process of categorization and category matching has been the subject of extensive research (see Gregson, 1975, Rosch & Lloyd, 1978, and Tversky, 1977, for discussions of basic properties of categories and of similarity and category-matching judgments), little of which has dealt with contexts such as PA. In this case, the context might make a difference, since performance evaluation is characterized by the use of a set of *ordered* categories (e.g., good, average, poor) rather than a set of qualitatively different categories. Qualitatively different categories might be used in the *perception* of performance (see Chapter Seven) but are unlikely to be used when the task is to map what has been seen onto a unidimensional evaluative scale.

The fact that the categories of evaluative judgment can be represented as points or regions on a single scale suggests that the matching process will have fewer degrees of freedom than in the typical social cognition experiment. First, behavior will be classified into one and only one category; the same incident will not be characterized as good, bad, *and* indifferent. Second, the number of categories is limited by their breadth. Since categories are aligned in order on a single scale, the use of broad categories necessarily implies the use of few categories. If a third of all behaviors fit into the "good" category and half of the behaviors fit into the "bad" category, there is not much room for a large number of intermediate categories.

Adjusting for the Environment   It is unlikely that standards are completely fixed. Rather, they are likely to include some provision for environmental variables that affect the likelihood of good or poor performance. Standards are probably least variable in stable environments (Thompson, 1967), but even when the environment is highly stable, situational variables can either depress or enhance performance. Standards might have to be adjusted to take this into account.

Peters and O'Connor (1980) called researchers' attention to the importance of considering situational constraints, such as the lack of the tools, supplies, equipment, or cooperation needed to perform a task, when evaluating performance or testing theories about the causes of job performance. Subsequent research has established the effects of situational constraints on both objective and subjective measures of performance (O'Connor, Peters, Pooyang, Weekly, Frank, & Erenkrantz, 1984; Peters, Fisher, & O'Connor, 1982; Steel & Mento, 1986). It is likely that the presence of situational constraints will cause a judge to shift his or her standard to a more realistic level. Thus, if workers usually produce 100 units but situational constraints make it impossible in a particular instance to produce more than 40, production of 39 units will not be judged as "poor." It is likely that the judge will adopt a sliding scale that takes into account unusual constraints or opportunities.

Very little is known about what happens when a supervisor adjusts his or her evaluative scale in reaction to the environment. For example, does the entire category shift downward or does the category move lower *and* become smaller? It is possible that the latitude of acceptance becomes narrower as the total range of behaviors shrinks, but at present there is little evidence one way or the other. Similarly, very little is known about which sorts of constraints lead to or fail to lead to shifts in standards. One might argue that workers are expected to overcome some situational constraints (e.g., lack of information) but not others (e.g., lack of materials). Some constraints probably lead to more adjustment than others but at present little is known about which ones or why.

Adjusting for Individuals   Norms do not apply equally to everyone (Jackson, 1965; Sherif & Sherif, 1969; Thibaut & Kelly, 1959); the same is probably true of standards. That is, there are probably systematic differences in the standards applied to different individuals, such that the same behavior is evaluated differently depending on who performs it.

The concept of in-groups and out-groups (Linville & Jones, 1980; Quattrone & Jones, 1980; see also Chapter Eight) is clearly relevant in discussing shifting standards for evaluating performance. Supervisors typically develop close working relations with some subordinates (in-group) and more distant, formal relationships with others (out-group). It is likely that the "good" category is broader for the in-group than for the out-group; the opposite is probably true for the "bad" category. The intensity of positive evaluation is probably greater for the in-group than for the out-group; the opposite is likely true for the intensity of negative evaluations. Research on the effects of affect and liking on performance appraisals is discussed in Chapter Seven. One way to explain these effects is in terms of differential standards. An individual might apply standards for people he or she likes different than standards for people he or she dislikes.

Returning once again to Sherif and Sherif's (1969) formulation, it is generally the case that standards are linked to the status of the target individual. The size of the latitude of acceptance is positively related to status, whereas the size of the latitude of rejection is negatively correlated with status. In performance evaluation, the set of subordinates evaluated by a supervisor is likely to occupy equivalent places in the formal status hierarchy, but its informal status (e.g., in-group versus out-group) will probably vary considerably. Employees often complain that their supervisors have different standards for evaluating different individuals; this claim may be well founded.

Current information regarding variation in the standards applied to different individuals does not encompass much beyond the rather obvious point that high-status, well-liked individuals are evaluated differently than low-status, disliked individuals. It does, however, suggest that much of the current cognitive and affective research dealing with this problem (see Chapter Seven) takes an overly narrow focus. Status and liking effects on evaluations are probably due in part to differential perceptions of behavior (this is the line followed in most recent research), but the possibility of radically different standards cannot be ruled out.

Anchoring and Adjustment

The preceding discussion assumes implicitly that one starts with behavioral information, aligns that information with an evaluative scale, and makes a judgment. Here, *standard* refers to the evaluative scale. However, there is another use of the term that treats *standard* as a starting point, the assumption being that behavioral information might move a person up (more favorable) or down (less favorable) from that standard point. Research on anchoring and adjustment processes in judgment is relevant to this use of the term *standard.*

Figure 6-6 illustrates the anchoring and adjustment phenomenon. If a standard provides a starting point, and the object or behavior to be judged deviates from that standard, research on anchoring and adjustment processes implies that the judgment will be closer to that standard than is warranted by the behavior (Lichtenstein, Slovic, Fischoff, Layman, & Combs, 1978; Poulton, 1968; Tversky & Kahneman, 1974; Wyer, 1976). If a standard represents what the judge usually expects, research on anchoring would suggest a chronic inability to evaluate deviant or unusual behavior accurately. When this behavior occurs, research on anchoring predicts an assimilation effect. If this is true, judges may habitually overestimate the stability of ratees' behavior. That is, they may evaluate unusual behaviors more conservatively (i.e., closer to the

Figure 6–6. Anchoring and Adjustment

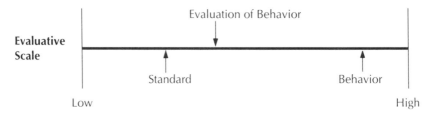

standard) than they should, and falsely conclude that performance rarely varies.

The possibility of assimilation effects is especially worrisome if past behavior defines the standard. Evaluation of the same person over several periods of time can be viewed as a Bayesian opinion-revision task, in which previous behavior defines prior expectations and new behavior may lead to a change in evaluations (Murphy et al., 1985). People are generally conservative in Bayesian tasks (c.f. Edwards, 1968), in the sense that they typically do not change their opinions as much as they should, given the new evidence. In the context of PA, this use of the term *standard* clearly implies that evaluations will not fluctuate as much as they should. It is possible that the persistence of first impressions can be explained in terms of anchoring or conservative opinion revision.

Athough the uses of *standard* referred to in this section may help to explain some phenomena in judgment, it is not clear whether they apply to evaluative judgment. Referring back to Figure 6-6, one might ask how behavior can be placed on the same scale as the standard. If the scale is an evaluative one (as in Figure 6-6), it would seem that some sort of standard matching would be necessary before one could get to the situation illustrated in the figure. Nevertheless, it is useful to consider that there may be multiple levels of standards and that some of these may apply only after the standard and the behavior have been mapped onto a common scale.

Summary

This chapter examined three issues that are rarely considered in psychological research on performance appraisal: (1) the nature of the external and internal standards that are used to determine whether a person's performance is good or bad, (2) the development and communication of these standards, and (3) the uniformity of precision of these standards, as they are applied to different persons or situations, or at different points in time. The research reviewed here suggests that the standards themselves and the ways in which raters use these standards to evaluate ratee behavior are affected by characteristics of the rater (i.e., his or her value system), the organization, the ratees (e.g., whether most subordinates are members of in-groups or out-groups), the organization (i.e., whether organizational norms encourage harsh or lenient evaluations), and the individual's progress in the organizational socialization process.

We believe that research on performance standards would provide important insights into a number of organizational phenomena. For example, disagreements between supervisors and subordinates over performance evaluations may not involve different views on *what* the individual did so much as they involve differences over whether it was good or bad. Similarly, conflicts between managers, or between a manager and his or her superior, may reflect, in part, differences in the standards that define good or poor performance.

There is a great temptation to make standards as explicit as possible. Most people want to know precisely what they need to do to be judged a good or poor worker. While clarity of standards is certainly a good thing, attempts to make standards objective can only be taken so far. For example, a subordinate who is an insensitive loudmouth or a busybody is probably not very effective in his or her work, and certainly will have a negative effect on the work of others. It is not clear what sort of an objective standard could be written to cover that behavior. When standards are made completely clear and explicit, there is a strong temptation to work to those standards and to ignore anything that is not covered in an explicit standard. Some ambiguity in the distinction between a good worker and a poor one is probably inevitable. The standards actually used by raters to evaluate performance are almost certainly fuzzy, and attempts to make them completely explicit and uniform may be doomed to failure.

Chapter Seven

Processes in
Evaluative Judgment

▶   This chapter is concerned with the psychological processes that are likely to be involved in evaluating the performance of subordinates. We concentrate on cognitive processes, or on the way in which raters mentally process information about ratees, but will also discuss research on emotional or affective bases of evaluation. This chapter draws more heavily than others on experimental research conducted in laboratory settings. The relevance of this research for rating and evaluation in organizations has been widely debated; several of the issues in this debate will be discussed in the chapter.

It is useful to keep in mind that our focus here is on the evaluation that the rater arrives at, not necessarily on the rating he or she records. The model we presented in Chapter One suggests that this evaluation is partly context bound and partly context free. That is, the organizational context helps to define which behaviors or outcomes are valued and helps to define the meaning of performance. However, concepts such as "good," "bad," "attractive," and so on exist independently of the organizational context, and judgments regarding performance will be heavily affected by these concepts. As we will discuss later, much of the research cited in this section is more relevant to the context-free aspects of judgment than to the context-bound aspects. This represents one of the potential barriers to generalizing from judgment research in the lab to actual judgments in organizations.

Cognitive Processes

The first topic that must be examined in discussing cognitive processes in evaluative judgment is the meaning of cognitive. A quick survey of relevant research suggests that *cognitive* is a very broad term that includes almost any activity involving the mental manipulation or storage of information. Thus, cognitive research might involve exploration of the basic processes in human memory (Craik & Lockhart, 1972; Tulving, 1974) or of person perception and social cognition (Wyer & Srull, 1986). Cognitive research also includes studies of the dynamics of halo error in rating (Cooper, 1981b), applications of personal construct theory (Borman, 1983), studies of attribution processes (Hogan, 1987; Kelley, 1971), research on the systematic distortion hypothesis (Shweder & D'Andrade, 1980), and examinations of the development and nature of tacit knowledge (Palermo, 1983; Wagner, 1986).

Given the wide range of things that might be included under the "cognitive" umbrella, it is a mistake to regard cognitive research in performance appraisal (PA) as a unitary field. Nevertheless, the majority of PA studies that would be labeled "cognitive" are concerned with the same basic issue — whether research in human information processing can be used to draw valid generalizations about the evaluation of job performance.

The rapid growth of research in cognitive processes in performance evaluation can be traced to several influential reviews that appeared between 1978 and 1982. Papers by Cooper (1981b), DeCotiis and Petit (1978), Feldman (1981), Landy and Farr (1980), and Wherry and Bartlett (1982) all called attention to the cognitive processes in appraisal and suggested ways of examining these processes and applying the results. Wherry and Bartlett (1982) described a model of rating developed by Wherry in the 1950s. Unfortunately, the paper describing the model was not published nor was the model widely known until it was described in Landy and Farr, 1980.

More recently, two models of the judgment processes in appraisal have emerged, one presented by Feldman and colleagues (Feldman, 1981; Ilgen & Feldman, 1983) and another presented by DeNisi and colleagues (DeNisi, Cafferty, & Meglino, 1984; DeNisi & Williams, 1988). Much of the current cognitive research draws on these two models for hypotheses and interpretations of experimental findings.

Although the two models referred to above are in some ways different, they (as well as other cognitive approaches that have been applied to PA) can be described in terms of the five basic processes shown in Figure 7-1. First, raters must observe behavior, sorting relevant from irrelevant information (Banks & Murphy, 1985). Second, they must mentally represent, or encode, that information. This representation is not necessarily a totally faithful replication of what they have seen; it may lack many of the details that were observed and it may contain details that were not in fact present in the stimulus. This representation must then be stored in memory. It is likely that some information is lost in the transition from working memory, where

Figure 7–1.   Basic Cognitive Model for Performance Evaluation

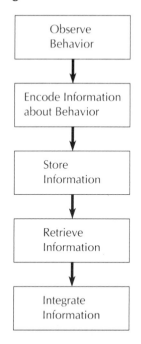

immediate processing takes place, and long-term memory, where the memory traced is stored.

At some later time, raters must retrieve information from memory. Since performance appraisals are frequently conducted at annual or semi-annual intervals, demands on memory may be substantial and raters might find it difficult to retrieve all of the relevant information. Finally, raters must somehow integrate all of the information they have about each ratee. As discussed in Chapter Five, raters may have to integrate information from several different sources, as well as from several different time periods. This last process, that of information integration, has received comparatively little systematic attention in cognitive models of performance appraisal, but has been a focus of considerable attention for judgment and decision researchers.

Information Acquisition

The process of information acquisition is active rather than passive. The rater does not simply bring in all of the available information from whatever he or she has an opportunity to observe. Rather, he or she selectively attends to some features of the ratees and their behavior and devotes little attention to others. Focusing for the moment on the perception of behaviors, cognitive research suggests that the attention devoted to any particular behavior is a function of three variables: (1) the behavior itself, (2) the context of observation, and (3) the purpose of observation. That is, some behaviors are likely to attract more attention, regardless of the context or purpose of observation.

Organizational norms and standards (see Chapter Six) define some behaviors as important, desirable, unacceptable, and so on. Behaviors that carry strong evaluative implications will likely receive attention, almost regardless of the local context (Murphy, 1982b; Wegner & Vallecher, 1977). Beyond this simple principle, cognitive research has had relatively little to say about the behaviors that are most and least likely to attract attention. Research in this area has concentrated most on the second two influences, the context of observation and the purpose of observation.

Research on context suggests two conclusions. First, the salience of most behaviors (i.e., the likelihood that they will be the focus of attention) varies across situations (McArthur, 1980; Taylor & Fiske, 1978). In part, this is due to differences in the evaluative implications of specific behaviors in different situations. For example, a loud, verbally aggressive style of conversation may not attract any attention among a group of heavy-equipment salespeople but might be very noticeable in a receptionist; the behavior is appropriate in one situation, but not in others.

Second, distinctive, novel features of the ratee or his or her behavior will be highly salient (Langer, Taylor, Fiske, & Chantowitz, 1976). Thus, gender might be a very salient characteristic in a office where there is only one female but may not be at all salient if half of the employees are female (Cleveland, Festa, & Montgomery, 1988). Behaviors that are infrequent might become salient through their novelty; behaviors that are important but commonplace may attract less attention.

Research on the purpose of observation, sometimes referred to under the heading of *observational goals,* is highly relevant for understanding what behaviors will or will not be attended to by raters in organizations. In laboratory studies, it is common for subjects to concentrate all of their attention on observing performance, for the sole purpose of evaluating the performance of the individuals they have observed. In organizations, this is rarely the case. Supervisors typically face multiple task demands and rarely have the luxury to devote all of their attention to behavior observation and evaluation (Balzer, 1986; Murphy, Philbin, & Adams, 1989). Thus, raters in organizations are likely to acquire information about ratees' performance while they are concentrating on tasks other than evaluation.

Murphy and associates (1989) demonstrated that the purpose of observation can have a direct impact on the accuracy of behavior ratings. In particular, they showed that raters who concentrate primarily on observing and evaluating ratees have a short-term advantage over raters for whom observation and evaluation is a secondary task. However, this advantage disappears over the long term. It may be that raters who concentrate on observation take in more information, both relevant and irrelevant, than raters for whom evaluation is a secondary task. In most organizational settings, raters may attend to relatively little information, but it is likely that what they do attend to will be relevant. A small amount of relevant information may lead to more accurate evaluations than a large amount of information that includes both irrelevant and relevant observations (Murphy & Balzer, 1986).

When raters *do* consciously seek out information about ratees, the purpose of observation will affect their information-acquisition activities. Raters will seek different information if they want information to find about people, tasks, or characteristics of the group (Murphy, Garcia, Kerkar, Martin, & Balzer, 1982; Williams, DeNisi, Blencoe, & Cafferty, 1985). For example, Cafferty, DeNisi, and Williams (1986) found that acquiring information in a person-blocked pattern (i.e., all information about ratee #1 before moving on to ratee #2), a task-blocked pattern (i.e., all information organized by task), or a mixed pattern had a direct effect on several measures of the accuracy of evaluations.

Most evaluations are concerned with assessing overall differences between persons — a purpose that might be most consistent with a person-blocked strategy (see Srull and Brand, 1983). However, this is not always the case. Raters who are trying to assess the training needs of their workgroup might focus on the overall strengths and weaknesses of the group; raters who are trying to decide which subordinate to recommend for which position might want to know about individual patterns of strength and weakness (Murphy, Garcia et al., 1982). The appropriate information search and acquisition strategy will depend on the demands of the task.

Before concluding this section, it is important to note that information-acquisition strategies have both conscious and unconscious aspects. That is, the rater might consciously develop a goal and might plan steps to acheive that goal (see Chapter Eight). However, features of the stimulus and the context of observation may also unconsciously shape the rater's information-acquisition activities. Ilgen and Feldman (1983) note that many important information-processing activities are done in an automatic mode, where little if any conscious deliberation is carried out.

One implication of this fact is that interventions to help direct the rater's attention to relevant and valid cues cannot concentrate solely on the conscious strategy the rater uses in searching for information, but must also attempt to deal with differences in the natural salience, the novelty, and the distinctiveness of relevant and irrelevant behaviors. In order to efficiently redirect the rater's attention to the most relevant or valid behavioral indicators, changes may be needed in both search and acquisition strategies *and* the context in which behavior is observed (Cleveland & Hollmann, 1988).

Encoding and Mental Representation

At one time, a movie camera served as a reasonable analogy for the way in which perception and the mental representation of information was assumed to work. That is, the mental representation of information was thought to be relatively automatic and faithful. The more current thinking in cognitive psychology, and in particular in social cognition, is that the mental representation of what one has observed involves a complex process of categorization, which may proceed automatically but often requires careful attention and mental effort. Furthermore, mental representations are not necessarily snapshots of what one has observed. Rather, some information may be lost when a stimulus is categorized.

In general, it is likely that one remembers the *category* rather than the *stimulus.* An example of this process is illustrated in Table 7-1. One mental category of people might represent persons who have the properties of (1) tall, (2) dark, and (3) handsome. An individual who is tall, dark, and average in appearance might be sufficiently similar to that category to be perceived as a member. If he or she is categorized in that manner, the information that will be later retrieved from memory is that the individual was tall, dark, and handsome (i.e., the person is now seen as having the properties of the category).

It is useful to distinguish between three related terms that are frequently encountered in research on encoding and categorization: category, prototype, and schema. A *category* is a group of related objects that takes the form of a "fuzzy set" (Rosch, 1977; Rosch, Mervis, Gray, Johnson, & Boyes-Braem, 1976). That is, categories do not have rigid boundaries but rather represent potentially unstable groups of objects that are held together by similarity or "family resemblance." A *prototype* is an exemplar of that category. It is an image that summarizes the typical and distinguishing features of a category. Thus, if the categories are "dependable economy car" and "American sports car," a Subaru and a Corvette might serve as prototypes of their respective categories. Finally, *schema* (or *schemata*) refers to higher-level memory structures that contain verbal or propositional information (Feldman, 1986; Ilgen & Feldman, 1983). Schema can be used to represent the self and/or well-known others in familiar situations (Ilgen & Feldman, 1983). One type of schema, referred to as a *script* (Abelson, 1976), pertains to a mentally stored representation of a familiar event (e.g., visiting a restaurant).

In the most general sense, categorization depends on the similarity between a target and each of the categories that are available to the rater (Rosch, 1978; Tversky & Gati, 1978). Thus, to understand the process of categorization, one must address two separate issues: how similarity judgments are made and how categories become more or less available to the rater.

Table 7–1. Effects of Categorization on Memory

Properties of the Stimulus	Properties of the Category	What Is Remembered
Tall	Tall	Tall
Dark	Dark	Dark
Average Appearance	**Handsome**	**Handsome**

Research on the similarity judgment process suggests that the process of assigning persons (or objects) to categories involves a comparison of the features of a person with the features of the prototype for each category. (Research in this area has not addressed *how* to compare stimuli and prototypes. The literature on similarity judgment (see Gregson, 1975) suggests that the similarity-matching process is not a simple one.)

Returning to our earlier example, a car will be classified as a "dependable economy car" if it shares many critical features with a Subaru. It will be classified as an "American sports car" if it shares many critical features with a Corvette. The features that are critical are those that best represent each category and that best distinguish between categories.

The concept of category accessibility is an essential one in this line of research. It is assumed that the set of all possible categories is extremely large and that individuals can work with only a subset of all the possible categories at any given point in time. The model of social cognition presented by Wyer and Srull (1986) suggests that *using* categories makes them more salient (see also Srull & Wyer, 1980). That is, if a person uses the category "American sports car" to classify the first car he or she sees, the likelihood that the person will use the same category for the next few cars is increased. Using a category also increases the accessibility of related categories. Thus, if the person does not categorize the second car he or she see as an "American sports car," the likelihood that the person will use a related category is increased.

The accessibility or availability of different categories may vary over time or situations. It follows that the same stimulus will not always be assigned to the same category. Figure 7-2 illustrates how this might occur. A person and five different categories are each described in terms of four properties. The match between the person and the category is a function of the number of properties the person and the category have in common. Of the five categories, the person fits category D the best, but that category is not currently available. As a consequence, the person will be classified as a member of category B. If, at some later time, the same person is encountered and category D is then available, the categorization of the object will change.

There is evidence from several studies that processes like those illustrated in Figure 7-2 may in fact occur (Higgins & King, 1981; Higgins, King, & Mavin, 1982; Posner, 1978). Typical studies in this area involve presenting subjects with persons or objects that could conceivably be placed into several different categories, "priming" one of those categories (e.g., by having the subject use a specific category in a preexperimental task), and later testing the subject's memory for what he or she has seen. These studies have shown that construct availability at the time of encoding leads to both short-term and long-term effects on memory for what was observed (see also Jeffrey & Mischel, 1979; Cohen & Ebbeson, 1979).

Several models of the cognitive processes involved in evaluative judgment distinguish between automatic and controlled processes in encoding and (less frequently) in retrieval (Bargh, 1984; Ilgen & Feldman, 1983; Lord,

Figure 7–2. The Category Matching Process

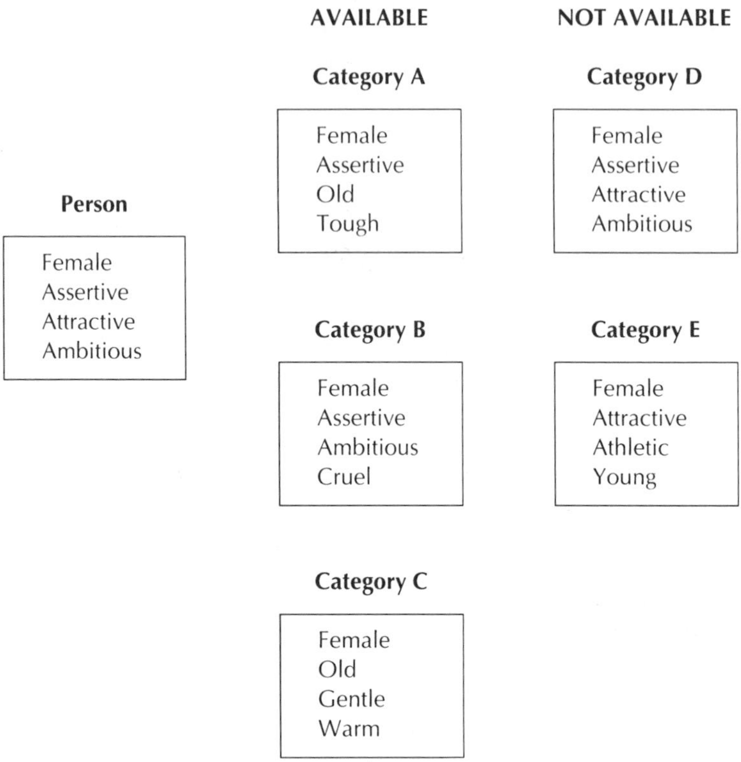

	AVAILABLE	NOT AVAILABLE

Category A

Female
Assertive
Old
Tough

Category D

Female
Assertive
Attractive
Ambitious

Person

Female
Assertive
Attractive
Ambitious

Category B

Female
Assertive
Ambitious
Cruel

Category E

Female
Attractive
Athletic
Young

Category C

Female
Old
Gentle
Warm

Note: Properties of the person and the categories are listed in boxes.

1985b; see also Motowidlo, 1986). There are three factors that distinguish automatic from controlled processes: (1) their development, (2) their demands, and (3) their consequences. First, automatic processes develop through what is referred to as *consistent mapping*, or repetition of a stimulus-response sequence. Controlled processes are activated when there is no well-learned stimulus-response link. In the context of performance appraisal, automatic processing will occur for observations that are repetitive, frequent, or simple, whereas controlled processing will occur for novel or unusual observations. Second, automatic processing makes only minimal demands on processing capacity, making it possible to perform on several well-learned activities simultaneously (e.g., driving a car while carrying on a conversation). Controlled processes demand conscious attention and involve serial rather than parallel processing. That is, the controlled process of encoding occurs when raters consciously attend to observations and effectively screen out surrounding activities.

Finally, and most important, the consequences of automatic versus controlled processes in encoding can be substantial. Automatic processing involves a simple, unconscious matching of objects and categories and involves the loss of information about the object that is not shared by the category. Thus, in the example shown in Figure 7-2, automatic processing would involve the loss of information about one of the properties of the person (i.e., attractive); subjects would remember the object as possessing properties female, assertive, ambitious, and confident (i.e., the properties of the category that most closely matches the object). Controlled processes involve an active search for information. The faithful representation of detailed information about the stimulus is probably more likely under controlled than under automatic processing.

The concepts of schema and prototypes have been applied to the area of leadership, as well as to PA (Lord, 1985b; Lord, Foti, & DeVader, 1984; Phillips & Lord, 1982). In fact, it is our opinion that the application of schematic theories has been more successful in the domain of leader perception and less successful in the domain of performance appraisal. The most obvious reason is that prototypes of leaders are more likely to exist and be similar across situations, than will prototypes of good workers or successful performers. For example, Foti and Lord (1987) studied memory for leader behavior at a board meeting, and were able to predict several important outcome variables using script and schema theory. One reason for this is that most people have at least a general idea of what behaviors are appropriate and expected from the leader of a meeting (i.e., scripts exist for this type of behavior). Thus, it is possible to determine which of the behaviors actually observed are or are not consistent with a schema and to make fine-grained predictions.

In contrast, PA studies are often carried out in contexts where the subjects will have no clear idea of what represents good, average, or poor performance. In the language of schema theories, studies of performance appraisal are often carried out in situations where schema, scripts, and even performance categories are not well defined. As a result, it is difficult to use schematic theories to make specific predictions about appraisal outcomes. One of the few studies that was successful in applying this approach in studying appraisal led to very mixed results (Nathan & Lord, 1983).

Content of Categories The outstanding weakness of schema and categorization theories as applied to PA has been a lack of attention to defining what performance-related categories look like. For example, is "good worker" a category? Is "average worker" another? Researchers in this area have argued both sides of this question but there has been little empirical work that addresses the content of job- or work-related categories (see, however, Blencoe, 1984, and Ostroff & Ilgen, 1986). Cardy, Bernardin, Abbott, Senderak, and Taylor (1987) have presented evidence suggesting that raters do have prototypes of good and poor workers but their research has not examined the content question in any depth.

Although Borman (1987) was not directly concerned with the content of the categories that are used in encoding performance-related behaviors, his research on the personal constructs, or "folk theories," that raters use to describe job performance is highly relevant. He found that general dimensions such as maturity/responsibility, organization, technical proficiency, and assertive leadership were among the personal constructs most often used by raters in their descriptions of work. One possibility is that categories are characterized by different levels of particular dimensions or by different profiles of levels on several dimensions. That is, the dimensions identified by Borman (1987) might define the properties of each category, in that categories might be defined in terms of the presence or absence of each property. For example, one category might be people who are (1) high on maturity, (2) low on organization, (3) average on technical proficiency, and (4) very high on assertive leadership. Other categories might be defined in terms of relative and absolute strengths on different dimensions.

It is likely that the categories used in defining job performance change over time, especially when new raters are compared to experienced raters. In general, experience with the task and/or with evaluating performance on the task leads to an increase in the number and sophistication of the categories that are used in evaluation (Cardy et al., 1987; Kozlowski & Kirsch, 1986). In addition to the number and the detail of job-related categories, the content of these categories is likely to change with experience. One of the several aspects of organizational socialization may be to develop a category system that is comparable to the one used by other members of the organization. As new managers learn their jobs, they are also likely to learn categories that are useful for mentally representing the work of their subordinates.

One dimension that is likely to be highly central in defining categories is the general evaluative dimension (Murphy, 1982b; Murphy & Balzer, 1986). That is, categorization is very likely to involve placing each person along a good-bad, preferred-nonpreferred continuum. Cognitive models have generally assumed that evaluation was the end product of the cognitive process, but there is evidence that evaluation is primitive and universal and that evaluation may occur at the same time as or even precede other information-processing activities (Kim & Rosenberg, 1980; Osgood, 1962; Wegner & Vallecher, 1977; Zajonc, 1980).

Research by Hastie and Park (1986) suggests that evaluations are stored at the time that behavior is observed, and that subsequent memory may be for evaluations rather than for behaviors. (Hastie and Park's distinction between on-line versus memory-based judgments is similar to the distinction Ilgen and Feldman, 1983, draw between stimulus-based and memory-based judgments.) One implication of this is that overall evaluations of individuals may not be greatly affected by the encoding-storage-retrieval process, whereas perceptions of specific behaviors may be directly affected. Raters may be highly accurate in remembering their evaluations but may have a great deal of difficulty in remembering supportive detail. Indeed, there is evidence that raters may *infer* behavioral details from their evaluations, rather than (as is generally assumed) basing their evaluations on the total set of behaviors they have observed (Murphy, Martin, & Garcia, 1982).

One final point about categories deserves attention. It is widely assumed that categorization simplifies perception and encoding. Ilgen and Feldman (1983) assert that "categorization is necessary to cognitive economy; it reduces the amount of information that must be processed and stored" (p. 155). The assumption that categorization is more economical, in terms of information-processing resources, depends on the untested assumption that the number of categories is small, relative to the number of stimuli that are encountered. In fact, the number of categories that might be used is potentially larger than the number of stimuli, since it is possible to construct categories that represent null sets. One such category of persons might be "female presidents of the United States" (hopefully, this category will not always be a null set).

It seems critical for proponents of the view that categorization is cognitively efficient and economical to demonstrate that this is in fact so. One way would be to show that stable categories exist only at a general level. For example, categorization will be economical if "good worker" and "bad worker" represent typical categories, but will not be economical if "good worker who sits at this desk and who is sometimes absent on Thursdays" represents a typical category.

Storage and Retrieval

Tulving (1983) noted that over 100 years of experimental research on human memory has failed to produce any clear consensus on how memory works or on how many different types of memory exist. Memory researchers generally agree that it is useful to distinguish between short-term working memory and long-term memory, but several researchers have proposed different models for each type of memory. Thus, it is important to realize that the models we will describe here are not universally accepted, and that alternative theories can lead to different predictions about what behaviors will or will not be remembered at the time of appraisal.

There are two principal distinctions between working memory and long-term memory: duration and capacity. Working memory is assumed to have a limited capacity, both in terms of the number of items that can be held in memory and in terms of the length of time they can be held. It is assumed that some information enters working memory, where immediate information processing activities occur, but is not transferred to long-term memory. Information that is not transferred to long-term memory within a very short period (often a few seconds) may be permanently lost.

Long-term memory is assumed to have effectively infinite capacity, both in terms of the number of items that can be stored and in terms of the length of time that they can be held. Although it is possible that the passage of time, as well as activities that intervene between storage and retrieval, may interfere with the ability to *retrieve* information from memory, it is assumed that information that is committed to long-term memory is not subsequently lost (Tulving, 1983).

One theory suggests that two separate memory systems exist: semantic and episodic memory (Tulving, 1983). More recent research suggests that transitional forms of memory that share both features of both semantic and episodic memory may also exist. Semantic memory provides storage for verbal, factual, and propositional information, whereas episodic memory provides storage for actions, occurrences, and experiences (both direct and vicarious). Information about a subordinate's performance may be stored in *both* semantic and episodic memory, which may have implications for the way in which this information is used. Integration of information from two separate memory systems may not be as easy as integration of several pieces of information from the same memory system.

Wyer and Srull (1986) present an alternative model — one that has had a significant impact on cognitive research in PA. Some of the aspects of this model are illustrated in Figure 7-3. A storage bin is used as an analogy for human memory. It is assumed that there are several bins, each of which are designed to hold different types of information. Each bin has a label (or a prototype) that describes its contents. Information is stored in a bin in the order of receipt; the same information may be stored in several different bins. Information that is at the top of each bin is most accessible, and information is retrieved by first locating the appropriate bin and then by searching through the bin. Bins in this model are similar to categories. One implication of this

Figure 7-3. A Storage-Bin Model of Memory

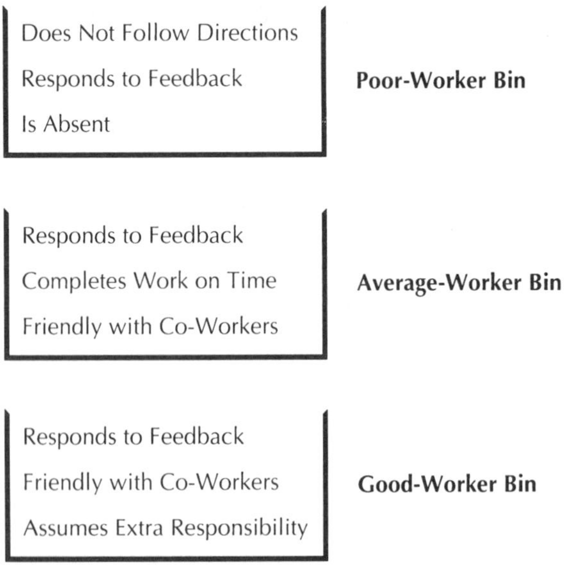

Does Not Follow Directions
Responds to Feedback   **Poor-Worker Bin**
Is Absent

Responds to Feedback
Completes Work on Time   **Average-Worker Bin**
Friendly with Co-Workers

Responds to Feedback
Friendly with Co-Workers   **Good-Worker Bin**
Assumes Extra Responsibility

model is that a memory search will not locate an individual piece of information unless the the the search includes the appropriate bin(s).

The model illustrated in Figure 7-3 suggests two major conclusions. First, some items (e.g., responds to feedback) can be found regardless of which bin is searched. Thus, categorization will not affect the *possibility* of retrieving this item, although it will be less accessible (i.e., the probability of locating the item will be lower) in a search of the poor-worker bin than in a search of the other two bins. Second, failure to search the correct bin(s) will result in a memory failure. Thus, if you search the average-worker or good-worker bins for the item "absent," you will report that you do not remember it; a search of the poor-worker bin is needed to locate that item.

Recognition, Recall, and Reprocessing   In describing retrieval procedures, it is useful to distinguish between *recall,* which represents a relatively unstructured effort to retrieve information from memory, and *recognition,* which represents an attempt to determine whether a stimulus that is present in working memory matches anything that is stored in long-term memory.

Recognition memory is typically better than recall (e.g., compare a multiple-choice test item to a short-answer item) but this is not always the case (Tulving, 1983). Murphy and Davidshofer (1988) suggest that some PA scales present the rater with a recall task, but other scales, particularly behavior-based scales, may present a recognitionlike task. Rating scales that ask about the occurrence of specific behaviors (e.g., Behavior Observation Scales [Latham & Wexley, 1977]; see this book's Appendix for an example) appear to present a more structured retrieval task than do global trait scales. One implication is that questions about the occurrence of specific behaviors may be easier to answer than unstructured questions about what has occurred.

Memory research in the area of social cognition and person perception has been primarily concerned with the effects of categorization on memory. Several studies have shown that subjects recall traits that are consistent with the category used to represent persons mentally, even when those traits were not in fact present (Cantor & Mischel, 1977; Hastie & Kumar, 1979; Wyer & Srull, 1986). Other studies have established that manipulating category accessibility at the time of encoding will systematically affect long-term memory (Cohen & Ebbeson, 1979; Higgins & King, 1981; Higgins et al., 1982; Jeffery & Mischel, 1979). At one point this research seemed to suggest that initial categorization determined the eventual contents of long-term memory. Recent studies of reprocessing suggest that this is not necessarily so.

DeNisi and Williams (1988) reviewed several studies of the effects of reprocessing on memory-related performance evaluation outcomes. Reprocessing occurs when information is obtained (and presumably encoded) for one purpose and subsequently used for another purpose. For example, Williams, DeNisi, Meglino, and Cafferty (1986) had subjects acquire information either for the purpose of making a designation decision (i.e., pick the best worker out of a group) or a deservedness decision (i.e., decide how well each worker performed), and then asked them, several days later, to rate all workers from memory. As expected, subjects in the deservedness condition were more accurate than those in the designation condition.

Williams and associates (1986) explain this finding by noting that subjects in the designation condition may have encoded workers' performance into two categories (such as "the best" and "not the best"). The subsequent PA task asked them to distinguish among all workers — something that was difficult to do for subjects who had initially categorized workers into two gross categories. However, it was not *impossible* for subjects in the designation condition to distinguish among workers they had previously categorized into the same group, which suggests that information about individuals' performance was not completely lost in categorization.

It is possible that reprocessing may lead to recategorization. The evidence is not clear on this point, but close examination of Williams and colleagues' (1986) results suggests that the initial decision task did not cause raters to lose all of the information that was not relevant to the category (e.g., differences in performance among workers in the "not the best" category). Although most models incorporate the assumption that categorization entails the loss of category-irrelevant information (Ilgen & Feldman, 1983), research on reprocessing suggests that this is not always the case. DeNisi and Williams (1989) suggest that the initial categorization of each person may involve at least two separate codes: a behavior code and an evaluation code. Recategorization may involve changing the emphasis on the behavioral versus evaluative information as a result of the demands of different tasks.

Memory Aids Behavior diaries have been suggested as a useful memory aid (Balzer, 1986; Bernardin & Walter, 1977). The rationale here is that it is very difficult for raters to remember all of the relevant behaviors they observe, and that consulting a behavior diary before rating could lead to more accurate evaluations. Although empirical evaluations of the effects of keeping a diary are somewhat mixed, there are some aspects of memory research that suggest that diaries may indeed be useful.

In order to understand the role of diaries, it is important to assess the precise nature of the memory problems that are most frequently encountered in rating. The problem is not that the information that is needed is not in the system; anything that is stored in long-term memory could, in principle, be retrieved at some later date. Rather, the problem is typically one of retrieval. The entries in behavioral diaries probably serve as retrieval cues. One implication is that a diary entry such as "Worker submitted a report that contained many typographical errors" will help to retrieve incidents of that behavior, and will also help in retrieving incidents of conceptually similar behaviors (e.g., behaviors that are stored in the same memory bin).

One unanticipated consequence of using behavior diaries may be a change in the method of categorization. Level-of-processing theories (e.g., Craik & Lockhart, 1972) suggest that consciously attending to and recording behaviors will shift categorization from an automatic to a controlled mode. This will imply more extensive searches for information and a greater likelihood of preserving specific details of what has been observed. It will also mean that raters may now process behavioral information in sequence, rather than engaging in parallel processing. In the automatic mode, raters can process many pieces of information simultaneously, but in the controlled mode, they will process only one piece at a time and will not encode information about other stimuli that are present at the time. It was argued elsewhere (e.g., Murphy & Balzer, 1986) that preserving all of the behavioral details one observes does not necessarily lead to more accurate evaluations, and may even detract from accuracy. Thus, the shift from automatic to controlled processing that may result from the use of behavioral diaries could be a mixed blessing.

Integration

Both the DeNisi and the Feldman models imply that integration of different pieces of information to form an overall judgment occurs after encoding, storage, and retrieval (see also Cooper, 1981b), although both models allow for the fact that previous information may effect subsequent encoding. This possibility has been examined in a series of studies by Murphy, Balzer, Lockhart, and Eisenman (1985) and by Murphy, Gannett, Herr, and Chen (1986). The main results of these studies are summarized in Table 7-2.

These studies showed that both previous and subsequent performance can affect evaluations of present performance. Also, the integration of information about present performance with information about previous and subsequent performance can lead to either assimilation or contrast effects. By

Table 7–2.   Effects of Previous and Subsequent Performance on Evaluations of Present Performance

Delay between Observation and Rating	Previous Performance	Subsequent Performance
Short	Strong Contrast Effect	Weak Assimilation Effect
Long	Weak Contrast Effect	Strong Assimilation Effect

Contrast: Ratings are biased in the opposite direction than that of previous performance.

Assimilation: Ratings are biased in the same direction as that of subsequent performance.

Sources: K. R. Murphy, W. K. Balzer, M. Lockhart, & E. Eisenman, Effects of previous performance on evaluations of present performance, *Journal of Applied Psychology, 70* (1985):72–84. Also: K. R. Murphy, B. A. Gannett, B. M. Herr, & J. A. Chen, Effects of subsequent performance on evaluations of previous performance, *Journal of Applied Psychology, 71* (1986):427–431.

itself, demonstration of assimilation and contrast effects in evaluation is neither new nor impressive but the overall *pattern* of results shown in Table 7-2 is highly informative.

First, previous performance sets up expectations for the future, and when present performance is different from previous performance, contrast effects occur. For example, if a worker usually does a very good job on a task, but this time does only an average job, that present performance will be perceived as poor rather than average. As memory demands increase, this contrast effect grows weaker. Second, when subsequent performance differs from present performance, assimilation effects occur. That is, if a worker is now performing at an above-average level, it is likely that one will remember that his or her previous performance was also above average, even though it was in fact not that good. Assimilation effects grow *stronger* as demands on memory are increased.

A study by Steiner and Raine (1989) suggests some boundary conditions for the conclusions reached by Murphy and colleagues (1985; 1986). They noted that the likelihood of assimilation versus contrast effects in evaluations of performance depended in part on the average performance level of the ratee. In particular, an employee whose performance is typically average but whose present performance is discrepant with the norm must be performing either very well or very poorly during the appraisal period. An employee whose typical performance is either very good or very poor and whose present performance is discrepant from the norm may be an average performer during the appraisal period. Contrast effects are more likely when the performance being evaluated is average; assimilation effects are more likely when their performance being evaluated is extreme (Murphy et al., 1985).

The studies summarized in Table 7-2 suggest an ongoing integration process, in that previous and subsequent performance affect two distinct information-processing activities. First, the expectations that are generated by previous performance direct one's attention to instances of present performance that differ from those expectations. In terms of the Feldman model, present performance that is different from previous performance may be processed in a controlled mode, whereas performance that is consistent with expectations may be processed in an automatic mode. Increasing one's attention to behaviors that violate expectations will lead raters to overestimate the differences between present and past performance, which results in a contrast effect.

Second, when subsequent performance is different from previous performance, one's *memory* for previous performance is biased; here, assimilation rather than contrast effects occur. The effects of subsequent performance on ratings of present performance cannot be due to biases in attention and encoding (Murphy et al., 1986), since present performance is encoded before subsequent performance even occurs. The fact that attention and encoding are ruled out, together with the pattern of results shown in Table

7-2, suggest that subsequent performance affects the retrieval of information about present performance from long-term memory.

The results summarized in Table 7-2 have clear implications for performance evaluations in organizations. Since performance appraisals are typically conducted at infrequent intervals, and are generally done from memory rather than using behavior diaries or other memory aids, results obtained when there is a relatively long delay between observation are most relevant. These results suggest that previous performance will have only a weak effect on evaluations, but that subsequent performance may lead to strong assimilation effects in rating performance that has occurred in the past.

In all, the results shown in Table 7-2 suggest that performance evaluations may lead to underestimates of the variability (over time) of a worker's job performance. If assimilation effects occur, raters will remember the past as being more similar to the present than is actually the case. Therefore, raters may have a very hard time accurately evaluating changes in their subordinates' performance.

Judgment Research   Although many cognitive models allow for the possibility of ongoing integration of information about performance (as described above), most models also assume that some summary integration is carried out at the time the performance is formally evaluated. Research on judgment and decision making has attempted to address processes that might be involved when judges are asked to integrate several pieces of information to arrive at a judgment.

Table 7-3 illustrates the type of task that is often used in studying judgment. Subjects are given multiple pieces of information about each person or object (in this case, about each bank), and are asked to make judgments on the basis of that information. Regression models, subjectively weighted models, and Bayesian opinion revision models have all been used in studying judgments of the type illustrated in Table 7-3 (Hammond, McClelland, & Mumpower, 1980; Slovic & Lichtenstein, 1971). Anderson and colleagues have applied more complex designs in studying algebraic models of human judgment (Anderson, 1971; Anderson & Alexander, 1971).

The approach illustrated in Table 7-3 uses an algebraic analogy to explain and explore information integration. That is, a judgment about a person or object is assumed to be the result of a weighting and averaging process. It is *not* assumed that people actually calculate the average of their evaluation of each property or cue when judging a person or object, but it is assumed that determining the weights assigned to properties will help to tell how much influence each property had on the final judgment. The term *policy capturing* is often used to refer to an approach in which a mathematical model of the judgment is used to infer the importance of each cue or property in judgment.

Although policy capturing has been used to study information integration in performance appraisal (Zedeck & Cascio, 1982), this approach is no longer as popular as it was in the 1960s and 1970s. The principal problem with policy

Table 7–3. Typical Task Used in Studying Information Integration in Judgment

The properties of several banks are described below. Rate each bank on a scale from 1 (not very desirable) to 7 (very desirable) in terms of how desirable each bank might be as a place to do business.

Rating

Bank #1 _____

Interest on Savings — very high
Charges for Checking — average
Accessibility — very easy to get to
Evening and Weekend Hours — very limited

Bank #2 _____

Interest on Savings — very low
Charges for Checking — very low
Accessibility — average
Evening and Weekend Hours — very often open

This task was used by K. R. Murphy, Assessing the discriminant validity of regression models and subjectively weighted models of judgments, *Multivariate Behavioral Research*, 17 (1982):354–370.

capturing is that the mathematical models employed frequently lead to ambiguous or unclear results. This can be illustrated with a simple example. Returning to the type of study illustrated in Table 7-3, the policy-capturing approach would entail the following:

1. Ask each subject to judge a large number of different banks (typically 50 to 100), each described in terms of the four properties included in Table 7-3.
2. Transform the verbal information about each property into scaled values (e.g., Charges for Checking — average would have a scale value of 4 on a 7-point scale).
3. Use the scores on the four cues as predictors and use the judgment about each bank as a criterion in a regression equation.

The regression weights in this equation are assumed to provide information about the importance of each cue in judgment (Lane, Murphy, & Marques, 1982). Thus, if the regression equation computed to predict a subject's judgments yielded regression weights of 1.0, 4.3, 0.20, and 0.33 for the four cues, respectively, you might conclude that (1) Charges for Checking are very important in your evaluation of a bank and (2) you also pay some attention to Interest on Savings, but do not really care about Accessibility or Evening and Weekend Hours.

The problem with the conclusions drawn above is that regression equations capture the *outcomes* of judgments, without necessarily capturing the *process*. That is, the regression equation will accurately predict the actual judgments, but that does not mean that the weights that define the equation were actually applied. Many studies have compared subjective weights, which are obtained by asking the subject how important each cue or property is in his or her judgment, with regression weights (see Hobson & Gibson, 1983; Murphy, 1979). There are two general findings in this literature. First, regression weights are often quite different from subjective weights. Second, subjective weights predict judgments just about as well as do regression weights. In fact, *any* weights are likely to work about as well as regression weights.

As long as cues are to some extent correlated, the choice of weights in a prediction equation has virtually no effect on the accuracy of predictions (Dawes & Corrigan, 1974; Wainer, 1976). Therefore, it is hard to argue that one particular set of weights captures the judgment process (i.e., the regression weights) when any other set of weights would do just as well in predicting judgments.

The relevance of judgment research for information integration in performance appraisal is doubtful. (For a different evaluation of policy capturing in PA research, see Hobson & Gibson, 1983). This research is useful for describing situations in which the decision maker is given several pieces of information at the same time and is required to make judgments solely on the basis of that information. The process of graduate admissions is an example of this. Here, each member of the admissions committee reads a folder describing each applicant in terms of a number of common properties (e.g., grade-point average, etc.) and makes a judgment about each one.

Performance appraisal does not involve a single summary evaluation, but rather probably involves an ongoing process of evaluation and opinion revision. Some decision research is relevant to this sort of ongoing evaluation process (Slovic & Lichtenstein, 1971) but policy-capturing research probably is not. Our conclusion is that we still know relatively little about the information integration processes involved in appraisal, and that policy capturing and related approaches are unlikely to provide an accurate description of these processes.

Applications of the Cognitive Approach

One of the most frequently encountered questions in cognitive research in performance appraisal is whether this approach has led or is likely to lead to advances in the *practice* of PA On the whole, this approach has not yet led to new advances in application, in part because researchers and practitioners have not cooperated fully (Banks & Murphy, 1985). Some of the areas where application has been tried have turned out to be blind alleys, whereas others have not yet been pursued on a sufficient scale to determine whether they will work.

In the areas where cognitive research *has* made a contribution, the contribution has often been negative. For example, behavioral anchors on rating scales have traditionally been regarded as useful guides for observing and evaluating ratee behavior (Bernardin & Smith, 1981). Murphy and Constans (1987) showed that behavioral anchors can be a source of bias rather than a source of validity in rating, and that anchors can misdirect attention and retrieval processes (see, however, Murphy & Pardaffy, 1989)

Other cognitive research (Ilgen & Feldman, 1983; Murphy et al., 1982) has served to further undercut the rationale that is typically put forth in arguing for behavior-based scales rather than for trait-based scales. This research suggests that the categories used in encoding and storage are more traitlike than behavioral, and the trait inferences cannot be avoided by simply phrasing scales in terms of behaviors. Rather, it is likely that people infer behavioral information from subjective trait judgments and that behavior-based scales are not as objective as they appear (Murphy et al., 1982).

At one time, it appeared that cognitive complexity would provide one key to improving the appraisal process. It was argued that individuals differ in their cognitive complexity, or their ability to sort persons and behaviors into many rather than few categories, and that appraisal would be most effective when the dimensional complexity of the rating form matched the level of cognitive complexity of the rater (Schneier, 1977). For example, if all work behavior is mentally sorted into 2 categories (e.g., task accomplishment and interpersonal relations), it will be difficult to rate subordinates using a form that requires performance to be separated into 15 dimensions.

Studies by Bernardin, Cardy, and Carlyle (1982) and Lahey and Saal (1981) cast doubt on the cognitive complexity hypothesis. One major problem with this line of thinking is the construct validity of the measures that are typically used to assess cognitive complexity. In our opinion, it is doubtful that there are stable individual differences in cognitive complexity (i.e., there may be no such thing as cognitive complexity). If there are, the construct is very difficult to measure.

Although the examples cited above suggest that, to date, applications of cognitive research have not advanced the practice of performance appraisal, there are reasons to be optimistic for the future. There are two areas where progress in cognitive research is likely to lead to progress in application.

The first area is in rating scale formats. Landy and Farr (1980) noted that the great majority of the studies of performance appraisal over the last 35 years have been concerned with determining whether one scale format was better than another. The contribution of this research has been so minimal (no one format is consistently better or worse than the others) that Landy and Farr (1980) called for an end to scale format research. However, Feldman (1986) and Murphy and Constans (1988) noted that previous research on scale formats has largely ignored cognitive issues. It is quite likely that different scales may involve different cognitive processes, which could have a definite impact on rating processes. Although no one scale is likely to be best in all situations, selecting the scale according to the cognitive demands imposed may lead to significant improvements in rating. For example, if the purpose of rating is to identify candidates for promotion, scale formats that concentrate on between-person differences (e.g., ranking rather than rating) may lead to more valid decisions than scales that concentrate on individual strengths and weaknesses.

A second area in which cognitive research has clear potential for improving practice is in the area of rater training. Feldman (1986) has suggested that training should provide raters with uniform and valid schema and prototypes. If all raters knew what good performance looked like and agreed in their definitions of good, average, and poor performance, it is likely that the quality of rating data would improve dramatically. Feldman's (1986) suggestions are similar to what is already done in frame-of-reference training (Bernardin & Beatty, 1984), and reflect ideas that were suggested in research on interviewing and on performance appraisals carried out in the 1950s. (See Wherry & Bartlett, 1982, and Webster, 1982, for reviews.) The advantage of the cognitive approach is that it provides methods of assessing the categories and prototypes that are currently being used (Lord, 1985b).

Assessment of the raters' current category systems represents one step in training needs assessment; if raters are already using valid schema and prototypes, training of this type may not be needed. However, in situations where prototypes vary over raters, or where the category of "good performance" is defined in ways that are inconsistent with organizational values and norms, this sort of training might be very useful.

Limitations of the Cognitive Approach

There are two very different criticisms of cognitive research in PA: (1) it is not good science and (2) it does not lead to good practice. The scientific criticism of this approach centers on shortcomings of schema-based and categorization-based theories. It is important to note that *direct* evidence for categorization processes of the sort featured in the DeNisi and Feldman models is hard to come by (Heneman, Wexley, & Moore, 1987; Ilgen & Feldman, 1983). Although research in this area has shown that categorization-induced errors *can* occur, there is little evidence that these errors are frequent or important (Funder, 1987). It is even more important to note that schematic theories themselves are open to attack. Alba and Hasher (1983) noted that schematic theories are not needed to account for many of the phenomena that are currently thought to result from categorization, and that some of the critical predictions of schema-based theories of memory have not been supported. Alba and Hasher's (1983) article asked the question, Is memory schematic? There is still no clear answer.

Social cognition research represents only one small section of the broader literature on human information processing. It is likely that cognitive research in performance appraisal will at some future point establish contact with that broader literature but this has not yet happened. The concepts that drive much of the current cognitive research described here are useful but they do not exhaust the possibilities. For example, an exchange of ideas with researchers in artificial intelligence (AI) would probably be fruitful for both groups. Much of the cognitively oriented research in AI is concerned with understanding the way in which experts make judgments and decisions. It is not known if raters in organizations could be considered experts in evaluation (Philbin, 1988), but even if they do not meet the standard definition of *expert,* many of the concepts from expert systems research may be useful for understanding performance appraisal.

Many other critics suggest that cognitively oriented research is too concerned with theory and not sufficiently concerned with application (Banks & Murphy, 1985; Ilgen & Favero, 1985; Latham, 1986; Wexley & Klimoski, 1984). Part of the problem is that the issues that are most often examined in cognitive research are not highly relevant to appraisal in organizations (Banks & Murphy, 1985).

There is even greater concern, however, over the issue of external generalizability. Cognitive research is almost always carried out in the laboratory, using college students as subjects. Although it is recognized that laboratory research can be used to make valid generalizations to the field (Locke, 1986), there is justifiable concern over the extent to which the typical lab study captures the essential features of appraisal in organizations. Bernardin and Villanova (1986) have described several critical features that are present in performance appraisals in organizations but are typically lacking in laboratory studies. These include: (1) the use of multiple ratees, (2) real consequences for the rater and the ratee, (3) time pressures, and (4) ratees who know the rater and who sign off on the rating form. The absence of these features may seriously restrict the generalizability of laboratory studies.

In our opinion, the debate over the external generalizability of lab studies of cognitive processes in appraisal has been somewhat misguided because of a failure to distinguish between performance *evaluation* (a private judgment) and performance *appraisal* (a public, written form that is submitted to the organization). Consequences for the rater and the ratee are the result of appraisals, not judgments. This suggests that points 2 and 4 above may not be relevant when laboratory studies are used to make inferences about *judgments* in organizations. On the other hand, point 3 is probably relevant to both judgments and appraisals.

For the most part, however, laboratory research is concerned with judgments rather than with decisions that have real consequences. It is incumbent on cognitive researchers to make this distinction and to clearly indicate what aspects of the overall appraisal process are or are not being examined in a particular study. It is incumbent on critics of cognitive research to recognize that laboratory studies do not have to mimic all of the features of performance appraisals in the field to provide useful information about the way in which raters transform their observations of ratee behavior to judgments about their effectiveness.

Affect and Performance Evaluation

Dipboye (1985) noted that recent research on the interview has addressed cognitive variables at length but has largely ignored several other important variables. In particular, both this literature and the PA literature have paid little attention to the issue of affect. Cognitive models portray evaluation as a "cold" process that does not explicitly involve emotion. It is more accurate to think of performance evaluation as an instance of "hot cognition," or of judgment that involves both cognitive and affective processes. Raters typically feel strongly about several of their subordinates and these feelings are likely to influence their evaluations. Although there have been few studies that directly examine affective processes in performance evaluation, it is worth briefly examining the relevant literature.

Unfortunately, *affect* is a fairly broad term. PA research that has examined affect has generally concentrated on liking (Cardy & Dobbins,1986; Dobbins & Russell, 1986). *Liking* can be thought of as directed affect — it represents an emotional reaction to a specific person. However, not all affect is directed toward a specific person. Rather, there are at least two categories of undirected affect: (1) mood — which represents transient undirected affect and (2) temperament — which represents chronic undirected affect. It is likely that both mood and temperament influence evaluations. A rater who is in a good mood at the time of observation and/or evaluation may give more positive evaluations than one who is in a sour mood. Raters who have a very positive, upbeat disposition may evaluate performance differently than raters whose temperament is surly or mean.

It is likely that raters' reactions to demographic cues (e.g., race, gender), physical attractiveness, and nonverbal behaviors are more affective than cognitive (Demuse, 1987). That is, a rater may have a "gut reaction" to a person of a different race or to a very attractive (or unattractive) person; this reaction will color the rater's evaluation. Zajonc (1980) has argued that affective reactions may, in some instances, occur independently of cognitive reactions. Thus, if a rater "knows" that an attractive person does not necessarily make a better secretary than an unattractive one, this may not prevent the rater from reacting positively to the attractive person and negatively to the unattractive one. Affective biases may be very difficult to detect and remove.

Affect and Cognition

Affect could influence cognition in many ways. First, one's affective reaction to a ratee could serve as one piece of information to be integrated with other pieces (e.g., observations of behavior, reports from customers). Thus, it is possible that affect directly influences evaluations (Isen, Shalker, Clark, & Karp, 1978). It is likely, however, that the influence of affect on evaluations is at least partially indirect. That is, affect may change the cognitive processes themselves, as well as serving as a cue to be cognitively processed.

Studies by Clark and Isen (1982) and Isen and Daubman (1984) have shown that mood can affect encoding and retrieval processes. There is some evidence for mood congruency effects (Bower, 1981; Teasdale & Fogarty, 1979), which occur when the similarity between one's mood at the time of encoding and one's mood at the time of retrieval is positively correlated with the likelihood of retrieving specific pieces of information. The reasoning here is that mood can serve as a retrieval cue. Although it has been shown that having the same cues available at both encoding and retrieval enhances memory (Tulving, 1983), it is still not clear whether mood congruency effects really occur, or if they do, whether they are strong enough to make any practical difference.

At one time, the existence of mood congruency effects led to the suggestion that learning might be state-dependent, in that material learned under one mood (e.g., a positive mood) would be more easily remembered while the learner was in that same mood than when the mood at learning was different from the mood at the time of testing (Bower, 1981). This suggestion is no longer considered a viable one; if congruency effects exist at all, they are likely to be too weak to substantially affect learning.

Affect influences the categorization process in two ways. First, affect increases the salience of some categories (Tajfel, 1969). It is possible that some categories are conceptually associated with affective states (e.g., a category of "things you detest"); the association between affect and categories may even result from classical conditioning. If a category of stimuli is repeatedly paired with aversive (or desired) outcomes, that category may develop a strong affective connotation. Affect also influences category breadth (Sinclair, 1988). There is evidence that positive affect leads to an increase in the breadth of categories, in such a way that persons in a positive affective state will classify more persons or objects into a given category than will persons in a negative affective state.

Although the precise explanation is not yet clear, there is evidence that interrater agreement is higher among raters with similar affect than among raters with dissimilar affect (Tsui & Barry, 1986; Zajonc, 1980). This may be due to the fact that affect itself is a piece of data that is integrated into the evaluation, but may also reflect the indirect influence of affect. That is, raters with similar affect may employ similar categorization strategies and may have similar retrieval cues available at the time of evaluation.

Research suggests that the effects of affect are not symmetric, in the sense that positive and negative affect do not necessarily lead to opposite outcomes (Isen, 1984). For example, positive affect is more strongly linked to halo than is negative affect (Williams & Keating, 1987). However, in one area (leniency) there is evidence of symmetric effects (Williams, Allinger, & Pulliam, 1988). Positive affect leads to lenient ratings, whereas negative affect leads to ratings that are unduly severe.

The current research on affective bases of performance evaluation and appraisal has barely scratched the surface of an important question. It seems reasonable that the influence of affect on evaluations can be as strong as or even stronger than the influence of cognitive variables. Managers like some of their subordinates, dislike others, and have no strong feelings about still others. Some managers have happy dispositions, whereas some focus on the negative sides of life. Managers are sometimes in good moods and sometimes in bad moods. All of these variables are likely to influence managers' judgments regarding the performance of their subordinates. Furthermore, affect effects the judgments of some raters but not others (Harris & Sackett, 1988). Current understanding of affective processes in performance evaluation and appraisal is not sufficiently advanced to allow us to predict the strength or direction of all of these effects, or to determine the circumstances under which affect will have a large or a small effect on evaluations. There is clearly need for more work in this area.

Summary

Information processing has become a central concern in many areas of psychology. During the 1980s, performance appraisal research was swept up in the so-called cognitive revolution. Most current PA studies are carried out in the lab, using college students as subjects and using a variety of tasks that appear to mimic features of appraisals in organizations. This research has advanced our understanding of evaluative judgment, but it is not clear whether it has contributed to our understanding of appraisals in organizations

Cognitive research has dealt with the acquisition, encoding, storage, and retrieval processes involved in judgment; less research has been devoted to the integration of information. One general conclusion that can be reached on the basis of this research is that the way in which information is initially categorized and encoded can have a substantial and perhaps decisive impact on the subsequent use of that information. This suggests that training raters to develop consistent and accurate categorization schemes (as in frame-of-reference training) is probably worthwhile.

Research on the influence of affect on appraisals is just beginning, but it is clear that affect is an important component of appraisal. The rater's mood, temperament, and like or dislike of individual ratees is almost certain to influence ratings.

The most significant challenge to cognitive and affective researchers is to develop applications for their findings. As we noted in this chapter, most of the applications of this research to date have been negative (i.e., demonstrations that existing techniques do not work). The field needs to move beyond this stage, which will require the active cooperation of researchers and practitioners. It may be several years before it is possible to determine whether research on cognition and affect will have an impact on performance appraisal in organizations.

Chapter Eight

Rater Goals

▶ Performance appraisal (PA) research has traditionally treated appraisal as a measurement process in which the principal goals were to provide reliable and valid measures of ratee performance. As a result, many of the deficiencies of appraisal systems are blamed on inadequate measurement instruments (i.e., rating scales), inadequate training, inappropriate schema and cognitive structures, and so on.

As discussed in Chapter One, it may be more useful to treat appraisal as a goal-directed *communication* process in which the rater attempts to use PA to advance his or her interests. Raters are not passive measurement instruments, and it is unwise to assume that they are always trying to provide accurate measures of each ratee's performance. This is not to say that the rater always, or even often, engages in cynical manipulation of appraisals. Rather, it is a simple recognition of the fact that raters are likely to consider the implications of the ratings they give, and may sometimes conclude that they *should* give ratings that do not correspond with their true evaluations of the ratee. (This topic is taken up in greater detail in Chapter Nine).

In this chapter, we discuss the nature and content of the goals that might direct the rater's behavior. Unfortunately, very little is known about the goals actually pursued by raters; most evidence at this point is anectdotal (Bjerke, Cleveland, Morrison, & Wilson, 1987; Longenecker, Sims, & Gioia, 1987). However, a great deal is known about the general ways in which goals influence behavior, and we can draw several hypotheses about rater goals from this literature. After discussing the nature of rater goals, we will examine the ways in which these goals develop, as well as the ways in which they are communicated to members of the organization. Next, we will discuss rater goals as a function of ratee performance levels. There is clear evidence that supervisors pursue different goals and use different strategies when working with good- versus poor-performing subordinates. Finally, we will discuss the relationship (or lack of relationship) between the goals of the rater and those of the organization.

Nature of Goals

The concept of goal-oriented action is as old as scientific psychology; this concept was central to the work of Wundt, Tolman, Lewin, and others (Frese & Sabini, 1985). The controversy over the use of goals as causal explanations for behavior is nearly as old. The principal objection to the use of goals as explanatory constructs is that it is teleological — it cites something in the future (i.e., the achievement of a goal) as the cause of behavior that occurs in the present. Although this argument suggests that goals themselves are not the cause of behavior, it does not preclude the possibility that goals direct and motivate behavior. The actual achievement of the goal is in the future, but goal-oriented theorists note that *anticipation* of goal achievement can and does occur prior to that behavior, and that a person's mental representation of a goal can be cited as one cause of the behavior that is used to achieve the goal.

Goals are central to action theory. For example, Sjoeberg (1981) distinguishes between behaviors that are not tied to a particular goal and actions that are goal directed. In Chapter Seven, we noted that the processes by which individuals divide a stream of behavior into discrete chunks could have implications for ratings. Action theory suggests that the processes of perceiving behaviors versus actions may be quite different. In observing behaviors, the individual must impose structure, whereas actions have an inherent structure. One implication may be that actions (i.e., goal-oriented behaviors) may be perceived similarly by most observers, whereas behaviors may be perceived differently. The action-behavior distinction has some interesting parallels in job analysis, specifically in the distinction between behaviors and tasks. Tasks are defined in terms of specific operations and endpoints (e.g., install generator), whereas behaviors are defined in more generic terms (e.g., supervise others). As in task analysis, it may be useful to analyze rating behavior by first asking about the purpose of the behavior.

The literature on goal-directed action is not always clear in defining exactly what constitutes a goal. For example, social learning theory (e.g., Bandura & Walters, 1963; Rotter, 1982) generally treats goals as endpoints. That is, the goal object is regarded as the source of reinforcement for goal-oriented behaviors. However, over time, the goal itself takes on reinforcement value that can persist even if the original goal object is withdrawn. In this literature, it is first the goal object and later the process of goal achievement itself that provides the motivating force for behavior. Rotter (1982) analyzed test faking in terms of differences in the goals envisioned by the examiner and by the respondent. Manipulation of ratings can be thought of as a sort of test faking and can be analyzed in analogous terms.

On the other hand, Rommetveit (1981) describes goals as means-end structures. That is, the goal not only implies the end to be pursued but also the methods that are used to pursue it. Finally, Stokols (1981) incorporates features of the environment in defining goals. Specifically, he notes that the environment can either facilitate or hinder the accomplishment of goals, and suggests that the motivating power of goals may depend on the degree to which they are seen as attainable.

We believe that there is a useful separation between environments, means, and ends when describing the types of goals that are likely to affect the behavior of raters. In part, this is because the choice of means and the evaluation of environments often involve consideration of subordinate goals or even goals that are not directly related to the end currently being sought by the rater. Thus, in this chapter we define rater goals in terms of the ends pursued rather than in terms of the environment in which they are pursued or the means used to pursue them.

Multiple Goals

Behavior is often influenced by several goals, which may or may not be compatible (Argyle, 1981; Cleveland, Murphy, & Williams, 1989; Reither & Staudel, 1985). These goals may operate sequentially or simultaneously, and the same behavior might be a part of several distinct actions. As a result, the use of goals to unitize behavior (i.e., classify behavior in terms of discrete actions) may not be simple; each rater behavior may reflect a complex set of goals. Furthermore, these goals may have different sources. Cleveland and associates (1989) note that the organization often imposes a number of goals on the rater (however, not all of these goals will be accepted by the rater). In addition, the rater might impose a number of his or her own goals. Some examples of goals that might be imposed by the organization or the rater are the following:

Organizational Goals

► Distinguish good from poor performers
► Provide developmental feedback
► Document and justify decisions
► Provide input for other personnel systems

Rater Goals

► Avoid interpersonal tension in workgroup
► Motivate poor performer
► Maintain current level of motivation in good performer
► Achieve or restore equity in workgroup
► Use ratings to convey *your* effectiveness as a supervisor

Some of these goals may be compatible (e.g., provide developmental feedback, motivate poor performer) but others are not (e.g., distinguish good from poor performers, avoid interpersonal tension in the workgroup).

When multiple goals exist, how do we determine which one(s) are influencing behavior? This may depend in part on the structure of the set of goals. Some researchers suggest that this organization is hierarchical in nature (Beach, 1985; Maslow, 1970), but Broadbent (1985) suggests a heterarchic structure. A heterarchy implies a more fluid arrangement than a strict hierarchy. It allows for the possibility that one goal can sometimes be more important and sometimes less important than a particular alternative. Regardless of the structure (i.e., hierarchy versus heterarchy), research on the organization of goals suggests that separate but compatible goals are grouped into relatively homogeneous categories. Therefore, it may be more useful to investigate the broad categories of goals pursued by raters, than to catalog the specific goals that are pursued.

The organization of multiple incompatible goals is more problematic. There is some speculation that when faced with incompatible goals, raters simply choose the goal that appears to be most important, and ignore the other alternatives (Bjerke et al., 1987). However, we do not know what determines the relative importance of goals or whether most or all raters make similar choices when confronted by incompatible goals.

Awareness of Rater Goals

A further complication in the study of goals is that individuals may not be aware of any or all of the goals they are pursuing (Argyle, 1981; Broadbent, 1985). One implication is that simply asking raters what they are trying to accomplish may not be sufficient, even if raters try to answer the questions truthfully and completely. Rather, it may be necessary to infer goals from behavior.

A research strategy similar to that used in construct validation may be appropriate here. That is, PA researchers may need to start with a set of hypotheses about the goals that are most likely to influence rater behavior, then proceed to deductions about events, behaviors, and so on that would occur if those goals were in fact being pursued, then determine whether those events, behaviors, and so on *had* occurred. If the answer is yes, this is evidence that the the hypothesized goals are indeed being pursued (Murphy & Davidshofer, 1988). As in any construct validation study, it may not be possible to *prove* that the hypotheses about rater goals are correct. However, as the body of evidence consistent with the hypotheses grows, the greater the likelihood that the hypotheses have captured at least some of the goals actually being pursued by the rater.

In Chapters One through Four, we discussed the influence of situational or contextual variables on rater behavior. Goals (both conscious and unconscious) may represent a very useful tool for analyzing and describing situations (Fuller, 1950; Magnusson, 1981; Pervin, 1981). That is, a description of the rating situation is more likely to convey useful information if it includes information about the goal or goals being pursued than if it does not. Furthermore, other characteristics of the situation may be used to make inferences about rater goals. For example, if the norms of the organization include a strong emphasis on maintaining good interpersonal relations in the workgroup, it is reasonable to infer that one goal that will affect the rater's behavior is that of avoiding negative interpersonal incidents. In this book, we use rater goals as an integral part of describing the context of rating in organizations.

Typology of Rater Goals

The specific goals pursued by raters will depend on a wide range of factors, including the values and experiences of the rater, the climate and culture of the organization, the performance level of subordinates, and the like. Several years of good descriptive research might be necessary in order to describe the goals that are most frequently pursued by raters. One way to structure this research is to propose a set of general categories of goals that raters are most likely to pursue. We believe that many of the most frequently pursued goals can be identified with one of four general categories: (1) task-performance goals, (2) interpersonal goals, (3) strategic goals, and (4) internalized goals.

Task-performance goals involve using performance appraisal to increase or maintain ratees' performance levels. Specific performance goals will necessarily depend on whether the ratee being evaluated is in fact (or in the rater's opinion) performing well. If the individual is performing well, the rater's goal might be to maintain that performance level. If the rater is performing poorly, the rater's goal might be to increase motivation or to identify and correct weaknesses. Finally, task-performance goals may be future-oriented. Raters may use appraisals to guide the development of employees in such a way that they will prepare themselves for future assignments or jobs.

Interpersonal goals are those that involve using appraisal to maintain or improve interpersonal relations between the supervisor and subordinates. The interpersonal goal that has been discussed most frequently in the literature (e.g., Mohrman & Lawler, 1983; Naiper & Latham, 1986) involves maintaining a positive climate in the workgroup. Because low ratings can lead to resentment and perceptions of inequity, the maintenance of a positive workgroup climate often involves rating inflation. It is interesting to note that some studies (e.g., Naiper & Latham, 1986) have questioned the extent to which raters are concerned with interpersonal relations. If the rater does not care what others think of him or her, this goal may not influence the rater's behavior.

Many interpersonal goals may involve efforts to achieve or restore equity. If a supervisor believes that a specific subordinate deserved some reward that he or she did not receive (e.g., a promotion or raise), subsequent ratings may be distorted to achieve those outcomes. If workgroup members believe that rewards have not been distributed equitably, the supervisor might have a strong incentive to restore perceptions of equity. Yet another class of interpersonal goals are those that involve attempts to establish or maintain interpersonal influence. For example, a rater who demonstrates that he or she can have a substantial influence on administrative decisions (e.g., salary) may have a great deal of power and influence over subordinates.

Strategic goals involve using appraisal to increase the supervisor's and/or the workgroup's standing in the organization. There are several ways to accomplish this. First, uniformly high ratings might reflect positively on both the rater and the workgroup, especially if the rater is viewed as a credible source. Second, the standing of both the rater and the workgroup may be enhanced if workgroup members are given widely sought promotions and assignments; raters may distort their ratings to increase the likelihood of these valued outcomes. Third, both the rater and the workgroup might look better if the supervisor succeeds in transferring poor performers to someone else's workgroup. Again, performance ratings may influence this type of decision.

Internalized goals are the product of the rater's values and beliefs. For example, a rater who believes that he or she should be honest in completing performance appraisals may turn in very different appraisals than a rater who believes that he or she should obtain value rewards for subordinates. The rater's self-image may also affect rating behavior. A rater who believes he or she is or should be a participative leader will probably devote more time and attention to feedback that will a rater whose self-image is more authoritarian.

Investigating Rater Goals

Raters are not always aware of their goals, and even when they are aware of them, they may not be willing to describe them. This does not mean self-reports are worthless for investigating rater goals but rather that these methods will probably not be sufficient. Fortunately, research in motivation and decision making provides a basis for some inferences about the content of rater goals.

Instrumentality theory (Porter & Lawler, 1968; Schwab, Olian-Gottlieb, & Heneman, 1979; Vroom, 1964) represents one of the most widely applied theories of work motivation. In its most basic form, the theory says that the motivation to work is a function of the value attached to the various outcomes of good performance and the individual's belief that specific levels of effort or specific behaviors will lead to those outcomes. This theory provides a useful framework for determining what goals are likely to operate in different organizational settings. First, the concepts of goal object and valued outcome are very similar. Second, the concepts of expectancy and instrumentality are closely related to the concept of means-end structure. We have chosen to focus on outcomes (i.e., goal objects) rather than on means used to reach goals, which means that the parts of the theory that deal with the value or valance attached to outcomes are most relevant.

In determining the probable content of rater goals, it is useful first to list the outcomes that might reasonably be associated with giving good, average, or poor ratings. Some of these outcomes will be valued by raters and these are likely to represent goal objects. Other outcomes might be valued by the organization but not by the rater (e.g., determining which member of the workgroup performed best this year). Raters will not necessarily direct their behavior toward achieving those goals.

Raters may find it difficult to describe the relative values of outcomes (assuming they are willing to try). Decision research provides methods that may prove useful for measuring rater values. For example, the first step in the assessment of multiattribute utility is often to ask questions about the values associated with different decision outcomes (Edwards, 1980; Edwards & Newman, 1982). This sometimes involves asking the decision maker to respond directly to a structured set of questions. It may also involve more indirect methods in which values (i.e., utilities) are inferred from the choices an individual makes (Raiffa, 1968). For example, raters might be presented with scenarios describing a variety of appraisal outcomes and asked to indicate their preferences among sets of outcomes. Raters who consistently choose one set of outcomes over another (e.g., high-quality feedback regarding strengths and weaknesses versus identifying best and worst performers) probably value that outcome more.

Communication Rules

Supervisors' and subordinates' role demands and constraints often make it difficult for them to pursue important goals openly. For example, a rater whose goal is to get rid of a poor-performing subordinate may not be able to turn in extremely low ratings; these ratings may lead to unfavorable reactions in the workgroup. Organizations (and units within organizations) frequently develop sets of unwritten rules that allow the supervisor to communicate the necessary information to the organization (i.e., that the ratee is a poor performer) without necessarily giving low ratings. Schall (1983) described these communication rules as "tacit understandings (generally unwritten and unspoken) about appropriate ways to interact (communicate) with others in given roles and situations; these are choices, not laws (although they constrain choice through normative, practical, and logical force), and they allow interactors to interpret behavior in similar ways" (p. 560).

Although formally not a part of the goal, communication rules are critical to the achievement of many goals, particularly goals involving subordinates who perform either very well or very poorly. For example, Bjerke and colleagues (1987) studied raters' approach to evaluating the performance of officers in the navy. Like many organizations, the navy is plagued by rating inflation; in some specialties, virtually everyone receives ratings at or near the top of the scale. However, raters were able to communicate their evaluations effectively in the narrative section of the appraisal. A poor-performing officer might receive high ratings, but the narrative section of his or her evaluation might be restricted to statements such as "is neat in appearance." A better performer might receive the same scores, but his or her narrative section might contain substantive comments about the most important aspects of the job.

In the example described above, raters developed a special language that allowed them to give high ratings and still discriminate between good and poor performers. We do not think this is unique to the navy, although there may be more uniformity in the armed services than in other large organizations. Very little is known about the communication rules that govern appraisal in organizations. However, appraisals are presumably more effective if there is widespread agreement about the appropriate communication rules, and presumably many of the deficiencies of appraisal systems involve incomplete or poorly understood communication rules. In particular, agreement regarding communication rules may make it easier to communicate the rationale behind ratings as well as the true meaning of the rating.

Development of Goals

When they first start their jobs, it is unlikely that supervisors have well-articulated goals that direct their behavior in performance appraisal. Indeed, this group might be unique in that they function in a way that some appraisal researchers assume *all* raters function — their principal goal might be to do the best job they can in honestly and accurately evaluating subordinates' performance.

With more experience, raters are likely to develop a more complex, sophisticated set of goals that reflect the realities of their organization, department, or workgroup. In part, these goals will be shaped by their own experiences on the job. That is, they will learn what outcomes to expect as the result of giving good or poor ratings, and will also learn which of these outcomes is of concern to the organization. However, this type of trial-and-error process is not the only one involved in acquiring goals and beliefs regarding PA. Organizations make formal and informal efforts to socialize their members, and one aspect of being socialized into the role of supervisor or manager is to learn the appropriate behaviors and strategies for evaluating subordinates.

Socialization Processes

Organizations are composed of a number of individuals who perform interlocking roles. Thus, it is important for newcomers quickly to learn the roles they are expected to carry out. Until newcomers learn their roles, co-workers whose jobs are in some way linked to theirs will find it more difficult to perform their jobs.

The socialization process refers to the transition from the status of a naive newcomer who knows little about the role, to that of a knowledgeable insider who understands the nuances of his or her role as well as the relationship between that role and the roles of others in the organization (Chao, 1988; Russo & Hartman, 1987). Much of this socialization occurs via the *role episode process*, in which other members of the role set (i.e., other persons with a vested interest in how well the newcomer performs his or her role) send information evaluating the focal person's role performance (Graen, 1976). Behaviors that are consistent with the role are met with approval, whereas behaviors inconsistent with the role are sanctioned.

The role socialization process can be intensive in the initial period in which an individual occupies a job. The critical experiences in organizational and job socialization typically occur during the first year (Buchanan, 1974). The model shown in Figure 8-1 (adapted from Feldman, 1976) illustrates the steps in the socialization process.

First, there is some anticipatory socialization that occurs before an individual enters the job. That is, individuals are likely to start with expectations about their role, as well as the behaviors appropriate for that role. Socialization itself begins with the process of accomodation, which involves initiation to both the task and the group, role definition, and the development of congruence between one's standards and the prevailing standards of the role set. Next comes role management, which involves resolution of conflicts between the work role and other roles (e.g., family roles), as well as resolution of conflicting demands presented by the work role. The outcomes of role

Figure 8–1.   Steps in the Socialization Process

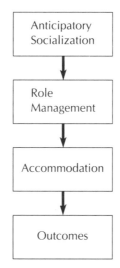

Adapted from D. C. Feldman, A contingency theory of socialization, *Administrative Science Quarterly, 21* (1976):443–452.

socialization range from job involvement and satisfaction to the development of influence in the organization.

The precise content of what is learned in role socialization will vary from job to job but there are some broad categories of learning that are likely to be present in most jobs (Fisher, 1986). First, and most obvious, the person must learn how to do the job. Thus, training activities (both formal and informal) are one component of socialization. Second, he or she must learn the values and norms of the immediate workgroup. Third, he or she must learn the values, culture, goals, and norms of the organization; these are not always the same as those of the workgroup. Finally, the individual must incorporate the new role into his or her identity or self-image. One implication of this final category of learning is that a fully socialized individual will not only learn the role but will also internalize at least some aspects of the role.

It is clear that some aspects of role socialization are easier than others. For example, expectations about the content of work are easily changed through experience (Wanous, 1980). Values and general work orientation are much less easily changed. In part this is because values are more firmly entrenched and more central than specific expectations about the content of work. However, there is another factor that influences the degree to which a person can be changed through socialization — the method of training.

Very few people object to participating in technical training that is designed to instruct them about how to do the job. Many people would object strenuously to training programs that were designed to mold their values or their orientation toward work, however. Therefore, it may be difficult to impart values and norms; these may require somewhat indirect methods of socialization. Weiss (1978), for example, suggests that organizational values are learned through modeling the behavior (and apparent values) of others. The ease of modeling probably depends on the number of opportunities the focal person has to make relevant observations of others' behavior, as well as the power and status of the role sender (Fisher, 1986).

Organizational Culture and Rater Goals

Modeling the behaviors of specific role senders is only one way in which newcomers acquire the values of the workgroup and the organization. These values and expectations that define the climate and culture of the organization influence most of the interactions between the focal person and other members of the organization (Rousseau, 1988; Schneider & Reichers, 1983); therefore, these values will probably influence the development of specific goals for performance appraisal.

Martin and Siehl (1983) note that the culture of an organization offers "an interpretation of an institution's history that members can use to decipher how they will be expected to behave in the future" (p. 52). Thus, the culture defines the behaviors that are either accepted or sanctioned, and the process of transmitting that culture (e.g., through stories or rituals) may serve as a powerful socializing force. In the context of performance appraisal, the culture might determine what approach to appraisal and what behaviors are evaluated positively or negatively in the organization.

Although evidence about the content of organizational cultures is fragmentary and contradictory, it is reasonable to expect that beliefs, values, and norms regarding PA will often be a part of the organization's culture. In some organizations, appraisal is treated as important; in others, it is treated as a joke. Feedback is the norm in some organizations and the exception in others. Ratings are a critical determinant of decisions in some organizations and are ignored in others. It is possible that all of these aspects of appraisal are influenced by the culture of the organization and that newcomers must learn that culture before they can use the appraisal system effectively to achieve their goals.

Organizational cultures can be described in terms of both the content and intensity of the values and beliefs that are part of that culture (Rousseau, 1988). The culture of an organization is most likely to affect the behavior of raters when (1) it includes beliefs, values, and so on that are directly relevant to appraisal; and (2) those values, beliefs, and so on are strongly held.

Returning to our earlier example of appraisal in the navy, there appears to be a strong norm in that organization that appraisals should be used to secure promotion for deserving subordinates (and for those who show promise of performing well in more responsible jobs). Most raters appear to accept this norm and fill out their appraisals with promotion in mind (Bjerke et al., 1987). These same conditions (i.e., strongly held beliefs about how appraisal should be done) may make it difficult to change the appraisal system in an organization without first changing its culture.

Goals as a Function of Subordinate Performance

To some extent, the rater's goals will be driven by the climate and culture that pervades the organization, as well as by the formal demands of the PA system. However, it is unlikely that a given rater pursues the same set of goals when evaluating each of his or her subordinates. Rather, there are likely to be very different goals when evaluating a chronically poor performer than when evaluating someone whose work is usually excellent. In the case of poor performers, the rater's goals might be to improve the performance, to improve the chances that the worker will be transferred to some other work unit, or to justify a decision to discipline or dismiss the worker. The choice among goals such as these may depend in part on the extent to which the workgroup accepts the evaluation and supports the impending action. In the case of good performers, the rater's goals will probably center on maintaining current performance; giving ratings that lead to raises, bonuses, or awards might be one mechanism for accomplishing this goal.

Although goals will be somewhat tailored to the subordinate, it is important to note that some goals are probably relevant to *all* subordinates (e.g., the goal of maintaining a positive workgroup climate) and probably do not vary as a function of the subordinate's performance level. The goals that are most likely to vary as a function of the ratee's performance are those in the categories we have labeled "task performance" and "strategic" goals.

Before discussing the specific goals that are pursued for good versus poor performers, it is useful to discuss a related but somewhat more complex distinction among the individuals who report to a given supervisor. That is, the members of the workgroup can often be divided into two categories: those in the in-group and those in the out-group. Raters probably pursue different goals when evaluating members of these two groups.

In-Group versus Out-Group

Supervisors do not treat all subordinates the same nor should they. One theory of leadership, the Vertical Dyadic Linkage (VDL) theory (Dansereau, Cashman, & Graen, 1973), suggests that each supervisor-subordinate dyad may involve a somewhat different style of interaction. However, the theory also suggests that dyads can be classified into those involving members of the in-group and members of the out-group.

Members of the in-group are chosen on the basis of (1) competence and skill, (2) the degree to which they can be trusted by the supervisor, and (3) their motivation to assume responsibility at work (Liden & Graen, 1980). In-group members perform the tasks that are most critical and challenging, whereas out-group members perform more mundane tasks. Furthermore, members of the in-group receive more information as well as more confidence and concern from supervisors than do those in the out-group (Dansereau, Graen, & Haga, 1975).

One way to characterize the difference between the in-group and the out-group is that in-group members are treated by supervisors as trusted assistants, whereas out-group members are treated as hired hands (Vecchio & Gobdel, 1984). That is, in-group members are treated as valued colleagues; out-group members are treated as if they are temporary employees who are not really the concern of the supervisor. Supervisors typically devote more attention, resources, and so on to in-group members, even though out-group members might have a greater need for assistance, information, and the like to perform their jobs.

Research on the VDL model suggests that supervisors adopt very different leadership styles when dealing with members of the in- versus the out-group (Dansereau et al., 1975). In general, supervisors are more participative when dealing with in-group members, and more directive or authoritarian when dealing with out-group members. In the context of performance appraisal, this suggests that supervisors will more readily incorporate information from in-group members in their evaluations, and will usually devote more time and effort to feedback for in-group as opposed to out-group members.

Research on in- versus out-groups has dealt with several issues that are directly relevant to performance appraisal. First, and most fascinating, there is evidence that in-group status is related to subjective ratings of performance but *not* to objective indices of performance (Vecchio & Gobdel, 1984). This implies that the perceived competence of in-group members may be an effect rather than the cause of their assignment to the in-group. It is possible that supervisors who feel that they can trust certain subordinates will perceive their performance as better than it actually is.

A second relevant finding is that out-group members typically receive more extreme evaluations than do in-group members (Linville & Jones, 1980). These evaluations are usually negative but the out-group member who actually does perform well may receive highly inflated ratings. One possible explanation for this effect is the fact that out-group members are expected to perform poorly. Performance that violates those expectations may attract more attention than performance that conforms to expectations (Hastie, 1980; Murphy, Balzer, Lockhart, & Eisenman, 1985).

Another finding in this research is that out-groups are seen as relatively homogeneous, whereas differences between in-group members are readily noticed by supervisors (Park & Rothbart, 1982). As a result, all out-group members may receive similar evaluations; stereotypes of the group as a whole may generalize to all group members. One implication of this finding is that performance evaluations may not provide feedback that is useful to out-group members; this feedback may reflect the group and may not be tailored to specific individuals in the group. Another implication is that there will often be range restriction in ratings of out-group members. Thus, raters who have small in-groups and large out-groups may be especially likely to provide ratings that do not discriminate among most subordinates.

The terms *in-group* and *out-group* are not synonymous with *good performer* and *poor performer*. Nevertheless, research on in- versus out-group status may be useful in forming hypotheses about the goals that raters are likely to have when rating subordinates who have performed well or poorly. In particular, this literature suggests that good and poor performers may differ not only in the ratings they receive but also in terms how they are treated by supervisors in the appraisal process (e.g., the degree to which developmental feedback is given). In particular, there might be substantial differences in the goals being pursued by the rater when the ratee is a good, average, or poor performer.

Goals for Superior Performers

As will be discussed in the next chapter, rating inflation is the norm in most organizations rather than the exception. One implication is that raters might find it difficult to give ratings to truly good performers that adequately reflect their actual performance level. If nearly everyone receives ratings at or near the top end of the scale, numerical ratings cannot be used to communicate to the ratee that he or she has really performed well. Thus, one goal that will often be relevant to the rater when evaluating a truly good performer will be to communicate to the ratee and the organization the fact that this individual's performance is in fact better than that of others who have received high ratings.

Raters may address this problem by developing a special vocabulary (Bjerke et al., 1987) or communication rules (Schall, 1983) that allow them to give ratings that are acceptable to all subordinates (in practice, this usually means giving inflated ratings to most ratees) and still communicate their evaluations of their subordinates. For example, a subordinate might receive a rating of 6 on a 7-point scale and may be described as "somewhat above average" in the narrative or comment section of the appraisal. However, a phrase such as "somewhat above average" might connote poor performance; phrases such as "excellent in all respects of the job" might be used to signal performance that is *actually* above average.

This process of developing special communication rules is especially likely to occur in organizations that have a strong and uniform culture. In such organizations, supervisors are probably well aware of what aspects of the job are treated as important, and are probably also aware of the special meanings that are given to specific evaluative terms in that organization. This phenomenon is familiar to anyone who must read large numbers of letters of recommendation in which comments tend to be uniformly positive. Special terms are sometimes needed to convey that a particular individual really *is* a superior candidate.

A second goal that is highly relevant when evaluating good performers is to guide their development in such a way that they will be prepared for promotion or complex assignments. The supervisor might accomplish this, for example, by giving feedback on aspects of performance that are not relevant for the subordinate's current job but that are highly relevant for the next higher job in the organization. The popular literature contains many descriptions of *mentoring;* this approach to PA may correspond closely to one of the roles of a mentor.

One strategic goal that might be pursued is to bring higher management's attention to the accomplishments of superior performers. Exceptional performance by subordinates is likely to enhance a supervisor's standing, this is particularly true in organizations where the evaluation of the supervisor depends in part on the performance of the subordinates. We expect that the probability that this goal will affect rater behavior will be positively correlated with the subordinate's performance level. The better the subordinate's performance, the more the supervisor has to gain by bringing that performance to the attention of others in the organization.

Goals for Average Performers

It is reasonable to assume that in a large workgroup the true distribution of job performance is reasonably normal. One implication is that the number of truly good or truly poor performers will be small relative to the number of individuals whose performance can best be described as average. Although average performers are the most numerous, we believe that raters do not pay a great deal of attention to their goals for evaluating average performers. There are several reasons for this. First, good performers are probably in the in-group and will therefore naturally receive much of the rater's attention and concern. Second, poor performers require attention; their low level of performance can directly affect the overall output of the workgroup, particularly if the work performed requires a high level of interdependence. Third, average performance is probably not as salient (or interesting) as either outstandingly good or outstandingly poor performance. As a result, average performers may not receive the attention they deserve.

There are a few goals that might become relevant for average performers, depending on the characteristics of both the person and the situation. First, there might be some individuals who, because of their trustworthiness and responsibility, would be good candidates for the in-group. The rater's goal when evaluating these individuals might be to improve their performance and bring it up to the level of other in-group members. Second, the rater might have a strong incentive to help improve the performance of individuals who are members of specific groups. For example, the supervisor whose values encourage affirmative action efforts might devote considerable time and attention to the development of members of protected groups whose performance is at or below the workgroup's average. On the other hand, the supervisor who is prejudiced against members of specific groups might be inclined to give them harsh ratings; the underlying goal may be to remove these individuals from the workgroup.

Goals for Poor Performers

The literature dealing with supervisors' reactions to poor performance is extensive. Although relatively few studies deal directly with performance appraisal, several conclusions can be drawn about the appraisal goals that might be pursued when evaluating poor performers.

It is clear that managers prefer to avoid dealing with the problem of poor performance (Mitchell & O'Reilly, 1983). In the context of appraisal, raters might avoid the problem by giving relatively high ratings, accompanied by vague and noncommittal comments. In this case, feedback is likely to be perfunctory, and little effort will be expended to improve the subordinate's performance. In many cases, however, it may be impossible to ignore poor performance, either because it is extremely bad or because there are situational factors (e.g., co-workers' resentment) that force the rater to attend to the problem of poor performance.

The rater's reaction to a poor-performing subordinate probably depends on the attributions he or she makes when deciding about the cause of that performance (Mitchell & O'Reilly, 1983). Mitchell, Green, and Wood (1981) described several different categories of attribution, including those that explain poor performance in terms of a lack of ability, a lack of values and standards, an unfavorable environment, or a variety of temporary barriers to performance (e.g., family crises). These specific categories of attributions can in turn be classified in terms of two dimensions that are frequently encountered in attributional research: (1) attributions to internal versus external causes and (2) attributions to stable versus temporary causes. The supervisor's response may be very different, depending on the type of attribution.

Attributions depend on a number of factors, including the behavior itself, and the values, standards, and inclinations of the supervisor (e.g., some supervisors make more internal attributions than others). Another factor that appears to influence the supervisor's attributions is the outcome of the behavior. The same behavior might be evaluated differently, and different causes might be cited for that behavior, depending on the seriousness of the outcomes of that behavior. For example, if two subordinates follow the exact same unsafe work practices and one of them causes or experiences an accident, they will probably be evaluated differently, with harsher evaluations for the person involved in the accident.

Research on attributions suggests systematic differences in the supervisors' versus subordinates' explanations for poor performance. In general, supervisors make more internal attributions (e.g., the person did not perform well because of poor work values), whereas subordinates are biased in favor of external attributions (e.g., constraints in the situation made it impossible to perform well) (Gioia & Sims, 1985; Ilgen, Mitchell, & Frederickson, 1981). The tendency of supervisors to make internal attributions increases the likelihood that their responses will involve discipline or punishment for the poor-performing subordinate.

Arvey and Jones (1985) note that the topic of discipline or punishment in organizational settings has been largely ignored by behavioral scientists. Studies that have examined punishment suggest that performance appraisal is sometimes used as a vehicle for administering discipline. For example, Jones, Tait, and Butler (1983) studied the degree to which different supervisory behaviors were perceived by subordinates as punishing. Behaviors that were cited as being very punishing included (1) telling a superior about a person's mistakes, (2) documenting the negative things the person does, and (3) publicly praising everyone in the group but that person. These and other punishing behaviors may be used differently in in-groups and out-groups (Arvey & Jones, 1985); in general, the frequency and severity of punishment will be lower in the in-group.

If the attribution is external, the supervisor may avoid punishing the subordinate. Task performance goals for poor-performing subordinates (assuming that the attributions are external) will probably involve efforts to develop the subordinate, to maintain or increase motivation, and to move the subordinate to circumstances that are more favorable (e.g., a less difficult assignment or a different, more supportive workgroup). The rater who intends to develop a poor-performing subordinate will probably (1) give higher ratings than deserved, in an effort to avoid organizational sanctions and maintain motivation; (2) devote more attention to feedback; and (3) identify weaknesses in feedback sessions, but not in the performance evaluation forms that are turned in to the organization.

When attributions are internal, strategic goals that involve getting rid of the poor-performing subordinate may strongly influence rating behavior. This will depend in part on how bad the performance really is. The worse the performance, the stronger the incentive to get rid of the subordinate. The strength of this goal may also depend on what specific aspects of performance are below standard. For example, supervisors might be more strongly inclined to get rid of subordinates whose poor performance reflects an inability to get along with co-workers than those whose performance reflects sincere effort but low ability. In general, performance deficiencies that may affect other co-workers may present a stronger incentive to get rid of the subordinate than will deficiencies that involve the individual only.

The exact rating strategy for accomplishing the goals described above will depend in part on the policies of the organization. For example, if the organization is very reluctant to fire poor performers, it may not be a good idea to give low ratings. If the subordinate consistently receives low ratings, it may be very difficult to persuade the organization to transfer him or her to another workgroup. The attractiveness of "dumping" a poor-performing subordinate on another workgroup will vary as a function of the nature and size of the organization. In a small organization, supervisors are more likely to know one another and to be friends. It may be very difficult, in this case, to transfer a poor-performing subordinate to someone else's workgroup without negatively affecting the relationship with that supervisor.

Rater Goals and Organizational Goals

It would be naive to expect that the goals pursued by the rater in performance appraisal are identical to those the organization wants him or her to pursue (Balzer & Sulsky, in press). However, it is also unrealistic to assume that the goals of the rater are completely inconsistent with those of the organization, even when the rater's behavior violates the organization's official policy. The personnel manual may state that accurate performance appraisals are expected, but if this will lead to friction, decreased motivation, and so on, the supervisor who skillfully inflates his or her ratings is acting in the organization's best interest. It is important to keep in mind that when organizational control systems such as PA make unrealistic demands or lead to unforseen, undesirable consequences, managers who subvert the system may contribute more to the organization than do managers who are faithful to the system.

One reason that rater goals are not always consistent with organizational goals is that the goals of the organization are not always themselves internally consistent. Organizations pursue a wide range of goals in several different areas, ranging from the highly general (e.g., profitability) to the highly specific (e.g., improve market share for a specific product) goals. Furthermore, some goals are explicitly stated, whereas others are implicit and are communicated to organization members through the culture of the organization. Cleveland and colleagues (1989) noted that the explicit goals of PA (e.g., distinguish between good and poor performers, provide valid feedback) are sometimes mutually incompatible. When implicit goals, such as maintaining a positive workgroup climate, are added in, it may be impossible to satisfy all goals.

Assume for the moment that there are no inconsistencies in the goals of the organization. In this case, it might be possible for the rater's goals to match closely the goals of the organization. This match is most likely when the rater is socialized to the extent that he or she internalizes the goals of the organization. At least one organization we have consulted with uses "extent to which individual accepts the values of the organization" as a dimension for assessing its managers. If value congruence leads to goal congruence in performance, there may be some utility to including values in the assessment program. We should note, however, that empirical evidence for the validity or relevance of ratings of this dimension is lacking.

Our discussion of goal conflicts points to two pressing research needs. First, more research is needed in describing the range and the content of the goals pursued by raters. The typology we have offered here is a first step in that direction but it is based on speculation rather than on data. Second, more knowledge about how raters deal with goal conflicts is needed. We believe that conflicts between the goals of the organization and those of the rater, as well as conflicts among the various goals pursued by the organization and the rater are the norm rather than the exception. We have reviewed some fairly limited data suggesting that raters choose one goal as primary and ignore the rest, but we do not know whether this always occurs, how raters make the choice, or whether those choices can be reversed. We regard the area of rater goals as a critical focus for future PA research.

Summary

Performance appraisal researchers rarely take the rater's perspective in analyzing performance appraisal processes and outcomes. Thus, when ratings fail to correspond with other performance measures or with reasonable assumptions about ratees' performance levels, this lack of correspondence is taken as evidence of rater errors or problems in the appraisal system. This diagnosis makes sense if the rater is treated as a passive measurement instrument, but makes much less sense when appraisal is treated as goal-directed behavior. Simply put, raters may distort their appraisals as a way to help achieve a variety of important goals.

It is useful to consider several classes of goals, including task performance goals, interpersonal goals, strategic goals, and internalized goals. Goals in each of these four categories may vary systematically as a function of the ratee's performance level.

Research on the development and application of rater goals represents several challenges. First, raters may not always be aware of the goals they are pursuing. Second, they may not be willing to admit that they are pursuing some goals (e.g., using performance appraisal to get rid of a poor performer). However, judgment research in several other areas (e.g., work motivation) has dealt successfully with similar constraints. Given the potential payoff of research on rater goals, the effort needed to mount a program of research is clearly worthwhile.

Chapter Nine

Rater Motivation

► One of the most frequent complaints regarding ratings is that they are inflated (Ilgen & Feldman, 1983; Landy & Farr, 1983; Longenecker, Sims, & Gioia, 1987). It is not unusual for the great majority of all employees to receive extremely high ratings. For example, when ratings are done on a 7-point scale, 80% of all ratings are often 6 or 7. This is particularly true in the military (Bjerk Cleveland, Morrison, & Wilson, 1987) but is also true in both the public and private sectors. Rating inflation of this sort is typically treated as evidence of rampant rater errors or of a breakdown in the performance appraisal (PA) system (Saal, Downey, & Lahey, 1980). The typical treatment for rating inflation is some adjustment in the scale format or perhaps a new training program for raters.

There is an alternative explanation for rating inflation that would have very different implications for both research and practice. It may be that the tendency to give uniformly high ratings is an instance of adaptive behavior that is, from the rater's point of view, an eminently logical course of action. That is, it may make no sense for the rater to give low ratings, except in extreme circumstances. It may make perfect sense to give high ratings, *regardless of the true performance levels of one's subordinates.*

This chapter considers the implications, for the rater, of giving high or low performance ratings, and seeks to explain rating inflation in terms of the rater's rational pursuit of sensible goals rather than explaining this phenomenon in terms of errors and mistakes. There are several facets of the rating context that may motivate raters to inflate their ratings. In order to obtain accurate ratings, the organization may have to structure the rating environment to provide raters with rewards for accurate rating.

The Psychology of Leniency

As will be discussed in Chapter Ten, research on performance appraisal is often characterized by the assumption that the rater is trying his or her best to evaluate performance accurately and just is not doing it very well. We believe that it is more reasonable to assume that raters are indeed capable of accurately evaluating performance, and that deficiencies in ratings are more likely to be a result of the rater's *willingness* to provide accurate ratings than of his or her *capacity* to rate accurately (Banks & Murphy, 1985). If the situation is examined from the rater's perspective, there are many sound reasons to provide inaccurate (typically, inflated) ratings. More important, there are surprisingly few good reasons for most raters to give accurate ratings. Thus, leniency may not be an error but rather a behavior that allows the rater to obtain rewards and avoid punishments.

Figure 9-1 illustrates the model we use to try and understand the forces that motivate a rater to provide ratings that are either an accurate reflection of his or her evaluation of each subordinate (see Chapter Seven) or that are distorted (i.e., inflated) and inaccurate. This motivational model is certainly not new (see DeCotiis & Petit, 1978; Mohrman & Lawler, 1983) but it does offer a different perspective than that which appears to dominate current PA research. The specific components of this model are discussed below.

Figure 9–1. **Model of Motivation to Provide Accurate versus Distorted Ratings**

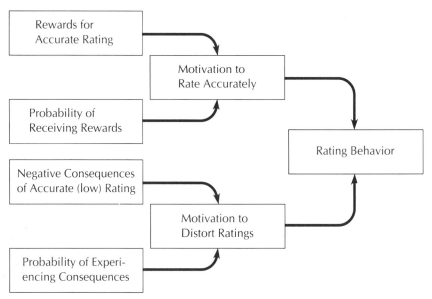

Rewards for Accurate Rating

The first question that needs to be addressed is why raters *should* devote the time and energy (and possibly suffer the negative consequences) needed to evaluate performance accurately. From an expectancy theory perspective, it might be predicted that raters will be motivated to rate accurately when (1) valued rewards are available for accuracy in rating and (2) the likelihood of acheiving those rewards is connected to the accuracy of the ratings given (Mohrman & Lawler, 1983).

Availability of Valued Rewards In most organizations, valued rewards are not available, at least with regard to extrinsic rewards such as pay or promotions. That is, there are typically no rewards from the organization for doing accurate appraisals and few if any sanctions for inaccurate appraisals (Carroll & Schneier, 1982; Naiper & Latham, 1986). Indeed, organizations seem to send mixed messages to raters regarding the value of the whole enterprise. Official company statements frequently stress the value of good performance appraisals but organizations typically take no concrete steps to reward this supposedly valued outcome. We know of no organizations that include the rater's accuracy as an evaluator of ratee performance as a part of *his or her* PA. A manager might infer that most organizations do not really care about the quality of PA data. If the organization is unwilling to reward good appraisers and sanction poor ones, we would argue that this inference is correct, regardless of the stated policy of the organization.

Even when the principal duties of a manager center around appraisal, as might be the case for an interviewer or a manager who is part of an assessment center staff, we know of no instances where raters are rewarded for accuracy or punished for inaccuracy. For most managers, performance appraisal represents an infrequent and unimportant activity. If the organization's willingness to provide rewards is taken as an indicator, we would conclude that most organizations feel exactly the same way.

Rewards Following Accurate Appraisal Suppose an organization sets aside a portion of each year's salary increase budget to reward accurate appraisers. The rater might still doubt that rewards will follow if he or she turns in accurate appraisals. There are two issues here — a criterion problem and a problem involving trust in the system.

It is a common finding that both raters and ratees distrust the organization's PA system (Bernardin & Beatty, 1984; Bernardin & Cardy, 1985). Ratees do not believe that providing accurate appraisals will be beneficial. Unfortunately, distrust of the PA system probably implies distrust for the reward system that is associated with the quality of one's performance appraisals. That is, raters who do not trust the system may not believe that promised rewards will follow desired behaviors.

When the problems in evaluating the accuracy of ratings are considered, a lack of trust might be well founded. As we will document more thoroughly in Chapter Ten, it is very difficult to measure the accuracy of the ratings that are given by a single rater. For example, suppose an evaluator rates 80% of his or her employees as "excellent." How does the organization determine whether the rater is providing accurate or inflated ratings? The people who receive high ratings may very well be excellent workers. On the other hand, the evaluator might be unduly lenient.

A manager has every right to feel that he or she is placed in a dilemma by efforts to reward accurate ratings, especially if accuracy is defined in terms of someone's preconceived notions regarding the true distribution of performance. We will develop our arguments more fully in the next chapter. It is sufficient here to note that there is no simple solution to the criterion problem in most organizations. It may be impossible for the organization to sort accurate from inaccurate raters; thus, efforts to reward good raters may be doomed. Later in this chapter, we will suggest some ways that organizations could approach the problem of rewarding good performance appraisals, but it is important to note that the problem of identifying good and poor raters is a formidable one, and raters may be right in distrusting the system.

Certain versus Uncertain Outcomes   Accurate performance appraisal presumably leads to some rewards and some costs (e.g., negative reactions from subordinates who receive low ratings). Many of the costs, or negative states, associated with accurate appraisals are reasonably certain. That is, if a rater gives ratings that cost a subordinate a promotion, an unpleasant work situation is almost certain to ensue. Rewards, on the other hand, are quite uncertain. Unless the rater believes that the organization can identify accurate and inaccurate raters, and is willing to provide rewards to those who evaluate performance accurately, the instrumentality of accurate ratings for achieving those rewards will always be less than perfect. Accurate PA may therefore be a behavior that carries certain costs and uncertain rewards. Unfortunately, this asymmetry in the certainty of costs and benefits could pose a serious barrier to achieving accurate appraisals.

Prospect theory (Kahneman & Tversky, 1979) provides a powerful tool for analyzing the effects of perceived costs and benefits on judgment and behavior. The theory suggests that (1) people undervalue gains and overvalue losses and (2) certain gains and losses receive more extreme values than corresponding uncertain gains and losses. Thus, a loss of $10 is more negative than a gain of $10 is positive; a certain loss of $10 is worse than a 50% chance of losing $20. This theory suggests that if rewards and costs were of objectively equal value, raters would *not* choose to provide accurate appraisals. In order to balance costs that are certain to be incurred, the rater must believe that the probable rewards are considerably more valuable than the certain costs. Since rewards are typically meager, if they exist at all, this condition may be only rarely met in organizations.

Negative Consequences of Accurate Rating ───────────

It is important to keep in mind that the specific problem most often cited in ratings is inflation. That is, if ratings were accurate, the ratings received by most or all individuals would typically be lower. There are several reasons why a rater might and should be reluctant to give lower ratings. We have grouped these reasons into four categories: (1) consequences for the ratee, (2) consequences for the rater, (3) avoidance of negative reactions, and (4) maintaining the organization's image.

Consequences for the Ratee The most common reason cited for rating inflation is that high ratings are needed to guarantee promotions, salary increases, prestigious assignments, and other valued rewards (Lawler, 1976). Low ratings, on the other hand, will result in these rewards being withheld from subordinates. McCall and DeVries (1977) suggest that the availability of resources affects rating inflation, in that inflation is most likely to occur when the supply of promotions, salary increases, and so on is either abundant or very restricted. When there are many resources available in the organization, the rater will be motivated to see that his or her subordinates receive their fair share. When resources are scarce, raters might be motivated to hoard them. In this context, this would mean trying to obtain valued resources (e.g., promotions) for one's subordinates.

The issue of consequences for the ratee has been examined most thoroughly in the voluminous literature on the effects of the purpose of rating. A number of studies have shown that ratings collected for administrative purposes (e.g., salary administration) are significantly higher than ratings of the same individuals collected for other purposes, such as feedback or research (Bernardin, Orban, & Carlyle, 1981; Heron, 1956; Reilly & Balzer, 1988; Sharon & Bartlett, 1969; Taylor & Wherry, 1951; Williams, DeNisi, Blencoe, & Cafferty, 1985; Zedeck & Cascio, 1982).

Some studies suggest that different psychological processes may be involved when ratings are collected for different purposes (Murphy, Balzer, Kellam, & Armstrong, 1984; Reilly & Balzer, 1988). Other studies have failed to find a main effect for purpose (Berkshire & Highland, 1953; Borreson, 1967; Murphy et al., 1984), but the failure to find an effect may be due to low power or weak manipulations of the purpose variable (Reilly & Balzer, 1988). All in all, this literature suggests that raters who believe that ratings will have an impact on administrative decisions are more lenient that raters who think that ratings will not have any impact on salary, promotion, and the like.

The literature on the effects of the purpose of rating provides what we regard as strong evidence for the hypothesis that raters consciously distort their ratings when they think that ratings are tied to valued outcomes. Raters who provide ratings for feedback or research purposes seem to have no problem in distinguishing between good and bad performers. When ratings are not used for administrative decisions, inflation and range restriction are not serious problems. We believe that raters whose appraisals are used in making administrative decisions are just as capable of distinguishing good from poor performers but simply refuse to do so. Purpose of rating may not affect the *evaluation* of performance (Murphy et al., 1984) but it is likely to affect what is reported by the rater.

There is one interpretation of the difference between ratings for administrative decisions and ratings for research that does not depend on conscious distortion. It is possible that the purpose of rating affects the standards that are used to judge performance (Murphy et al., 1984; see also Chapter Seven). Thus, the same behavior might be evaluated favorably for one purpose (i.e., under one set of standards) and evaluated unfavorably for another. We do not know of any direct test of this hypothesis but it is an interesting one. Hypotheses about performance standards are quite difficult to test (Constans, 1987) but this hypothesis could explain a variety of phenomena, ranging from interrater disagreements (raters see the same behaviors but are applying different standards) to instability in ratings (the same rater applies different standards at different points in time).

Why should the rater care whether his or her subordinates receive valued rewards? We think there are two related reasons. First, raters are very concerned with establishing and maintaining high levels of motivation. Many raters believe that telling a poor worker that he or she is performing poorly will not be motivating and could discourage the poor performer (Longenecker et al., 1987). Negative ratings could represent a self-fulfilling prophecy, in that they discourage employees, who from then on perform at substandard levels.

Concerns over ratee motivation lead many raters to do two separate performance appraisals — a public appraisal that is turned in to the personnel department and a private, verbal appraisal that is shared with the worker during his or her appraisal interview (Longenecker et al., 1987; Mohrman & Lawler, 1983). The discrepancy between the written appraisal and the oral appraisal can itself be used as a motivational device. That is, the rater can inform the ratee that he or she knows about the ratee's poor performance but is still turning in good ratings. This may serve as an incentive or perhaps as a warning.

The second reason that raters should care whether ratees receive valued rewards is that raters and ratees have to work together. Raters often must maintain good interpersonal relations with subordinates to perform their jobs (McCall & DeVries, 1976), and even when good interpersonal relations are not required, raters are likely to strongly prefer a positive work atmosphere to a negative one. It is unlikely that relations will be good if the supervisor is seen as the reason why workers did not receive valued rewards (Smith, 1976).

From the rater's point of view, the ability to maintain positive interpersonal relationships with his or her subordinates might be viewed as much more important than turning in accurate performance appraisals. Poor performance appraisals, especially if the organization's norm is to turn in high ratings for everyone, will probably lead to resentment, which may in turn make it impossible for the subordinate and the supervisor to work together effectively.

The idea that raters will give high ratings to avoid bad interpersonal relations with ratees seems quite reasonable. However, Naiper and Latham (1986) note that there is little empirical evidence of raters showing concern over the aversive interpersonal consequences that accompany low ratings. This finding must be interpreted cautiously, since there might be a strong social desirability factor present in research that examines raters' concerns over ratees' reactions to performance appraisals. A rater might be unwilling to admit that he or she is worried about the resentment that is likely to accompany low ratings that result in the loss of desirable outcomes such as raises or promotions. Nevertheless, their criticism must be taken seriously.

Consequences for the Rater   The second reason that raters may be motivated to give inflated ratings is that the ratings received by subordinates say something about the *rater's* job performance. One of the duties of a manager is to develop his or her subordinates and to get the best performance possible out of them. If a manager consistently rates his or her subordinates as poor performers, it will eventually appear as if the manager is not doing his or her job. This is particularly true in organizations where the manager's peers routinely turn in high ratings. Thus, the simplest explanation for rating inflation may be that high ratings make the rater look good and low ratings make the rater look bad.

There are some reasons to believe that accuracy in rating is in fact tied to the rater's true level of performance. Landy and Farr (1983) note that studies in the 1950s and 1960s indicated that better performers gave more accurate ratings. Since inaccuracy is not random but rather is manifest in the form of rating inflation, this line of research implies that the correlation between the rater's level of performance and the ratings he or she gives should be negative. That is, the better the rater, the higher the likelihood of low ratings. High ratings may be a signal that the rater wants to *look* good; low ratings may be a signal that the rater *is* good.

The rewards a manager receives are sometimes tied to the performance of his or her workgroup. Ilgen, Mitchell, and Frederickson (1981) showed that when supervisors' rewards are tied to the performance of subordinates, rating inflation occurs. One interpretation of this finding is that raters intentionally distort their ratings to maximize their own rewards. Evidence of intentional distortion is hard to come by, although anecdotal evidence has been collected (Longenecker et al., 1987). More information is needed about the contingencies raters perceive between the ratings they give and the rewards they receive. If raters believe that there is a strong link, this might motivate them to inflate their ratings.

Even if ratings are not tied to the rewards received by the rater, there is still a strong possibility that self-interest will lead to rating inflation. Longenecker and associates (1987) note that raters show little concern over whether their ratings are accurate but are greatly concerned about the consequences of the ratings they give for the future performance of their subordinates. That is, raters consider whether a high or low rating will be more effective in increasing the subordinate's future level of performance. They must also consider whether a high or a low rating will make it easier for them to perform *their* jobs in the future. It may be very reasonable to conclude that high ratings do more to facilitate future performance and low ratings only complicate the rater's life. It may make more sense, from the raters point of view, to give the ratings that will do the most good for the workgroup's future effectiveness (i.e., high ratings) than to give accurate ratings that only interfere with the smooth functioning of the group.

Research on self-serving biases in attribution (Gioia & Sims, 1985; Mitchell, Green, & Wood, 1981; Miller & Ross, 1975) suggests another mechanism for explaining rating inflation. It is well known that individuals attribute their own successes to internal factors (e.g., ability, effort) and their own failures to external causes (e.g., situational constraints). However, individuals attribute *others'* successes to external causes (e.g., luck, superior resources available to others) and others' failures to internal causes (e.g., they didn't work hard enough). In the case of performance appraisal, the supervisor may see himself or herself as an important external cause of subordinates' success. Therefore, if subordinates are evaluated as successful, the manager may attribute that success to his or her own ability as a manager, in effect taking credit for subordinates' performance. Note that this explanation probably operates at the unconscious level rather than involving conscious distortion. That is, it is unlikely that raters (1) know their subordinates are performing poorly, (2) consciously distort their ratings upward, and (3) take credit for the success of their employees.

Another possible explanation for unconscious distortion comes from research that shows that raters tend to view subordinates as more similar to themselves than they actually are (Rand & Wexley, 1975). Since most individuals attempt to retain positive self-images, it follows that the supervisor who sees similarities between subordinates and himself or herself will tend to rate subordinates favorably. Raters who commit the similar-to-me error (Rand & Wexley, 1975) will probably also inflate their ratings.

One final way in which self-interest can lead raters to inflate their ratings is through peer pressure. In an organization where the norm is to give high ratings, the rater who defies the norm might experience disapproval from his or her peers. There is a long history of research on the effects of peer pressure on the performance levels of workers (Sherif & Sherif, 1969, review this research, much of which was carried out prior to 1960); the same phenomenon is probably present in management. Shop-floor workers put a great deal of pressure on "rate busters," whose level of performance makes them look bad. Managers probably react in exactly the same way when another rater makes them look bad. Pressures for conformity may be a significant factor in rating inflation.

Avoidance of Negative Reactions   Another reason why raters might tend to inflate their ratings is that they wish to avoid the negative reactions that accompany low ratings (Latham, 1986). This phenomenon is particularly relevant in understanding the performance feedback process. Negative feedback typically results in defensive reactions from ratees (Kay, Meyer, & French, 1965), which can create a very stressful situation for the rater. The simplest way to avoid unpleasant or defensive reactions in appraisal interviews is to give uniformly positive feedback (i.e., give inflated ratings). There is evidence that raters do indeed inflate their ratings when they believe they will be required to provide face-to-face feedback (Landy & Farr, 1983).

Both supervisors and subordinates dislike giving and receiving feedback (Fisher, 1974). In part, this may be due to the expectation on the part of both the rater and the ratee that subordinates will not be satisfied with the feedback they receive. Earlier, we noted that self-appraisals tend to be more favorable than appraisals from others (see Chapter Five), and suggested attributional mechanisms that would account for this effect (i.e., self-serving biases in attribution). As a result, the rater's own inflated rating might not be as favorable as the ratee's self-evaluation. There are some reasons to believe that poor performers evaluate their own performance less accurately than good performers (Mitchell et al., 1981). If this is true, it may also mean that truly poor performers are the most likely to be dissatisfied with the feedback they receive. Evidence from several studies suggests that the favorability of the PA is one of the major determinants of ratees' reactions to the rating process (Dipboye & dePontbriand, 1981; Landy, Barnes, & Murphy, 1978; Landy, Barnes-Farrell, & Cleveland, 1979).

There several aspects of the rating process that, independent of the rating level, may influence subordinates' reactions to performance feedback. Performance feedback is most likely to be accepted by the ratee when:

1. Appraisals are frequent.
2. There is widespread agreement concerning job duties.
3. Feedback from any given source is consistent with feedback from other sources.
4. There is widespread agreement regarding what constitutes good and poor performance (Ilgen, Fisher, & Taylor, 1979; Landy et al., 1978; Landy et al., 1979).

It may be that when these conditions are met, negative feedback does not provoke a negative reaction. Greenberg (1986) notes that performance feedback is more likely to be accepted when the requirements of procedural justice are fulfilled (i.e., when procedures that appear reasonable and fair to *ratees* are followed). We suspect that the conditions specified above are typically *not* met in organizations. Therefore, a rater who gives low ratings might quite rightly be concerned over how feedback based on those ratings will be received.

Feedback acceptance may be important to the rater, even if feedback results in no behavior change. When the rater *does* give negative feedback, he or she runs the risk that it will be discounted or ignored by the ratee. In this case, the rater is likely to encounter all of the negative facets of giving low ratings and will not experience any benefits. Thus, the rater who believes that poor feedback will not be accepted may be likely to avoid giving poor feedback (i.e., to inflate the ratings).

Maintaining the Organization's Image Our final explanation for rating inflation is one that does not assume any conscious distortion of ratings but rather involves the inferential processes that are used to process information about job performance (see Chapters Five through Seven). We assume that many, if not most, raters have a reasonably positive image of the organization in which they work. That is, it is reasonable to assume that most managers think of their company as one that employs good people and that does a good job producing the goods and services the company provides. The mere fact that an individual is a member of the organization therefore conveys some information (probably favorable) about the person's performance. The fact that an individual has been able to get and keep a job in that organization may be used to infer that he or she must be a good worker (Ilgen & Feldman, 1983). The longer an individual stays with an organization and the higher he or she rises in the ranks, the more likely this effect.

The image of an organization is not necessarily uniform throughout the organization. Some parts of any organization are likely to be perceived as high-status areas that have high standards, whereas other parts of the organization are regarded as the dumping ground for substandard employees. If the image of each part of the organization influences evaluations, one might expect more rating inflation in high-status areas and more accurate appraisals in low-status areas. There is anecdotal evidence that this in fact occurs.

Bjerke and colleagues (1987) noted that high-status combat communities in the navy (e.g., nuclear submarine community) were more likely to suffer from rating inflation than were low-status support communities (e.g., supply and tanker fleets). In the high-status community, the mere fact that an individual is a member of the community is enough to justify ratings of "excellent" on many dimensions. We do not know of any research on this phenomenon in the private sector but we would make two predictions. First, mean rating in each department of an organization should be correlated with that department's position in the status hierarchy. Second, the variance of the mean ratings calculated for each department in an organization should be positively correlated with the status differentiation within that organization. If some departments are very high in status and others are very low, we would expect that the average rating in the low-status area will be much lower than the average rating in the high-status area. In some high-technology firms, there appears to be little differentiation in the status of different levels or functions in the organization. In those organizations, the mean rating is probably similar in all departments.

A person's reputation as a good or poor performer is one source of information that might be used in evaluating his or her performance (see Chapter Five). We suspect that the inferential process that is involved in evaluating an individual who has a reputation as a good or poor performer is similar to the inferential process involved when evaluating a person who works in an area where most workers are thought to be superior performers. In both cases, the reputation is a source of a prior hypothesis about the person's performance, and information about his or her behavior provides data that may be used to revise that hypothesis (Murphy, Balzer, Lockhart, & Eisenman, 1985). The effect of an individual's reputation are probably stronger than the effects of an organization's or a department's reputation, but in either case the ratings will probably be inflated when the reputation is a particularly good one.

A Framework for Research on Rating Inflation

We have suggested several reasons why raters might be motivated to inflate their ratings. However, it is important to realize that not all raters inflate their ratings. Among those who turn in inflated ratings, there is substantial variability in the extent to which ratings are inflated. In predicting who will inflate ratings and to what degree, we find a combination of ideas from expectancy theory and techniques derived from decision research especially useful. In particular, we think that Edwards's (1980) Multiattribute Utility Technology (MAUT) (see Edwards & Newman, 1982, for a review) provides a framework for organizing research on the psychological processes involved in rating inflation.

MAUT represents a tool that can be used to structure evaluations of alternate courses of action that may affect several valued outcomes or attributes. In the context of rating inflation, MAUT might be used to describe and study the processes of choosing between providing inflated ratings or providing accurate ratings. This technique can easily be applied to a wider range of courses of action (e.g., the rater might choose among different levels of rating inflation), but it can be best illustrated by examining the decision of whether or not to inflate one's ratings.

In its simplest form, MAUT can be described in terms of the following five steps

1. Identify the courses of action to be evaluated.
2. Determine the relevant attributes or value dimensions of the outcomes that may follow each action.
3. Determine the relative importance of each of the values.

4. Determine the probability that each course of action will result in valued outcomes.
5. Integrate importance measures from step 3 with value measures from step 4. (See Edwards & Newman, 1982, for a more complete description.)

The usual applications of MAUT are ones in which the values, importance weights, and so on are known and are integrated to recommend which of several courses of action should be followed. The same technology may be applied to predict which course of action the rater will follow, as we will illustrate below.

First, assume that the set of alternatives was limited to two — to inflate ratings or not to inflate ratings. The research reviewed above provides a starting point for the second step in the MAUT process, the specification of relevant valued outcomes. Table 9-1 summarizes the outcomes that have been cited in this chapter that might be affected by the decision to inflate or not inflate ratings. Note that these outcome states are arranged hierarchically, indicating that some outcomes represent combinations or effects of achieving lower-level outcomes. Note also that some of these outcomes are positively valued, whereas others have a negative value. Different courses of action have different probabilities of producing each outcome. Utility theory assumes that individuals choose the course of action that maximizes the likelihood of receiving positively valued outcomes and minimizes the probability of achieving negatively valued ones. (Expectancy theory makes the same assumption.)

To predict an individual's choice, we need to know (1) the perceived probability of each outcome for each course of action and (2) the value

Table 9–1. Valued Outcomes That Are Affected by Rating Inflation

Outcome	Value
1. Organizational rewards for accurate ratings	+
2. Ratees receive valued rewards	+
a. Good interpersonal relations maintained	+
b. Ratee motivation is maintained	+
3. Raters look good	+
a. Rater's performance evaluated positively	+
b. Rater's job is easier to do	+
c. Rater enhances self-image	+
d. Rater experiences peer pressure	−
4. Negative reactions from ratees	−
a. Defensive reaction to feedback	−
b. Feedback is not accepted	−
5. Organization's image is maintained	+

assigned to each outcome. The overall utility of each course of action is then determined by multiplying the probability estimates by the values, and summing over outcomes.

For example, assume that probability estimates and value judgments were obtained from two raters (the values are shown in Table 9-2). For the sake of simplicity, only the highest level of outcomes (outcomes 1-5) are listed. The values are scaled so that the probability of outcomes sums to 1.00. Values are scaled so that numerical ratings are proportional to the relative value of outcomes (e.g., value ratings of 40 and 20 would indicate that the first outcome is twice as valuable as the second), and the absolute values for the five outcomes sum to 100.

The values shown in Table 9-2 were used to compute the utility of each course of action for each rater. The outcomes of these calculations are shown in Figure 9-2. These figures indicate that for both raters, inflating ratings makes more sense than providing accurate ratings. That is, rating inflation is a course of action that maximizes rewards (positively valued outcomes) and minimizes punishments (negatively valued outcomes). However, the motivation to inflate ratings is stronger for rater B than for rater A, as is indicated by the difference in the utilities of the two courses of action considered by each rater. Thus, rating inflation could be predicted for both raters but the prediction is more likely for rater B.

It is instructive to describe why the utilities for the two raters differed. In part, this difference reflects a difference in values. Rater A attaches considerable value to the rewards that might be obtained for accurate ratings. He or she also

Table 9-2. Values and Probability Estimates for Two Raters

		Rater A		Rater B	
		p	v	p	v
Course of Action — Inflate Ratings					
Outcome:	1	.05	40	.10	10
	2	.65	10	.40	30
	3	.10	15	.25	10
	4	.05	25	.05	45
	5	.15	10	.10	5
Course of Action — Give Accurate Ratings					
Outcome:	1	.10	40	.10	10
	2	.05	10	.20	30
	3	.05	15	.05	10
	4	.70	25	.60	45
	5	.10	10	.05	5

p = probability of achieving outcome
v = value (absolute) of outcome

Figure 9–2.   Estimated Utility of Inflating Ratings for Two Raters

	Rater A	Rater B
Inflate Ratings	10.25	13.75
Give Accurate Ratings	−11.25	−19.25

To calculate the utility for Rater A of inflating ratings, use the following:
utility = $(.05 \times 40) + (.65 \times 10) + (.10 \times 15) - (.05 \times 25) + (.15 \times 10)$

Note that the fourth term is subtracted from the rest, indicating that the outcome (negative reactions from ratees) has a negative value.

places a strong value on avoiding negative reactions from ratees (remember that this attribute is a negatively valued one). Rater B also shows concern over negative reactions and he or she values the ability to secure rewards for subordinates. These raters not only differ in their values, they also differ in their beliefs about the strength of the links between rating inflation and valued outcomes. Rater A believes that the principal outcome of accurate ratings will be negative reactions from ratees (rater B also emphasizes this outcome). Rater B believes that rating inflation had a noticeable impact on evaluations of his or her own performance. If ratings are inflated, the probability of "looking good" is five times as great as will be acheived with accurate ratings. Thus, it might be inferred that rater B is more concerned than rater A with using ratings as a vehicle for impression management.

Our presentation has simplified many of the highly important technical issues that are dealt with by Edwards (1980) and has adjusted other concepts to fit the current problem of predicting and explaining rating inflation. Nevertheless, we think the MAUT framework provides a powerful tool for studying the problem. First, it directs attention to issues that have not been considered in depth in research on rating inflation, such as the attribute dimensions considered by individual raters, individual differences in values, and the origin and alteration of beliefs about the links between rating inflation and valued outcomes. Second, it provides a basis for describing the rater's approach to the rating task that we think may bring us much further than the approaches that have dominated the literature to date.

By eliciting the perceived probability of outcomes and the values of outcomes from raters, useful insights may be obtained about the rater's perception of the PA context. For example, it would be possible to develop a simple index of the degree to which the perceived probabilities of the set of relevant outcomes varies as a function of the course of action the rater follows (e.g., the squared distance between probabilities under accurate rating versus rating inflation would provide one index). We expect that some raters see strong links between their choice of a rating strategy and valued outcomes, whereas others do not. The stronger the perceived link between rating behavior and valued outcomes (i.e., the greater the change in outcome probabilities with different rating strategies), the stronger the motivation to distort ratings, assuming that distorted ratings have higher utility than accurate ones. Examining the values that the rater emphasizes might provide information about the goals the rater is pursuing in rating (see Chapter Eight for a discussion of rater goals). For example, the rater who places a high value on avoiding negative outcomes will be motivated to act differently than a rater who values the rewards the organization provides to accurate raters.

Mohrman and Lawler (1983) advocated applying expectancy theory to the problem of understanding rater motives. The MAUT approach provides a technology that will acheive that goal and may allow us to approach the problem of rating inflation from an entirely different angle. Rating inflation is often a highly rational course of action, from the point of view of the individual rater. The best hope for curing rating inflation may involve changing values and instrumentality beliefs rather than simply exhorting raters to avoid leniency.

Strategies for Reducing Rating Inflation

The first issue an organization should consider is whether it really *wants* to reduce rating inflation. We have discussed many of the negative outcomes that might be associated with giving accurate ratings. The organization should not take steps to reduce rating inflation unless the benefits outweigh the costs. In many situations, the benefits of accurate ratings might be minimal; assessment of the benefits of accuracy depends largely on the uses to which ratings are put (see Chapter Ten). For example, if the organization uses ratings to determine promotions, the most relevant criterion will be the extent to which ratings sort incumbents into two categories: promotable and nonpromotable. Accuracy beyond this gross sorting may be irrelevant to the organization's actions (Feldman, 1986).

Assuming that the organization *does* want accurate ratings and is willing to pay the costs that may be associated with accuracy, three issues need to be addressed:

1. Valued rewards must be tied to rating behavior.
2. Negatively valued outcomes of accuracy must be reduced.
3. Raters must see clear links between their rating behavior and valued outcomes.

These issues are discussed below. The chapter ends with a brief discussion of units of analysis involved in attempts to reduce rating inflation.

Rewarding Accuracy

Few organizations incorporate the ability to evaluate subordinates accurately as a criterion for evaluating the supervisor's performance. If an organization really cares about accuracy, it should be willing to provide substantial rewards for accuracy in rating. That is, salary increases, promotions, assignment to choice positions, and so on should depend partly on the manager's ability to evaluate subordinates' performance accurately.

The key issue in any system that attempts to reward PA accuracy is the same criterion problem that has plagued PA research. At present, there are few measures that can be applied in organizations that convincingly indicate accuracy in rating. (See Chapter Ten for a detailed critique of existing measures.) One practical approach we can recommend is to evaluate ratings in terms of the procedures followed by the rater. Does the rater have access to relevant information about the ratee's performance, and is there evidence that he or she has made efforts to obtain that information? Has the rater collected careful records of relevant observations? Has the rater been adequately trained, and has there been any meaningful followup to determine the transfer of training? The more closely the rater's strategy for evaluating performance corresponds to procedures that are likely to produce accurate ratings, the higher the likelihood that ratings will be accurate.

Another approach for evaluating raters is a variant of the approach one might take to assess the construct validity of ratings (see Chapter Ten). The performance of individual workers should have implications for a variety of nonjudgmental indices of the group's performance and productivity. For example, one would suspect inaccuracy if all workers were rated high, but the group's productivity was lower than that of comparable groups in the organization. If ratees receive high marks for dimensions such as "time management," there should be few instances of products or reports that are turned in late, there should be little use of overtime, and there should be few complaints about the timeliness of workers in performing their tasks.

The assessment of accuracy will be easiest when the organization can identify specific outcomes that should follow as the result of good or poor performance in specific aspects of subordinates' jobs. If the actual outcomes correspond closely to those that would be expected on the basis of the ratings, this is one piece of evidence that the ratings are accurate. If expected and actual outcomes differ, this might be evidence of inaccuracy. If rating inflation is indeed present, actual outcomes can be expected to be less favorable than those predicted on the basis of the ratings.

Research on scale development suggests that one of the principal benefits of developing behaviorally anchored scales is that it gets many raters involved in the design of the appraisal system, which leads to increased levels of acceptance and trust in the system (Landy & Farr, 1983). It is critical to develop high levels of trust, since providing accurate appraisals is a very risky behavior. An organization might use scale development as a tool to increase raters' awareness and acceptance of the PA system. The scales that are developed probably matter less than the possibility of changing raters' attitudes toward performance appraisal.

Reducing Negative Outcomes

Many of the negative outcomes of accurate performance appraisal are the result of the subordinates' perception that the rater is responsible for them receiving a poor evaluation, and that the rater is to blame if they fail to receive valued rewards (e.g., pay raises) from the organization. One strategy for reducing negative outcomes would involve diffusion of responsibility. That is, the ratee might not react as negatively if the rater was seen as only a part of the evaluation process rather than the sole judge of ratee's performance.

The use of multiple raters has been advocated for a variety of reasons, ranging from increased control over rater biases (Murphy, 1982b) to increased flexibility in developing criteria (Saal et al., 1980). This strategy may also have the benefit of reducing the perceived responsibility of the supervisor for the ratings received. If ratings are the product of multiple, independent evaluations, the immediate supervisor cannot be seen as the sole reason for a low rating. Having multiple raters may take the heat off of the immediate supervisor, and may leave the worker who is dissatisfied with his or her ratings no clear target at which to vent his or her anger.

Rater training might provide another method of diffusing the responsibility for low ratings. For example, frame-of-reference training (Bernardin & Buckley, 1981; Bernardin & Beatty, 1984; McIntyre, Smith, & Hassett, 1984), which involves exposing raters to vignettes of good, poor, and average performance and giving them feedback on the accuracy of their ratings of vignettes, could serve two purposes.

First, it could be used as a means of communicating information about the norms and standards the organization uses for evaluating performance (see Chapter Six). Second, and this is more germane to the problem of reducing negative outcomes, this type of training externalizes norms and standards. That is, the rater who has received extensive training in identifying good, average, and poor performance might be able to tie low ratings to the standards that are set by the organization. This will not resolve all of the ratee's complaints when ratings are low, but it will reduce the likelihood that ratees attribute their low ratings to the arbitrary standards of their supervisors.

A different strategy for reducing the negative consequences of accurate ratings is to reduce the links between the ratings a worker receives and the organizational rewards he or she receives. In the extreme case, ratings might be used solely for research or feedback, without linking them in any way to raises, promotions, and so forth. We would not advocate going this far. It might be possible, however, to reduce the link between any *particular* rating and organizational rewards. We are familiar with several academic departments that reward employees on the basis of their average performance over periods of several years, with the idea that one unusual year should not have a strong influence on one's salary. One benefit of this type of system is that it may reduce ratees' concerns over the ratings they receive in any one year; with this system, ratees may react less vehemently to a low rating.

A third strategy for reducing negative reactions to accurate appraisals comes from Meyer, Kay, and French (1965). They suggested that performance feedback and discussions related to salary increases should be done separately. This might be taken a step further by having separate PA systems for the purposes of feedback and administrative decision making (Cleveland, Murphy, & Williams, 1989). Rating inflation may not be a problem in salary administration; salary increases are often determined on the basis of factors other than performance (e.g., seniority, equity). Therefore, it may not be important whether the ratings turned in to the Human Resources department are accurate; the accuracy of the feedback given to employees may be more important than the accuracy of the numerical ratings that are turned in.

This strategy is especially appealing since it is already a *de facto* policy in many organizations. Raters often have one set of ratings that they turn in to the organization and another set that is used for giving feedback (Longenecker et al., 1987). It may be worthwhile institutionalizing this process, at least to the extent that developmental feedback is separated from evaluations of performance. (However, there may be legal problems with maintaining two sets of ratings, particularly if they are discrepant.)

Several facets of the PA process, including the frequency of appraisals and the credibility of the source, affect subordinates' perceptions of the fairness and accuracy of appraisals. User acceptance may be a critical issue in reducing the negative reactions that accompany accurate appraisals. As Bernardin and Beatty (1984) note, when ratees do not accept or trust the appraisal system, it is unlikely that the system will function well.

The culture of an organization (Mitroff, 1983) may be an important determinant of the consequences of accurate rating. Some cultures support distinguishing between individuals in terms of their performance, whereas others do not. An organizational culture that stresses teamwork and group goals might discourage raters from distinguishing among their subordinates. Cultures that stress individual achievement might more readily support performance appraisals that recognize individual differences in performance. Cultures may also affect the power and authority structure of the organization, which will in turn have implications for the acceptability of accurate versus inflated ratings. Organizations with a clearly defined power structure and significant power differentials between levels of the organization may be more supportive of systems designed to produce accurate ratings than organizations with very flat and democratic power structures.

Linking Rating Behavior to Valued Outcomes

The preceding section outlined some methods of reducing the links between negatively valued outcomes and appraisal behavior. However, it is not enough to reduce the motivation to rate inaccurately. The organization must also provide good reasons to rate employees accurately. The issue of providing rewards for accurate appraisals was discussed previously. In this section, we concentrate on methods of building strong links between rating behavior and rewards and sanctions.

The best way to convince raters that they will be rewarded for accurate ratings is to give rewards, as publicly as possible, to raters who comply. If it is clear that people *do* receive better raises, promotions, and so on when they rate accurately than when they distort ratings, motivation to rate accurately will increase. We have made the point many times in this chapter that the organization's willingness to reward accurate appraisals is a good measure of the real importance of accuracy. Here, we are suggesting that one step toward achieving accuracy is to provide and publicize rewards for accurate raters.

An organization might use the concept of profit sharing to increase the links between rating behavior and valued outcomes. Ratings have a direct bearing on many of the decisions an organization makes, and the success of those decisions is sometimes measurable. This is particularly true for promotion decisions. The rater who correctly identifies high-potential employees should receive some reward, which could be tied to the success of the people who are promoted on the basis of his or her performance ratings.

For example, a rater who correctly identifies an employee who rises quickly through the ranks or who makes an important contribution to the organization's success might receive a bonus. On the other hand, the rater who gives high ratings to people who routinely fail after being promoted might receive a pay cut or some other sanction. Making the raters share in the subsequent success or failure of their subordinates might lead to more careful attention to performance appraisals and promotion recommendations.

Policies such as pay secrecy can work against achieving accurate performance appraisals. If the organization keeps both the method it uses to make salary decisions and the results of those decisions secret, it may be difficult for the rater to develop any well-informed opinion about the links between rating behavior and organizational rewards. Strongly perceived behavior-reward links are most likely when raters are well aware of the rewards or punishments that others have received for turning in accurate or inaccurate ratings. Organizations are most likely to create conditions that motivate raters to provide accurate ratings when they can establish and implement a clear policy linking the quality of rating data to rewards.

Changing the Rater
versus Changing the Context

The final issue in this chapter involves the choice of a unit of analysis for interventions in the PA process. In the past, performance appraisal researchers have intervened by either changing features of the task (e.g., by changing the rating format) or by changing the rater (e.g., through rater training). We think that a better strategy is to change the rating context. That is, we do not believe that much can be achieved much by changing the rater or the task if the context dictates that ratings will be inflated.

Performance appraisal researchers agree that approaches that focus on the rating scale have not been successful (Landy & Farr, 1983). There is also some disenchantment with rater training, since training often fails to change rating behavior in organizations (Bernardin & Beatty, 1984). This issue is sometimes discussed under the heading of *transfer of training,* but we think that the problem is more fundamental than one of simply transferring information learned in training to the work setting.

We suspect that the traditional diagnosis of the underlying problem in performance appraisal is incorrect. Raters do not fail to give accurate ratings because they are incapable of accuracy but rather because they are unwilling to rate accurately (Banks & Murphy, 1985). This problem will not be solved by increasing their capability; the environment must be modified in such a way that raters are motivated to provide accurate ratings.

Changing the rating environment is likely to be a formidable undertaking. Accurate rating is most likely in a context where the following conditions exist:

1. Good and poor performance are clearly defined.
2. The principle of distinguishing among workers in terms of their levels of performance is widely accepted.
3. There is a high degree of trust in the system.
4. Low ratings do not automatically result in the loss of valued rewards.
5. Valued rewards are clearly linked to accuracy in performance appraisal.

We know of organizations in which *none* of those conditions are met; we do not know of any in which *all* of them are met.

Changing the rating context may involve changing the value structure of the organization, the administrative procedures of the organization (e.g., pay secrecy versus publicizing rewards), or the beliefs of individual raters about behavior-reward contingencies. At present, very little is known about the strategies that might be effective for acheiving any of these goals. We see a clear need for more and better research on contextual factors in performance appraisal, and we think that the ultimate solution to the problem of rating inflation will come through changing the context rather than changing the rater.

Summary

Rating inflation is a way of life in most organizations. From the rater's point of view, there are often many good reasons to turn in inflated ratings, and few good reasons to turn in ratings that reflect his or her honest appraisal of each subordinate. The consequences of giving low ratings to subordinates are often negative and immediate, whereas the rewards for turning in accurate ratings are often uncertain. It is therefore not surprising that most supervisors quickly learn to inflate their ratings.

Rating inflation has traditionally been treated as a rater error. This chapter suggested that inflation should be treated as an adaptive behavior. That is, accurate ratings can lead to a variety of negative outcomes. In the worst case, accuracy in evaluation could make it difficult for supervisors and subordinates to work together, and in the long run, it could lower the actual performance of everyone in the workgroup. An organization that is successful in stamping out rating inflation may, in the long run, be worse off than a similar organization in which rating inflation is the universal norm.

Research in the areas of decision making and work motivation provides a variety of frameworks for analyzing and understanding rating inflation. This research also suggests that the best way to counteract rating inflation (assuming that one is indeed interested in accurate ratings) is to create conditions that reward accuracy in rating and punish inaccuracy. The fact that organizations rarely attempt to create those conditions suggests that accuracy in performance appraisal may not be an important organizational goal. Unless organizations are willing to reward accuracy in rating and sanction inaccuracy, it is unreasonable to expect that raters will turn in anything but inflated ratings.

Chapter Ten

Error and Accuracy Measures

▶ It is important to know whether performance ratings provide an accurate reflection of the performance of the individuals being rated. The need for criteria against which ratings can be assessed is most obvious when evaluating an existing performance appraisal (PA) system or choosing among alternative systems. Presumably, some methods of PA are better than others. To make an informed choice, it is necessary to know which system is best and how much better one system is than another.

This chapter opens our discussion of the methods that are or might be used to evaluate the quality of rating data. We concentrate here on what are typically referred to as *psychometric characteristics* of ratings. In the chapter that follows, we will discuss alternative methods of evaluating ratings that examine the *uses* of rating data rather than the ratings themselves. There are advantages and disadvantages to both psychometric criteria and user-oriented (or decision-oriented) criteria. The chapter that follows will consider the issues involved in choosing among these two types of measures.

Criteria for Criteria

Measures of the psychometric qualities of rating data can be classified into three broad groups: (1) traditional psychometric criteria, such as reliability, construct validity, and interrater agreement; (2) indices of rater errors that reflect response biases on the part of the rater that are thought to limit the accuracy of ratings; and (3) direct measures of the accuracy of ratings.

Rater error measures are the most common indices of the accuracy of ratings. Psychometric criteria are still employed, although their use appears to be declining. A variety of procedures for directly measuring accuracy, rather than inferring it from the absence of rater errors or psychometric deficiencies, have been employed in studies of rater training (McIntyre, Smith, & Hassett, 1984), cognitive processes involved in rating (Murphy & Balzer, 1986; Murphy, Garcia, Kerkar, Martin, & Balzer, 1982), and judgmental processes in the interview (Vance, Kuhnert, & Farr, 1978). To date, these accuracy measures have been confined to the laboratory, although it may be feasible (as we will note later in this chapter) to generalize these measures to the field.

Bernardin and Beatty (1984) list a number of specific measures that have been used in research to evaluate ratings; some of these criteria are the following:

Psychometric

- ► Reliability and internal consistency
- ► Interrater agreement
- ► Equivalence of alternate forms
- ► Convergent validity
- ► Discriminant validity
- ► Construct validity
- ► Criterion-related validity
- ► Utility

Rater Errors

- ► Leniency
- ► Central tendency and range restriction
- ► Halo error
- ► Correlational bias (distortion of correlations to fit implicit theories)
- ► Scale unit bias
- ► Distortion (inappropriate weighting of dimensions in forming judgments)

Rating Accuracy

- ► Elevation
- ► Different elevation
- ► Stereotype accuracy
- ► Differential accuracy
- ► Halo accuracy
- ► Distance accuracy

Balzer and Sulsky's (in press) review indicates the extent to which different criteria are actually used to evaluate ratings. They surveyed the dependent

Table 10–1. **Dependent Measures in Performance Appraisal Studies**

	1976	1986
Reliability/Validity	31%	10%
Rater Error	54%	30%
Rater Accuracy	0%	15%
Recall/Recognition	0%	10%
Other	16%	70%

Since multiple criteria were used in several studies, columns total to more than 100%.

From W. K. Balzer and L. M. Sulsky, in K. R. Murphy and F. E. Saal (Eds.), *Psychology in Organizations: Integrating Science and Practice* (Hillsdale, NJ: Erlbaum, in press).

measures used in published research on performance appraisal in 1976 and in 1986; the results of their survey are summarized in Table 10-1. First rater error measures appear to be the most common criteria for evaluating ratings, although their use declined between 1976 and 1986; psychometric criteria (reliability and validity) showed a similar decline. Second, the direct measurement of rating accuracy is still relatively rare. If recall/recognition measures are pooled together with accuracy measures, the percentage of studies employing accuracy measures as criteria is still relatively small (25% or less). Third, these results suggest that there is no clear consensus among PA researchers regarding the measures that are most appropriate for evaluating ratings. In part, this is because some measures are method bound (i.e., accuracy measures are confined to the laboratory), but it also indicates that none of the measures commonly employed to evaluate ratings are so obviously good that they dominate the others. To understand our apparent failure to develop widely accepted standards for evaluating rating data, it is necessary to examine in depth the measures currently used in evaluating ratings.

Indirect Measures of Accuracy

Both indices of the psychometric quality of rating data and measures of rating errors can be thought of as indirect measures of rating accuracy. In fact, it seems more logical to regard these approaches as indices of *inaccuracy.* The argument for using these measures as indicators of accuracy is when raters cannot agree, or give unreliable ratings, or give ratings whose distributions make no sense, they must not be providing accurate measures of performance. For the most part, then, accuracy is inferred in the absence of psychometric deficiencies or apparent rater errors. As we will note later, this approach to indirectly inferring accuracy depends on some extremely restrictive assumptions about the true distribution of performance in organizations. These assumptions are so implausible that they may call into question the majority of the criteria that are presently used in evaluating rating data.

Psychometric Criteria

Establishing the reliability and validity of ratings has proved to be a very challenging task. The assessment of reliability has been hampered by disagreements over the most appropriate type of reliability for different purposes. Criterion-related validity studies are often difficult. Ratings themselves are often the best available measures of performance, and the criteria against which ratings are evaluated are often dubious. Construct validity has been difficult to establish, since there is no consensus on the nature or the boundaries of the construct "job performance" (Murphy & Kroeker, 1988). Although traditional psychometric criteria are conceptually appealing, they have not been used as the principal criterion for evaluating rating data. It is useful to consider why.

Reliability The most difficult issue in determining the reliability of performance ratings is to decide which definition of reliability to employ. The most common method for evaluating the reliability of psychological tests is to examine the internal consistency of the items (Murphy & Davidshofer, 1988) but this model does not apply to typical PA scales. Unlike test items, the dimensions included on PA scales are not chosen to represent a single dimension or construct. On the contrary, many of the uses of performance appraisal make it clear that each dimension on the scale provides what is thought to be unique information (Cleveland, Murphy, & Williams, 1989). Since most performance appraisals employ a single item (or a very small number of items), to measure each dimension, internal consistency reliability estimates will be misleading. In a typical performance appraisal, a valid measure of performance would be expected to exhibit *low* internal consistency.

Validity generalization research (Hunter & Hunter, 1984; Schmidt & Hunter, 1977) has employed a test-retest model, and has typically used a reliability coefficient of .60 to characterize the long-term stability of job performance measures (see Schmidt, Hunter, & Caplan, 1981). In essence, this research incorporates the assumption that 40% of the variance in job performance measures can be attributed to random errors of measurement. This assumption has been criticized as unrealistic (Schmitt & Schneider, 1983), and the correction for attenuation used in validity generalization research has been shown to be biased in the direction of supporting validity generalization (Paese & Switzer, 1988).

One conceptual problem that plagues the test-retest approach is that is confounds the effects of measurement error with those of true changes in job performance. This approach is reasonable only if it is believed that the *relative* levels of job performance of different individuals do not change over time.

However, accepting that assumption, it is difficult to justify the practice of annual or semiannual appraisals. If apparent changes in individuals' performance levels are due to primarily to measurement error, frequent measurement of job performance will only add to inaccuracy.

Interrater agreement is sometimes used as a criterion for evaluating ratings (Saal, Downey, & Lahey, 1980). It is not at all clear whether this criterion provides information about the reliability of ratings, the validity of ratings, or both. For example, the research reviewed in Chapter Five leads us to conclude that disagreements between raters (especially those at different levels in the organization) cannot be attributed solely to random measurement error; different raters observe different aspects of the same ratee's performance and will sometimes honestly disagree in their evaluations Therefore, the correlation between ratings obtained from different sources provides only partial information about the reliability of ratings. Although the case for using interrater agreement as an index of validity is somewhat stronger, even here, there are problems. Raters who share common biases (e.g., two supervisors who do not approve of female subordinates) will agree in their ratings but this is hardly evidence that the ratings are accurate.

Generalizability theory represents the most comprehensive framework for defining reliability (Cronbach, Gleser, Nanda, & Rajaratnam, 1972). The theory suggests that there is no single figure that represents *the* reliability of a measure. Rather, there are as many potential reliability coefficients as there are uses for the information that a test provides. Generalizability theory suggests that the problem of evaluating and interpreting reliability indices cannot be solved in a vacuum but rather must be based on the uses to which information obtained from performance measures are put. As a result, it is impossible to determine *the* correct model of reliability for PA research; different models are appropriate for different purposes. We will return to this point in the chapter that follows.

Validity   The validity of ratings is difficult to establish. Several researchers have attempted to establish criterion-related validity by comparing ratings to objective or results-oriented criteria (Heneman, 1986; Landy & Farr, 1976, 1983; Roach & Wherry, 1970). In general, the correlations between subjective and objective measures of job performance are small, indicating a low level of validity. However, it is not clear what is being validated. Objective measures are often unreliable and often provide only partial coverage to the domain of job performance. (See Landy and Farr, 1983, for a review.) It is quite feasible that the correlations between subjective and objective measures would be significantly higher if objective indices were better measures of job performance.

As is often the case, criterion-related validity studies are used in this area to help establish the construct validity of ratings. Although the construct-oriented model for validating ratings has long been advocated (Astin, 1964; James, 1973; Smith, 1976), empirical research on the construct validity of ratings has been rare (Murphy, in press; Murphy & Kroeker, 1988). There have been several studies of the convergent and discriminant validity of ratings (Dickinson, 1987; Kavanaugh, MacKinney, & Wolins, 1971; Lawler, 1967) but convergent and discriminant validity are not synonymous with construct validity. That is, convergent and discriminant validity are desirable but they are neither necessary nor sufficient to establish construct validity.

Consider, for example, convergent validity. If one method provides a perfect measure of performance and another does not, the two will fail to converge. On the other hand, two measures that share common measurement biases *will* converge. Discriminant validity is more a function of the traits chosen than of the measurement procedures that are being evaluated. If different dimensions of performance are conceptually distinct, discriminant validity is likely. If performance dimensions overlap, discriminant validity is unlikely.

Unless the construct of performance is described in some detail (i.e., unless the construct is explicated), progress in construct validation research is difficult (Murphy & Davidshofer, 1988). To date, there has been virtually no research that carefully describes the construct of job performance and then attempts to determine whether a particular index provides an adequate measure of that construct (Murphy & Kroeker, 1988). Therefore, the question of whether ratings are valid measures of job performance is still an open one. However, as noted below, there is a good deal of incorrect evidence of construct validity.

Construct Validity Evidence   Although there are few studies directly concerned with the construct validity of ratings, there are many studies that provide indirect evidence. First, there are studies indicating that raters agree and, in particular, that raters at different levels in the organization show considerable consistency in their ratings. Although ratings obtained from different sources often differ in *level* (e.g., self-ratings are usually higher than supervisory ratings [Meyer, 1980; Thornton, 1980]), there is substantial agreement among ratings from different sources with regard to the relative effectiveness and performance of different ratees. For example, in a meta-analysis of research on rating sources, Harris and Schaubroeck (1988) found an average correlation of .62 between peer and supervisory ratings (self-supervisor and self-peer correlations were .35 and .36, respectively). Mount (1984a) reports some evidence for the reliability and validity of rating obtained from subordinates, and notes that when supervisors, subordinates, and the target individual all provide ratings (the last source is a self-rating), supervisors and subordinates agree more closely with one another than either source agrees with self-ratings.

A second category of evidence comes from research on the utility of various personnel programs (this research is reviewed in Chapter Eleven). Utility estimation often involves asking supervisors to determine the worth of highly successful versus highly unsuccessful performers to the organization.

There is considerable evidence that these judgments are accurate (see Bobko, Karren, and Kerkar, 1987, for a review and critique of this research), which suggests that supervisors can identify good and poor performers. If they were unable to tell who was doing well or poorly, it is hard to see how they would be able to evaluate accurately the value of the goods, services, and so on produced by good versus poor performers.

Another category of relevant research examines the correlations between ratings and other measures of performance. For example, Heneman (1986) showed that ratings are positively correlated with a variety of objective measures of job performance, although the correlations are often small. It is hard to tell whether the small correlations indicate any deficiencies in ratings as criteria, because the objective measures against which ratings are usually compared are themselves incomplete measures of job performance.

A fourth category of evidence comes from studies of the effects of performance feedback. There is clear evidence that appraisal feedback leads to increases in worker productivity, measured in terms of criteria such as production, error rate, backlogs, and so on (Guzzo & Bondy, 1983; Guzzo, Jette, & Katzell, 1985; Kopelman, 1986; Landy, Farr, & Jacobs, 1982). The fact that performance feedback has a consistent and positive effect suggests that raters are reasonably accurate in the feedback they give.

A final category of evidence comes from the large number of validity studies that use supervisory ratings as criteria for validating selection tests. This literature shows that scores on most selection tests, particularly those that measure cognitive ability, are correlated with supervisory ratings (Hunter & Hunter, 1984). Furthermore, the validities for these tests for predicting subjective criteria (such as ratings) are as large as the validities for predicting objective measures of job performance (Nathan & Alexander, 1988; Schmitt, Gooding, Noe, & Kirsch, 1984). In theory, the abilities measured by these tests *should* be related to job performance. The fact that the validity coefficients obtained using supervisory ratings are consistently large (both in an absolute sense and in comparison with validities obtained using objective measures) suggests that ratings have some validity.

Caution must be observed in evaluating the evidence on the construct validity of ratings. This evidence shows that raters *can* provide reasonably valid judgments of the overall performance levels of their subordinates, and can reliably identify their best and worst workers. As noted in several of the preceding chapters, this does not mean that raters *will* provide valid ratings.

Rater Error Measures

There are several well-known phenomena that suggest that performance ratings are flawed measures. First, it is not unusual to find that 80 to 90% of all employees are rated as "above average." (This phenomenon has been referred to by educators as the "Lake Wobegon Effect" since it is often found that all the children are "above average.") Second, differences in the ratings received by different employees often seem small, given the obvious differences in their performance. Third, ratings on conceptually distinct aspects of performance are often highly correlated. One explanation for these phenomena is that raters make systematic errors in their evaluations of performance.

Discussion of the three most common rater errors, leniency, range restriction, and halo error, can be traced back over 60 years (Kingsbury, 1922, 1933). These concepts still strongly influence the ways in which rating data are analyzed (Balzer & Sulsky, in press; Saal et al., 1980) and have provided the foundation for a large body of research. We find it useful to deal separately with two classes of so-called rater errors: distributional errors and correlational errors.

Distributional Errors   The rater errors of leniency/severity, range restriction, and central tendency are thought to be present when the distribution of ratings differs from the (assumed) distribution of job performance. For example, if the mean of all the ratings given by a particular rater differs substantially from the scale midpoint, the rater is thought to be either overly severe (low mean rating) or overly lenient (high mean rating). The assumption implicit in the above statement is that the true mean level of performance corresponds roughly to the scale midpoint. Similarly, if ratings cluster near the scale midpoint, central tendency errors are assumed. The assumption here is that the true distribution of performance is normal and that the true variability of performance is substantial. Finally, if the variability of ratings is small, range restriction is assumed.

The assumptions that characterize typical measures of leniency, range restriction, and central tendency have been criticized. First, the true distribution of performance is almost always unknown, and there is typically no empirical justification for the assumption that it is normal and centered around the scale midpoint. Statistical convenience appears to be the only justification for assuming this true distribution (Bernardin & Beatty, 1984). Second, organizations exert considerable effort to assure that the distribution of performance is *not* normal. Saal and associates (1980) point out that a variety of activities, ranging from personnel selection to training, are designed to produce a skewed distribution of performance. Any rational personnel manager would be pleased if all of the employees in a company were exceptional workers.

Third, these assumptions imply that there is no variation, from workgroup to workgroup, in terms of their actual performance (Murphy & Balzer, 1989). Thus, if rater A gives ratings whose mean is 5.0 (7-point scale) and rater B gives ratings whose mean is 4.1, rater A is likely to be labeled as the more lenient rater. However, it is entirely possible that rater A's subordinates *are* better performers than those of rater B. There is a substantial literature on leadership that assumes that workgroups *will* differ in their performance, depending in part on the effectiveness of the leader (Landy, 1985). It seems illogical to assume that all groups perform at the same level, regardless of their resources, their leadership, their tasks, and so on.

The literature on rating errors contains a good deal of speculation about the causes of distributional errors. Saal and Knight (1988) list several possible explanations for leniency/severity effects, including (1) a desire to be liked, (2) unwillingness to give negative feedback, (3) fear that other raters inflate their ratings, and (4) abnormally high or low standards.

Similarly, central tendency and range restriction errors are often attributed to (1) an unwillingness to stick one's neck out, (2) inadequate opportunities to observe, and (3) an unwillingness to justify high or low ratings to the organization or the ratee. Although there is no lack of speculation, we know of little empirical work on the reasons behind apparent rater errors. The reasons cited above represent hypotheses that seem to be widely accepted, but to date they have not been adequately tested.

There are two reasons to be concerned about the use of distributional error measures to infer that ratings are accurate or inaccurate. First, as noted above, the true distribution of performance is almost never known. Indeed, if there were means available to determine the true distribution of performance, it is hard to see why ratings would be needed at all. It is doubtful that anyone would favor the use of subjective criteria *if valid objective criteria were available.* They typically are not, meaning that the assumptions that underlly distributional error measures are inherently untestable. We believe that they are also implausible. Second, ratings whose distributions *did* correspond to the (unknown) true distribution of performance are not necessarily more accurate than those whose distributions are obviously wrong.

Figure 10-1 illustrates how this could happen. Rater X's distribution very closely matches the true distribution, whereas rater Z seems unduly severe (i.e., his or her ratings are systematically lower). However, rater Z is obviously more accurate in determining who is better or worse at their jobs. Although rater X showed the "correct" distribution, that was one of the few things about the ratings that *was* correct. Although exhibiting obvious rater errors, rater Z is clearly more accurate. That is, rater Z ranked the 11 ratees in an order that corresponds almost exactly with their true performance levels (e.g., ratee A, who was the best performer, received the highest ratings), whereas rater A was clearly off base (e.g., he or she rated ratee H as better than ratee A).

Correlational Errors   It has long been known that raters tend to give similar evaluations to separate aspects of a person's performance, even when those dimensions are clearly distinct (Thorndike, 1920; Newcomb, 1931). The result is an inflation of the intercorrelations among dimensions and is referred to as halo error. Cooper's (1981b) review suggests that halo is likely to be present in virtually every type of rating instrument.

Halo is typically described in terms of (1) the rater's tendency to let global evaluations color ratings on specific dimensions or (2) the rater's unwillingness to discriminate among separate aspects of a ratee's performance (Saal et al., 1980). The first explanation more clearly corresponds with the name of the error; a positive evaluation could be thought of as a "halo" that colors the evaluation of specific dimensions. Building on this idea, Landy,

Figure 10–1. Why Distributional Errors Do Not Necessarily Indicate Accuracy

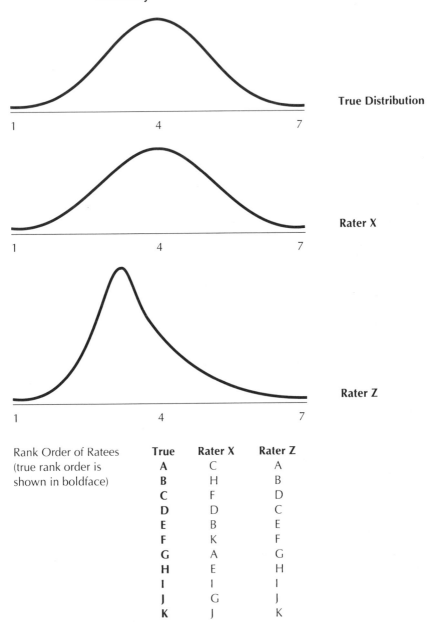

Rank Order of Ratees	**True**	**Rater X**	**Rater Z**
(true rank order is	**A**	C	A
shown in boldface)	**B**	H	B
	C	F	D
	D	D	C
	E	B	E
	F	K	F
	G	A	G
	H	E	H
	I	I	I
	J	G	J
	K	J	K

Vance, Barnes-Farrell, and Steele (1980) suggested that halo could be statistically controlled by partialling out an overall rating from ratings of separate performance dimensions (see also Ritti, 1964). Harvey (1982), Hulin (1982), and Murphy (1982b) pointed out shortcomings of this method and suggested that it does more harm than good. Nevertheless, Landy and colleagues' (1980) suggestion is conceptually appealing to those who adopt the first definition of halo.

A second explanation is that halo is a function of the conceptual similarities among the dimensions being rated. The systematic distortion hypothesis suggests that raters tend to distort their ratings so that the correlations among dimensions correspond with the conceptual similarity among dimensions, regardless of the actual similarity of the behaviors being rated (Shweder, 1975; Shweder & D'Andrade, 1980). Although conceptual similarity has been used in several studies to predict halo levels (Cooper, 1981b; Murphy & Reynolds, 1988a), this approach has not always been successful. In carefully designed experiments, both Cooper (1981a) and Murphy and Jako (1989) failed to find substantial conceptual similarity effects. Thus, the current status of the systematic distortion hypothesis is unclear.

In addition to conceptual similarity, Cooper (1981b) reviews several possible causes of halo, including (1) failure to attend to hit rates, (2) confirmatory biases, and (3) discounting of inconsistent information. In addition to these cognitive distortions, halo is probably a function of the amount of information the rater has when making evaluations. Kozlowski, Kirsch, and Chao (1986) have shown that halo error is related to familiarity with the ratee and with job-related knowledge.

Bingham (1939) was probably the first to distinguish between valid and invalid halo. Cooper (1981b) used the terms *true halo* and *illusory halo* to refer to these two explanations for the correlations among rating dimensions. One reason why ratings on separate dimensions may be correlated is that the behaviors being rated, although conceptually distinct, really *are* correlated. This is referred to as *true halo.* For example, if teachers were asked to evaluate the verbal ability and the quantitative ability of 10th-grade students, these ratings would undoubtedly be correlated. Although verbal and quantitative ability are distinct constructs, they are nevertheless correlated phenomena. It is assumed in this literature that *illusory halo,* or the part of the correlation that is due to cognitive distortion on the part of the rater, combines with true halo to produce the observed correlation among ratings. In essence, this formulation parallels the classic formulation of reliability theory, in which an observed score is partitioned into true score and error components.

Although it seems obvious that observed correlations reflect, in part, the true correlations among the behaviors being rated, it is difficult to demonstrate empirically the effects (if any) of true halo. Murphy and Reynolds (1988a) varied the true halo levels of sets of videotapes so that the behaviors to be rated would have average intercorrelations of .07 (low true halo), .43 (medium true halo), and .76 (high true halo). They found that the true halo levels of the stimuli being rated had an effect on the observed intercorrelations among rating dimensions, albeit a *very* small one, on observed levels of halo. In particular, observed halo was higher when the true correlations among dimensions was extremely high than when the true correlation was near zero, but the variance accounted for by true halo levels was hardly impressive, considering the extreme variation in true halo levels ($\omega^2 = .05$). Murphy and Reynolds' (1988a) results were replicated by Murphy and Jako (1989).

To understand why true halo is so weakly related to observed halo, it is useful to speculate about the conditions that would be necessary for true halo levels to have any real effect on rating behavior. The first and simplest condition is that raters must somehow be able to detect the level of true halo. This does not imply that they must be consciously aware of the intercorrelations among the dimensions they are rating, but they must also not be oblivious to that information.

Research suggests that subjects have difficulty estimating the correlation between variables, even when this information is reduced to a simple form, such as a scatterplot or a 2×2 contingency table (Peterson & Beach, 1967; Ward & Jenkins, 1965). Research on performance in multiple-cue judgment tasks suggests that judgment behavior is not affected by the true correlations among cues (Dudycha & Naylor, 1966; Lane, Murphy, & Marques, 1982; Slovic, 1966). Taken together, these studies suggest that subjects could not validly infer the level of true halo in complex behavior, even if detecting true halo was their primary task. Thus, we conclude that the idea that observed correlations among ratings represent a combination of true and illusory halo is not a useful one. One implication of this conclusion is that efforts to eliminate illusory halo without disturbing true halo (e.g., Landy et al., 1980) are likely to fail.

Although true halo may have little or no effect on ratings, the concept is still useful for interpreting measures of halo error. As noted earlier, halo has usually been defined in terms of a tendency to give ratings whose correlations are *higher* than the true correlations. Recent research suggests that this definition is not adequate. Observed intercorrelations tend to be artificially high only when the true intercorrelations are low. Conversely, raters tend to *underestimate* true halo (i.e., give ratings whose intercorrelations are too low) when the true correlations among dimensions are high (Kozlowski & Kirsch, 1986; Murphy, Balzer, Kellam, & Armstrong, 1984; Murphy & Jako, 1989; Murphy & Reynolds, 1988a).

This finding suggests that many of the traditional explanations for halo are probably incorrect. For example, if halo was the result of letting one's overall evaluation color evaluations of specific dimensions, observed correlations should be larger than true halo levels, regardless of whether true halo levels are high or low. Similarly, a failure to attend to hit rates, a confirmatory bias, or a tendency to discount disconfirmatory information (Cooper, 1981b) should lead to consistent overestimation of the true correlations among dimensions. The evidence reviewed above suggests that this does not occur.

One very simple explanation for halo error in ratings might be the demand characteristics of most rating tasks. The dimensions on a PA scale presumably all relate to overall performance, and thus will also be (at least conceptually) related to one another (Murphy, 1982b). On the other hand, the dimensions are unlikely to be seen as *completely* independent; if they are unrelated, how can they be put together to represent overall performance? We suspect that a rater who had no valid information on which to base his or her ratings would give ratings that showed moderate levels of intercorrelation, which would be interpreted as halo if true correlations are thought to be low.

Operational Definitions of Rater Errors Saal and colleagues (1980) cataloged a variety of operations of each of the rater errors described above. The most frequently encountered definitions of the three types of rater errors are:

Leniency

- ► Shift of mean rating away from scale midpoint
- ► Skew of rating distribution
- ► Rater main effect in Rater × Ratee × Dimension ANOVA

Range Restriction/Central Tendency

- ► Standard deviation across ratees within dimensions
- ► Kurtosis of rating distribution
- ► Ratee main effect in Rater × Ratee × Dimension ANOVA

Halo

- ► Intercorrelations among dimension ratings
- ► Percentage of variance accounted for by first principal component
- ► Standard deviation of ratings across dimensions
- ► Rater × Ratee interaction in Rater × Dimension ANOVA (Saal et al., 1980)

Although the availability of multiple operational definitions of a construct is usually thought to be desirable (Murphy & Davidshofer, 1988), the existence of several operational definitions for common rating errors is problematic. There is clear evidence that different definitions of the same rater are not equivalent (Saal et al., 1980). For example, Murphy and Balzer (1989) performed a meta-analysis of studies employing the two most common operational definitions of halo, leniency, and range restriction. The average correlation between alternate measures of the same rater error was .08.

If the conclusion is accepted that alternate definitions of rater error measures are not equivalent, it becomes important to develop methods of choosing among the alternatives. The merits of alternate definitions of halo have received the most attention. Pulakos, Schmitt, and Ostroff (1986) make a strong case for defining halo in terms of the averaged observed correlation coefficient, and make an even stronger case for abandoning the use of the standard deviation across dimensions as a halo index. As we will note later, their argument is weakened by its reliance on some debatable assumptions, but we do agree with their warning about the use of the standard deviation.

In choosing among alternate definitions of halo, leniency, and range restriction, two considerations are relevant. First, the operational definition should correspond with the conceptual definition of the construct. Second, the operational definition should not involve arbitrary cutoffs or decisions. The first requirement is met by some of the definitions shown on the previous page, but the second requirement is not really met by *any* of those definitions. For example, how high do the intercorrelations among dimensions have to be before they are judged to be too high? In Murphy and Reynolds (1988a), the observed average intercorrelation was .50 in the high true halo condition. This figure would probably be regarded by most individuals as a high correlation, but in this case it seriously underestimated the true halo level (average $r = .76$). How much variance does the first principal component have to account to signal a high level of halo? How much skew and kurtosis is needed to indicate leniency and range restriction?

We do not know of any clearly defensible way of choosing one operational definition of leniency, range restriction, or halo. Rather than concentrating our efforts on this task, we suggest that researchers stop using rater error measures altogether. Our rationale is outlined below.

Are Rater Error Measures Useful as Criteria?   Our answer is no, they are not useful criteria for evaluating performance ratings. We believe that ratings that show normal distributions, large standard deviations across ratees and dimensions and low intercorrelations among dimensions, are not necessarily (or even likely to be) better measures than ratings that show all of the traditional rater errors.

We have two concerns regarding rater error measures. First, the unit of analysis for these measures is often defined incorrectly. For example, if halo is defined as a *rater* error, the individual rater should be the unit of analysis. However, halo is frequently defined at the organizational level (Murphy, 1982b). Although this may seem like quibbling, the example shown in Table 10-2 suggests that it can be an important problem.

Rater X gives a 7 to all ratees on all dimensions, whereas rater Z gives a 1 to all ratees on all dimensions. The average intercorrelation among dimensions for each individual rater would be .00, since for each rater there is no variance in ratings. However, if data are pooled over raters, the average intercorrelation among dimensions is 1.00. This unit of analysis problem may not be as severe for other rater error measures, but it is disconcerting to see apparently arbitrary choices when defining the unit of analysis for measuring rater errors.

Our most serious concern is over the assumptions that are implied by different rater error measures. Suppose the mean rating, the standard deviation across ratees within dimensions, and the average intercorrelation for three raters were calculated and the results were as shown in Table 10-3. It might be concluded that rater Y is the most lenient, that rater Y is most guilty of range restriction, and that both raters X and Y have high levels of halo in their ratings. Unfortunately, these data do not support those conclusions, since these

Table 10–2. Illustration of the Effects of Unit of Analysis on Halo Measures

Ratee	A	B	C	D	E	
1	7	7	7	7	7	
2	7	7	7	7	7	**Rater X**
3	7	7	7	7	7	
4	7	7	7	7	7	
5	1	1	1	1	1	
6	1	1	1	1	1	**Rater Z**
7	1	1	1	1	1	
8	1	1	1	1	1	
9	1	1	1	1	1	

The column group header is **Dimension** (over A B C D E).

Average:
Rater X = .00
Rater Z = .00
Overall = 1.00

Table 10–3. Hypothetical Results Illustrating Assumptions of Rater Error Measures

	Rater X	Rater Y	Rater Z
Mean rating	4.0	5.2	3.7
Standard deviation across ratees	2.0	.09	1.9
Average observed intercorrelation	.50	.67	.09

Ratings were obtained using a 7-point scale.

interpretations depend on the assumption that the true performance levels of the workers supervised by raters X, Y, and Z are equivalent in every respect. What if the workers assigned to rater Z really are worse than average and really are worse than those assigned to raters X and Y? It is not unreasonable to assume that workgroups vary in their true levels of performance. More important, we know of no justification for the implicit assumption that the true level of performance is constant across workgroups (see also Murphy & Balzer, 1981, 1989).

Similar problems exist in interpreting measures of range restriction and halo. Is it reasonable to assume that the true variability in workers' performance is constant across groups? We believe it is more likely that true individual differences in performance are small in some groups and large in others. Is it reasonable to believe that the true correlations among performance dimensions are constant across groups? (Pulakos and associates, 1986, make this assumption.) We believe it is more likely that the true correlations among the behaviors being rated vary from group to group and from time to time.

Researchers have long debated possible confounds between true halo and illusory halo. There is a similar confound between true leniency (sometimes everyone *did* perform well) and the rater error of leniency. The same principle applies to range restriction/central tendency. Some range restriction may reflect true differences (or the lack thereof) in performance, whereas other instances of range restriction may reflect real rater errors. It is time to face the fact that much of what has been labeled *rater error* in the past may not be an error at all (Burnaska & Hollmann, 1974; Carroll & Schneier, 1982; Murphy, 1982b; Murphy & Balzer, 1981, 1989).

Our overall conclusion is that rater error measures should be abandoned. They are based on arbitrary and often implausible assumptions, and there are too many nonequivalent definitions of each one. Fortunately, there are some alternatives to rater error measures. These alternatives are reviewed in this chapter and in the chapter that follows.

Direct Measures of Rating Accuracy

The direct measurement of rating accuracy requires some standard against which ratings can be evaluated. This standard is often referred to as a *true score* and is thought to represent the rating that would be expected from an unbiased, careful rater who completed the rating task under optimal conditions. Questions have been raised about the adequacy of operational definitions of such true scores (Heneman, Wexley, & Moore, 1987; Sulsky & Balzer, 1988) and about the meaning of accuracy in rating (Balzer & Sulsky, in press; Sulsky & Balzer, 1988). Nevertheless, accuracy measures have become increasingly popular in recent years.

Two distinct types of accuracy measures have appeared in the literature: behavior-based measures and judgmental measures. Behavior-based measures are considerably simpler and are often based on the rater's accuracy in recognizing specific behavioral incidents (Cardy & Krzystofiak, 1988; Lord, 1985a). For example, Murphy, Philbin, and Adams (1989) studied the effects of purpose of observation on behavior-recognition accuracy. They asked raters to indicate whether each of 36 behavioral incidents had or had not occurred in the videotapes of performance they had observed. Since the true status of each behavior can be determined (here, 18 behaviors actually occurred and 18 did not), it was possible to measure observational accuracy in terms of true positives, true negatives, false positives, and false negatives. When responses are coded as true positives, true negatives, and so on, signal detection theory can be employed to derive measures of response bias and sensitivity (Lord, 1985a).

Although behavior-based measures are both simple and highly useful for testing several propositions from cognitive theories of evaluation, they are limited in their application. They rely on the rater's recognition of a short list of critical incidents. They do not incorporate any explicit evaluation of the behaviors nor do they guarantee comprehensive coverage of the performance domain. Further, the rater's task in studies involving behavior-based measures is not at all similar to the typical rater's task in real performance appraisals. It is hard to conceive of a PA system that consisted of a checklist of behaviors in which the rater's task was simply to indicate whether each behavior had occurred. On the whole, judgmental measures of accuracy seem more relevant and useful.

Measures of accuracy in judgment have been widely used, especially in cognitively oriented research on performance appraisal (Becker & Cardy, 1986; Borman, 1977, 1978, 1979; Cardy & Dobbins, 1986; McIntyre et al., 1984; Murphy & Balzer, 1986; Murphy et al., 1984; Murphy, Garcia, et al., 1982; Pulakos, 1986). Sulsky and Balzer (1988) reviewed a variety of operational measures of accuracy, which can be broken down into three main types: (1) distance accuracy, (2) accuracy components, and (3) correlational measures of differential accuracy.

Operational Definitions The simplest definition of accuracy is in terms of the distance (or squared distance) between ratings and true scores. This definition of accuracy has been employed in several studies (Bernardin & Pence, 1980; Heneman & Wexley, 1983; McIntyre et al., 1984) but there are serious drawbacks to this measure (Sulsky & Balzer, 1988). In a classic article, Cronbach (1955) showed that when N individuals are each rated on k traits, the distance between ratings and true scores (or any standard) is a function of several distinct types of accuracy, and that the interpretation of an overall distance accuracy measure is exceedingly difficult.

Cronbach (1955) recommended describing accuracy in terms of four separate components: (1) elevation, (2) differential elevation, (3) stereotype accuracy, and (4) differential accuracy (see Wiggins, 1973). *Elevation* refers to the accuracy of the average rating, over all ratees and dimensions. *Differential elevation* refers to accuracy in discriminating among ratees, averaging over dimensions. *Stereotype accuracy* refers to accuracy in discriminating among performance dimensions, averaging over ratees. (For example, if dimensions include "Planning" and "Oral Communication," stereotype accuracy involves accuracy in determining whether a group of workers is better at Planning or at Oral Communication.) Finally, *differential accuracy* refers to accuracy in detecting ratee differences in patterns of performance (i.e., accuracy in diagnosing individual strengths and weaknesses). If the rating data to be analyzed is structured in a ratee $\times$ dimension ($N \times k$) matrix, elevation can be thought of as the accuracy of the grand mean. Differential elevation refers to the accuracy of the row marginals, whereas stereotype accuracy refers to the accuracy of the column marginals. Differential accuracy refers to the accuracy of the row $\times$ column interaction.

Elevation reflects the difference between the observed and true grand means. Cronbach's (1955) remaining three accuracy measures reflect both accuracy in rank-ordering ratees, dimensions, or ratees within dimensions and accuracy in evaluating the variability of performance (Balzer & Sulsky, in press; Becker & Cardy, 1986; Wiggins, 1973). That is, they contain both correlational components and variance components. For example, a rater who accurately rank-orders employees but drastically underestimates the extent to which different ratees' performance actually differs might receive a poor score for differential elevation. Some researchers have questioned the practice of confounding accuracy in rank-ordering and accuracy in estimating the variance of performance (Balzer & Sulsky, in press; Becker & Cardy, 1986; Sulsky & Balzer, 1988). As we will note in Chapter Eleven, solution to this controversy depends entirely on the uses to which ratings will be put.

Borman (1977) has advocated concentrating on the correlational component of differential accuracy (see also Becker & Cardy, 1986; Wiggins, 1973). His index of rating accuracy is obtained by correlating ratings with true scores for each dimensions, and then taking the average of those correlations. This operational definition is somewhat different from Cronbach's (1955) definition of the correlational component of differential accuracy (Sulsky & Balzer, 1988) but the concepts behind the two definitions are quite close.

Researchers' preference for Borman's measure (as opposed to the four accuracy components described earlier) can be explained in terms of simplicity and a belief that this measure represents the most important component of accuracy (Borman, 1977; Wiggins, 1973). It is hard to dispute the claim that one measure is simpler than four, but we disagree with the claim that Borman's index is a measure of the most important aspect of accuracy.

Murphy, Garcia, and colleagues (1982) argued that differential elevation is much more important than differential accuracy. If administrative decisions, such as promotions or salary increases, are based on performance ratings, it is differential elevation, not differential accuracy, that determines the accuracy of those decisions. Differential accuracy is important only in situations where different decisions might be made, depending on the pattern of performance. For example, if ratee A is high on "Planning" and low on "Oral Communication" and ratee B shows the opposite pattern, accuracy in detecting this difference is important only if ratee A is to be treated differently than ratee B. That is, differential treatment based on patterns of performance is justified only if an Aptitude × Treatment Interaction (ATI) exists (Cronbach & Gleser, 1965; Cronbach & Snow, 1977).

In the rating context, an ATI would exist if someone with ratings of 4 and 6 on the dimensions "Time Management" and "Planning" and someone with ratings of 6 and 4 on those same dimensions should be treated differently. ATIs are rarely found in educational settings (Cronbach & Snow, 1977) and we suspect they are even rarer in industry. If a researcher must concentrate on a single accuracy measure, we would advocate differential elevation rather than differential accuracy.

Our recommendation that attention be directed at accuracy in distinguishing among ratees, as opposed to accuracy in distinguishing among ratees within dimensions, has interesting implications for research on halo error. As we noted earlier, it is doubtful that halo error (as it is typically measured) really is an error. Even if halo *was* an error, the preceding paragraph suggests that it may not be a bad or costly one. In fact, it may be better to make halo errors than to avoid them, in that halo errors make it easier to distinguish among ratees.

To understand why this is so, it is useful to note that the variance of a linear combination of *p* variables is a function of the variance of each variables and the sum of the covariances among the variables. High halo will lead to large correlations among variables, which means large covariances. All things being equal, the rater who commits halo errors will give ratings that more clearly discriminate between ratees than will the rater who avoids halo error. Although halo error restricts one's ability to differentiate among ratees whose overall levels of performance are equivalent, but whose patterns of performance differ, the loss may be trivial when compared to the gain in differential elevation. Murphy and Balzer (1986) have empirically demonstrated how halo error contributes to accuracy in rating.

The proliferation of accuracy measures has been noted in several reviews (Balzer & Sulsky, in press; Becker & Cardy, 1986; Heneman et al., 1987; Sulsky & Balzer, 1988). Research suggests that the different accuracy measures are not highly correlated (Sulsky & Balzer, 1988). For example, Murphy and Balzer (1981) noted that the average correlation among Cronbach's (1955) four measures is essentially zero. This is not as serious a problem as with rater error measures, since the different accuracy indices are designed to measure distinct facets of accuracy. Nevertheless, it is disconcerting to note that one's results may depend more on the choice of accuracy measures than on the phenomenon being studied (Becker & Cardy, 1986).

At present, there is no clear consensus among researchers regarding the best or most appropriate accuracy measures. Our recommendation is that multiple measures should be used if at all possible. In most cases, the researcher who has the data needed to compute one type of accuracy will have the data needed to compute several types. Situations in which the use of a single accuracy measure would be optimal are likely to be few and far between.

True Score Estimation   The validity of any accuracy measure depends primarily on the quality of the standards, or true scores, that are used to judge the ratings. In evaluating the procedures that have been or might be used to generate estimates of true scores, it is necessary to understand what is meant by *true score.* In the classical theory of reliability, this term has taken two distinct meanings. Some researchers define true scores in terms of objective reality (Platonic true scores). Thus, if a person's true score is 7 on a 7-point scale, he or she really is an excellent performer. Others define true scores as the expected values of observations obtained from a particular population (Cronbach et al., 1972; Lord & Novick, 1968). Here, the population could be a population of raters, occasions, and so on.

The Platonic true score concept has not proved useful in psychometrics

(Lord & Novick, 1968) and is probably even less useful in the context of performance appraisal. Performance evaluation is, in the final analysis, a value judgment. It seems illogical to argue that a particular person *really* is a 7.0 and not a 6.9 or a 6.8; the exact evaluation of the individual's performance depends in part on the values of the rater. We prefer to define true score in terms of the expected value one would obtain from a specific population. The question that must then be answered is which population.

The most widely used procedure for computing true score estimates was developed by Borman (1977) (see also Murphy, Garcia et al., 1982). This procedure involves the use of multiple expert raters who evaluate performance under optimal conditions. For example, in Murphy, Garcia, and colleagues (1982), 13 graduate students served as expert raters of videotaped lectures. Videotapes were designed to exemplify specific levels of performance on each of several dimensions; these levels are sometimes referred to as *intended true scores*. Raters were given copies of the lecture scripts and had multiple opportunities to view the tapes before rating them. Estimated true scores were computed for each tape and dimension by averaging over these 13 raters. These true scores showed evidence of convergent and discriminant validity, as well as high correlations with intended true scores (see also Borman, 1978).

This procedure implicitly defines the population of raters in terms of their expertise with the task, as well as the conditions under which performance is observed. It would be possible to develop true scores from other populations with less expertise or who had fewer opportunities to observe performance, but it unlikely that any other population would be regarded as superior to the population of raters used in Borman's (1977) procedure. Although there has been some criticism of this approach to developing true scores (Heneman et al., 1987; Sulsky & Balzer, 1988), we think this approach is the best available. The problem with this approach is that it limits the study of rating accuracy to the laboratory (Latham, 1986). This approach requires that the same behavior that is viewed by raters must also be viewed by experts, which is practical only when the performance to be evaluated consists of short videotaped vignettes.

There is an alternative method of defining true scores that might allow for the study of accuracy in the field; to our knowledge, this method has not yet been applied. If m raters each evaluated N ratees on k dimensions, it would be possible to define true scores for each ratee and dimension by taking the mean across all m raters. Taking the mean provides a reasonable estimate of the expected value for this population of raters. That is, the true score could be defined as the expected value of the rating obtained from the population of raters who are actually engaged in performance appraisal.

This definition of true score has several interesting implications. First, this definition identifies accuracy closely with interrater agreement. If all raters agree in their evaluations, ratings must, by this definition, be accurate, since any rater will be close to the mean of all raters. Second, the components of accuracy are defined in terms of how far a particular rater deviates from the mean of all raters. Thus, the mean square for raters provides an overall index of the amount of elevation present in the ratings; each rater's elevation is measured by his or her deviation from the grand mean. Similar interpretations can be drawn for other accuracy measures. For example, the mean square for ratees provides one index of differential elevation; the mean square for dimensions provides one index of stereotype accuracy. (Dickinson, 1987, provides a similar method of analysis that incorporates externally defined true scores in a Rater $\times$ Rater $\times$ Dimension design.)

There are two potential objections to the method outlined above. First, does the mean over a group of raters really define a person's true level of performance? We would argue that it does, as long as the precise meaning of *true* is kept in mind. That is, the average over a set of raters is a reasonable approximation of what a person would receive if his or her performance was evaluated by every possible rater in the organization. Proponents of the Platonic true score concept might argue that the mean over all possible raters did not define the "real" performance level, but this position is a hard one to support. Even if it is accepted, it may not be relevant, since we are interested in defining the "real" *evaluation* of performance, not merely its "real" level.

Second, and more important, this approach may not be practical. It might be very difficult to assemble more than a few individuals who are qualified, in terms of their job knowledge and their opportunities to observe performance, to evaluate an individual's performance. The use of the observed mean as an estimate of the expected value is justified primarily by application of the law of large numbers. If the number of qualified raters is two, we cannot place much faith in the mean as a true score estimate.

Vance, Winne, and Wright (1983) suggest a practical alternative to the fully crossed Rater $\times$ Ratee $\times$ Dimension design described above. They note that ratees are often nested within raters (i.e., are evaluated by a single supervisor) at any single point in time, but are sometimes partially crossed with raters (i.e., are evaluated by multiple raters) over longer periods of time. It is possible in this partially nested design to estimate both rater and ratee effects. More important, this design provides for multiple raters per dimension, which makes it possible to estimate expected-value true scores.

Rater Errors and Rating Accuracy   For those researchers who are already skeptical about the use of rater error measures as criteria for evaluating ratings, research on the relationship between rater errors and rating accuracy will drive the last nail into the coffin of rater error measures. The general trend in this literature is clear — rater error measures are largely unrelated to direct measures of the accuracy of ratings (Becker & Cardy, 1986; Bernardin & Pence, 1980; Borman, 1977; Murphy & Balzer, 1981, 1989).

As discussed earlier, rater error measures are used to infer accuracy indirectly. The presence of rater errors is generally taken to indicate inaccurate ratings and the absence of rater errors is seen as an indication of accuracy. Until the development of direct measures of rating accuracy (Borman, 1977), the validity of this inference was impossible to evaluate. Several recent studies have measured the correlation between different measures of rater errors and rating accuracy. The results of Murphy and Balzer's (1989) meta-analysis, shown in Table 10-4, illustrate the relationships between error and accuracy measures.

Murphy and Balzer (1989) computed accuracy component scores and the two most common measures of each of three rater errors (halo, leniency, and range restriction) for each of 854 raters, drawn from eight separate studies. They calculated the correlations between error and accuracy measures in each study and then averaged the eight correlation matrices, weighting for sample size. The mean of the correlations shown in Table 10-4 is small and negative ($r = -.09$). Furthermore, the only substantial correlations between error and accuracy scores are negative. If the absence of error indicated accuracy, these correlations should be positive. (Accuracy scores are deviation measures where small deviations indicate high levels of accuracy.) Thus, if there is any relationship between rater errors and rating accuracy, it is a paradoxical one in which rater errors contribute to rating accuracy.

The unusual relationship between errors and accuracy has been noted most often in research on halo error (Becker & Cardy, 1986; Cooper, 1981b; Murphy & Balzer, 1986) and has been labeled the *halo-accuracy paradox*. The data in Table 10-4 suggest that the strongest relationships between errors and accuracy do indeed involve halo and accuracy measures, and are in the opposite direction that would be predicted if rater errors were valid indicators of accuracy. Fisicaro (1988) suggested that this paradox is due in part to the definitions of halo and accuracy commonly used in the literature, and showed

Table 10–4.   Correlations Between Rater Error and Rating Accuracy Measures

	Elevation	Differential Elevation	Stereotype Accuracy	Differential Accuracy
Halo				
Median correlation	−.11	−.14	−.16	−.31
Variance within ratees	−.01	.02	−.34	−.60
Leniency				
Difference between mean and scale midpoint	−.26	−.04	−.03	.00
Skew of ratings	.17	.15	.00	.00
Range Restriction				
Standard deviation across ratees	.11	−.25	−.18	−.22
Kurtosis of ratings	.06	−.14	−.06	−.09

that it disappears when different definitions are employed (see also Becker & Cardy, 1986).

We think that a better resolution of the halo-accuracy paradox is to admit that there is no paradox at all. The halo-accuracy relationship is paradoxical only if one assumes that the typical operational definitions of halo error are valid representations of the construct. We think there are sufficient problems with current operational definitions of *all* of the frequently cited rater errors to question their validity, and that there is no need for an elaborate theory to explain apparent paradoxes in measures of such dubious validity.

One final indication of the dubious relationship between rater errors and rating accuracy comes from the rater training literature. A favorite method of training has been to inform raters of the existence and nature of rater errors, and exhort them to avoid those errors. This method does indeed reduce rater errors but it also reduces the accuracy of ratings (Bernardin & Beatty, 1984; Bernardin & Pence, 1980; Borman, 1979; Landy & Farr, 1983). It appears that rater error training leads raters to substitute an invalid rating bias (avoid rater errors) for whatever strategy they were using before rating. Avoiding errors simply does not address the question of accuracy.

Psychometric Criteria and Accuracy We know of little empirical research on the relationship between the reliability, construct validity, and accuracy of ratings, although in theory these concepts should be related. In particular, reliability probably places an upper limit on accuracy; ratings that are plagued by random measurement error are unlikely to be accurate. Construct validity probably also places some limits on accuracy, although the relationship is not so direct. For example, ratings might not provide valid information about separate dimensions of performance but might still provide a valid indication of ratees' overall level of performance. Here, a lack of construct validity would limit the stereotype accuracy and the differential accuracy of ratings but would not necessarily limit their differential elevation.

Sulsky and Balzer (1988) make the point that reliability and validity might be necessary but would not be sufficient to assure accuracy. One reason for this is that many accuracy measures reflect both rank-ordering accuracy and accuracy in estimating the variability of performance. Sulsky and Balzer (1988) maintain that the first type of accuracy is a function of reliability and validity, but that the second is not. One solution is to separate the correlational components of accuracy from the variance components (Becker & Cardy, 1986). This approach is especially appealing if ratings are to be used solely to rank-order ratees (e.g., to determine priority for promotion) but will not always be appropriate. Pay-for-performance plans attempt to reward individuals in relation to their contribution to the organization. In this case, the best worker should receive a higher bonus if he or she is vastly superior to all other employees than if he or she is marginally better that other workers.

There is a need for more research on the reliability and construct validity of ratings. We believe that reliability and validity indices *will* be related to rating accuracy. Furthermore, the strength and pattern of this relationship will help in the future in choosing among the bewildering array of accuracy measures that are currently in use (Balzer & Sulsky, in press).

Research Design Issues

In most applications of performance appraisal, each individual is evaluated on several dimensions by a single rater (i.e., the supervisor). If the Analysis of Variance (ANOVA) were used to analyze these data, the design would be a nested one (Ratee × Dimension, nested within Raters). This design makes it empirically impossible to separate rater effects from ratee effects (Vance et al., 1983). For example, if a rater gives ratings of "excellent" to all ratees, it is impossible to tell if the rater is lenient or if the ratees really are excellent.

A fully crossed Rater × Ratee × Dimension design is needed to understand rating data. This design is impractical for most organizations since it is unlikely that all raters are qualified to rate all ratees, but a smaller-scale version of this design might be achieved by having each rater evaluate all ratees who he or she has observed, and then constructing separate Rater × Ratee × Dimension matrices for all possible groupings of raters and ratees. This would provide multiple (but nonindependent) replications of the basic Rater × Ratee × Dimension design, and if a sufficient number of raters was available for each ratee, it would be possible to separate rater biases from ratee differences. Another possibility for analyzing data from such a study is to perform a Rater × Ratee × Dimension × Group analysis, where each group consist of ratees who are evaluated by the same raters (Saal et al., 1980).

Saal and colleagues (1980) recommend the use of a Rater × Ratee MANOVA (Multivariate Analysis of Variance) in analyzing data from a Rater × Ratee × Dimension design. They suggest four criteria that should be used in evaluating the ratings.

1. The overall mean rating should be near the scale midpoint.
2. The ratee effect should be large; there should be clear differences in the mean ratings assigned to different ratees.
3. The rater effect should be small; there should *not* be sizable differences in the mean ratings from different raters.
4. The number of latent roots (i.e., eigenvalues of the correlation matrix that are sufficiently large to indicate the presence of a substantive factor) should be large.

Saal and associates (1980) suggest that the number of latent roots indicates the extent to which ratees are rank-ordered differently on different dimensions (i.e., the amount of halo in rating).

There are two difficulties with the approach outlined above. First, some criteria seem arbitrary. For example, the number of latent roots might indicate whether dimensions have been chosen that are similar to or different from one another, and may not provide useful information about the quality of the rating data. Second, these recommendations imply that the organization should serve as the unit of analysis. There is some merit to this position. This unit of analysis allows one to determine whether or not the PA system as a whole is working in the way one would expect from a valid and accurate system. However, this approach does not provide information to or about individual raters. Perhaps the best approach is to use *both* the rater and the organization as units of analysis. A Rater × Ratee MANOVA could provide information about the PA system as a whole, whereas an analysis for each individual rater could provide valuable diagnostic information. In the event that the system as a whole is deficient, an analysis of each rater's data could help determine whether the problem is systemic or whether it is concentrated in some group of raters. This rater-level analysis could serve as a type of individual needs analysis when deciding who to assign to rater training programs.

In addition to untangling rater and ratee effects, it is often important to untangle ratee effects from the effects of the group in which the rater works. Research clearly shows that the performance of other workgroup members affects evaluations of the performance of each member of the group (Grey & Kipnis, 1976; Liden & Mitchell, 1983; Mitchell & Liden, 1982). Yammarino, Dubinsky, and Hartley (1987) suggest analytic methods for separating individual effects from group effects in rating. Their methods are conceptually similar to those that might be employed in a Rater × Ratee ANOVA, in which ratees are nested within groups. They propose interpreting within-group and between-group differences as indices of specific rater errors. As with most other rater error measures, this method depends heavily on implicit assumptions about the true distribution of performance (e.g., that individuals differ more than groups differ) that are debatable and that have not been demonstrated empirically.

The final research design issue that needs serious consideration involves the choice of dimensions for the appraisal instrument. As we have noted elsewhere, indices of convergent and discriminant validity are difficult to interpret unless the proper relationship among dimensions is known. We would be more impressed with modest evidence of discriminant validity for dimensions that are conceptually similar than for dimensions that were obviously unrelated. Likewise, we would be more impressed with evidence of convergent validity for unrelated dimensions than for conceptually similar ones. When dimensions are redundant, convergent validity depends solely on the differences in the average level of performance of employees.

The choice of dimensions for a PA scale has generally been dictated by a careful job analysis (Bernardin & Beatty, 1984). We think that job analysis is important but that it is not enough. More attention is needed about the explication of the construct of job performance (Murphy & Kroeker, 1988) and the important parts of the performance domain that may not show up in a job analysis. For example, maintaining at least adequate interpersonal relations with co-workers is frequently critical but it is unlikely to appear on any task analysis. Research on the criteria that should be used to evaluate performance appraisals will continue to be flounder unless more progress is made in the area of the construct validity of job performance ratings.

Summary

It is surprisingly difficult to determine whether or not performance ratings provide valid and accurate indications of individuals' performance. Several methods and measures have been proposed over the years, including a variety of indices drawn from psychometric theory, a number of so-called rater error measures, and, more recently, direct measures of rating accuracy.

Over the last 30 years, rater error indices have been the most common measures of the quality of rating data. The popularity of these measures seems to be declining, in part because of research questioning the relationship between rater errors and rating accuracy. Direct accuracy measures have become more common, but are limited almost exclusively to laboratory experiments. As noted in this chapter, it might be possible to measure rating accuracy in the field, although this will require substantial changes in the way in which ratings are done in most organizations. In particular, it will require the routine use of multiple raters.

Psychometric criteria continue to be important and should probably be used in more studies. Research on the psychometric characteristics of ratings is both scarce and fragmented. Nevertheless, a substantial body of indirect evidence for the construct validity of ratings exists. This research suggests that supervisors are indeed capable of telling who is performing well or poorly. However, this does not necessarily mean that their ratings will reflect the judgments they have made. Raters' tendency to distort their evaluations when filling out performance appraisal forms may continue to be the most difficult issue in evaluating the validity and accuracy of ratings.

Chapter Eleven

Criteria That Reflect the Uses of Ratings

▶ Chapter Ten examined the criteria that are most often used to evaluate ratings: rater error and rating accuracy measures. Both of these classes of measures attempt to address the question Are ratings any good? Neither of these measures does a completely adequate job. We think the problem is not with the specific measures themselves but rather with the underlying question. Rather than asking Are ratings any good?, it is more accurate to ask What are they good for?

As discussed in several earlier chapters, it is the organizational context that defines the form and function of a performance appraisal (PA) system. Methods of evaluating rating data that are context free (e.g., rating accuracy scores) are not likely to provide an adequate basis for evaluating ratings. It is possible to envision situations in which ratings were highly reliable and valid, and showed no leniency, halo, or central tendency, but still were absolutely useless to the organization. On the other hand, ratings that do poorly on all of the criteria outlined in Chapter Ten could still be make a substantial contribution to the organization's ability to function and survive.

Balzer and Sulsky (in press) noted the growing proliferation of measures that are used to evaluate rating data, and noted further that there are no clear guidelines for choosing among measures. This chapter will provide guidelines for evaluating rating data that incorporate contextual factors as well as psychometric ones.

We open this chapter with a review of research on the utility of accurate performance ratings. We will note that utility and usefulness are not necessarily the same thing, and that utility formulations may lead us to a narrow focus on only a few aspects of the organizational context. Next we will review literature that considers the match between the uses of rating data and the selection of criteria for evaluating these data. Consideration of this link could help move us from context-free to context-determined criteria, by shifting our attention from a global evaluation of ratings to the question of whether they efficiently accomplish a specific purpose in an organization. Finally, we will consider the problem of integrating information from several distinct criterion measures to form an overall evaluation of a PA system.

Utility

Very few people are interested in tests or other psychological measures solely as exercises in measurement. Rather, measurement is a critical social concern because test scores are used to make important decisions. The same principal applies to performance appraisals. No rational manager is or should be interested in measurement for measurement's sake. Performance appraisal is an important activity because it affects a wide range of organizational and individual decisions. Utility theory represents a decision-oriented method of evaluating appraisal systems or procedures that can be applied to assessing the value of accurate ratings, well-structured feedback, and so on to the organization. There is substantial literature applying utility theory to employment testing (Boudreau & Berger, 1985; Cascio, 1982; Cascio & Ramos, 1986; Cascio & Silbey, 1979; Hunter & Hunter, 1984; Wyer, 1988). Landy, Farr, and Jacobs (1982) applied this same approach to the evaluation of performance appraisal systems (see also Landy and Farr, 1983).

The basic equation for assessing utility can be traced to the early work of Brogden (1949), and Cronbach and Gleser (1965), both of whom were concerned primarily with personnel selection. The increase in utility associated with using a valid test in personnel selection is given by:

$$\text{Gain in utility} = N_s r_{xy} (\phi/p) SD_y - C \qquad (1)$$

where:

N_s = number of persons selected

r_{xy} = correlation between test scores and performance

p = selection ratio (number of positions/number of applicants)

ϕ = ordinate of the normal curve that corresponds to p

SD_y = standard deviation of performance

C = cost, per person, of testing

Equation 1 is nothing more than a simple regression equation. The term ϕ/p corresponds to the average standard score (z score) of those who are selected. Since candidates with the highest test scores are hired and candidates with the lowest scores are typically rejected, it follows that ϕ/p will generally be positive and will increase as the ratio of applicants to positions increases. (For example, if the selection ratio is .15, $\phi/p = 1.55$; if $SR = .10, \phi/p = 1.76$). Thus, ϕ/p represents the increase in the average test score if the highest-scoring candidates are hired rather than hiring people at random (Murphy, 1986).

When this z score is multiplied by r_{xy}, the result is the expected increase in Y (performance), measured in standard score units. Thus, if $SR = .15$ and $r_{xy} = .50$, using the test to select applicants will result in an average increase in performance of .775 standard deviation units, per person hired. Multiplying this figure by the number selected (N_s) gives the total increase, in standard deviation units. Multiplying this figure, in turn, by the standard deviation gives the increase in utility in whatever units are used to measure the standard deviation (usually, the dollar value of performance).

Finally, the costs of testing should be subtracted from the total utility estimate to obtain a comprehensive estimate of net gain. However, in most testing applications, these costs are so low that they can effectively be ignored (Murphy, 1986). Elaborate procedures, such as those used at some assessment centers, may involve more substantial costs.

Utility is typically expressed in dollar terms. This is accomplished by measuring the standard deviation of performance in terms of dollars, which can be done either through cost-accounting methods (Cronbach & Gleser, 1965) or by using supervisory judgments (Schmidt, Hunter, McKenzie, & Muldrow, 1979). For example, if the value of the goods and services produced by a highly superior worker (i.e., someone in the 85th percentile) is $60,000, and the value of the goods and services produced by an average worker (i.e., someone in the 50th percentile) is $40,000, this difference provides a concrete measure of SD_y. The 85th percentile is approximately one SD above the 50th percentile in a normal distribution, so the standard deviation of performance, measured in dollar terms, is approximately $20,000. However, dollars are not the only metric that might be used. For example, if the standard deviation of performance were measured in terms of the number of units produced per year, Equation 1 would give you a way of predicting the increase in production associated with the use of a valid test to select employees.

There is a substantial body of literature on the validity of utility estimates obtained by applying Equation 1. (See Bobko, Karren, and Kerkar, 1987, and Boudreau, in press, for discussions of the boundary conditions of utility equations and SD_y estimation.) Caution must be observed in evaluating the results of analyses of selection utility. Nevertheless, utility analyses suggest that the productivity gain associated with valid selection could be substantial. For example, Hunter and Hunter (1984) estimate that the use of valid selection tests for entry-level federal jobs would result in savings of $15 billion per year.

Applications to Performance Appraisal Landy and colleagues (1982) noted that if a poorly designed PA system were replaced with one that provided workers with valid feedback about performance, there should be an increase in productivity. Equation 1 can be adapted to estimate the size of this increase. The annual gain to an organization associated with the installation of a valid performance appraisal and feedback system is given by:

$$\text{Gain in utility} = N_T/p \ (r_1 - r_2) \ SD_y \ (\phi/p) - N_T/p \ (C_1 - C_2)$$

(2)

where:

r_1 and r_2 = validity of the new and the old appraisal systems, respectively

C_1 and C_2 = costs, per person, of the new and the old appraisal respectively

N_T = total number of persons involved

p = proportion who receive new appraisal

Equation 2 is simply a more general case of Equation 1. The validity of a PA system (r_1) can be thought of in terms of analysis of variance (ANOVA) as the square root of η^2, where η^2 refers to the percentage of the total variance in responses accounted for by differences in the responses of those who use the new PA system and those who do not.

Equation 1 is based on the assumption that the current selection system has no validity whatsoever (i.e. selection is done at random), which implies that r_2 is zero. If selection is done at random, the costs of the old system (C_2) will also be zero. The only other difference between the two equations is that N_s is replaced by N_T/p. In most settings, all incumbents will receive the new appraisal system, which means that $p = 1.00$ and $N_T = N_S$.

Landy, Farr, and Jacobs (1982) suggest that utility analyses can be more easily understood if the effect of the appraisal system is expressed in terms of the difference in the mean levels of performance as the result of a new appraisal system (d_t), rather than expressing this same difference in correlational terms $(r_1 \times \phi/p)$. The term d_t is approximately twice the size of $r_1 - r_2$. Since p generally equals 1.00 (i.e., all employees typically participate in a new appraisal program), the term ϕ/p drops out of the equation. If the validity of the old appraisal system equals zero (or, if there was no previous system), and the new system is used with all employees, Equation 2 reduces to:

$$\text{Gain in utility} = N_T([2 \ r_1 \ SD_y] - C_1)$$

(3)

Landy and associates (1982) illustrate the application of Equation 3 in a hypothetical organization with 500 managers, where the validity of a new system is .30, SD_y = $20,000, and C_1 = $700. Equation 3 yields an estimated gain of $5.3 million per year.

Research on utility estimation has generally treated job performance as a unitary dimension. There is typically one r_{xy} value in a utility formula that represents the correlation between the X variable (e.g., a test or a new performance appraisal system) and overall job performance. This approach appears to embrace a concept that has been largely abandoned by PA researchers — the concept of the "ultimate criterion" (Thorndike, 1949). Job performance is more likely to be multidimensional, and the concept of overall job performance may have no meaning (Murphy & Kroeker, 1988). As we will note below, the failure to consider the multidimensional nature of performance may represent a serious problem in current approaches to utility estimation.

Credibility of Utility Estimates Suppose an individual had just carried out the utility analysis described above. Based on those figures, should the individual conclude that there is now an extra $5.3 million to spend? We think the answer is no. First, there are some technical objections to the procedures typically used to estimate SD_y (Bobko et al., 1987). Although the literature generally supports the validity of those estimates, there is also evidence of bias in the judgments that go into estimating SD_y. In particular, SD_y judgments may be based in part on the salary level of the job (Bobko et al., 1987). Thus, if workers in two separate plants do exactly the same thing but receive different salaries (e.g., if one plant is unionized and the other is not), higher SD_y estimates could be expected where the salary levels are higher.

Second, the equations do not account for the possibility that some employees may use the new program and others may not (Murphy, 1986). In personnel selection, some applicants who receive job offers may turn them down. In performance appraisal, some raters might be more willing to provide valid feedback than others. Murphy (1986) showed that utility equations, such as Equations 1, 2, and 3, typically overestimate the actual gain that can be expected as the result of a new test or appraisal system.

Third, and most important, it is uncertain that the outcomes of implementing a new PA system can adequately be summarized in terms of either a single validity coefficient (r_1) or in terms of a single outcome variable (dollar value of the increase in performance). There are multiple outcomes associated with any new system, some of which will be positive and others of which will be negative. The following list shows a number of outcomes that might reasonably be expected if a managerial PA system was instituted in a company that previously had no system.

Positive Outcomes

▶ More awareness of performance level
▶ More awareness of strengths and weaknesses
▶ Better development plans
▶ More effort to address current weaknesses

Negative Outcomes

- ▶ Interpersonal strain between managers and their superiors
- ▶ Perceptions of inequity (if rewards are not commensurate with ratings)
- ▶ Discouragement (average and poor performers see fewer opportunities for promotions and other rewards)
- ▶ Less willingness to help peers

Presumably, the value of these outcomes would vary (both in terms of sign and the magnitude) and the "validity" of the appraisal system for producing each outcome would also vary. For example, effort by managers to address current weaknesses may be more valuable to the organization than awareness of one's performance level. The tendency of an appraisal system to reduce a manager's willingness to help peers (under the new system, peers may be seen as competitors for promotions, salary increases, etc.) might be seen as a more harmful than increasing interpersonal strain between managers and their supervisors.

Differences in the values of outcomes would not be a problem if the likelihood of each outcome was the same. Unfortunately, it is likely that there will be a different validity coefficient (r_{xy}) for each outcome variable. For example, valid feedback will, by definition, almost certainly lead to higher awareness of strengths and weaknesses. However, this does not necessarily mean that the quality of developmental plans will also increase. In utility theory terms, performance appraisal and feedback may have more validity when the outcome variable is awareness of strengths and weaknesses than when the outcome variable is the quality of developmental plans.

More realistic estimates of utility will require the identification of multiple outcome variables, estimation of the dollar value of each, and estimates of the validity of the proposed appraisal system in relation to each important outcome variable. Multiattribute Utility Technology (MAUT) (Edwards & Newman, 1982) provides some methods for identifying important outcome variables and estimating their relative value.

For example, applying MAUT methods might lead to the identification of the three outcome variables listed in Table 11-1. In this case, a new PA system might be likely to lead to better awareness of strengths and weaknesses ($r = .60$). Workers who are highly aware of their strengths and weaknesses might produce goods and services that are worth $3,000 more than workers whose awareness of strengths and weaknesses is only average. If there are 500 participants, Equation 3 suggests that the utility for this outcome variable has a value of $1.2 million. The new system has considerably less validity for increasing the quality of developmental plans ($r = .15$) but the difference in performance of someone with highly superior versus average developmental plans is substantial ($17,000). The net utility for this outcome is $225,000.

Finally, the new system has some potential for leading to perceptions of

Table 11–1. Utility Estimation with Multiple Outcome Variables

	Outcome Variable		
	Awareness of Strengths and Weaknesses	Better Development Plans	Perceptions of Inequity
N_T	500	500	500
Validity (r_1)	.60	.15	−.20[a]
SD_y	$3,000	$17,000	$10,000
Cost per person (C_1)	$600	—[b]	—[b]
Gain or loss in utility	$1.2 million	$225,000	−$2 million

[a] Negative validity coefficient indicates that people with higher perceptions of inequity perform worse than those who perceive little inequity.

[b] The cost of the system does not increase if there are multiple outcome variables, and should be subtracted from only one of the utility estimates.

inequity. Since this outcome is negative, the validity coefficient for this outcome should also be negative ($r = -.20$). Workers who perceive a high level of inequity will not perform as well as workers who are at the mean in their perceptions of inequity; the difference in their levels of productivity leads to a SD_y estimate of $10,000 for this outcome variable. Equation 3 suggests that the utility for this outcome will be a *negative* $2 million. In other words, considering the effects of the new performance appraisal system on perceptions of inequity, it may be concluded that one is worse off with the new system than without it.

In this example, the utility estimates for three outcome variables were $1.2 million, $225,000, and −$2 million, respectively. It is not clear how to go about combining these estimates to arrive with an overall utility estimate. Simply adding them together gives an estimate of −$575,000, which implies that the system will do more harm than good. Unfortunately, simply adding the separate estimates for each outcome variable might not result in an accurate estimate, since outcome variables are not likely to be independent. For example, the extent to which an appraisal system leads to better developmental plans is almost certainly correlated with the extent to which the system makes workers aware of strengths and weaknesses. Thus, some of the gain is associated with better awareness of strengths and weaknesses, as is illustrated in Figure 11-1. The net gain for these two outcomes is almost certain to be less than the sum of the separate utility estimates. More research is needed on methods of combining separate estimates.

The most critical problem in multiattribute utility estimation is determining all of the important outcomes of implementing a performance appraisal system. It is possible that outcomes that are of concern to the organization *not* listed in Table 11-1 might also result from the introduction of a PA system, and failure to include those outcome variables could lead to substantial distortions in utility estimates.

Figure 11–1.   Overlap in Gain Associated with Awareness of Strengths and Weaknesses and Better Developmental Plans

Gain from Awareness of Strengths and Weaknessess

Gain from Better Developmental Plans

In our opinion, accurate estimation of utility is not possible unless most of the important outcome variables can be identified. The most reasonable way to identify important versus unimportant outcomes might be to examine SD_y estimates. If SD_y is small, that outcome variable cannot have much impact on productivity; workers who are at the top of the distribution of that variable will not perform much better than workers who are near the middle.

Usefulness of Utility Estimates   Assuming that accurate estimates of the utility of different performance appraisals were available, it might be argued that utility estimates that are ignored or discounted by organizations are not useful. Although there is a growing body of research on utility estimation itself, the question of whether utility estimates are in fact used by organizations has not received much attention.

Organizations rarely ask for utility estimates expressed in dollar terms. There are reasons to believe that utility estimates are more impressive to researchers than to managers in organizations. For example, although expressed in dollar terms, these estimates typically do not account for a variety of factors that would be routinely considered by accountants and financial managers, such as the tax rate or the interest that could be earned on money that is devoted to the personnel program under consideration (c.f. Cronshaw & Alexander, 1985). Thus, the projected gain obtained from a utility equation is, at best, likely to be viewed by managers as a rough approximation (and probably an overestimate).

In the area of performance appraisal, utility estimates clearly have had little impact on organizational decisions. There are two lines of evidence to support this contention. First, although the estimated utility of valid performance appraisal is probably substantial (Landy et al., 1982), many organizations *act* as if performance appraisal is not very important. As noted in Chapter Nine, organizations rarely reward supervisors for doing good performance appraisals or punish supervisors for doing bad ones. Longenecker, Sims, and Gioia (1987) interviewed 60 executives to assess their perceptions of PA. A quote from one of these people very neatly summarizes the attitude of many managers and supervisors toward performance appraisal: "At some places, the PA process is a joke — just a bureaucratic thing that the manager does to keep the IR (industrial relations) people off his back." If organizations really believed that valid performance appraisal could lead to savings in the millions, they would hardly treat performance appraisal in such a cavalier fashion, and would not tolerate executives who regarded appraisal as a joke.

An examination of PA practices in organizations provides another type of evidence that managers either are not aware of or do not accept estimates of the utility of performance appraisal. Longenecker and Gioia (1988) note that although performance appraisal is nearly universal in the lower ranks of organizations, it is only rarely carried out for top-level executives. However, utility theory suggests that the potential gain, per person, from a valid performance appraisal system is greatest at the top levels of an organization. Top-level executives typically have large budgets and considerable discretion. The difference between the achievements of an average top executive and those of an excellent or poor executive should be correspondingly large. (SD_y estimates are usually proportional to the salary level of the job. An executive whose salary is $200,000 will probably recive an SD_y estimate that is roughly four times as large as a manager whose salary is $50,000.) The fact that appraisal becomes *less* likely, rather than more likely, as one moves up in the organization suggests that top-level executives either are not aware of or do not accept existing estimates of the utility of performance appraisal.

We believe that estimates of utility are more useful in making choices among alternatives than in projecting the real savings that will result from a valid PA system (Murphy, 1986). If two different PA systems with estimated utilities of $2 million and $5 million per year are being considered, we would be more confident in our choice of systems (choosing the latter) than in the prediction that there will be $3 million more available next year as the result of adopting the better performance appraisal system. It is interesting to note that the use of a dollar metric has no effect whatsoever when choosing among programs. The same choice will be made if SD_y is measured in dollars, time saved, increased output, or any other metric. Thus, the sizable literature on SD_y estimation (see Bobko et al., 1987) may be dealing with a question that is entirely academic.

At present, utility estimates appear to be useful but rarely used. Latham (1986) notes that researchers' emphasis on estimating financial gain is not shared by many managers; managers rarely ask social scientists for utility estimates. It may be that the present emphasis on the financial impact of personnel programs *decreases* the credibility of results. Estimates of financial gain that do not take into account the rudiments of accounting are not likely to impress a sophisticated business manager. They are more likely to reinforce the stereotype that social science researchers do not understand the realities of management and business. We believe that future research should emphasize estimating the *comparative* utility of alternative appraisal systems rather than trying to estimate the dollar savings expected as the result of a particular system.

Choosing among Criteria

Utility estimates are certainly informative but they do not necessarily indicate whether a performance appraisal system is useful to the organization. A PA system that yields an estimated gain of several million dollars might still fail to fulfill its major functions in an organization. In this section, we will consider some alternatives to utility estimates. First, however, we must discuss principles involved in choosing appropriate criterion for evaluating a performance appraisal system.

Appraisal Goals and the Choice of Criteria

Traditional criteria, such as reliability, validity, and even utility, are deficient in that they do not fully consider the actual purpose of performance appraisal. Reliability and validity would be highly relevant criteria if PA was solely concerned with measurement (Murphy & Davidshofer, 1988; Sulsky & Balzer, 1988). However, performance appraisal is *not* concerned solely with measurement; its purpose of may be to increase employee motivation and performance, or it may be used as a control mechanism or as an aid in making administrative decisions. Reliability and validity may be largely irrelevant to many of these uses of performance appraisal (Balzer & Sulsky, in press; Kane & Lawler, 1979).

Consider the case in which a PA system is used to make promotion decisions. Reliability, validity, and accuracy are not completely relevant in deciding whether the performance appraisal system is fulfilling it function (Sulsky & Balzer, 1988). Feldman (1986) notes:

> The practical level of accuracy needed is only great enough to support decisions in the same way that the ideal system would if it were available. That is, if it is necessary to divide employees into promotable and nonpromotable groups . . . a less than perfect appraisal system may be able to generate this dichotomy with the same level of accuracy as a schematically perfect one (p. 77).

In other words, a system that did nothing more than allowing an individual to make correct promotion decisions would be a good system, even if the indices used to measure performance were inaccurate or measured the wrong set of constructs. In a similar vein, Schmitt and Schneider (1983) note that if an appraisal system is used primarily to rank-order workers, accuracy in multidimensional evaluations is not really a relevant criterion. Rather, the system must be evaluated in terms of its ability to validly rank-order workers.

In Chapter Ten, we noted that the criteria most often used in evaluating ratings are defined independently of the context or purpose of rating. That is, criteria such as reliability, validity, accuracy, and freedom from rater errors are assumed to be important for assessing *any* PA system. Since there is a wide variety of criterion measures, all of which are supposedly relevant, PA researchers and practitioners seem to face a dilemma in choosing criteria, in that the choice of any specific set of measures can be criticized as arbitrary (Balzer & Sulsky, 1988).

We think that an entirely different approach needs to be taken to the choice of criterion measures for evaluating performance appraisal systems. Rather than relying on the same context-free criteria for evaluating each system, the context must be carefully considered and the criteria chosen accordingly. The central assumption here is that *the choice of criteria should be determined by the goals of the PA system.* The goals of the system will, in turn, be determined by the organizational context and, in particular, by the implicit and explicit purpose(s) of performance appraisal in that organization.

Cleveland, Murphy, and Williams, (1989) surveyed literature on the uses of performance appraisal in organizations and suggested that 20 different uses could be identified. They grouped these uses into four categories that help indicate the major goals associated with each use of performance appraisal. Thus, one group of uses is concerned with distinguishing between individuals (e.g., for salary administration, promotion). The major goal of appraisal systems whose primary purpose falls within this first category will be to indicate overall levels of performance for the individuals rated. In some cases (e.g., promotion), it will be sufficient simply to rank-order ratees. For other purposes (e.g., salary administration), the system must also validly estimate the intervals between individuals.

The second group of uses is concerned with within-individual comparisons, such as providing feedback about strengths and weaknesses. The main goal of the system is not to compare different people but rather to compare performance in different areas by the same person. The major goal of this group of uses is to estimate *patterns,* rather than levels, of performance.

The third group is concerned with using performance appraisal to help maintain and run different personnel systems in organizations. Examples include using PA to identify organizational development needs or organizational training needs. If the primary use of performance appraisal falls within this category, the appraisal system should be evaluated in terms of its contribution to the smooth functioning of the personnel systems it serves.

Finally, there are several uses of performance appraisal that suggest that the primary goal is to document personnel actions or decisions. If the primary purpose of performance appraisal is to provide a "paper trail," or a justification for a personnel decision, the system should be evaluated in those terms.

The categories discussed by Cleveland and associates (1989) represent explicit goals that might be set by the organization for a PA system. There are also several implicit goals that are set by the users of the system, and these goals will also be relevant in choosing criteria for evaluating a performance appraisal system. For example, Longenecker and colleagues (1987) note that raters often use performance appraisal as a motivational tool. If this is true, a PA system that gives completely inaccurate measures of performance but that motivates workers to perform better may be a very good rating system.

Bjerke, Cleveland, Morrison, and Wilson (1987) noted that the implicit goals shared by raters are often a product of the culture or climate of the organization. They cite as an example the PA system used for officers in the navy. Although several explicit goals have been identified by the navy, interviews with raters make it clear that raters are pursuing one and only one goal — to help secure promotion for some ratees and deny promotion to others. It follows that the quality of promotion decisions should be a primary criterion for evaluating this appraisal system.

Studies of political factors in performance appraisal (e.g., Longenecker et al., 1987; Patz, 1975) suggest that the the presence of implicit goals (or unwritten rules) for performance appraisal is the norm rather than an abberration. It seems reasonable to conclude than in many organizations, there might be widely shared implicit goals that govern the PA process. These implicit goals are one feature of the organization's culture. An accurate evaluation of the performance of a PA system must take into account these implicit goals, as well as the explicit goals that are set by the organization. For example, the organization might state that performance appraisal is used solely to make promotion decisions, but raters in the organization might in fact use performance appraisal as a motivational tool. A system that does a relatively good job of meeting both goals might be preferable to one that does an excellent job of meeting the goal of validly determining promotions but that has no effect on ratee motivation.

Table 11-2 illustrates the process of linking the choice of criteria to the goals of the appraisal system, as applied to several of the uses of performance appraisal reviewed by Cleveland and associates (1989). The first step is to define the goal in terms of the measurement principles that apply. For example, a system that is used solely to make promotion decisions implies an ordinal system of measurement in which the major criterion for evaluating the system is its validity in rank-ordering candidates. A system that is designed to give feedback about strengths and weaknesses must allow one to scale different performance dimensions on a comparable scale that allows for meaningful comparisons among performance levels in qualititatively different areas. A system that is is used to identify organizational development needs must provide a valid measure of *overall* strengths and weaknesses in an organization. A system that is used to document personnel decisions or actions must provide a detailed and relatively objective record of the individual's past performance. The best criterion for evaluating such a system may be the amount of specific information about performance that can be recorded rather than the accuracy of performance evaluations.

Cleveland and colleagues (1989) suggest one final problem in determining and specifying the goals of performance appraisal. They note that performance appraisal is often viewed as a multipurpose tool, and that it is quite common for there to be multiple goals for any given PA system. Unfortunately, performance appraisal systems often try to achieve goals that are in conflict with one another. For example, the goals of making valid comparisons between persons versus within persons are largely incompatible,

Table 11–2. **Using the Goals of the Appraisal System to Determine Criteria**

Purpose of Appraisal	Major Goal of System	Criteria That Are Most Appropriate for Evaluating the System
Promotion	Rank ratees	Rank-order correlation between ratings and true overall performance level
Feedback on strengths and weaknesses	Scale performance in different areas using a common metric	Stereotype accuracy Comparability of scores on different dimensions (e.g., ability to measure all dimensions on a common evaluative scale)
Determine organization's developmental needs	Scale *average* performance level on each dimension on a common metric	Stereotype accuracy of the *mean* rating on each dimension Comparability across dimensions
Document personnel actions	Provide detailed, objective record of past performance	Amount and apparent objectivity of supporting information

but performance appraisal systems nevertheless often try to achieve both goals (Cleveland et al., 1989).

The presence of multiple conflicting goals will greatly complicate the evaluation of a PA system and will place a ceiling on how well the system can work. If a system pursues two mutually incompatible goals, it cannot succeed in both; the best that can be expected is to succeed in meeting one goal and to fail in meeting the other. The worst-case scenario is one in which the presence of mutually incompatible goals will make it impossible to achieve *any* of the goals of the system.

Defining the Goals of a Performance Appraisal System

The system for choosing criteria illustrated in Table 11-2 is based on two assumptions: (1) there are few goals and (2) these goals are known. Research on the use of performance appraisal (e.g., Cleveland et al., 1989) suggests that these conditions are seldom met. Multiple goals, some of which are not explicitly defined, will drive the appraisal system in most organizations. Therefore, it is unlikely that an external consultant could examine most PA systems and determine all of the goals that the system is designed to meet.

What is needed is a systematic procedure for eliciting goals from those individuals who use the PA system. Balzer and Sulsky (in press) suggest a general framework for eliciting goals and selecting criteria that are relevant to those goals. Their approach is quite similar to procedures used in decision research (Edwards & Newman, 1982) and is illustrated in Figure 11-2. First, the set of individuals who have a stake in the PA system must be identified. Balzer and Sulsky (in press) assume that there will be groups of individuals who share common goals; these are referred to as *constituent groups*. Raters, ratees, and personnel or human resource departments might define three separate constituencies, each of which is pursuing different goals. Our earlier discussion of explicit versus implicit goals suggests that explicit goals, such as making better promotion decisions, will be pursued by the human resource department, and that implicit goals will be defined by the raters and ratees.

Once constituents, or stakeholders, are identified, the set of goals pursued by each constituent group must be identified. Edwards and Newman (1982) discuss a variety of methods of eliciting values and goals from stakeholders. This process may involve nothing more than asking each group what goals they are pursuing in performance appraisal, and clustering together related groups of goals. Goals can then be arranged into hierarchically organized sets that represent the valued end states that the users of the system are attempting to reach. However, it is possible that members of constituent groups are not fully aware of the goals they are pursuing. Group discussion formats, in which members have an opportunity to add to or disagree with

Figure 11–2. Framework for Identifying Goals and Choosing Criteria

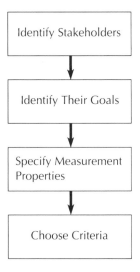

Adapted from W. K. Balzer and L. M. Sulsky, in K. R. Murphy and F. E. Saal (Eds.), *Psychology in Organizations: Integrating Science and Practice* (Hillsdale, NJ: Erlbaum, in press).

statements of other group members, are probably preferable to questionnaires for eliciting goals.

The third step is to specify the measurement properties that will enable the PA to meet the goals defined in the second step. We do not know of any algorithm that can be applied to all goal sets to derive measurement properties (i.e., there is no "cookbook" for accomplishing this phase of the process). The success of this step will depend largely on the ingenuity of the investigator. This step will be easier if there is one overriding goal; it will be more difficult if there are many goals or goals that are in conflict.

The final step illustrated in Figure 11-2 is to choose criteria. This step entails matching operational measures to the measurement properties specified in the previous step. Once again, there is no "cookbook" for doing this, and the choice of criteria will depend somewhat on the investigator's ability to translate general principles into practical measures. The more detail about desirable measurement properties that can be specified in the third step, the easier it will be to choose appropriate criteria for evaluating a PA system in this final step.

Some Neglected Criteria

The dominance of psychometrically-oriented criteria (e.g., reliability, halo) and, more recently, accuracy-oriented criteria (e.g., rating accuracy, behavior recognition accuracy) has directed the attention of researchers and practitioners away from a number of "soft" criteria that might be highly critical in evaluating whether a performance appraisal system has met its major goals. In particular, little recent attention has been given to three classes of criteria that might be extremely important in determining the success of an appraisal system: (1) reaction criteria, (2) practicality criteria, and (3) criteria that reflect the contributions of the appraisal system to the *process* of making decisions.

Reaction Criteria Kirkpatrick (1967) suggested that one type of criterion that could be used to evaluate the effectiveness of a training program would deal with reactions to the program. This criterion is also highly relevant when evaluating a performance appraisal system. Regardless of the technical sophistication of an appraisal system, the system will not work if the raters and ratees do not accept or believe in the system.

We noted earlier that some managers regard performance appraisal as a joke (see Longenecker et al., 1987). We would regard this type of reaction as a potentially fatal flaw in a PA system and would predict that a system that is regarded as pointless pencil-pushing by the raters will not be effective in meeting important goals. On the other hand, a system that is well accepted by raters and ratees *may* work well, although there is no guarantee of this. Reactions to a performance appraisal system probably place a ceiling on the possible effectiveness of the system, in that acceptance of the system by raters and ratees may be necessary but not sufficient for the system to be effective.

Acceptance by the raters and ratees is a function of both the process and the outcomes of performance appraisal. In order to convince raters and ratees that the appraisal system is a reasonable one, the system must refer to relevant and important dimensions of work behavior, and raters must be in a position to provide well-informed judgments about the aspects of performance measured. In addition, there must be clear and visible support for performance appraisal in the organization. If appraisal systems deal with irrelevant aspects of performance, or require raters to make judgments they plainly are not qualified to make, or if appraisal is treated as an unimportant activity by most organization members, reactions to the PA system are likely to be negative.

A second important component of reactions to performance appraisal is the acceptability of the *outcomes* of using the appraisal system. Some outcomes are politically more acceptable than others, and an appraisal system that leads to unacceptable outcomes will not be useful or successful in an organization. For example, if performance appraisals are used for salary administration, and high-rated employees in one job grade receive higher pay than low-rated employees in a higher pay grade, this outcome might be unacceptable and, as a result, the appraisal system may fail.

Most of the research on reaction criteria has concentrated on factors that affect perceptions of the fairness and accuracy of appraisal systems (Bernardin & Beatty, 1984; Dipboye & dePontbriand, 1981; Dorfman, Stephan, & Loveland, 1986; Landy, Barnes, & Murphy, 1978; Landy, Barnes-Farrell, & Cleveland, 1980; Lawler, 1967; Mount, 1984b; Waldman, Bass, & Einstein, 1987). In general, this research suggests that performance appraisals are most likely to be perceived as accurate and fair when the following criteria are met:

1. Appraisals are conducted frequently.
2. There is a formal system of appraisal.
3. Supervisors have a high degree of job knowledge.
4. Ratees have an opportunity to appeal or to express their concerns over ratings.
5. The performance dimensions are seen to be highly relevant.
6. Action plans are formed for dealing with present weaknesses.

Although this literature does not deal at any length with the facets of organizational climate and culture that lead to perceptions of fairness and accuracy, it seems reasonable to expect that performance appraisals will be received better if the climate is cooperative rather than competitive, if supervisor-subordinate relations are close, and if trust is a valued norm within the organization.

The literature on perceptions of justice in organizations may provide a rich theoretical framework for further research on factors that affect perceptions of fairness and accuracy (Greenberg, 1986; Thibaut & Walker, 1975). This literature suggests that there are two dimensions to the perceived justice of any act or policy: procedural justice and distributive justice (Folger &

Greenberg, 1985; Greenberg & Folger, 1983). These two types of justice correspond nicely with the distinction made above between reactions to the process of appraisal and reactions to the outcomes of appraisal. The research on perceptions of justice suggests that both of these facets must be present in many instances in order to guarantee that the act or policy will be perceived as fair. Thus, an appraisal system that follows sensible procedures but leads to unacceptable outcomes might fail. A system that leads to completely acceptable outcomes but follows procedures that are not accepted by raters or ratees may also fail.

Another reaction criterion that has received some attention in the research literature is the perceived utility of performance appraisals. Davis and Dickenson (1987) studied features of the organizational context, such as job standardization, leader trust and support, and climate for innovation, that determined the extent to which PA was perceived as useful for making both salary administration and promotion decisions. They found that the perceived utility of performance appraisal for these two purposes was related to (1) the extent to which the organization encouraged participation in decision making and had open lateral and vertical communications (interestingly, these two factors were *negatively* related to the perceived utility of performance appraisal); (2) to the extent to which the climate encouraged innovation; and (3) the extent to which planning for goals is formal and structured.

Although we encourage more research on perceptions of fairness, utility, and accuracy, it is important not to lose sight of the fact that these perceptions represent only a few dimensions of a complex set of reactions to performance appraisal. That is, a system may be seen as basically fair and may lead to acceptable outcomes, but still might not be well-received. As discussed in Chapter Two, both individuals and cultures vary in the extent to which they are likely to view the whole process of appraisal as acceptable or unacceptable. An individual who is basically uncomfortable with rigid authority structures might react negatively to *any* appraisal system. An organization in which the climate is highly democratic and participative might react negatively to the typical top-down appraisal system.

One reason that performance appraisal so often receives reactions ranging from indifference to disgust is that organizations, regardless of their stated policies, treat PA as a joke. As discussed in Chapter Nine, organizations rarely reward good raters or punish bad ones. Performance appraisal often occupies only a minimum of the busy supervisor's time, and organizations rarely take concrete steps to encourage more thorough or deliberative appraisals. Organizations do not bother to provide appraisals to top management, who represent their most influential employees. None of these practices is likely to lead to the perception that accurate performance appraisal is important or that the judgments of the raters will have any real impact on the actions of the organizations.

The first question that should be faced by organizations that consider reaction criteria in their evaluations of appraisal system is whether there is any good reason for a positive reaction. If the appraisal system is seen by most raters and ratees as a waste of time, it is hard to see how the appraisal system will aid in accomplishing any worthwhile goals. Reaction criteria are almost always relevant, and an unfavorable reaction may doom the most carefully constructed appraisal system. One of the most difficult challenges that may lay ahead of PA researchers will be to convince organizations to (1) take reaction criteria seriously and (2) create conditions in their organization that will lead to favorable reactions to the performance appraisal system.

Practicality Criteria   With a few exceptions (e.g., Cascio, 1987) the issue of practicality is rarely discussed in evaluating appraisal systems. However, practicality concerns are likely to influence strongly an organization's decisions regarding a new appraisal system, particularly one that is unusually complicated or involved. An appraisal system that calls for multiple raters, at different levels in the organization, all using detailed behavior diaries and behavior-based rating scales might represent the technical state of the art, but it is likely to be rejected on the simple ground that it is impractical.

Practicality concerns are considered, to some degree, in utility estimates. As discussed earlier, one of the formulas widely used in utility estimation can be expressed as:

$$\text{Gain in utility} = N_T(2\,[r_1 - r_2] \times SD_y - [C_1 + C_2]) \qquad (4)$$

Practicality concerns are represented by the cost terms (C_1 and C_2). One implication of Equation 4 is that when two alternative appraisal systems are being considered, differences in the costs of the alternatives must be offset by differences in validity to justify the choice of the more costly system. (One possibility is to compare the costs and benefits of a single appraisal system, with the alternative course of action being no performance appraisal. In this case, Equation 4 reduces to Equation 3.)

For example, suppose one system uses multiple raters and new, complex scales that cost $1,500 per person to implement, and another system employs supervisors as raters and uses existing scales that cost $200 per person. Practicality considerations suggest that the complex system should not be adopted unless it leads to some benefit that offsets the additional cost.

The differences in validity, multiplied by SD_y, provide a measure of the differences in the value of the benefits of the two systems. In the example cited above, if SD_y is equal to $10,000, the validity of the complex system (i.e., the correlation between using the system and attaining valued goals) must be .065 larger than the validity of the simpler system (i.e., if $r_2 = .45$, r_1 must be .515) to justify the choice of the more complex system. Otherwise, choice of the more valid but more expensive system will lead to a net loss in utility.

Utility equations are useful for capturing some aspects of practicality but they may ignore or underestimate some important variables that distinguish highly practical from highly impractical systems. For example, some appraisal systems require substantial commitments of time on the part of both the raters and the ratees. To our knowledge, the raters' and ratees' investment of time is not typically fully factored into the costs that are considered in utility equations. The tendency of some systems to lead to unacceptable outcomes can also be considered a facet of practicality. A system that is politically unacceptable to the organization is not practical and will not succeed.

Ease of installation is yet another facet of practicality that is not always factored into utility equations. Some systems require long training periods. Other systems have complex reporting requirements that require many workers at all levels to readjust their schedules and routines. In general, an appraisal system that can be installed in an organization with a minimum of disruption of the organization's routine will be preferable to a more disruptive one, unless the disruptive alternative is substantially more valid than the simpler one.

Decision Process Criteria   One final criterion that is frequently overlooked is the extent to which PA contributes to the decision-making process in organizations. Utility equations estimate the effect of alternative systems on the *correctness* (or the dollar value) of decisions. There are two additional ways that performance appraisal might affect the decision-making process. First, several characteristics of the appraisal system will affect the degree to which decisions are accepted by the members of the organizations. Second, the characteristics of a PA system will have a considerable impact on the ease with which specific decisions are made.

In our brief discussion of procedural and distributive justice, we noted that the perceived fairness and accuracy of appraisal system can be an important determinant of its success. The fairness of decisions (e.g., raises, promotions) made on the basis of performance appraisals must also be carefully considered. An appraisal system that does a poor job of measurement but that leads to decisions that are accepted as fair by organization members may be preferable to one that provides accurate measures that lead to decisions that are not accepted by raters or ratees.

Throughout this book, we have argued that performance appraisal should be viewed as a decision aid rather than as a measurement tool. One way that performance appraisal can contribute to the organization is to streamline and rationalize the process of making administrative decisions. The extent to which a PA system contributes to the ease of decision making is a direct function of the match between the measurement properties of the system and the goals of the different constituent groups.

For example, a manager might use performance appraisal as a tool for deciding which 3 of his or her 10 subordinates should be promoted. The only measurement characteristic that is relevant to that goal is that the appraisal system should allow the rater to separate quickly and easily the total group into two subgroups: the promotable group ($N = 3$) and the nonpromotable group ($N = 7$). An appraisal system that does not allow the rater to separate these two groups, or one that requires substantial effort or calculation on the part of raters to decide who should and should not be promoted, may not make a worthwhile contribution to the process of making administrative decisions.

The contribution of a PA system to the decision-making process may be more a matter of perceptions than reality. If organizational members *believe* that a performance appraisal system makes decisions easier and better, the system will have some benefits regardless of its actual contribution to the ease and the quality of decisions. As we noted earlier, the procedural justice literature may provide a framework for research on the contributions of a performance appraisal system to perceptions of equity. Survey research might provide some clues to the facets of PA systems that contribute to the perception that appraisals simplify the decision-making process.

Integrating Multiple Criteria

Since most performance appraisal systems are driven by multiple goals, multiple criteria will generally be needed to evaluate an appraisal system fully. One problem the researcher or practitioner must face is to integrate the evaluations reached on the basis of each individual criterion into an overall evaluation of the PA system. Research on multiattribute evaluation (Edwards, 1980; Edwards & Newman, 1982) and on decisions with multiple objectives (Keeney & Raiffa, 1976; Raiffa, 1968) provides some useful guidelines for this sort of integration.

Consider the case illustrated in Table 11-3. Here, a performance appraisal system whose primary goals are to help make promotion decisions, to document personnel actions and decisions, and to motivate employees is

Table 11–3.   Evaluating a Performance Appraisal System Using Multiple Criteria

Criteria	Evaluation	Percentile[a]
Rank-order correlation between ratings and some externally validated measure of promotability	$r = .50$	50th
Amount and specificity of information recorded about each ratee	Little information but highly specific	70th
Change in levels of motivation to perform well	Motivation to perform increases by 25%	85th

[a] Percentile: Location of the appraisal system on a scale where 0 = worst possible value of this criterion measure and 100 = best possible value of this criterion measure.

being evaluated in terms of three criteria that can be derived from those goals: (1) the rank-order correlation between ratings and some externally validated measure of promotability, (2) the amount and specificity of the information recorded about each ratee, and (3) the change in levels of motivation. Since these criteria are qualitatively different, they will need to be put on a common scale before they can be sensibly integrated. One simple approach, which is illustrated in Table 11-3, might be to express each criterion in terms of where the obtained value would be located on a percentile scale ranging from the worst possible value for that criterion (i.e., 1st percentile) to the best possible value for that criterion (i.e., 99th percentile).

For example, the worst possible value for the rank-order correlation between ratings and some externally derived measure of promotability is $r = .00$ (assuming that a system with negative validity would never be seriously considered). The best possible value is $r = 1.00$. One interpretation of the correlation coefficient is in terms of the distance between the best possible decision and decisions made at random. Therefore, the correlation of .50 can be expressed as a score of 50 on a 100-point scale. The score of 85 for the third criterion, changes in levels of motivation, indicates that the observed change is nearly as large as the increase in motivation that would result if the best possible system were instituted.

Although the percentile-based approach illustrated in Table 11-3 solves some problems, it does not provide a basis for integrating the values of different criteria. The reason for this is that criteria vary in their importance, as well as in the relative value that might be assigned to the same percentage score on different criteria. For example, a validity coefficient of .10 might be an indicator that a PA system is not very useful for making promotion decisions, whereas an increase in motivation that has a percentile value of .10 might be considered worthwhile.

To further complicate things, the difference between the value of a given score on one criterion and the value of the same score on another criterion might not be constant. For example, a value of .20 on the the motivational criterion might be twice as good as a value of .20 on the validity for promotion criterion. A value of .60 on the motivational criterion might be five times as valuable as a value of .60 on validity for promotion, since motivational changes affect all workers but promotions affect only a small number of workers. In order to integrate multiple criteria, more is needed than a common scale of measurement (e.g., the percentile scale). In particular, a common scale is needed for the *value* of the outcomes associated with each criterion.

Decision theory (Keeney & Raiffa, 1976; Raiffa, 1968) provides a method for scaling qualitatively different outcomes on a common value scale. This method allows one to predict value tradeoffs and to aggregate value indices for different attributes or outcomes. The method involves the use of *indifference curves,* which can be constructed by asking an individual or a group of decision makers for their preferences among outcomes (see Figure 11-3). For example,

Figure 11–3.   Indifference Curve Comparing Promotion versus Motivational Criteria

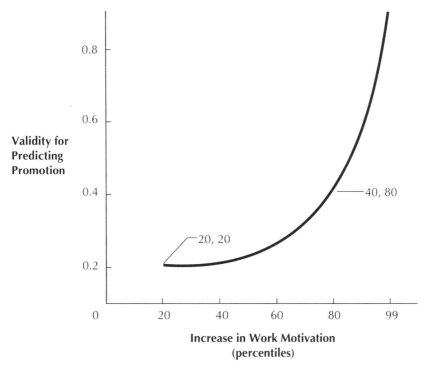

Area above the curve: Promotion outcome preferred to motivational
Area below the curve: Motivational outcome preferred to promotion
Curve itself: Value of promotion and motivational outcomes is equal

a group of managers might be asked a series of questions in the following form:

Which outcome would you prefer or value more?
1. A promotion validity of .20 (20th percentile)
   or
2. An increase in motivation at the 25th percentile

For some questions, the preponderant majority will prefer one of the two alternatives (e.g., here, 85% of the managers may prefer item 2). However, for other questions, approximately 50% of the managers will prefer item 1 and approximately 50% will prefer item 2. According to decision theory, if the group is indifferent about receiving 1 versus 2, these two outcomes must have equivalent value. (See Raiffa, 1968, for a highly accessible introduction to this technique and its applications in multiattribute evaluation.)

   The indifference curve represents a plot of those alternatives that have equal value to the respondents. For example, Figure 11-3 implies that a validity for promotion of .20 and an increase in motivation at the 20th percentile are equally valuable. Similarly, a validity of .40 and an increase in motivation at the 80th percentile are seen as equally valuable. All points above the curve (e.g., validity of .60 and increase in motivation at at the 25th percentile) represent tradeoffs where the promotion outcome has more value than the motivational outcome. All points below the curve represent choices where the motivational outcome is more valuable than the validity for promotion outcome.

The indifference curve allows one to rescale different outcomes on a common value scale. For example, Table 11-3 includes values of 50 and 85 for the promotion and motivational criteria, respectively. The indifference curve suggests that a validity coefficient of .5 is equal in value to an increase in motivation that is approximately at the 88th percentile. When the two outcomes are expressed on a common scale, it becomes clear that the evaluation of this appraisal system in terms of its effect on promotion validity is very similar to the evaluation of the system in terms of its impact on work motivation levels (scores of 88 and 85, respectively), and that the system does a very good job of meeting both goals. If the remaining criterion dimension (amount and specificity of information) was also scaled on this value dimension (this would require another indifference curve), it would be possible to measure the effectiveness of the appraisal system with multiple criteria that all shared a common value scale.

In principle, any one dimension can be chosen to provide a common value metric. In practice, it is best to choose a dimension that is both important and highly concrete. For example, organization members might find it easier to evaluate an appraisal system that is scaled in terms of its motivational impact than one that is scaled in terms of the specificity and amount of behavioral information provided. Once all criterion dimensions are measured on a common value scale, the only remaining issue is to combine the dimensional assessments into an overall assessment. This can be done by forming a weighted linear combination of scores on the separate dimensions, where the weights are proportional to the relative importance of each criterion.

The method of forming indifference curves to express value tradeoffs is not only useful for multiattribute evaluation, it is also useful for comparing different appraisal systems that address totally different goals. For example, suppose that one system did a good job of improving motivation and a moderately poor job of assisting in making salary decisions. Suppose that another system did a good job of identifying promotable workers and did a fair job at providing a detailed record of each individual's performance. The use of indifference curves will allow one to sensibly compare these two systems and to choose the one that best meets the most important set of goals. To our knowledge, indifference curves and related methods from decision theory have not yet been applied to the evaluation PA systems. We think these methods have great potential and expect that they will be more widely used in the future.

Summary

The most common criteria for evaluating PA systems (e.g., rater error and accuracy measures) do not take into account the actual use(s) of ratings in organizations. This chapter reviewed several methods of evaluating PA systems that reflect the degree to which PA helps the organization achieve or advance important goals. For example, utility formulations allow one to estimate the impact of good versus poor appraisal systems on the productivity of the workforce. It is much more important to know whether or not PA contributes to productivity than to know merely whether or not appraisals are accurate.

Several challenges await researchers and practitioners who attempt to develop criteria that reflect the impact of appraisal systems on the organization. The most obvious challenge is to identify the goals (both explicit and explicit) that PA systems are designed to serve. It is likely that different groups (e.g., raters, ratees, upper management) have very different goals in mind when participating in appraisal. Indeed, it is likely that each individual will pursue multiple goals in appraisal. The identification of relevant goals and the reconciliation of inconsistent goals may be the most important step in evaluating PA systems.

There are numerous criteria, including measures of reactions to performance appraisal systems, measures that reflect the practicality of PA systems, and measures of the contribution of appraisal to decision-making processes in organizations, that are usually dismissed as "soft" criteria that are of secondary importance. These criteria are often critically important, and the acceptability, practicality, and apparent contribution of PA systems to fair and accurate decisions may be the *most* important criteria. PA systems that are highly accurate but that appear to produce unfair outcomes or that are cumbersome and expensive to install and use may be doomed from the start.

One final problem considered in this chapter is the integration of different criteria in evaluating PA systems. Every PA system serves multiple goals and is more relevant to some goals than to others. This chapter suggested some ways of adapting the methods of decision research to the problem of integrating information about the impact of PA on the various goals that appraisal systems serve.

Chapter Twelve

Directions
for Research

▶   In this chapter we will identify promising directions for future research in performance appraisal (PA). We will discuss 73 specific questions that could be addressed to increase understanding appraisal in organizations. Some of these questions lead directly to hypotheses that are amenable to immediate empirical investigation, whereas others will require researchers to modify and clarify the constructs and theories they use to structure their knowledge of psychological processes involved in appraisal before empirical investigations can begin.

This chapter and Chapter Thirteen are organized in terms of the four-component model of appraisal presented in Chapter One and articulated in Chapters Two through Eleven. First, we will discuss the research that is needed to advance our understanding of contextual influences on appraisal. Second, we will suggest a number of possibilities for future research on evaluative judgments of job performance. Next, we will discuss the type of research that is needed to advance our understanding of rating behavior in organizations. Finally, we will examine questions that need to be answered to evaluate the validity, accuracy, and usefulness of a PA system.

Context

The effects of context variables on appraisal processes and outcomes have been the object of speculation but have not been empirically examined in the detail that these effects warrant. This lack of attention to context is hard to understand, since industrial/organizational psychology is itself defined by a context (i.e., the organization) rather than by specific content. We believe that context is the key to understanding appraisal in organizations, and believe that several specific questions can be posed that will advance our understanding of this critical variable.

Levels of Context

The first set of issues that require attention are those that revolve around defining the various levels of context that may affect appraisal. *Context* refers to a set of qualitatively different variables that exist in the immediate and distal environment. It is important to know more about the way in which people respond to different levels of context. Three questions that should be addressed in this area are:

1. How many levels of context do people respond to? Are there some individuals who are sensitive to the immediate context only and others who focus on more distal levels? Do some individuals attend to many levels of context simultaneously?

2. How do people cope with inconsistencies between different levels of context? Suppose, for example, that the market is generally tight for computer manufacturers but one division of a manufacturer has access to a large market in which the competition is minimal. Which level of context most strongly affects behavior?

3. Distal context variables, by definition, do not affect behavior directly. What are the intervening variables between distal context and rater and ratee behavior? What comes between distal factors such as the national economy or the current legal climate and rater/ratee behavior?

Context Effects

The next set of issues concern the effects of several specific context factors on appraisal processes and outcomes. In particular, the appraisal literature has mentioned three distal variables that are thought to be highly relevant to appraisal: (1) the perceived performance of the organization, (2) the performance of the organization relative to its competitors, and (3) the culture and values of the organization. Three questions that should be addressed in this area are:

4. How does the performance of the organization affect performance appraisal? Do raters and ratees behave differently if they think the organization is doing well or poorly? What defines organizational success or failure in their eyes? If they believe that the organization is doing poorly, do they focus on different goals than if they think it is doing well?

5. Do performance standards vary as a function of distal environment factors? Are standards set more stringently when the competition is tight? When the organization is not doing well?

6. How do organizational cultures and values affect the definition of job performance? How do they affect the perceived difference between good and poor performance?

Technological Context

Changes in the technology of work are likely to have a significant impact on performance appraisal. In particular, computer-based technologies often allow employees to work with minimal supervision, perhaps even working at home and communicating with the office via modem. In other cases, supervision is still required but supervisors may be less familiar with the technology than are the individuals they are asked to evaluate. Three questions could be posed regarding the effects of technological changes on appraisal processes and outcomes:

7. Does advanced technology undermine the role of the supervisor in performance appraisal? This is particularly likely to happen if the technology is one that the employees understand but the supervisor does not. In this case, the supervisor might lose "expert power" and may not be perceived as a competent judge of the subordinates' performance. This may also occur if the new technology allows or requires the employee to work with little or no direct supervision.

8. How does automatic monitoring of employees' behavior affect appraisals? For example, it is possible to collect a minute-by-minute analysis of the work of a person who works at a computer terminal? How does this type of record influence the appraisal process? One possibility is that supervisors will feel compelled to bring their evaluations in line with the objective counts, even if they know that the workers who spend the most time at their desks may not be the best performers.

9. How do the technologies mentioned in question 8 affect employee reactions to appraisal? It seems likely that automatic monitoring will be regarded negatively by employees, but little is known about the conditions under which it will either cause major problems (e.g., employee stress, morale) or cause only trivial problems in the organization.

Organizational Goals

The next set of issues are those that are raised by considering the strategic goals of the organization, the climate of the organization, and possible inconsistencies between the two. This set of questions is predicated on the assumption that some organizational climates are better than others for achieving specific goals. For example, an organization that requires its members to develop creative solutions to complex problems (e.g., a new computer manufacturer) is more likely to succeed if the climate encourages risk taking and entrepreneurship than if it encourages conservative, rule-bound approaches to problems. Three questions emerge when considering the simple and joint effects of these two related variables:

10. How do the strategic goals of the organization affect the appraisal process? Are links consciously made between the goals of the organization, the definition of good and poor performance on the job, and the procedures used to assess performance, or is the link between strategic goals and appraisal practices a haphazard one?

11. How does the climate of the organization affect appraisal processes and outcomes? What are the mechanisms (or intervening variables) linking organizational climate to rater goals?

12. How do raters deal with inconsistencies between strategic goals and the climate of the organization? Is this conflict salient for raters? The answer to this question may depend on the level(s) of climate to which raters respond. Strategic goals are more distal than the perceived climate of the organization. The conflict may depend on whether raters focus on proximal context, distal context, or both.

Norms

Moving to more proximal aspects of context, we think it would be very useful to study and understand the process by which norms regarding performance (e.g., What constitutes a fair day's work?) and norms regarding performance appraisal (e.g., Should poor performers receive low ratings?) are developed and applied. Four questions should be addressed:

13. What is the appropriate unit of analysis for studying norms regarding performance appraisal? Do the same norms permeate the entire organization or are there different norms for different departments, areas, or workgroups?

14. If appraisal norms support the use of appraisal for development and feedback, will they also *discourage* the use of appraisal to make distinctions among employees? Cleveland, Murphy, and Williams (1989) suggest that these two uses of appraisal are mutually incompatible. If norms also recognize this incompatibility, it might be difficult to win rater and ratee acceptance of an appraisal system that appears to serve incompatible goals.

15. Can research on procedural and distributive justice help in understanding perceptions of fairness and accuracy in appraisal? Is there any way to determine a priori what procedures or outcomes will be perceived as fair? How do norms develop regarding the fairness or unfairness of specific policies or actions?

16. Are self-evaluations of performance primarily a function of internalized standards or are they driven by the standards and norms of superiors

and co-workers? Can experiences of success and failure in organizations override workgroup norms? In other words, what happens when a worker is regarded as successful by the workgroup and unsuccessful by the organization?

Purpose of Rating

One contextual variable that has been examined in depth is the effect of the purpose of appraisal on appraisal outcomes. This research is useful but is limited in two important ways. First, it has focused on only a small number of purposes that are explicitly defined by the organization. Second, it has generally considered the effects of only one purpose at a time. Appraisals in organizations often serve a number of purposes, some of which are explicitly defined by the organizations and others that are implicitly defined by the rater. Furthermore, some purposes are incompatible with others. Our understanding of research on the effects of purpose of rating suggests that there are five questions that should be considered:

17. What are the implicit purposes of performance appraisal? Is there consensus regarding these purposes or is there wide variation in the implicit purposes that different raters and ratees believe exist?

18. If raters differ in their perceptions of the purpose of rating, will systematic differences in ratings emerge? The research on the effects of purpose frequently shows that raters are more lenient or severe depending on the perceived purpose of appraisal. However, this research has been restricted to a consideration of the effects of a single, explicit purpose (typically contrasting appraisal for research only with appraisal that is linked to administrative decisions), and has not considered implicit purposes. It is possible that much of what we dismiss as "rater error" is in fact the result of differences in the perceived purposes of appraisal.

19. What are the psychological consequences of conflicting purposes for appraisal? We have noted earlier that one way to resolve this problem is to focus on one purpose, to the virtual exclusion of the others. Is this what raters actually do or are there other ways of solving the problem?

20. What happens when information about ratee performance is collected for one purpose but used for another? Research by DeNisi, Williams, and their colleagues has demonstrated reprocessing effects. Murphy, Philbin, and Adams (1989) demonstrate that the purpose of observation affected both behavior recognition and the accuracy of judgments. At present, little is known about the strength, duration, or boundaries of these effects. Does the purpose of observation have any measurable effect on appraisals in organizations?

21. In what way does position in the organization, defined both in terms of level and functional area (e.g., production versus personnel), affect the rater's perception of the purpose of appraisal? We suspect that implicit and explicit purposes of appraisal are increasingly similar as one moves up in the organization but we know of no research on this question.

Judgment

Review papers by Feldman (1981), Landy and Farr (1980), and DeNisi, Cafferty, and Meglino (1984) have stimulated a significant body of research dealing with cognitive processes involved in evaluative judgments about job performance. This cognitive research is useful and contributes to our overall understanding of appraisal, but we should not ignore aspects of judgment that fall outside of the traditional realm of cognitive psychologists. We believe that significant progress could be made by exploring issues such as the nature and communication of performance standards, the nature of the comparison processes involved in evaluation, the sources of information considered in appraisal, and the way in which raters use descriptive versus evaluative information about their subordinates' performance. The suggested directions listed below include some research questions that are clearly within the cognitive domain and others that have not been considered by cognitively oriented researchers.

Cognitive Processes

The first set of issues are those concerning cognitive processes in appraisal, and in particular those concerning the generalizability of laboratory research to evaluative judgment in organizations. Eight questions need to be considered here:

22. Are individual differences in chunking large enough to make any difference in performance appraisal? Chunking ongoing observations into discrete units is a cognitive process that has been examined in great detail in cognitive research, although little of this research has been applied directly to appraisal. There are individual differences in chunking strategies but little is known about whether they are large enough to ever make any difference in performance evaluations. This issue applies to many of the cognitive processes studied in the laboratory. Funder (1987) reminds us that psychologists tend to overemphasize errors that can be made in judgment, and pay relatively little attention to whether these errors lead to any observable differences in actual judgments. Categorization errors, memory errors, errors in integrating information, and so on *can* happen but little is known about *how often* they happen or how serious they are.

23. Do behavior-based and trait-based rating systems evoke different cognitive processes? No one format is uniformly better than the others (Landy & Farr, 1980) and different formats often yield similar outcomes but little is known about what processes are triggered by the demands of different formats. For example, research on behaviorally oriented rating scales has examined the effects of formats on the psychometric characteristics of ratings but has had little to say about the psychological processes involved in using behavior-based versus nonbehavioral rating scales. Murphy and Davidshofer

(1988) and Murphy and Constans (1988) suggest that behavior-oriented formats may trigger different processes than are triggered by trait-oriented formats.

24. Can theories from cognitive psychology and social cognition be used to make valid predictions about important phenomena in performance appraisal? If so, what are the important boundary conditions? For example, Hartel (1988) used the two-process theory of attention to make a number of specific predictions about behavior rating and behavior recognition in a simulated appraisal task. Her study carefully controlled for many of the potential confounds and involved the careful development of scales and procedures specifically defined to test hypotheses derived from two-process theory. Virtually none of the predictions held up; observed results were virtually the opposite of what would be predicted by the theory. Does this indicate a weakness in the study or a weakness in the theory? We suspect that even more serious problems will be encountered when attempting to apply more modern theories (e.g., parallel distributive processing models of cognitions) whose key constructs are still being defined.

25. Can policy-capturing methods shed significant light on the integration processes raters use in performance appraisal? It is not reasonable to believe that raters actually go through the sort of weighted averaging process implied by the regression models typically employed in policy capturing. Thus, the statistics that can be calculated in a policy-capturing study cannot be interpreted as the weights actually applied to behavior. On the other hand, they should provide *some* information about psychological processes. At present, little is known about what information is or is not provided.

26. When information is obtained for multiple purposes, which cognitive processes are affected by (a) the purpose of observation and (b) the purpose of rating? The issue here is once again one of external validity. Purpose of observation and purpose of rating *can* affect ratings, but *do* they?

27. How do the results of behavior affect the evaluation and perception of that behavior? It is likely that there are hindsight effects (Baron & Hershey, 1988); favorable outcomes are likely to lead to the impression that the behaviors were appropriate. Once again, it is important to estimate the strength and frequency of these effects.

28. What aspects of evaluation are totally context free, partially context bound, or fully context bound? In other words, which aspects of evaluation are universal and which are tied to the particular context? We suspect that different processes might be involved in context-free versus context-bound evaluations. For example, attractive people are evaluated more favorably in virtually all contexts than are equally deserving but unattractive people. The cognitive and affective processes that are responsible for attractiveness biases may be quite different from those that allow one to distinguish successful from unsuccessful behavior in a specific context.

29. Is there a single, global evaluative dimension or are there qualitatively different evaluative dimensions for different types of judgments? Can we

meaningfully compare the evaluations given to different persons holding different jobs?

Categorization

Much of the recent cognitive research in performance appraisal has examined the process of categorization and its implications for memory and judgment. This is particularly true for studies growing out of schematic theories. The application of these concepts to performance appraisal has been hampered by a lack of understanding of the nature and the content of the categories that are likely to be used in appraisal. We think that more progress could be made if the following four questions were addressed:

30. What do performance schema look like? What is the content of the cognitive categories that are used to represent performance on the job? For example, are good performer and poor performer two separate categories that are used by most raters or are these judgments the result of applying more complexly defined categories?

31. What methods are best for examining and describing the content of cognitive categories in appraisal? A principal weakness of schematic theories of perception, categorization, and memory is the failure to develop methods of assessing the contents of categories, schema, and scripts. Schema are usually inferred post hoc; schematic theories would be more convincing and useful if schema could be defined a priori.

32. How do raters develop and use "folk theories" of the job or performance? Borman's (1987) paper is one of the few attempts, to our knowledge, to assess and describe systematically the contents of the category system used to assess workers' performance. His results suggest that implicit theories of the job can be assessed and that they are useful for understanding performance evaluations. It would be useful to go beyond this descriptive level and investigate the way in which the rater learns or develops a theory of the job. The cognitive categories used to classify observations are probably at a more primitive level than these theories but the theory of the job will still probably have an impact on the development of categories.

33. What do performance norms look like? Do they represent thresholds separating good from bad performance? Do they represent implicit scales? Do they represent implicit distribution theories?

Data Sources

A topic that has not been adequately considered in research on performance evaluation is the *way* in which information is obtained. Included under this category are issues such as the source of the appraisal (e.g., peers, supervisors, etc.), the form of the information that is considered (e.g., descriptive statements versus evaluations from others), and the use of direct observation versus indirect observation as a method of obtaining information about ratee performance. Five questions that fit into this category are listed below:

34. How does the source, the medium, and the form of the report, as well as the apparent motivation behind the report, affect the rater's evaluation and use of indirect observations about their subordinates' performance?

35. What is the frequency with which raters obtain data from different direct and indirect sources? Good descriptive research on the ways in which raters obtain the information they use to evaluate subordinates' performance is lacking and would make a clear contribution to our understanding of appraisal in organizations.

36. Is information obtained from direct versus indirect observation represented differently in memory? Is Tulving's distinction between semantic and episodic encoding relevant here? If so, what are the consequences?

37. What aspects of performance are most accurately evaluated by supervisors, peers, subordinates, and self? It is clear that some compelling argument will be needed to convince many organizations to involve persons other than the direct supervisor in performance appraisal. We believe that this task would be easier if one could point to specific advantages that would follow from incorporating multiple sources rather than simply arguing that it increases accuracy. For example, if it was known that peers were better judges of present performance than supervisors but that supervisors were better judges of potential, this would argue for the use of both sources and for orienting each source toward the tasks they were most qualified to perform.

38. How do raters process descriptive versus evaluative information about their subordinates' behavior? Do the same variables (e.g., source, motivation) affect both descriptive and evaluative information? Is it possible to separate description from evaluation or are all descriptions partly evaluative?

Performance Standards

The standards that define good versus poor performance and the processes by which individual ratees are compared to those standards have received little attention in research on evaluative judgments of performance. This may be an extremely fruitful area for research; the question of developing, communicating, and using performance standards pervades many of the daily issues faced by practitioners in organizations. These range from the acceptance of feedback (negative feedback is more likely to be accepted if the standards for evaluating performance are clear) to the minimization of stress on the job (ambiguous standards may be a source of stress). Identified here are ten questions that should be addressed to advance the understanding of the nature, the communication, and the use of performance standards in organizations. These are:

39. What psychological processes are used in comparing a person to a standard? Possibilities include anchoring, averaging, or comparisons that require the difference between ratee performance and the standard to exceed some threshold. Does this vary by rater, ratee, or type of standard?

40. Evaluation involves comparing a person with a standard. How large does the deviation from standard have to be to trigger a change in evaluation? If an employee has been evaluated over a long period, is a larger deviation needed?

41. How do raters reconcile inconsistencies between internal and external standards? If their own standards are different from those the organization, department, or workgroup, how do raters reconcile these differences? Under what circumstances do raters use their own versus the someone else's standards?

42. In adjusting for environmental constraints, what changes in judgment rules and strategy are made? Does this involve changing the standard? Changing the latitude of acceptance and rejection?

43. Some standards refer to procedures; others refer to results. How do raters deal with inconsistencies between these (e.g., worker follows the correct procedures and fails; worker fails to follow procedures and succeeds)?

44. What individual difference variables are useful for predicting the extent to which the rater internalizes performance standards that are defined by the organization or by other members of the organization?

45. Do performance standards reflect leadership styles? For example, it is possible that Theory X leaders will be characterized by very rigid standards in which the latitude of acceptance is small, whereas Theory Y leaders may have much more flexible standards? Can we use performance standards as a tool for assessing leadership style? Can we use leadership measures to infer standards?

46. Will supervisors who have risen through the ranks have more rigid standards or more tolerant standards than those who have not? Attribution theory suggests that raters who have risen through the ranks will have a distorted perception of how well *they* performed in the job (they will readily recall good performance and will discount poor performance), which may lead to unrealistically high standards.

47. Is the ambiguity of performance standards a significant source of stress? Can work-related stress be reduced by clarifying standards and making them more explicit? Role theory suggests that role ambiguity is a serious issue; clarifying standards may help to remove role ambiguity.

48. Is the latitude of standards related to an individual's performance level? For example, it is likely that the standards that are applied to poor performers are more rigid than those applied to good performers. The same objective change in performance may be evaluated differently for a good performer than for a poor one. Does this make it more difficult for a poor performer to improve (or to be seen as improving)?

Rating

The failure to distinguish clearly between judgment and rating represents the most significant barrier to the successful application of much of the recent research on performance appraisal. This distinction is not unique to our model; Banks and Murphy (1985) make a similar distinction between the rater's capacity to evaluate employees and his or her willingness to record accurate ratings (see Mohrman & Lawler, 1983). Nevertheless, we think that the single most important contribution our model makes in clarifying PA research is to distinguish between the rater's own judgment and the ratings he or she records. Previous researchers, to the extent that they considered this distinction at all, have regarded differences between judgments and ratings as a nuisance variable and a source of error variance. We disagree. We believe that potential discrepancies between judgment and ratings represent a unique opportunity to study a wide variety of psychological processes in organizations. Comparisons between judgments and ratings may shed light on issues ranging from the level of trust in the appraisal system to the importance of good interpersonal relations between supervisors and subordinates.

Rater Goals

Our analysis of rating behavior focuses on the goal-directed behavior of the supervisor, and treats performance rating as a communication process rather than as a measurement process. From this perspective, the task of psychologists is to decipher the message that raters are trying to send and to understand the individual and contextual forces that shape that message. The first set of issues to be considered here are those dealing with the nature of rater goals and the integration of multiple goals. Three questions that should be considered in this area are:

49. Are raters aware of the goals they are pursuing in appraisal? If not, would they embrace these goals if they could be made aware of them? Although performance rating is regarded as an instance of goal-directed behavior, it is not necessary to assume that raters are fully aware of any or all of the goals they are pursuing when filling out rating scales and other appraisal forms. For example, the rater who has experienced a dramatic decline in the quality of interpersonal relations in the workgroup as the result of giving unfavorable ratings might adopt a goal of avoiding these problems in the future, without ever being fully conscious of the goal itself.

50. Are the goals pursued by raters stable over time (i.e., does the rater have a reasonably constant agenda?) or do they vary? If so, what causes them to vary? Another way of thinking about this question is to ask whether rater goals are characteristics of the person or characteristics of the situation. Considerable stability could be expected if goals reflect core values held by the

rater; goals that are defined by the context will probably change whenever the context changes.

51. How do raters set priorities among incompatible goals? For example, raters might accept the organization's goal of maximizing performance but they might also be concerned with maintaining good interpersonal relations at work. Under what conditions do raters allow their goal to override the organization's goal?

Goals and Ratee Performance Level

A second set of issues emerges when the rater's goals are considered in the light of the ratee's true performance level. The same rater may be pursuing very different goals for good performers (e.g., using appraisal as a developmental tool) than for poor performers (e.g., using appraisal to improve performance in the present job). Four questions should be considered:

52. If the ratee's performance is truly good, what will the rater attempt to communicate to the organization?

53. If the ratee's performance is truly bad, what will the rater attempt to communicate to the organization?

54. If the ratee's performance is neither good nor bad, what will the rater attempt to communicate to the organization?

55. What variables moderate the relationship between the ratee's performance level and the rater's goals? Research on affective influences on appraisal may provide a starting point for attacking this question. It is likely that the rater develops different goals when evaluating two substandard performers, one of whom the rater likes and the other who the rater dislikes.

Rating Outcomes

The goals pursued by raters can be defined in terms of the desired or anticipated outcomes of giving high, average, or low ratings. Several motivation theories, especially expectancy theory and its derivatives, suggest that raters will consider the value of several outcomes and the likelihood of achieving each outcome when deciding what types of ratings to give. Two questions should be addressed in this area:

56. How do raters develop perceptions of the links between the ratings they give and the consequences for the ratee? How do ratees develop the same perceptions? How do raters develop perceptions of the consequences for themselves of giving high, average, or low ratings to their subordinates?

57. What positive and negative outcomes of giving accurate appraisals are viewed as certain, probable, or improbable by raters? Research on prospect theory (Kahneman & Tversky, 1979) suggests that we pay too much attention to negative outcomes and to outcomes that are certain to occur. If

negative outcomes are viewed as relatively certain and positive outcomes are viewed as highly uncertain, it may take a substantial number of potentially positive outcomes to offset a few certain negatives.

Rater and Ratee Expectations

A related set of questions concerns rater and ratee expectations regarding performance appraisal. Suppose, for example, that workers have received inflated ratings in the past. Giving honest ratings now may lead to very negative reactions; workers may come to regard high ratings as an entitlement and may regard low ratings as a breach of the unwritten agreement between raters and ratees. Three questions related to rater and ratee expectations are:

58. How do norms regarding procedural justice in appraisal develop and how can they be modified? Is it possible to give low ratings without suffering negative consequences if the procedures involved in evaluating performance are accepted by ratees as fair and accurate?

59. How do norms regarding distributive justice in appraisal develop and how can they be modified? We suspect that ratees will be more concerned with outcomes than with procedures. Also, appraisal procedures that are regarded as fair but produce results that are regarded as unfair will not be easily accepted by ratees.

60. What leads a ratee to expect either inflated ratings or ratings that accurately reflect his or her level of performance? Are there aspects of the context that either create or discourage ratees' expectations that ratings will be inflated?

Rater Motivation

The last set of issues to be considered in this section span the boundary between research and practice. Two questions about the approach that should be taken in assessing and modifying raters' outcome expectations, goals, and behaviors are:

61. Is the multiattribute utility framework (e.g., MAUT) useful for analyzing rater motivation? Can this approach or other analogous approaches derived from decision research predict rating behavior?

62. If raters are not motivated to provide accurate ratings, should attempts be made to change the rater or change the context?

Evaluation

The last component of our four-component model represents the complex set of issues that arise when one attempts to evaluate a performance appraisal system. In our judgment, researchers' inability to evaluate PA systems sensibly represents the single greatest barrier to the application of the results of psychological research on performance appraisal. There are two main issues that need to be addressed before performance appraisal systems can be evaluated in any systematic fashion: (1) the choice of criteria for evaluating the system and (2) the operationalization of measures of these criteria.

Choice of Criteria

In choosing criteria for evaluating appraisal systems, seven questions need to be addressed:

63. Can a theory of job performance be developed that describes what a valid measure of performance *should* look like? This is a prerequisite for the use of criteria such as adequacy in covering the domain or construct validity in evaluating rating systems. Murphy and Kroeker (1988) suggested one approach to developing such a theory (i.e., using position goals to define performance dimensions) but little progress has been made in mapping the performance domain for most jobs in the workforce. In the absence of such a theory, little can be said about whether the appraisal system is measuring the right dimensions or whether it will produce valid measures of the construct performance. Most evaluations of construct validity depend exclusively on the multitrait-multimethod approach to assessing convergent and discriminant validity (e.g., see Vance, MacCallum, Coovert, and Hedge, 1988) but this may not be enough. If specific criteria cannot be specified in advance for how measures of different aspects of performance *should* be related, there is no meaningful way to assess construct validity (Murphy & Davidshofer, 1988).

64. What is the relationship (if any) between accuracy in recognizing what has occurred, accuracy in reporting the frequency of behaviors, and accuracy in evaluating performance? Murphy, Garcia, Kerkar, Martin, and Balzer (1982) suggested that accuracy in reporting the frequency of behavior is not related to accuracy in judgment. Hastie and Park (1986) suggest that memory accuracy is often unrelated to the accuracy of judgments. Do *all* of the major definitions of accuracy refer to unrelated phenomena (Sulsky & Balzer, 1988)?

65. How does the performance level of the group affect the evaluations of a particular member of the group? If the performance of the group *does* affect individual evaluations, which is the appropriate unit of analysis for evaluating ratings — the individual or the group?

66. What is the utility of reaction criteria? Under what circumstances are these criteria either more or less important than results-oriented criteria? Should organizations care about rater and ratee reactions to appraisal systems?

67. How does the accuracy of an appraisal affect reactions to that appraisal? Landy, Barnes, and Murphy (1978) studied perceptions of fairness

and accuracy and suggested that these are overlapping constructs. Perhaps accuracy is necessary but not sufficient for the raters and ratees to regard the system as a fair one. If so, are there some facets of accuracy (e.g., between-person accuracy) that have a stronger impact than others (e.g., within-person accuracy)?

68. If there are multiple outcomes associated with each possible appraisal system, how is information about each outcome integrated to arrive at an overall evaluation? Are indifference curves appropriate here? Are there simpler methods that might provide the same information? Does it depend on the degree to which different outcomes are correlated or redundant?

69. Are the value tradeoffs individuals are willing to make regarding different outcomes of appraisal stable over time? Is there wide individual variation or is there consensus regarding value tradeoffs?

Operational Definitions

Four questions seem most pressing when assessing the various operational definitions of criteria that are used in evaluating rating systems. They are:

70. What is the best model for assessing and evaluating the reliability of ratings? Validity generalization research is based in part on the premise that the test-retest model is best. Is this always true or does the choice of a method depend on the purpose of rating?

71. How can rating inflation be separated from true ratee differences? Are there reasonable alternatives to a fully crossed Rater $\times$ Ratee design? Are the assumptions behind these alternatives reasonable?

72. Are there reasonable alternatives to rater error measures? Accuracy measures are very difficult to obtain in nonlaboratory settings and there are conceptual problems with many of the traditional criteria. Although rater error measures are riddled with problems, is it better to use them than to abandon (or at least postpone) evaluating ratings?

73. How can the criterion-related validity of an appraisal system be estimated? What should the criterion be?

Linking Appraisal Research to Appraisal in Organizations

The last issue to be considered in this chapter is whether the type of research that is outlined above is likely to help in understanding appraisal processes and outcomes in actual organizations. That is, the concern here is with the issue of external validity.

The debate over the external validity of appraisal research has usually been framed in terms of comparisons between laboratory and field studies. One inference drawn from this debate is that laboratory studies are thought by many appraisal researchers to have little external validity and that field studies are thought to have substantial external validity. In other words, in order to understand appraisal in organizations, many researchers feel that research should be conducted in the field, not in the lab.

A book edited by Locke (1986) examined in detail the question of whether lab research in industrial/organizational psychology generalizes to the field. It is clear from the material reviewed in this book that the issue of external validity is more complex than the simple lab versus field dichotomy. Indeed, several authors argue that such a debate is pointless and that it only serves to distract researchers from the more important question of whether research explains anything about the phenomena researchers are trying to understand (Campbell, 1986; Ilgen, 1986). Empirical examinations of lab versus field studies strongly support this argument.

For example, Locke (1986) compared the outcomes of lab and field studies in 14 separate areas of industrial/organizational psychology to determine whether the direction of the effects and the size of the effects were similar or different. In over 92% of the comparisons made, Locke (1986) concluded that the size and/or the direction of the effects found was either highly similar or virtually identical in lab and field studies. Dipboye and Flanaghan (1979) suggested that the generalizability of a lab study to the field was no smaller or greater than the generalizability of any one field study to other field settings.

Murphy and colleagues (1986) compared the outcomes of laboratory studies of performance appraisal using a method that should minimize internal and external validity (i.e., studies in which hypothetical ratees were described in written vignettes) with the outcomes of studies, usually conducted in organizations, using a method that should have much more fidelity (i.e., studies in which direct observations of ratee behavior served as the basis for appraisals). They found only small differences in the sizes of the effects (mean d values of .42 and .30, respectively) and almost perfect consistency in the direction of the effects.

If the choice of methods (i.e., lab versus field) does not govern external validity, what does? Several researchers suggest that boundary conditions must be set that describe the potential limits to the generalizability of research results (Fromkin & Streufert, 1976; Ilgen, 1986; Locke, 1986). These boundary conditions reflect critical variables that may affect the direction or magnitude of research findings (Fromkin & Streufert, 1976). For example, if researchers wanted to study the effects of raters' expectations regarding the outcomes of appraisal on rating behavior, it would be important to structure a study in which the type and the importance of the outcomes were similar to those encountered in the field. In this case, a laboratory study in which there were no real rewards or punishments for giving high or low ratings would probably not provide generalizable information.

Some researchers have attempted to solve external validity problems through cosmetic changes in their methods. For example, Ilgen (1986) notes that studies involving business students as subjects are incorrectly thought by some to be more generalizable than studies using college sophomores. Bernardin and Villanova (1986) attempted to apply a more systematic approach to outlining the variables that characterize appraisal in organizations. They were able to identify 15 variables that described the modal setting for collecting appraisals in organizations:

1. More than six ratees.
2. Ratees see the ratings.
3. The rater's supervisor sees the ratings.
4. Ratees are aware of the evaluations their peers receive.
5. Ratings are done on an annual basis.
6. Ratings are used to make important administrative decisions.
7. Raters do not have adequate time to appraise ratees.
8. The performance of the ratees affects the evaluation the rater receives.
9. Raters have experience performing major components of the ratees' jobs.
10. Countable results are unavailable.
11. Raters feel that they are above average in the accuracy of their ratings.
12. Raters dislike giving appraisals.
13. Supervisors do not use formal appraisals to determine the feedback they give to ratees.
14. Raters evaluate ratee traits.
15. Ratings, rather than rankings, are done.

Some of these characteristics would be relatively easy to capture in a lab or field experiment (e.g., items 1, 7, 10, 14), whereas others would be very difficult to capture in a study and would be present only in real rating situations (e.g., item 5). Bernardin and Villanova (1986) suggest that external validity is most likely to be high when most or all of the characteristics listed above are present in a study, and that studies that do not include these characteristics are less likely to generalize.

Although we applaud Bernardin and Villanova's (1986) efforts to identify boundary conditions for external validity, we disagree with some of their conclusions. First, we are not sure whether the question of external validity can be asked in the abstract; the critical boundary conditions for generalizing the results of a study must surely depend in part on the phenomenon' being studied. Thus, a single list of boundary conditions will probably set conditions that are irrelevant in some studies and omit conditions that are critical in others. Second, the list is descriptive but not evaluative. We could probably add many other modal features to this list. For example, most ratings are done by white males. Is this a critical characteristic? The answer probably depends on the purpose of the study. It may be necessary to consider this fact when researching certain questions (e.g., effects of rater and ratee race).

The key to specifying boundary conditions for establishing external validity is to understand clearly (1) the phenomenon being studying, (2) the context in which it will be studied, and (3) the context in which results will be applied. The key variable, in our opinion, is the investigator's (and the field's) understanding of the phenomenon being studied. Boundary conditions are essentially moderator variables; it is hard to see how moderators can be correctly identified if the effects of the variables being studied are not well understood. One implication is that it may not always be possible to identify nonarbitrary boundary conditions. For example, if the processes that are involved in relating rating scale formats to rating behavior are unknown, it is hard to know how to identify variables that will moderate those processes.

By virtue of their training, industrial/organizational psychologists should have some general knowledge of both the context of research and the context in which that research is applied. That is, most Ph.Ds in the field will receive extensive training in research methods, which hopefully gives them some insight into the context of their own research. These same individuals are also likely to engage in a number of activities that are designed in part to increase their understanding of the organizational context. These include internships, consulting projects, and field research projects. One way to translate this general knowledge into specific knowledge about the similarities and differences between the research context and the organizational context may be to engage in roleplaying. Bernardin and Villanova's (1986) list of modal characteristics is useful for describing what typically happens in appraisal. The descriptive level could be expanded upon by asking what psychological processes are likely to be triggered by each of these characteristics. Putting oneself into the role of a manager in this modal situation may help highlight the psychological effects of the 15 variables.

A second application of roleplaying techniques is to put oneself in the role of a subject in one's own study. Are the psychological processes evoked in the study comparable to those that are likely to be found in the organizational context? The answer to this question is clearly a matter of more than the cosmetic similarity of the two contexts. For example, laboratory research in PA tends to follow one of two strategies: (1) have the subjects play the role of managers, doing a task that is similar to that done by managers; or (2) have the subjects do a familiar task that is in some way comparable to a task done by managers. We would argue that either strategy could yield generalizable results and that the choice of a strategy should depend primarily on the researcher's comparison between the psychological processes that are likely to occur in the research context and those that are likely to occur in the organization. (See research by Williams, DeNisi, Blencoe, and Cafferty, 1985, for an example of the first approach, and Murphy, Martin, and Garcia, 1982, for an example of the latter.)

Many reviews have expressed doubt about the generalizability of psychological research (particularly laboratory research) on performance appraisal (e.g., Latham, 1986). We are more optimistic. In the final analysis, the generalizability of different types of research is an empirical issue; analyses such as those presented by Locke (1986) suggest that generalizability is more often the rule than the exception.

Chapter Thirteen

Practical Applications

▶   Throughout this book, we have focused on research in the social sciences that we believe is relevant for understanding performance appraisal (PA) in organizations. We think that this research is valuable for two reasons. First, it helps to advance the science of psychology by increasing understanding of several aspects of behavior in organizations. Second, this research suggests a number of ways of improving performance appraisals. Thus, we believe that this research is useful for both scientists and practitioners. (Banks and Murphy, 1985, note that the terms *scientist* and *practitioner* often refer to distinct roles that a person enacts rather than referring to distinct individuals.) The purpose of this chapter is to suggest ways in which this research can be applied to increase the reliability, validity, effectiveness, and utility of performance appraisals.

Many of the suggestions made here are quite different from the type of suggestions a competent personnel manager might give. One reason is that our perspective in developing suggestions for application is that of a psychologist rather than a manager. There is a good deal of controversy in industrial/organizational psychology over whether practitioners' goals should be to become better managers or to become better psychologists (Murphy & Saal, in press). We ascribe to the latter point of view and believe that we can make a better contribution, in the long run, by thinking of ourselves as psychologists who work in or with organizations than to think of ourselves as managers who also know a good bit about psychology.

One implication of this perspective is that we say much less about *how* to improve appraisal than might be found in a good book on personnel administration (e.g., Famularo, 1972). We focus more on *what* needs to be done to apply the research reviewed in this book. As a result, our suggestions do not always address problems that appear most pressing to managers, and they do not always tell the manager exactly what to do in solving the problems to which they are addressed. They do, however, suggest several avenues that should be pursued to use the research reviewed here in improving appraisals in organizations.

This chapter contains a number of specific proposals for applying the results of psychological research on performance appraisal. Some of these are suggestions for immediate application; others represent questions that need to be resolved before theories or research results can be applied. As with Chapter Twelve, this chapter is organized in terms of the four-component model we presented in Chapter One. First, we will suggest several ways in which psychologists could improve appraisals through the assessment and modification of key contextual variables. Second, we review applications of current research on performance evaluation and judgment. Third, we suggest ways in which research on rating behavior, as distinct from judgment, can be applied to improve appraisals. Finally, we suggest a number of avenues that practitioners might pursue in developing methods of evaluating performance appraisal systems.

Specific suggestions for improving performance appraisals in organizations are discussed. We suggest a variety of ways to address issues related to contextual influences on appraisal, improving the quality and the understanding of evaluative judgments, understanding and shaping rating behavior, and improving the ability to evaluate PA systems.

Context

If, as we suggest, context is the most important determinant of appraisal outcomes, there are clear advantages to knowing what context factors are or are not present in a given rating situation and, further, how they are likely to affect rater and ratee behavior.

Measuring the Context

The first set of suggestions to be considered are for developing methods of measuring key contextual variables. Two avenues would be worth pursuing:

1. Develop measures for assessing distal context variables (e.g., sociopolitical or technological context) that are likely to affect appraisal. It is useful here to note that distal variables, by definition, do not affect behavior directly. Rather, rater and ratee *perceptions* regarding these variables are likely to be

the important determinant of rating behavior. One implication is that self-report measures might be appropriate for measuring perceptions of these distal variables and their effects.

2. Develop measures for assessing proximal context variables (e.g., timing and purpose of appraisal) that are likely to affect appraisal. There may be more latitude in measuring proximal than distal context factors. Self-reports will still be useful but a variety of objective measures may also be available for assessing these factors. For example, one set of context factors deals with the administration of appraisals (e.g., Annual or more often? Supervisor only or multiple sources?); it may be possible to classify objectively these facets of context.

Technological Context

In some jobs, the technology of work is changing rapidly, and the technological environment could have a substantial effect in appraisal. For example, changes in technology could affect the nature of good versus poor performance. In some simple technologies, performance is primarily a function of effort, whereas in some complex technologies, performance is primarily a function of the strategy chosen for completing tasks. Technological changes could also undermine the role of the rater, particularly if the ratees understand the new technology but the rater does not. Two suggestions for application that are related to the technological context of work are:

3. Describe the dimensions of job performance for groups of jobs in the organization. Organizations frequently invest considerable time and effort in job analysis. Some of this effort should be devoted to a description of what separates a good performer from a poor performer in a particular job. It is important to integrate information about technological change and its implications for appraisal more fully into PA systems. If the technology changes quickly, there may be the need for ongoing job analytic efforts.

4. Develop training programs to increase supervisors' understanding of and ability to evaluate performance in technologically complex jobs. This should be an integral part of the organization's program to update workers (Kozlowski & Farr, 1988). That is, supervisors will need to keep up to date in their own jobs as well as the jobs of the individuals they supervise.

Rater Goals

In the model presented in Chapter One, we assumed that context factors are one key determinant of the rater's goals, which in turn determine his or her behavior. It would be useful to know what goals raters are pursuing; we suggest an approach to this problem below. It might be even more useful to modify existing rater goals and to guide the development of new raters' goals in such a way that rater goals are consistent with the goals of the organization. Three suggestions are:

5. Determine the best way (and the optimum frequency) to assess rater goals. Here, self-reports may be somewhat useful but their validity will be limited by the extent to which raters are able and willing to state their goals. It may be possible to use characteristics of the ratings themselves to infer goals. For example, a rater who inflates all of his or her ratings is probably attempting to use ratings either to (a) motivate employees or (b) avoid negative ratee reactions. Another possibility is to compare ratings to the feedback the ratee receives. If there are discrepancies between ratings given to the organization and the feedback given to employees, this may give some insight into the rater's goals. If feedback is given in written form, these discrepancies may be easy to assess. If not, ratee's self-reports will be informative but not definitive. Discrepancies could result from differences between what the rater tells the ratee and what the rater tells the organization, or they could reflect distortions and misunderstandings on the part of the ratee.

6. Determine ways of modifying the climate of the organization to (a) ensure uniform rater goals and (b) ensure that raters' goals are consistent with those of the organization.

7. Design socialization programs to develop, in the shortest time possible, rater goals that are consistent with those of the organization.

Purpose of Rating

The purpose of rating is widely assumed to be a critical aspect of the rating context (Landy & Farr, 1980). Several opportunities for applying this research exist. In particular, reliable ways are needed of assessing the purpose of rating, as it is perceived by raters, ratees, and other organization members. Also needed are ways to match the procedures we use for appraising performance to the intended, actual, and perceived purposes of rating. Six suggestions for applications of research on the effects of purpose of rating are:

8. Measure the perceived purpose(s) of rating. Raters, ratees, and the top management of the organization should all be surveyed. These groups may differ substantially in their perceptions of the purpose of rating.

9. Determine the maximum number of purposes that can be adequately served by a single PA system. This figure will depend in part on the specific set of purposes that are being served. If several purposes are compatible or conceptually related, the system might be effective in serving a relatively large number of purposes. If different purposes require very different types of information, the system is likely to serve a smaller number of purposes adequately.

10. Determine which purposes are mutually incompatible. Uses of

appraisal that concentrate on between-person differences (e.g., using appraisal to determine promotions) may be incompatible with uses that concentrate on within-person differences (e.g., using appraisal to give feedback regarding strengths and weaknesses). Although this is probably true in a general way, it may not apply to all possible combinations of between- and within-person uses of appraisal. For example, rating a person's promotability may not interfere with giving valid feedback about strengths and weaknesses.

11. Determine which scale format is best for any given purpose. Some formats are *not* appropriate for specific purposes (e.g., mixed-standard scales may be inappropriate for giving performance feedback); however, it is not known if there is some specific format that is best for each of the major purposes of appraisal.

12. Develop rater training programs that convey the purposes that are actually being pursued by the organization in performance appraisal. This will require a careful examination of both the explicit and the implicit purposes of appraisal. Thus, a valuable side benefit of developing such a training program may be a greater awareness of exactly what goals are and should be pursued.

13. Determine what happens when information about ratee performance is *provided* for one purpose but used for another. In Chapter Twelve, we suggested that it would be useful to study the psychological processes involved when information is *collected* for one purpose and used for another. In this chapter, we have a somewhat different concern — the fact that the rater's purpose might not be the same as the purpose the organization imposes. It is not yet known if information that is provided for one purpose but used for another is easier or harder to use than information that is provided for the same purpose for which it is used.

Feedback

One of the most crucial purposes for doing performance appraisals is that they provide feedback to ratees. This feedback should both activate and shape ratee behavior; Landy and Farr (1983) review empirical evidence showing that feedback does have a substantial effect on performance. Two things psychologists in organizations could do to increase the utility of feedback are:

14. Develop procedures for maximizing the utility of negative feedback. This will entail reducing defensiveness and distortion, but it also includes considerations such as the optimal timing of negative vversuspositive feedback.

15. Determine whether and when inflated self-evaluations reduce the credibility and utility of feedback. If ratees have a difficult time accepting negative feedback, and their evaluations of their own performance are inflated, a completely accurate evaluation (e.g., lower ratings than they think they

deserve) may be perceived negatively. In some cases, it can be argued that inflated self-evaluations help maintain self-esteem. A loss of self-esteem might have a more negative effect on performance than will the inflated self-evaluation.

Rater and Ratee Reactions

Finally, raters' and ratees' reactions to the performance appraisal system are critical contextual determinants of appraisal processes and outcomes. To help guarantee a favorable or constructive reaction to appraisal practices, two avenues might be pursued:

16. Determine what appraisal practices are either accepted as legitimate or rejected by major constituencies in the organization. These constituencies will often be defined in terms of level in the organization but this is not always the case. Thus, there is also a need to develop procedures for identifying major constituencies.

17. Develop training programs or strategies for communicating the organization's rationale for following appraisal practices that are not viewed favorably by raters or ratees. Organizations will not want to retain policies that do little more than anger employees. Thus, there is likely to be a well-defined rationale for adopting and retaining appraisal practices that are not received well. This rationale is not always communicated well to the users of the appraisal system.

Judgment

Most of the recent research on cognitive processes in appraisal deals with judgment. This research has been criticized on the grounds that it provides few solutions to practical problems in organizations (Banks & Murphy, 1985), although some practical suggestions have been put forth (Feldman, 1986). We believe that the key to increasing the practical relevance of research on judgment and cognition is to broaden the scope of our inquiry. It is important to continue to pursue questions that emerge when applying theories of encoding, storage, retrieval, and so on to performance judgments, but it is also important to pursue several lines of research that are somewhat outside of the traditional domain of cognitive psychology. For example, how do supervisors obtain the information they need to make judgments and how we might facilitate the process? How do raters and ratees define good and poor performance and might the congruence of these definitions be increased? How might raters be trained to make good judgments? Finally, how and when does cognitive research provide information that is useful for understanding appraisal in organizations?

Acquiring Information ────────────────────────────

The first set of suggestions deals with the type of information that is available to the rater at the time he or she does appraisals. Two main issues arise. First, what type of information is or should be obtained directly by the supervisor? Second, when information is obtained from some source other than direct observation, how is it evaluated and effectively used? Five suggestions related to this topic are:

18. Develop strategies to increase the acceptability of using sources such as peers, subordinates, or the ratee himself or herself as sources of information in performance appraisal. Organizations are losing a great deal of potentially relevant information by not attending to these sources. What steps can be taken to make the use of these sources more acceptable? One possibility, mentioned earlier, is to identify what each source does well or poorly. One way to do that is to ask what sorts of information are available to different sources. If information that is critical for making important decisions is unavailable to the supervisor, this provides some incentive to use sources other than the direct supervisor in performance appraisal.

19. Determine what sort of information is collected via direct versus indirect observation. What is needed here is an analysis of the "job" of rater. How does the rater collect information about performance? Good descriptive research in this area would contribute to both science and practice.

20. Determine what sorts of information should be collected via direct versus indirect observation. Two issues need to be considered here. First, is there something about the information itself that requires one source or the other to be used? For example, if the organization needs to know how customers react to a salesperson, the customers rather than the supervisor should be the source of that information. Second, is there something about the context that requires one source or the other to be used? For example, direct observation may not provide valid information about interpersonal relations among members of a workgroup; the presence of the supervisor might change the ratees' behavior.

21. Develop procedures to increase the reliability and usefulness of secondhand observations of ratee performance. In part, this will involve training supervisors to regard the evaluation of *all* employees as their job, thus increasing the frequency of valid secondhand reports.

22. Develop methods of direct observation that do not violate ratees' privacy or that do not lead to the feeling that privacy is being violated. Technology is probably not the answer here. In many jobs, the technology exists to obtain detailed unobtrusive observations of each ratee's behavior. Reactions to this technology are almost universally negative. A better approach might be one that is widely used in organizational development. Raters might negotiate a *psychological contract* with ratees that specifies what behaviors the rater should observe and what observations constitute an

invasion of privacy. (Golumbiewski, 1972, refers to a more elaborate version of this process as "role negotiation.")

Norms

Judgment is a comparison process. In performance appraisal, raters form judgments by comparing ratees to a norm or a set of norms. Thus, one key to understanding performance judgments is to understand how norms are developed, communicated, and used. Five suggestions for application that relate to performance norms are:

23. Develop programs to facilitate the communication of performance norms from (a) top management to supervisors, (b) peers to supervisors, and (c) supervisors to subordinates. Different methods may be required for each of these. One issue that will need to be addressed here is to define the *content* of performance norms (see suggestion 31 in Chapter Twelve). Different methods of communicating norms might be best if they represent implicit distributions than if they represent thresholds between ordered categories of performance (e.g., good, average, and poor performer).

24. Develop programs to help new managers quickly identify the appropriate reference groups for defining performance standards. New managers may not know who sets the standards; socialization activities for new managers should include attempts to help them identify appropriate reference groups.

25. Use programs that recognize individual employees (e.g., employee-of-the-month programs) to communicate performance standards. To do this, one will need to determine how best to communicate information about what the effective employee did (or what the ineffective employee failed to do) that determined the performance level.

26. Develop methods for assessing the norms and standards that are accepted by each rater. Individual differences in performance norms are expected. These differences could be a significant source of friction between workers and supervisors and could also be a source of interrater disagreements.

27. Determine whether organizations can affect workers' norms regarding "a fair day's work" and, if so, how? It is uncertain whether it is possible for the organization to intervene in this area or even whether it *should* intervene. Nevertheless, ratee performance norms that discourage superior performance have long been recognized as a potentially serious problem in organizations (Sherif & Sherif, 1969). Where norms exist that limit performance and productivity, it would be worthwhile to attempt to change the norms.

Cognitive Processes

Research on cognitive processes in appraisal has been criticized as irrelevant to appraisal in organizations. We disagree. We believe that cognitive process research can make a useful contribution in three areas: (1) comparing different rating scale formats, (2) developing technologies and techniques to minimize the effects of shortcomings in cognitive processes on the accuracy of judgments, and (3) designing rater training programs. Four specific suggestions for applying cognitively oriented research to appraisal in organizations are:

28. Determine whether there is any practical reason to continue to develop and employ behavior-oriented (as opposed to trait-oriented) PA scales. Murphy and Constans (1987, 1988) summarize research that suggests that including behavioral information on rating scales does not improve (and can reduce) the accuracy of judgments. However, accuracy is not the only criterion that is relevant to the organization. Behavior-based scales may be viewed more favorably by ratees and by other relevant constituencies (e.g., in litigation involving appraisal, the courts have consistently favored behavior-based scales). A tradeoff needs to be made between the time and expense involved in developing behavior-based scales versus the benefits that these scales convey.

29. Much of the research on cognitive processes in appraisal has examined issues relating to the encoding/categorization process. It would be useful to assess the categories raters actually use when assessing their subordinates. Thus, it might be worthwhile to develop methods for assessing raters' "theories of the job." Raters may differ in their conceptions of what is important on the job and in terms of their conceptions of good and poor performance.

30. Develop training programs that will help all raters adopt consistent categories (and consistent definitions of each category) for classifying what they observe. This recommendation is consistent with recommendations made over 35 years ago by researchers who were studying the selection interview (Webster, 1982). These researchers noted that interview decisions are often based on stereotypes. Since it is very hard to change basic decision processes, they suggested that interviewers should be trained to develop and use valid, consistent stereotypes of good, average, and poor performance.

31. Develop training programs to minimize the impact of irrelevant information (e.g., attractiveness) on evaluations. Banks and Murphy (1985) suggested that the need for good "forgetting aids" is even more pressing than the need for good memory aids. There is considerable evidence that factors such as race, age, attractiveness, and gender can influence social judgments, although Wendelken and Inn (1981) and Murphy, Herr, Lockhart, and Maguire (1986) suggested that this influence was not large. We do not know of any effective method of training raters to overlook or forget irrelevant information but such training would obviously be worthwhile.

External Validity

The last issue to be considered here is the external validity of research on evaluative judgment of performance. It would be useful to know if and under what circumstances this research will yield generalizable results. Three suggestions for determining whether this research generalizes to the field are:

32. Assuming that different psychological processes are evoked by different formats, determine whether (and under what circumstances) these differences are sufficiently large to have any effect on the outcomes of appraisal. There is good reason to believe that different scale formats do indeed evoke different psychological processes. At present, very little is known about the size or even the direction of this effect. It is entirely possible that there is a systematic effect but that it is too small to be important in the field.

33. Determine the frequency and severity in organizational settings of categorization errors that are known to occur in laboratory studies of categorization. Once again, researchers know that these errors *can* occur but they do not know whether or when they *do* occur. This is another instance in which good descriptive research would contribute both to science and practice.

34. Determine the critical variables that demonstrate the extent to which a laboratory study generalizes to the field. Locke (1986) argues that the obvious differences between the lab and the field are not always the important ones, and that some laboratory studies will generalize better to the field than a study conducted in one organization will generalize to another organization.

Rating

There are two key issues that practitioners must face when analyzing and shaping rating behavior. First, there is often a discrepancy between judgments and ratings. Practitioners must decide how to reduce this discrepancy and whether attempts to reduce this discrepancy will do more harm than good. Second, rating is a communication process. Practitioners must devise ways to determine what the rater is trying to communicate and to facilitate the accurate communication of critical information to the organization.

Rating Inflation

The first issue to be examined is rating inflation. It is well known that ratings are skewed in a positive direction and that many ratees receive higher ratings than they deserve. Traditionally, this phenomenon has been treated as just another rater error. Attempts to reduce this problem have focused on developing scales or rater training programs that would combat inflation. It is probably more useful to examine rating inflation from a motivational standpoint. In most rating contexts, strong incentives exist to inflate ratings and few incentives exist to report accurate ratings. Five suggestions for reducing rating inflation are:

35. Identify the outcomes that are valued (positively or negatively) by raters, and assess the value and perceived probability attached to each outcome. Some outcomes are relevant to all raters, whereas others are important to some raters and not to others. Some outcomes are viewed as highly likely (e.g., giving low ratings is very likely to lead to strained interpersonal relations), whereas others may be viewed as very uncertain. Expectancy theories of motivation suggest that both outcome value and outcome probability must be assessed to understand motivation to pursue a specific course of action.

36. Determine what rewards should be available to raters. In some contexts, the organization may decide that accurate ratings are not sufficiently important to justify large rewards for accurate raters. In others, accurate ratings may be truly important. An analysis of values of key members of the organization will be useful here but assessing stated values will not be enough. Decision theorists suggest that if accurate ratings are highly valued, the organization will give rewards for accuracy and sanctions for inaccuracy. Thus, the organization's willingness to reward accuracy in rating will be a clear indicator of the value attached to accurate evaluations of ratee performance.

37. One outcome that is likely to be highly salient to raters is their own discomfort with giving negative feedback. Therefore, it would be useful to develop methods of delivering negative feedback that are less stressful for the *rater*. Training represents one approach to the problem but others might include changes in the nature and structure of performance feedback. For example, negative feedback may be easier to give and receive if there are multiple raters who all agree in their evaluations.

38. Determine the circumstances under which raters should be trained to use distortion in ratings as a motivational tool. As noted above, this will entail a careful comparison of costs and benefits of accurate ratings versus higher levels of motivation. This will require research in at least two areas. First, it will be necessary to determine whether and when rating inflation works as a motivational tool. Second, it will be necessary to determine what benefits the organization receives if accurate ratings are given. For example, if it is concluded that rating inflation was a moderately effective motivator and that the organization would not do anything different with accurate ratings than it now does with inflated ratings, it would *not* be worthwhile to reduce rating inflation.

39. Develop methods to increase raters' and ratees' trust in the appraisal system; high levels of trust in the system are likely to increase the match between judgments and ratings. One way to increase trust in the system is to communicate clearly and honestly to raters and ratees what is done with performance evaluations and what the consequences of high versus low ratings really are. Trust is likely to be higher if the system is developmental in its orientation (e.g., ratings are used to help improve performance) than if it is punitive in orientation (e.g., ratings are used to weed out poor performers).

Ratings as Communication Tools

The next set of suggestions involve determining precisely what the rater is trying to communicate when giving ratings. Two suggestions relevant to this issue are:

40. Develop methods the organization can use to tell whether the rater thinks the ratee is a good or poor performer. We have noted the distinction between judgment and rating and have also noted that organizations ordinarily have access to ratings (which may be inflated or distorted) but not to judgments. Are there any ways of gaining better insights into the private opinions of the rater?

41. Develop ways of clearly separating evaluations of present performance from recommendations concerning outcomes (e.g., salary increases, promotions, etc.). One possibility is to develop and articulate policies that make it clear that present performance is *not* the sole determinant of outcomes such as raises and promotions.

Improving Communication

The final set of suggestions in this section are focused on improving the rater's ability to communicate clearly to the organization via performance appraisals. Four specific suggestions are:

42. Determine the best way to elicit and communicate information about the absolute and relative performance levels of ratees. For some purposes (e.g., promotion), the organization needs to know who are the best performers. For others (e.g., workforce planning), the organization needs to know how well workers perform their jobs. It is important to determine what the organization needs to know about the ratee's performance. Presumably, some of the potential uses of appraisal are unimportant and some of the information provided in a typical appraisal is of little value to the organization. Appraisals that focus on truly important purposes would be preferable to those that do not.

43. Determine what the ratee needs to know about his or her perormance and then structure feedback accordingly. Again, depending on the purpose of performance appraisal, the ratee might need to know his or her (a) absolute level of performance, (b) relative level, or (c) relative strengths and weaknesses.

44. Help make raters aware of the goals they are now pursuing and of the goals the organization is trying to acheive with appraisal. Communication is likely to be clearer if the rater is aware of both his or her goals and the goals of the organization.

45. Train managers to recognize and deal effectively with political factors in performance appraisal. Researchers often note, with apparent

disapproval, the political nature of appraisals in organizations (see, for example, Longenecker, Sims, and Gioia, 1987). However, the fact that appraisal is partly political is neither good nor bad. What is bad is the fact that some managers are *ineffective* politicians, who do not know what they should do to achieve their goals in appraisals. Training all raters to be effective politicians in organizations might be strongly preferable to leaving this critical but maligned managerial skill to chance.

Evaluation

Organizations need to evaluate the effectiveness of all personnel programs, including performance appraisal. That is, they need good criteria for criteria or, more broadly, good procedures for determining whether appraisal systems acheive their important goals. Problems with current methods for evaluating appraisal systems may represent the most pressing set of practical problems facing practitioners. Two distinct issues should be considered here. First, how can one determine whether an appraisal system is any good or which system is best for a given organization? Second, how can these evaluations be used to influence the policy of the organization (i.e., to increase the likelihood that systems that best meet relevant criteria are adopted)?

Criteria for Criteria

The first issue to be considered in this section is the evaluation of ratings. Research reviewed in Chapters Ten and Eleven suggests that the psychometric indices and rater error measures that are most often used to evaluate ratings are not adequate criteria for criteria. Are there any realistic alternatives? Four possibilities are suggested below:

46. One type of evidence for the quality of ratings is the documentation that is available to support good, average, or poor evaluations. Documentation will not by itself guarantee accuracy; raters are very good at specifying a post hoc rationalization for the ratings they give. However, if documentation can be obtained from multiple, independent sources, the value of this evidence increases substantially. It will be important to determine the most cost-effective way to collect and retain detailed information documenting workers' performance levels. In a number of contexts, particularly those in which performance appraisals might lead to unfavorable outcomes (e.g., dismissal), detailed documentation is necessary. The simplest solution is to collect detailed information about all workers but this is unlikely to be cost-effective.

47. Develop methods for measuring the accuracy of ratings in organizations. The most formidable problem here is that although most organizations designate the supervisor as the sole rater, accuracy measurement in organizations will require the use of multiple raters (see Chapter Ten). Murphy

(1982b) suggested that only a small number of raters (three to six) would be necessary to combat halo errors; this same number might also be sufficient for assessing accuracy.

48. Not all aspects of accuracy are relevant. Thus, it is important to determine the aspects of accuracy that are most relevant to various uses of performance appraisal. For example, if ratings are used to make salary decisions, accuracy in distinguishing between persons is relevant and accuracy in distinguishing individual strengths from weaknesses is not.

49. Determine the conditions under which so-called rater errors are beneficial versus harmful. For example, it is known that halo facilitates between-person comparisons (Murphy & Balzer, 1986); it is reasonable to assume that halo also interferes with some of the potential uses of rating data (e.g., using ratings to make placement decisions). Similarly, it is likely that leniency sometimes serves a valid purpose (e.g., increasing motivation); in other cases, it might interfere with the organization's ability to make important decisions (e.g., promotion decisions are more difficult if large numbers of ratees receive near-perfect appraisals).

Value Tradeoffs

The evaluation of different appraisal systems often involves a tradeoff between the advantages and disadvantages of each system. Research on decision making provides a number of ways of describing and carrying out these tradeoffs. Two specific suggestions can be derived from decision research:

50. Develop practical methods for establishing indifference curves among qualitiatively different outcomes of appraisal. One set of issues that needs to be addressed is who should serve as judges for establishing these curves. A related issue is the amount of data that is needed to define these curves adequately.

51. Develop a method of monitoring changes in the values of organization members that will necessitate changes in the appraisal system. The idea here is that a system may be perfectly consistent with the present values of key members of the organization, but changes in personnel or in the goals of the organization may decrease the fit between the appraisal system and the goals of the organization.

Utility Estimation

The last set of issues to be considered here are those related to the credibility and completeness of utility estimates that are computed for appraisal systems. Two problems should be examined: Have all of the relevant criteria been considered? Are the estimates derived from utility equations credible? Two specific suggestions for dealing with these questions are:

52. Determine whether reaction criteria are important. If so, how should these criteria be integrated with quantitative evaluations of ratings? We believe that these criteria *are* important and that they are typically ignored in utility estimates. Utility estimates that focus on short-term results of appraisal systems without considering the reactions to the system are likely in the long run to be the cause of inaccurate ratings. For example, the introduction of an electronic system for recording ratee's behavior (e.g., number of minutes per day spent at the keyboard) may lead to an immediate rise in the class of behaviors recorded, but may also increase negative reactions to the appraisal system and the organization. In the long run, these reactions might have a significant negative effect on performance.

53. Determine whether utility estimates provide useful and credible information to organizational decision makers. If not, determine what is missing and whether it can reasonably be obtained. For example, we suspect that many organizations do not regard utility estimates as useful. In some cases, this is because procedures that are normally followed by the organization (e.g., accounting procedures) have not been applied to the estimates. In other cases, managers may not accept the data (e.g., validity estimates) that underly these estimates. The solution to the problem of credibility will be quite different in these two cases.

Integrating Science and Practice

At the beginning of this chapter, we noted that psychologists often serve an anomalous role in organizations. That is, they are likely to be regarded as managers first and psychologists second (if at all). One effect of this type of role definition is that it will be difficult for psychologists in organizations to directly apply the knowledge gained from psychological research. In some cases, a psychologist has no choice but to accept this limitation and to do his or her best in the organizational context. In others, it might be very feasible to more fully integrate science and practice. Several prerequisites for acheiving this integration are discussed below.

Prerequisites for Integrating Science and Practice

The successful application of psychological research in organizations depends on a careful (or fortuitous) match between the characteristics of psychologists and the characteristics of the settings in which they do and apply research. Three essential prerequisites can be identified. First, psychologists (and students of psychology) must have values that are compatible with the dual roles of scientist and practitioner. Second, they must have the skills to do and apply scientific research. Third, and perhaps most important, the settings in which they work must allow them opportunity to do relevant research and/or to apply the results of research.

Values The role of applied psychologist requires the integration of two distinct value systems, one that emphasizes precision and scientific caution and the one that emphasizes action and the solution of practical problems (Spence, 1987). This integration is especially difficult for clinical and other health-service areas of psychology, since the humanistic value system that often characterizes practice is fundamentally different from the scientific value system that usually characterizes research (Kimble, 1984). However, this integration is probably difficult in *any* applied area of psychology. As Spence (1987) notes, few psychologists have the inclination or the flexibility to be comfortable in both scientist and practitioner roles.

It is easier to describe value systems that would prevent one from effectively integrating the roles of scientist and practitioner than to describe the value system that would allow this integration. First, there is the belief, sometimes expressed by psychologists in nonapplied fields, that applied psychology is not real psychology. There is some merit to this point of view; virtually all applications of psychology involve activities, interventions, and so on that are not solely psychological in nature. For example, a psychologist who designs a PA system strictly on the basis of the most recent research on cognition and judgment will not be successful. A successful application of psychology in this instance will require the psychologist to be aware of and to take into account organizational realities, and it is unlikely that the system that is best for use in the real world will be the same as the system that is best for scientific research.

Value systems that are sometimes associated with practice can also prevent the successful integration of science and practice. In particular, the belief that the *process* of doing research is irrelevant to one's activities as a practitioner appears to be widespread, and will clearly hinder the integration of science and practice. One's beliefs about the fundamental causes of behavior might also have direct implications for the value that is attached to research. The belief that the causes of behavior are completely idiosyncratic and that they can be understood only from the subjective perspective of the actor will make it impossible for one to do psychological research or to use the results of other peoples' psychologists. Being an effective applied psychologist requires that the individual believes that research is possible and that research can help solve practical problems.

A related value system is common among managers and, to a lesser extent, among practitioners. Personal experience is often viewed as a necessary and sufficient prerequisite for solving practical problems. This value system has two components: (1) knowledge, results, and so on from other settings do not apply in your setting; and (2) people learn to solve problems simply by being repeatedly exposed to them. Both components will lead one to distrust research as a process for addressing real-world problems and will greatly hinder the integration of science and practice.

Skills The second requirement for the effective integration of science and practice is that psychologists have the skills necessary to perform successfully in both roles. Research skills would include skills in (1) problem definition, (2) operationalization, (3) design of experiments and studies, (4) data collection, and (5) data analysis and interpretation. Most graduate students in psychology receive some training in all five areas, although the amount of coursework involved and the centrality of these skills to the students' training vary considerably across different areas of psychology. Even in graduate programs that offer a professional degree rather than a Ph.D. (e.g., programs that offer a Psy.D.), students are likely to receive some exposure to these topics. Thus, it is safe to assume that most psychologists will have *some* skills as researchers, although many may lose seldom-used skills over time.

The set of skills that are needed to apply psychology will depend greatly on the context in which the psychologist works. The skills needed to work effectively in a large organization may be different than those needed to function in a small one. An industrial/orgnizational psychologist working as an external consultant to a large organization may need different skills than one who is working as an internal consultant in the same organization. Because of the diversity of skills required in different settings, we will focus on one type of psychologist and on one setting, and will discuss skills required of industrial/organizational psychologists employed either as members of an organization's human resources department or as an external consultant to that department.

Howard (1984) describes the role of the psychologist in industry and notes that several skills that are not taught in graduate school are highly relevant to success in organizations. First, psychologists must convince other organizational members or units that their services will be useful in solving practical problems. As psychologists in organizations quickly learn, there is usually little spontaneous demand for their services, nor is there clear recognition of the types of problems psychologists might be able to solve. Second, psychologists in organizations usually function as managers rather than as autonomous professionals. Therefore, they must be skilled in supervising others, delegating authority and tasks, planning, and other typical managerial functions.

Next, psychologists must be able to communicate the results and implications of their work to a nonprofessional audience and must be able to translate jargon into understandable prose. Fourth, and perhaps most important, they must understand the context. That is, psychologists must learn or know how the organization functions and why, and must understand the goals, the culture, and the climate of the organization. Understanding the context is essential to recognizing and avoiding constraints on one's ability to address problems in the organization effectively.

Skills in problem definition and diagnosis are especially critical for external consultants. It is common for consultants to find that the *real* problem is substantially different than the problem that is presented to them when they are contacted by the organization. For example, what managers describe as a problem with their PA scales may in fact reflect problems with rater motivation or with communication between different levels of the organization. External consultants are less likely to know, in any detail, the context of the organization (although they may know the contexts of organizations in general), and thus cannot draw upon their knowledge of the particular situation to diagnose organizational problems.

Opportunities No matter what one's values or skills are, science and practice cannot be integrated effectively if the setting in which one works does not allow this. For example, many psychologists working in organizations have few if any opportunities to do research; instead, they must devote all of their time to solving practical problems. Similarly, a clinician in private practice may not have access to the data needed to test his or her hypotheses. Many academics have limited opportunities to apply their knowledge of psychology (or are discouraged from devoting time and energy to application).

Although opportunities to do both research and practice may be rare, the limitations this places on one's ability to integrate science and practice should not be overemphasized. A psychologist working in an organization may not have the opportunity to do research but there is nothing to prevent him or her from basing the practice as a psychologist on others' research findings. Similarly, some academics and employees of research units may have few opportunities to actually practice psychology in organizations. This does not prevent them, however, from doing research on problems that are relevant to the practice of industrial/organizational psychology.

Although doing both research and practice is desirable, it is not essential for the effective integration of science and practice. Thus, limitations on one's ability to do research or to practice are barriers to their integration but these barriers are not insurmountable. Recognition of the constraints that are often placed on a psychologist's ability to do research *and* apply this research in organizations may help practitioners to develop more realistic expectations about applying psychological research in organizations and may also point toward recommendations for minimizing those constraints.

Appendix

Rating Scale Formats

▶ If the number of studies devoted to various topics in performance appraisal (PA) since 1950 were counted, one would probably conclude that the format of the rating scale was one of the most important issues in appraisal. Although there is still some interest in the psychological processes that are engaged by different formats (Murphy & Constans, 1987, 1989), current PA research pays little attention to the question of which format is best. This is a direct result of Landy and Farr's (1980) review, in which they concluded that formats have only a minimal effect on the quality of ratings and that no one format was consistently better than the others. Their call for a moratorium on rating scale format research was heeded by most researchers; as a result, the topic that accounted for the majority of studies from 1950 to 1980 now receives little attention. Nevertheless, it is useful to examine some of the features of widely used scale formats.

In this Appendix, we discuss several scale formats, including graphic scales, behaviorally anchored rating scales (BARS), mixed standard scales (MSS) and behavior observation scales (BOS), as well as methods of defining performance criteria (e.g., Performance Distribution Assessment, Management by Objectives, and employee comparison methods). We will not go into the question of which format or method is best overall but we will comment on factors that might lead a person to adopt one format rather than another. In addition, we will briefly discuss several methods for comparing or ranking employees. Although these are not rating scales per se, they are frequently included in performance appraisals and form the basis for some personnel decisions.

Graphic Rating Scales

The simplest scale format asks the rater to record his or her judgment about some specific aspect of the ratee's performance on a scale that can be used to obtain numeric values that correspond with the rater's evaluation of the ratee. Several examples of a graphic scale that might be used to record ratings of a performance dimension are presented in Figure A-1.

This type of scale format provides little structure for the rater in recording his or her judgment. Graphic scales can range from those like our example 1, which contains no definitions of what is meant by very poor, very good, or intermediate levels of performance, to those that define each level in terms of some label (e.g., our example 3), or even in terms of a brief description of what is meant by each level of performance.

The principal advantage of this scale type is simplicity. The disadvantage of this format, which led to efforts to develop alternative formats, is the lack of clarity and definition. First, the scale does not define what is meant by *Time Management*. Different supervisors might include very different behaviors under this general heading. Second, the scale does not define what is meant by Poor, Average, and so on. Supervisors might apply very different standards in evaluating the same behaviors. Behaviorally Anchored Rating Scales and Mixed Standard Scales attempt to solve these problems by defining performance dimensions and performance levels in behavioral terms.

Figure A–1

Time Management

1.
Very
Poor   Very
                                                                    Good

2.
1   2   3   4   5
Very   Very
Poor   Good

3.
1   2   3   4   5
Very   Poor   Average   Good   Very
Poor   Good

Behaviorally Anchored Rating Scales

The development and use of Behaviorally Anchored Rating Scales (BARS) accounted for much of the research on performance appraisal in the late 1960s and the 1970s. These scales use behavioral examples of different levels of performance to define both the dimension being rated and the performance levels on the scale in clear, behavioral terms. The process of scale development can be long and complex but it will usually result in scales that are clearly defined and well accepted by both raters and ratees. An example of a BARS used by Murphy and Constans (1987) in one of their studies of teacher rating is presented in Figure A-2.

Much of the rating format research of the 1970s seemed to reflect the assumption that BARS were more objective than graphic scales and that defining performance in behavioral terms would result in more accurate ratings. This assumption was not supported in subsequent research, which has led many researchers and practitioners to question the utility of BARS. This question is especially relevant because the process of developing BARS can be time-consuming and expensive. However, BARS appear to have one advantage that was not fully anticipated by early BARS researchers — they are accepted by the users. The reason for this is that most BARS development procedures incorporate feedback from large numbers of raters (and sometimes ratees) in the process of constructing scales. As a result, many of the raters and ratees are likely to feel that they have some personal investment in the scales. As a result, many of the raters and ratees are likely to feel that they have some

Figure A–2

Response to Questions

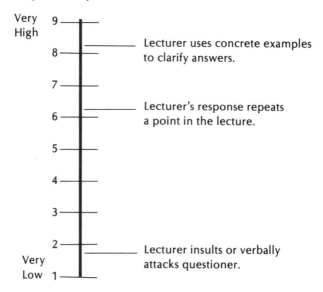

personal investment in the scales. Even those raters and ratees who do not participate in scale development may view the scales favorably because of the heavy reliance of their colleagues' feedback.

Mixed Standard Scales

Mixed Standard Scales (MSS) also incorporate behavioral examples but they employ a different response format than that used in BARS. An example of a MSS will help illustrate the similarities and differences. A MSS designed to measure two performance dimensions (Response to Questions and Speaking Style), again taken from Murphy and Constans's (1987) research, is shown in Figure A-3. Here, items 1, 4, and 5 refer to behaviors that represent "Response to Questions." Items 2, 3, and 6 refer to behaviors that represent "Speaking Style."

By carefully examining the examples, it can be seen that for each dimension, there is one item describing good performance, one item describing average performance, and one item describing poor performance. The rater responds to a MSS by noting, for each item, whether the ratee's performance is better than, about equal to, or worse than the behavior described in each item. Several algorithms exist for translating these ratings into an overall numeric score for each dimension.

One apparent advantage of MSS is that it may simplify the rater's task. Rather than evaluating each lecturer's performance by using vague, undefined terms (e.g., good), raters have only to compare the ratee with the example. However, it is important to note that research on MSS does not strongly support this claim. The complexity of the MSS scoring system is the source of one of its greatest disadvantages. Raters typically do not know which items measure which dimensions (they may not know what dimensions are measured) or how their ratings are translated into numeric scores. As a result, the rater using MSS will find it very difficult to give meaningful feedback. If a subordinate asks why he or she received a low rating on "Speaking Style," the rater may not be able to answer.

Figure A–3

1. _____ Lecturer's response repeats a point in the lecture.
2. _____ Lecturer stands behind the podium.
3. _____ Lecturer misses words when reading from notes.
4. _____ Lecturer insults or verbally attacks questioner.
5. _____ Lecturer uses concrete examples to clarify answers.
6. _____ Lecturer varies pitch and tone of voice to emphasize points.

Behavior Observation Scales

A final variation on the use of behavioral examples in evaluating performance is the Behavior Observation Scale (BOS). This type of scale uses the same class of items as the MSS but it asks for a different sort of judgment. Rather than asking for evaluations of each ratee, the BOS asks the rater to describe how frequently each behavior occurred over the period covered by appraisal. Proponents of BOS suggest that this method removes much of the subjectivity that is usually present in evaluative judgments. Unfortunately, research into the cognitive processes involved in responding to BOS (Murphy & Constans, 1988; Murphy, Martin, & Garcia, 1982) suggests that the process of judging behavior frequency is every bit as subjective as the process of forming evaluative judgments. In fact, behavior frequency ratings may be *more* subjective than trait ratings or overall judgments; overall evaluations of the ratee's performance appear to serve as a critical cue for estimating behavior frequencies. Thus, the use of BOS probably does not allow the rater to avoid the subjectivity of overall impressions or judgments.

We cited potential advantages for graphic scales, BARS, and even MSS; however, we are not as enthusiastic about BOS. The behavioral orientation of these scales appears, on the surface, to be a decided advantage, but there are several reasons to believe that raters do not respond to these scales in terms of behaviors. Rather, they use their overall, subjective evaluations to guide their behavior ratings. This type of scale might actually disguise the inherent subjectivity of evaluative judgment by phrasing judgments in an apparently objective behavioral language. Our rather negative evaluation of this type of scale may reflect our biases as much as it reflects shortcomings in BOS. One of the authors of this book (Murphy) has been involved in much of the research questioning BOS and it is possible that this evaluation of BOS is not shared by other researchers.

Performance Distribution Assessment

Performance distribution assessment (PDA) represents a more sophisticated version of the basic approach exemplified by BOS. In PDA, raters must indicate the frequency of different outcomes (e.g., behaviors, results) that indicate specific *levels* of performance on a given dimension. For example, the scale might describe the most effective outcome and the least effective outcome that could reasonably be expected in a particular job function, as well as several intermediate outcomes. The rater is asked to estimate the frequency of each outcome level for each ratee. One of the potential advantages of this format is that it allows the rater to consider the distribution or the variability of performance as well as the average level of performance in forming an evaluation. PDA involves some fairly complex scoring rules and results in measures of the relative effectiveness of performance, the consistency of performance, and the frequency with which especially positive or negative outcomes are observed. (A concise description of PDA is presented in Bernardin and Beatty, 1984. Also, software now exists for PDA scoring.)

Our evaluation of PDA is similar to our evaluation of BOS. Both depend on the rater's ability to indicate accurately the frequency of specific behaviors or outcomes. In our view, cognitive research suggests that raters are simply incapable of performing this task in an objective way. It is very likely that raters infer the frequency of different behaviors or outcomes from their global evaluations of individuals, and that when one asks for data on the frequency of effective or ineffective behaviors, what one actually gets is a restatement of the rater's overall evaluation. Thus, we do not believe that assessments obtained using PDA or BOS will be more specific, objective, or behavior-based than assessments obtained with much simpler scales.

Management by Objectives

Management by Objectives (MBO) is not a performance appraisal system per se; rather, it represents a method for defining goals, objectives, and priorities. However, MBO includes an appraisal component in the sense that a person working under an MBO system is evaluated in terms of the goals and objectives he or she (together with the supervisor) has previously defined. Thus, the MBO process defines objectives for a given period of time and defines the relevant dimensions and criteria for evaluating performance at the end of that period. MBO represents the most common format for evaluating managerial performance.

One danger of MBO is that goals and objectives will be set that are (1) easily quantified, (2) easily achieved, and (3) not really central to the job. This simplifies the process of performance appraisal but also implies that appraisals will be virtually worthless. However, it is important to note that goals do not always have these characteristics and that MBO *can* work. The effectiveness of MBO depends on the skills of both the supervisor and subordinate in defining appropriate goals and objectives. For this reason, it is somewhat difficult to evaluate MBO as a system. The same MBO program might work very well for some supervisor-subordinate dyads and poorly for others.

Employee Comparison Methods

There is a useful distinction between rating and ranking (i.e., employee comparison). *Rating* involves comparing a person to a standard. This standard might be undefined or subjective (e.g. a scale in which the anchors of good, average, and poor are undefined) or it might be defined in exact behavioral terms. *Ranking* involves comparing a person to another person. We believe that the psychological processes involved in rating versus ranking may be different (Murphy & Constans, 1988). Even if this is true, however, ratings and rankings often lead to similar conclusions about the performance of a group of ratees.

To illustrate ranking procedures, consider the example of a supervisor who evaluates eight subordinates. One possibility is simply to rank-order those eight individuals, from the best performer to the worst. With small numbers of ratees, this should not be difficult. However, as the supervisor's span of control increases, ranking of all subordinates can become tedious and sometimes arbitrary. Although it might be easy to pick out the best and the worst performers out of a group of 30 workers, it can be very difficult to distinguish the 15th best from the 16th, 17th, or 18th. The forced-distribution ranking procedure provides a partial solution to this problem.

A forced-distribution scale requires supervisors to sort subordinates into ordered categories. An example of such a scale is given in Figure A-4. A supervisor using this scale to evaluate eight subordinates would have to decide who his or her two best and two worst performers are; the remaining subordinates will fall in the middle category. This procedure is particularly useful if administrative rewards correspond to the categories. For example, the supervisor who must designate two subordinates out of eight for promotion does not need to rank all eight subordinates. The forced-distribution scale illustrated in Figure A-4 would be sufficient.

The principal distinction between a forced-distribution scale and a scale that requires all subordinates to be ranked is that in a full ranking, the number of categories is equal to the number of persons being evaluated. In a forced-distribution scale, the number of categories is less than the number of persons. The choice between these two methods depends in part on the specificity of the information required. If there are different outcomes for each individual (e.g., the 6th best performer will get a larger raise than the 7th best), full ranking is worthwhile. Otherwise, a forced-distribution scale might be easier to use.

There is one more procedure that should be considered, especially if the rater or the organization requires precise information about the rank order of employees, as well as the size of the differences in performance among employees. The pair-comparison method allows the rater to scale subordinates with some precision on a ratio-level scale of overall performance. An example

Figure A–4

Sort subordinates into these three categories

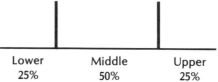

| Lower | Middle | Upper |
| 25% | 50% | 25% |

of a pair-comparison scale for a supervisor with four subordinates (A, B, C, and D) is shown in Figure A-5.

If the number of comparisons is sufficiently large, scaling procedures can be applied that transform these comparisons into a ratio scale that establishes both the ranking and the extent to which subordinates differ in their performance. The principal drawback of this method is that the number of comparisons expands geometrically as the number of subordinates increases. In the example shown in Figure A-5, 6 comparisons were needed to evaluate 4 subordinates. If there were 10 subordinates, 45 comparisons are needed. With 20 subordinates, 190 comparisons are needed.

There is a real dilemma for users of a pair-comparison scale. The accuracy of the scaling is a direct function of the number of comparisons that are made. Thus, if the number of comparisons is sufficiently small to be easily carried out, the scaling may not be precise. If the number of comparisons is sufficiently large to yield accurate measurement, the pair-comparison procedure may be extremely time consuming. For this reason, pair-comparison procedures seem to have attracted more attention in the basic research literature than in the field.

Figure A-5

Circle the better performer in each pair:

A or B	B or C
A or C	B or D
A or D	C or D

References

Abelson, R. P. (1976). Script processing in attitude formation and decision making. In J. Carroll & J. Payne (Eds.), *Cognition and social behavior*. Hillsdale, NJ: Erlbaum.

Adams, J. S. (1965). Inequity in social exchange. In L. Berkowitz (Ed.), *Advances in experimental social psychology, Vol. 2*. New York: Academic Press.

Adams, J. S. (1976). The structure and dynamics of behavior in organizational boundary roles. In M. Dunnette (Ed.), *Handbook of industrial and organizational psychology*. Chicago: Rand McNally.

Agervold, M. (1975). Swedish experiments in industrial democracy. In L. Davis & A. Cherns (Eds.), *The quality of working life, Vol. 2*. New York: Free Press.

Alba, J. W., & Hasher, L. (1983). Is memory schematic? *Psychological Bulletin, 93*, 203-231.

Alluisi, E., & Morgan, B. (1976). Engineering psychology and human performance. *Annual Review of Psychology, 27*, 320-365.

Anderson, N. (1971). Integration theory and attitude change. *Psychological Review, 77*, 153-170.

Anderson, N., & Alexander, G. (1971). Choice test of the averaging hypothesis for information integration. *Cognitive Psychology, 2*, 313-324.

Argyle, M. (1981). The experimental study of the basic features of situations. In D. Magnusson (Ed.), *Toward a psychology of situations: An interactional perspective*. Hillsdale, NJ: Erlbaum.

Argyris, C. (1980). *Inner contradictions of rigorous research*. New York: Academic Press.

Arvey, R. D., & Faley, R. (1988). *Fairness in selecting employees*. Menlo Park, CA: Addison Wesley.

Arvey, R. D., & Jones, A. P. (1985). The use of discipline in organizations: A framework for future research. In L. Cummings and B. Staw (Eds.), *Research in organizational behavior, Vol. 7*. Greenwich, CT: JAI Press.

Ashford, S. J., & Cummings, L. L. (1983). Feedback as an individual resource: Personal strategies of creating information. *Organizational Behavior and Human Performance, 32*, 370-398.

Astin, A. (1964). Criterion-centered research. *Educational and Psychological Measurement, 24*, 807-822.

Backburn, R. (1981). Lower participant power: Toward a conceptual integration. *Academy of Management Review, 6*, 127-131.

Balcazar, F. E., Hopkins, B. L., & Suarez, Y. (1985-86). A critical objective review of performance feedback. *Journal of Organizational Behavior, 7*(3-4), 65-89.

Balzer, W. K. (1986). Biases in the recording of performance-related information: The effects of initial impression and centrality of the appraisal task. *Organizational Behavior and Human Decision Processes, 37*, 329-347.

Balzer, W. K., & Sulsky, L. M. (1988). *Performance appraisal effectiveness and productivity*. Presented at Conference on Industrial Organizational Product Psychology and Productivity, Rennsselaer Polytechnic Institute, Troy, NY.

Balzer, W. K., & Sulsky, L. M. (in press). Performance appraisal effectiveness and productivity. In K. Murphy & F. Saal (Eds.), *Psychology in organizations: Integrating science and practice*. Hillsdale, NJ: Erlbaum.

Bandura, A., & Walters, R. H. (1963). *Social learning and personality theory.* New York: Holt, Rinehart and Winston.

Banks, C. G., & Murphy, K. R. (1985). Toward or narrowing the research-practice gap in performance appraisal. *Personnel Psychology, 38,* 335-345.

Bargh, J. A. (1984). Automatic and conscious processing of social information. In R. Wyer & T. Srull (Eds.), *Handbook of social cognition, Vol. 2.* Hillsdale, NJ: Erlbaum.

Barley, S. R. (1986). Technology as an occasion for structuring: Evidence from observations of CT scanners and the social order of radiology departments. *Administrative Science Quarterly, 31,* 78-108.

Barnes, J. L., & Landy, F. J. (1979). Scaling behavioral anchors. *Applied Psychological Measurement, 3,* 193-200.

Baron, J., & Hershey, J. C. (1988). Outcome bias in decision evaluation. *Journal of Personality and Social Psychology, 54,* 569-579.

Barrett, G. V., & Kernan, M. C. (1987). Performance appraisal and termination: A review of court decisions since Brito v. Zia with implications for personnel practices. *Personnel Psychology, 40,* 489-503.

Barrett, R. S. (1966). *Performance rating.* Chicago: Chicago Science Research Association.

Barrett, R. S. Taylor, E. K., Parker, J. W., & Martens, L. (1958). Rating scale content: I. Scale information and supervisory ratings. *Personnel Psychology, 11,* 333-346.

Bass, A. R., & Turner, J. N. (1973). Ethnic group differences in relationships among criteria of job performance. *Journal of Applied Psychology, 57,* 101-109.

Bass, B. M., & Franke, R. H. (1972). Societal influences on student perceptions of how to succeed in organizations. *Journal of Applied Psychology, 56,* 312-318.

Bassett, G. A. (1979). PAIR records and information systems. In D. Yoder and H. G. Heneman (Eds.), *ASPA handbook of personnel and industrial relations.* Washington, DC: Bureau of National Affairs.

Bazerman, M., Beekum, R., & Schoorman, F. (1982). Performance evaluation in a dynamic context: A laboratory study of the impact of a prior commitment to the ratee. *Journal of Applied Psychology, 67,* 873-876.

Beach, L. R. (1985). Action: Decision-implementation strategies and tactics. In M. Frese and J. Sabini (Eds.), *Goal directed behavior: The concept of action in psychology.* Hillsdale, NJ: Erlbaum.

Beatty, R. W., Schneier, C. E., & Beatty, J. R. (1978). An empirical investigation of perceptions of ratee behavior frequency and ratee behavior change using behaviorally anchored rating scales (BARS). *Personnel Psychology, 30,* 647-658.

Becker, B. E., & Cardy, R. L. (1986). Influence of halo error on appraisal effectiveness: A conceptual and empirical reconsideration. *Journal of Applied Psychology, 71,* 662-671.

Bellows, R. M., & Estep, M. F. (1954). *Employment psychology: The interview.* New York: Rinehart.

Bem, D. J. (1981). Assessing situations by assessing persons. In D. Magnusson (Ed.), *Toward a psychology of situations: An interactional perspective.* Hillsdale, NJ: Erlbaum.

Bem, D. J. (1982). Person's, situations, and template matching: Theme and variations. In M. P. Zanna, E. T. Higgins, & C. P. Herman (Eds.), *Consistency in social behavior: The Ontario symposium, 12* (pp. 173-187). Hillsdale, NJ: Erlbaum.

Bem, D. J., & Funder, D. C. (1978). Predicting more of the people more of the time: Assessing the personality of situations. *Psychological Review, 85,* 485-501.

Bendig, A. W. (1952a). A statistical report on a revision of the Miami instructor rating sheet. *Journal of Educational Psychology, 43,* 423-429.

Bendig, A. W. (1952b). The use of student ratings scales in the evaluation of instructors in introductory psychology. *Journal of Educational Psychology, 43,* 167-175.

Bendig, A. W. (1953). The reliability of self-ratings as a function of the amount of verbal anchoring and the number of categories on the scale. *Journal of Applied Psychology, 37,* 38-41.

Bendig, A. W. (1954a). Reliability and number of rating scale categories. *Journal of Applied Psychology, 38,* 38-40.

Bendig, A. W. (1954b). Reliability of short rating scales and the hetereogeneity of the rated stimuli. *Journal of Applied Psychology, 38,* 167-170.

Berger. C. J., & Cummings, L. L. (1979). Organizational structure, attitudes and behaviors. In B. Staw (Ed.), *Research in organizational behavior, Vol. 1* (pp. 169-208). Greenwich, CT: JAI Press.

Berkshire, H. & Highland, R. (1953). Forced-choice performance rating: A methodological study. *Personnel Psychology, 6,* 355-378.

Bernardin, H. J. (1977). Behavioral expectation scales versus summated rating scales: A fairer comparison. *Journal of Applied Psychology, 62,* 422-427.

Bernardin, H. J., Alvares, K. M., & Cranny, C. J. (1976). A recomparison of behavioral expectation scales to summated scales. *Journal of Applied Psychology, 61,* 564-570.

Bernardin, H. J., & Beatty, R. W. (1984). *Performance appraisal: Assessing human behavior at work.* Boston: Kent.

Bernardin, H. J., & Buckley, M. R. (1981). Strategies in rater training. *Academy of Management Review, 6,* 205-212.

Bernardin, H. J., & Cardy, R. (1982). Appraisal accuracy: The ability and motivation to remember the past. *Public Personnel Management Journal, 11,* 352-357.

Bernardin, H. J., Cardy, R. L., & Carlyle, J. J. (1982). Cognitive complexity and appraisal effectiveness: Back to the drawing board? *Journal of Applied Psychology, 67,* 151-160.

Bernardin, H. J., & Klatt, L. A. (1985). Managerial appraisal systems: Has practice caught up with the state of the art? *Public Personnel Administrator,* November, 79-86.

Bernardin, H. J., LaShells, M. B., Smith, P. C., & Alvares, K. M. (1976). Behavioral expectation scales: Effects of developmental procedures and formats. *Journal of Applied Psychology, 61,* 75-79.

Bernardin, H. J., Orban, J., & Carlyle, J. (1981). Performance ratings as a function of trust in appraisal and rater individual differences. *Proceedings of the 41st annual meeting of the Academy of Management,* 311-315.

Bernardin, H. J., & Pence, E. C. (1980). Effects of rater error training: Creating new response sets and decreasing accuracy. *Journal of Applied Psychology, 65,* 60-66.

Bernardin, H. J., & Smith, P. C. (1981). A clarification of some issues regarding the development and use of behaviorally anchored rating scales. *Journal of Applied Psychology, 66,* 458-463.

Bernardin, H. J., & Villanova, P. (1986). Performance appraisal. In E. Locke (Ed.), *Generalizing from laboratory to field settings.* Lexington, MA: Lexington Books.

Bernardin, H. J., & Walter, C. S. (1977). Effects of rater training and diary keeping on psychometric error in ratings. *Journal of Applied Psychology, 62,* 64-69.

Bialek, H., Zapf, D., & McGuire, W. (1977, June). *Personnel turbulence and time utilization in an infantry division* (HumRRO FR-WD-CA 77-11). Alexandria, VA: Human Resources Research Organization.

Bingham, W. V. (1939). Halo, valid and invalid. *Journal of Applied Psychology, 23,* 221-228.

Bjerke, D. G., Cleveland, J. N., Morrison, R. F., & Wilson, W. C. (1987). *Officer fitness report evaluation study.* Navy Personnel Research and Development Center Report, TR 88-4.

Blanz, F., & Ghiselli, E. E. (1972). The mixed standard scale: A new rating system. *Personnel Psychology, 25,* 185-199.

Blencoe, A. G. (1984). *An examination of raters' cognitive processes in performance appraisal: A laboratory investigation.* Unpublished dissertation, University of South Carolina.

Block, J., & Block, J. H. (1981). Studying situational dimensions: A grand perspective and some limited empericism. In D. Magnusson (Ed.), *Toward a psychology of situations: An interactional perspective.* Hillsdale, NJ: Erlbaum.

Blum, M. L., & Naylor, J. C. (1968). *Industrial psychology.* New York: Harper & Row.

Bobko, P., Karren, R., & Kerkar, S. (1987). Systematic research needs for understanding supervisory-based estimates of SDY in utility analysis. *Organizational Behavior and Human Decision Processes, 40,* 69-95.

Boice, R. (1983). Observational skills. *Psychological Bulletin, 90,* 218-244.

Borman, W. C. (1974). The rating of individuals in organizations: An alternative approach. *Organizational Behavior and Human Performance, 12,* 105-124.

Borman, W. C. (1977). Consistency of rating accuracy and rater errors in the judgment of human performance. *Organizational Behavior and Human Performance, 20,* 238-252.

Borman, W. C. (1978). Exploring the upper limits of reliability and validity in job performance ratings. *Journal of Applied Psychology, 63,* 135-144.

Borman, W. C. (1979). Format and training effects on rating accuracy and rater errors. *Journal of Applied Psychology, 64,* 410-421.

Borman, W. C. (1983). Implication of personality theory and research for the rating of work performance in organizations. In F. Landy, S. Zedeck, and J. Cleveland (Eds.), *Performance measurement and theory.* Hillsdale, NJ: Erlbaum.

Borman, W. C. (1987). Personal constructs, performance schemata, and "folk theories" of subordinate effectiveness: Exploration in an Army Officer sample. *Organizational Behavior and Human Decision Processes, 40,* 307-322.

Borman, W. C., & Dunnette, M. D. (1975). Behavior-based versus trait-oriented performance ratings: An impirical study. *Journal of Applied Psychology, 60,* 561-565.

Borman, W. C., & Vallon, W. R. (1974). A review of what can happen when behavioral expectation scales are developed in one setting and used in another. *Journal of Applied Psychology, 59,* 197-201.

Borreson, H. (1967). The effects of instructions and item content on three types of ratings. *Educational and Psychological Measurement, 27,* 855-862.

Boudreau, J. W. (in press). Utility analysis for decisions in human resource management. In M. Dunnette (Ed.), *Handbook of industrial and organizational psychology.* Palo Alto, CA: Consulting Psychologist Press.

Boudreau, J. W., & Berger, C. J. (1985). Decision-theoretic utility analysis applied to employee separations and acquisitions. *Journal of Applied Psychology, 70,* 581-612.

Bower, G. (1981). Mood and memory. *American Psychologist, 36,* 129-148.

Bowers, K. S. (1973). Situationism in interaction psychology. Analysis and critique. *Psychological Review, 80,* 307-336.

Brewer, M. B. (1979). In-group bias in the minimal intergroup situations: A cognitive-motivational analysis. *Psychological Bulletin, 86,* 307-324.

Brito v. *Zia Company* (428 F.2d 12001 [10th cir. 1973]).

Broadbent, D. E. (1985). Multiple goals and flexible procedures in the design of work. In M. Frese and J. Sabini (Eds.), *Goal directed behavior: The concept of action in psychology.* Hillsdale, NJ: Erlbaum.

Brogden, H. (1949). When testing pays off. *Personnel Psychology, 2,* 171-183.

Brown, G. E., Jr., & Larson, A. F. (1958). Current trends in appraisal and development. *Personnel, 34,* 51-58.

Brown, R., & Herrnstein, R. J. (1975). *Psychology.* Boston: Little, Brown.

Brunswick, E. E. (1952). *The conceptual framework of psychology.* Chicago: University of Chicago Press.

Buchanan, B. (1974). Building organizational commitment: The socialization of managers in work organizations. *Administrative Science Quarterly, 19,* 533-546.

Buchholz, R. (1978). An empirical study of contemporary beliefs about work in American Society. *Journal of Applied Psychology, 63,* 219-227.

Burchett, S. R., & DeMeuse, K. P. (1985). Performance appraisal and the law. *Personnel, 62,* 29-37.

Bureau of National Affairs. (1974). Management performance appraisal programs. *Personnel Policies Forum Survey, 104.*

Burnaska, R. F., & Hollmann, T. D. (1974). An empirical comparison of the relative effects of rater response biases on three rating scale formats. *Journal of Applied Psychology, 59,* 307-312.

Caffert, T. P., DeNisi, A. S., & Williams, K. J. (1986). Search and retrieval patterns for performance information: Effects on evaluations of multiple targets. *Journal of Personality and Social Psychology, 71,* 672-678.

Calder, B. J., & Schurr, P. H. (1981). Attitudinal processes in organizations. In L. L. Cummings & B. Straw (Eds.), *Research in organizational behavior, Vol. 3.* Greenwich, CT: JAI Press.

Campbell, J. P. (1982). Editorial: Some remarks from an outgoing editor. *Journal of Applied Psychology, 67,* 691-700.

Campbell, J. P. (1983). Some possible implications of "modeling" for the conceptualization of measurement. In F. Landy, S. Zedeck, & J. Cleveland (Eds.), *Performance measurement and theory.* Hillsdale, NJ: Erlbaum.

Campbell, J. P. (1986). Labs, fields, and straw issues. In E. Locke (Ed.), *Generalizing from laboratory to field settings.* Lexington, MA: Lexington Books.

Campbell, J. P., Crooks, L. A., Mahoney, M. H., & Rock, D. A. (1973). *An investigation of sources of bias in the prediction of job performance: A six-year study.* Final Project Report No. PR-73-37. Princeton, NJ: Educational Testing Service.

Campbell, J. P., Dunnette, M., Lawler, E., & Weick, K. (1970). *Managerial behavior, performance and effectiveness.* New York: McGraw-Hill.

Cantor, N. (1981). Perception of situations: Situation prototypes and person-situation prototype. In D. Magnusson (Ed.), *Toward a psychology of situations: An interactional perspective.* Hillsdale, NJ: Erlbaum.

Cantor, N., & Mischel, W. (1977). Traits as prototypes: Effects on recognition memory. *Journal of Personality and Social Psychology, 35,* 38–48

Cantor, N., & Mischel, W. (1979). Prototypes in person perception. In L. Berkowitz (Ed.), *Advances in experimental social psychology.* New York: Academic Press.

Cantor, N., Mischel, W., & Schwartz, J. (1982). A prototype analysis of psychological situation. *Cognitive Psychology, 14,* 45–77.

Cardy, R. L., Bernardin, H. J., Abbott, J. G., Senderak, M. P., & Taylor, K. (1987). The effects of individual performance schemata and dimension familiarization on rating accuracy. *Journal of Occupational Psychology, 60,* 197–205.

Cardy, R. L., & Dobbins, G. H. (1986). Affect and appraisal accuracy: Liking as an integral dimension in evaluating performance. *Journal of Applied Psychology, 71,* 672–678.

Cardy, R. L., & Krzystofiak, F. J. (1988). *Observation and rating accuracy: WYSIWYG?* Presented at Annual Convention of Society for Industrial/Organizational Psychology, Dallas.

Carroll, S. J., & Schneier, C. E. (1982). *Performance appraisal and review systems: The identification, measurement and development of performance in organizations.* Glenview, IL: Scott, Foresman.

Cartwright, D., & Zander, A. (1968). *Group dynamics: Research and theory* (3rd ed.). New York: Harper & Row.

Carver, C. S., & Scheier, M. F. (1981). *Attention and self-regulation: A control theory approach to human behavior.* New York: Springer-Verlag.

Cascio. W. F. (1982). *Costing human resources: The financial input of behavior in organizations.* Boston: Kent.

Cascio, W. F. (1987). *Applied psychology in personnel management* (3rd ed.). Englewood Cliffs, NJ: Prentice-Hall.

Cascio, W. F., & Bernardin, H. J. (1980). *An annotated bibliography of court cases relevant to employment decisions.* Mimeo. Tampa, FL.

Cascio, W. F., & Bernardin, H. J. (1981). Implications of performance appraisal litigation for personnel decisions. *Personnel Psychology, 34,* 211–226.

Cascio, W. F., & Ramos, R. A. (1986). Development and applications of a new method for assessing job performance in behavioral/economic terms. *Journal of Applied Psychology, 71,* 20–28.

Cascio, W. F., & Silbey, V. (1979). Utility of the assessment center as a selection device. *Journal of Applied Psychology, 64,* 107–118.

Cederbloom, D. (1982). The performance appraisal interview: A review, implications, and suggestions. *Academy of Management Review, 7,* 219–227.

Chadwick-Jones, J. K., Brown, C., Nicholson, N., & Sheppard, A. (1971). Absence measures: Their reliability and stability in an industrial setting. *Personnel Psychology, 24,* 463–470.

Chadwick-Jones, J. K., Nicholson, N., & Brown, C. (1982). *The social psychology of absenteeism.* New York: Praeger.

Chao, G. T. (1988). *Organizational socialization and role design features on job and career outcomes.* Presented at Annual Conference of Society for Industrial/Organizational Psychology, Dallas.

Christal, R. E. (1974). *The United States Air Force occupational research project* (AFHRL-TR-73-75). Lackland AFB, TX: USAF, AFHRL, Occupation Research Divsion.

Clark. C. L., & Primoff, E. J. (1979). Job elements and performance appraisal. *Management: A magazine for government managers, 1,* 3-5.

Clark. M. S., & Isen, A. M. (1982). Toward understanding the relationship between feeling states and social behavior. In A. Hastorf & A. Isen (Eds.), *Cognitive social psychology.* New York: Elsevier.

Cleveland, J. N., Festa, R. M., & Montgomery, L. (1988). Applicant pool composition and job perceptions: Impact on decisions regarding an older applicant. *Journal of Vocational Behavior, 32,* 112-125.

Cleveland, J. N., & Hollmann, G. (in press). Context and discrimination in personnel decisions: Direct and mediated approaches. In J. R. Meindl, R. L. Cardy, & S. Puffer (Eds.), *Advances in information processing in organizations.* Greenwich, CT: JAI Press.

Cleveland, J. N., & Landy, F. J. (1983). The effects of person and job stereotypes on two personnel decisions. *Journal of Aplied Psychology, 68,* 609-619.

Cleveland, J. N., Morrison, R., & Bjerke, D. (1986). *Rater intentions in appraisal ratings: Male-volent manipulation or functional fudging.* Presented at First Annual Conference of the Society for Industrial and Organizational Psychology, Chicago.

Cleveland, J. N., Murphy, K. R., Barnes-Farrell, J. L., & Banks, C. G. (1988). *Analyzing appraisal as goal-directed behavior: An alternative approach to peformance appraisal research and practice.* Unpublished manuscript, Department of Psychology, Colorado State University.

Cleveland, J. N., Murphy, K. R., & Williams, R. E. (1989). Multiple uses of performance appraisal: Prevalence and correlates. *Journal of Applied Psychology, 74,* 130-135.

Cline, V. B. (1964). Interpersonal perception. In B. A. Maher (Ed.), *Progress in experimental personality research, Vol. 1.* New York: Academic Press.

Cocheu, T. (1986). Performance appraisal: A case in points. *Personal Journal, 65,* 48-55.

Cohen, C., & Ebbeson, E. B. (1979). Observational goals and schema activation: A theoretical framework for behavior perception. *Journal of Experimental Social Psychology, 15,* 305-329.

Connolly, T., Conlon, E. J., & Deutsch, S. J. (1980). Organizational effectiveness: A multiple constituency approach. *Academy of Management Review, 5,* 211-217.

Constans, J. I. (1987). *Scale and weight bias in behaviorally anchored rating scales.* Unpublished thesis, Colorado State University.

Cooper, W. (1981a). Conceptual similarity as a source of illusory halo in job performance ratings. *Journal of Applied Psychology, 66,* 302-307.

Cooper, W. (1981b). Ubiquitous halo. *Psychological Bulletin, 90,* 218-244.

Cornelius. E. T., Hakel, M. D., & Sackett, P. R. (1979). A methodological approach to job classification for performance appraisal purposes. *Personnel Psychology, 2,* 283-297.

Craik, F. M., & Lockhart, R. S. (1972). Levels of processing: A framework for memory research. *Journal of Verbal Learning and Verbal Behavior, 11,* 671-684.

Craik, K. (1973). Environmental psychology. *Annual Review of Psychology, 24,* 403-422.

Cronbach, L. J. (1955). Processes affecting scores on "understanding of others" and "assumed similarity." *Psychological Bulletin, 52,* 177-193.

Cronbach, L. J. (1970). *Essentials of psychological testing* (3rd ed.). New York: Harper & Row.

Cronbach, L. J., & Gleser, G. C. (1965). *Psychological tests and personnel decisions* (2nd ed.). Urbana: University of Illinois Press.

Cronbach, L. J., Gleser, G. C., Nanda, H., & Rajaratnam, N. (1972). *The dependability of behavioral measurements: Theory of generalizability for scores and profiles.* New York: Wiley.

Cronbach, L. J., & Snow, R. E. (1977). *Aptitudes and instructional methods: A handbook for research on interactions.* New York: Halstead.

Cronshaw, S. F., & Alexander, R. A. (1985). One answer to the demand for accountability: Selection utility as an investment decision. *Organizational Behavior and Human Decision Processes, 35,* 102-118.

Crowder, R. G. (1976). *Principles of learning and memory.* Hillsdale: NJ: Erlbaum.

Cummings, L. L., & Schwab, D. P. (1973). *Performance in organizations: Determinants and appraisal.* Glenview, IL: Scott, Foresman.

Daft, R. L. (1986). *Organizational theory and design.* St. Paul, MN: West Publishing.

Dalton (1955). Cited in Whyte, W. *Money and Motivation.* New York: Harper and Row.

D'Andrade, R. G. (1965). Trait psychology and componential analysis. *American Anthropologist, 67*, 215-228.

Dansereau, F., Cashman, J., & Graen, G. (1973). Instrumentality theory and equity theory as complementary approaches in predicting the relationship of leadership and turnover among managers. *Organizational Behavior and Human Performance, 10*, 184-200.

Dansereau, F., Jr., Graen, G., & Haga, W. J. (1975). A vertical dyad linkage approach to leadership within formal organizations: A longitudinal investigation of role-making processes. *Organizational Behavior and Human Performance, 13*, 46-78.

Darley, J., & Fazio, R. (1980). Expectancy confirmation processes in the social interaction sequence. *American Psychologist, 35*, 867-881.

Davis, D. D., & Dickinson, T. L. (1987). *Organizational and contextual determinants of perceived utility of performance appraisals.* Presented at Annual Conference of American Psychological Association, New York.

Dawes, R. M., & Corrigan, B. (1974). Linear models in decision making. *Psychological Bulletin, 81*, 95-106.

DeCotiis, T. (1977). An analysis of the tracts external validity and applied relevance of three rating formats. *Organizational Behavior and Human Performance, 19*, 247-266.

DeCotiis, T., & Petit, A. (1978). The performance appraisal process: A model and some testable propositions. *Academy of Management Review, 3*, 635-646.

Demuse, K. P. (1987). A review of the effects of non-verbal cues on the performance appraisal process. *Journal of Occupational Psychology, 60*, 207-226.

DeNisi, A. S., Caffery, T., & Meglino, B. (1984). A cognitive view of the performance appraisal process: A model and research propositions. *Organizational Behavior and Human Performance, 33*, 360-396.

DeNisi, A. S., & Stevens, G. E. (1981). Profiles of performance evaluations and personnel decisions. *Academy of Management Journal, 24*, 592-602.

DeNisi, A. S., & Williams, K. J. (1988). Cognitive approaches to performance appraisal. In G. Ferris and K. Rowland (Eds.), *Research in personnel and human resource management, Vol. 6.* Greenwich, CT: JAI Press.

DeVries, D. L. (1983). *Viewing performance appraisal with a wide angle lens.* Presented at Annual Conference of the American Psychological Association, Anaheim, CA.

DeVries, D. L., Morrison, A. M., Shullman, S. L., & Gerlach, M. L. (1986). *Performance appraisal on the line.* Greensboro, NC: Center for Creative Leadership.

Dickinson, T. L. (1987). Designs for evaluating the validity and accuracy of performance ratings. *Organizational Behavior and Human Decision Processes, 40*, 1-21.

Dickson, J., & Buchholz, R. (1977). Managerial beliefs about work in Scotland and the U.S.A. *Journal of Management Studies, 12*, 80-101.

Dipboye, R. L. (1985). Some neglected variables in research on discrimination in appraisals. *Academy of Management Review, 10*, 116-127.

Dipboye, R. L., & dePontbriand, R. (1981). Correlates of employee reactions to performance appraisals and appraisal systems. *Journal of Applied Psychology, 66*, 248-251.

Dipboye, R. L., & Flanaghan, M. F. (1979). Research settings in industrial and organizational psychology: Are findings in the field more generalizable than in the laboratory? *American Psychologist, 34*, 141-150.

Dipboye, R. L., Stramler, C. S., & Fontenelle, G. A. (1984). The effects of the application on recall of information from an interview. *Academy of Management Journal, 27*, 261-275.

Dobbins, G. H., Cardy, R. L., & Platz, S. J. (1988). *The moderating effects of organizational characteristics on the relationships between appraisal characteristics and appraisal satisfaction.* Unpublished manuscript.

Dobbins, G. H., Cardy, R. L., & Truxillo, D. M. (1986). Effects of ratee sex and purpose of appraisal on the accuracy of performance evaluations. *Basic and Applied Social Psychology, 7*, 225-241.

Dobbins, G. H., Cardy, R. L., & Truxillo, D. M. (1988). The effects of individual differences in stereotypes of women and purpose of appraisal on sex differences in performance ratings: A laboratory and field study. *Journal of Applied Psychology, 73*, 551-558.

Dobbins, G. H., & Russell, J. M. (1986).The biasing effect of subordinate likeableness on leaders' reactions to poor performers: A laboratory and a field study. *Personnel Psychology, 39,* 759-777.

Dorfman, P. W., Stephan, W. G., & Loveland, J. (1986). Performance appraisal behaviors: Supervisor perceptions and subordinate reactions. *Personnel Psychology, 39,* 579-597.

Dornbusch, S. M., & Scott, W. R. (1975). *Evaluation and the exercise of authority.* San Francisco: Jossey-Bass.

Drucker, P. F. (1954). *The practice of management.* New York: Harper.

Dudycha, L. W., & Naylor, J. C. (1966). Characteristics of the human inference process in complex choice behavior situations. *Organizational Behavior and Human Performance, 1,* 110-128.

Duncan, R. (1972). Characteristics of organizational environments and perceived environmental uncertainty. *Administrative Science Quarterly, 17,* 313-327.

Duncan, R., & Weiss, A. (1979). Organizational learning: Implications for organizational design. In B. Staw (Ed.), *Research in organizational behavior, Vol. 1,* pp. 75-124. Greenwich, CT: JAI Press.

Ebbeson, E. B., & Allen, R. B. (1979). Cognitive processes in implicit personality trait inferences. *Journal of Personality and Social Psychology, 37,* 471-488.

Edwards, A. L. (1957). *Techniques of attitude scale construction.* New York: Appleton-Century-Crofts.

Edwards, W. (1968). Conservatism in human information processing. In B. Kleinmuntz (Ed.), *Formal representation of human judgments.* New York: Wiley.

Edwards, W. (1980). Multiattribute utility for evaluation: Structures, uses, and problems. In M. Klein and K. Teilmann (Eds.), *Handbook of criminal justice evaluation.* Beverly Hills: Sage.

Edwards, W., & Newman, J. (1982). *Multiattribute evaluation.* Beverly Hills: Sage.

Ekehammar, B. (1974). Interactionism in personality from a historical perspective. *Psychological Bulletin, 81,* 1026-1048.

Endler, N. S. (1982). Interactionism comes of age. In M. P. Zanna, E. T. Higgins, & C. P. Herman (Eds.), *Consistency in social behavior: The Ontario symposium, Vol. 2,* pp. 209-250. Hillsdale, NJ: Erlbaum.

Endler, N. S., & Magnusson, D. (1976). Toward an interactional psychology of personality. *Psychological Bulletin, 83,* 956-974.

Etzioni, A. (1975). *A comparative analysis of complex organizations* (rev. ed.). New York: Free Press.

Eulberg, J. R., O'Connor, E. J., Peters, L. H., & Watson, T. W. (1984). *Performance constraints: A selective review of relevant literature.* (AFHRL-TP-83-48). Brooks AFB, TX: Manpower and Personnel Division, Air Force Human Resources Laboratory.

Evan, W. M. (1966). The organization-set: Toward a theory of interorganizational relations. In J. D. Thompson (Ed.), *Approaches to organizational design.* Pittsburgh: University of Pittsburgh Press.

Famularo, J. F. (1972). *Handbook of modern personnel administration.* New York: McGraw-Hill.

Farh, J., & Werbel, J. D. (1986). Effects of purpose of the appraisal and expectation of validation on self-appraisal leniency. *Journal of Applied Psychology, 71,* 527-529.

Farr, J. L., O'Leary, B. S., & Bartlett, C. J. (1971-1977). Ethnic group membership as a moderator of the prediction of job performance. *Personnel Psychology, 24,* 609-636.

Feild, H. S. & Holley, W. H. (1982). The relationship of performance appraisal system characteristics to verdicts in selected employment discrimination cases. *Academy of Management Journal, 25,* 392-406.

Feldman, D. C. (1976). A contingency theory of socialization. *Administrative Science Quarterly, 21,* 443-452.

Feldman, J. M. (1981). Beyond attribution theory: Cognitive processes in performance appraisal. *Journal of Applied Psychology, 66,* 127-148.

Feldman, J. M. (1986). Instrumentation and training for performance appraisal: A perceptual cognitive viewpoint. In K. Rowland and J. Ferris (Eds.), *Research in personnel and human resources management, Vol. 4.* Greenwich, CT: JAI Press.

Finn, R. H. (1972). Effects of some variations in rating scale characteristics on the means and reliabilities of ratings. *Educational and Psychological Measurement, 32,* 255-265.

Fisher, C. D. (1974). Transmission of positive and negative feedback to subordinates: A laboratory investigation. *Journal of Applied Psychology, 64,* 533–540.

Fisher, C. D. (1986). Organizational socialization: An integrative review. In K. Rowland and G. Ferris (Eds.), *Research in personnel and human resources management, Vol. 4.* Greenwich, CT: JAI Press.

Fisicaro, S. A. (1988). A reexamination of the relationship between halo error and accuracy. *Journal of Applied Psychology, 73,* 239–244.

Fitzgibbons, J., & Moch, A. (1980). *Employee absenteeism.: A summary of research.* Washington, DC: Educational Research Service.

Flanagan, J. C. (1949). Critical requirements: A new approach to evaluation. *Personnel Psychology, 2,* 419–425.

Flanagan, J. C. (1954). The critical incidents technique. *Psychological Bulletin, 51,* 327–358.

Fleishman, E., & Quaintance, M. (1984). *Taxonomies of human performance: The description of human tasks.* New York: Academic Press.

Folger, R., & Greenberg, J. (1985). Procedural justice: An interpretive analysis of personnel systems. In K. Rowland & G. Ferris (Eds.), *Research in personnel and human resources management, Vol. 3.* Greenwich, CT: JAI Press.

Forehand, G. A. (1968). On the interaction of persons and organizations. In R. Taguire & G. Litwin (Eds.). *Organizational climate: Explorations of a concept.* Boston: Harvard Business School.

Form, W. (1987). On the degradation of skills. *Annual Review of Sociology 13,* 29–47.

Foster, S. L., & Cone, J. D. (1980). Current issues in direct observation. *Behavioral Assessment, 2,* 313–338.

Foti, R. (1988). *Differences in performance schemata as a function of subordinate and superior rank.* Presented at Annual Convention of Academy of Management, Anaheim.

Foti, R. J., & Lord, R. G. (1987). Prototypes and scripts: The effects of alternative methods of processing information on rating accuracy. *Organizational Behavior and Human Decision Processes, 39,* 318–340.

Fox, S., & Thornton, G. C. III (1987). *Implicit distribution theory: The influence of schematic perception of differentiation on actual ratings.* Unpublished manuscript, Bar-Ilan University, Israel.

Fredericksen, N. (1962). Factors in in-basket performance. *Psychological Monographs, 76* (22, Whole No. 541).

Frederiksen, N. (1972). Toward a taxonomy of situations. *American Psychologist, 27,* 114–123.

Fredericksen, N., Jensen, C., & Beatrin, A. (1972). *Prediction of organizational behavior.* Elmsford, NY: Pergamon.

Freeberg, N. F. (1969). Relevance of rater-ratee acquaintance in the validity and reliability of ratings. *Journal of Applied Psychology, 53,* 518–524.

Freedom, J. L., Sears, D. O., & Carlsmith, J. M. (1981). *Social psychology* (4th ed.). Englewood Cliffs, NJ: Erlbaum.

French, J., & Caplan, R. (1973). Organizational stress and individual strain. In A. Morrow (Ed.), *The failure of success.* New York: Amacon.

French, J., & Raven, B. (1959). The bases of social power. In D. Cartwright (Ed.), *Studies in social power.* Ann Arbor: Institute for social Research, University of Michigan.

Frese, M., & Sabini, J. (1985). Action theory: An introduction. In M. Frese and J. Sabini (Eds.), *Goal directed behavior: The concept of action in psychology.* Hillsdale, NJ: Erlbaum.

Friedlander, F., & Pickle, H. (1968). Components of effectiveness in small organizations. *Administrative Science Quarterly, 13,* 289–304.

Friedman, B. A., & Cornelius, E. T. (1976). Effects of rater participation in scale construction on the psychometric characteristics of two rating scale formats. *Journal of Applied Psychology, 61,* 210–216.

Friedman, M. (1986). 10 steps to objective appraisals. *Personal Journal, 65,* 66–71.

Fromkin, H. L., & Streufert, S. (1976). Laboratory experimentation. In M. Dunnette (Ed.), *Handbook of industrial and organizational psychology.* Chicago: Rand-McNally.

Fry, L. (1982). Technology-structure research: Three critical issues. *Academy of Management Journal, 25,* 532–552.

Fuller, J. L. (1950). Situation analysis: A classification of organism-field interactions. *Psychological Review, 7,* 3-18.

Funder, D. C. (1987). Errors and mistakes: Evaluating the accuracy of social judgment. *Psychological Bulletin, 101,* 75-90.

Garber, B. D., & Miller, M. L. (1986). On beasties and butterflies: Evidence for the stability and domain-specificity of individual differences in categorization. *Journal of Personality, 54,* 647-658.

Gaudet, F. J. (1963). *Solving the problem of employee absence.* New York: American Management Association.

Ghiselli, E. E. (1964). *Theory of psychological measurement.* New York: McGraw-Hill.

Ghordade, J., & Lackritz, J. R. (1981). Influences behind neutral responses in subordinate ratings of supervisor: A methodological note. *Personnel Psychology, 34,* 511-522.

Gibson, J. L., Ivancevich, J. M., & Donnelly, J. H. (1983). *Organizations: Structure, processes, behavior.* Dallas: Business Publications.

Gioia, D. A., & Sims, H. P. (1985). Self-serving bias and actor-observer differences in organizations: An empirical analysis. *Journal of Applied Social Psychology, 15,* 547-563.

Goldman, P. (1983). A sociohistorical perspective on performance assessment. In F. Landy, S. Zedeck, & J. Cleveland (Eds.), *Performance measurement and theory.* Hillsdale, NJ: Erlbaum.

Goldstein, I. L., & Mobley, W. H. (1971). Error and variability in the visual processing of dental radiographs. *Journal of Applied Psychology, 55,* 549-553.

Golumbiewski, R. (1972). *Renewing organizations: The laboratory approach to planned change.* Itasca, IL: Peacock.

Gordon, M. E. (1970). The effects of the correctness of the behavior observed on the accuracy of ratings. *Organizational Behavior and Human Performance, 5,* 366-377.

Gorman, C. D., Clover, W. H., & Doherty, M. E. (1978). Can we learn anything about interviewing real people from "interviews" of paper people? Two studies on the external validity of a paradigm. *Organizational Behavior and Human Performance, 22,* 165-192.

Graen, G. (1976). Role-making processes within complex organizations. In M. Dunnette (Ed.), *Handbook of industrial and organizational psychology.* Chicago: Rand-McNally.

Green, B. F. (1980). Note on Bem and Funder's scheme for scoring Q-sorts. *Psychological Review, 87,* 212-214.

Greenberg, J. (1986). Determinants of perceived fairness of performance evaluations. *Journal of Applied Psychology, 71,* 340-342.

Greenberg, J., & Folger, R. (1983). Procedural justice, participation, and fair process effects in groups and organizations. In P. Paulus (Ed.), *Basic group processes.* New York: Springer-Verlag.

Gregson, R. A. (1975). *Psychometrics of similarity.* New York: Academic Press.

Grey, R. J., & Kipnis, D. (1976). Untangling the performance appraisal dilemma. The influence of perceived organizational context on evaluative processes. *Journal of Applied Psychology, 61,* 329-335.

Guilford, J. P. (1954). *Psychometric methods* (2nd ed.). New York: McGraw-Hill.

Guion, R. M. (1961). Criterion measurement and personnel judgments. *Personnel Psychology, 14,* 141-149.

Guion, R. M. (1965). *Personnel testing.* New York: McGraw-Hill.

Guzzo, R. A., & Bondy, J. S. (1983). *A guide to worker productivity experiments in the United States 1976-1981.* Elmsford, NY: Pergamon Press.

Guzzo, R. A., & Gannett, B. A. (1988). The nature of facilitators and inhibitors of effective task performance. In F. D. Schoorman & B. Schneider (Ed.). *Facilitating work effectiveness.* Lexington, MA: Lexington Books.

Guzzo, R. A., Jette, R. D., & Katzell, R. A. (1985). The effects of psychologically-based intervention programs on worker productivity. *Personnel Psychology, 38,* 275-293.

Haberstroh, C. J. (1965). Organization design and systems analysis. In J. March (Ed.), *Handbook of organizations.* Chicago: Rand-McNally.

Hackett, J. D. (1928). Rating legislators. *Personnel, 7*(2), 130-131.

Hackman, J. R. (1976). Group influences on individuals. In M. Dunnette (Ed.), *Handbook of industrial and organizational psychology,* Chicago: Rand-McNally.

Hackman, J. R., & Morris, G. G. (1975). Group task, group interaction processes, and group performance effectiveness. In L. Berkowitz (Ed.), *Advances in experimental social psychology, Vol. 7.* New York: Academic Press.

Hackman, J. R., & Oldham, G. R. (1980). *Work redesign.* Reading, MA: Addison-Wesley.

Hackman, J. R., & Porter, L. W. (1968). Expectancy predictions of work effectiveness. *Organizational Behavior and Human Performance, 3,* 417-426.

Hakel, M. D. (1986). Personnel selection and placement. *Annual Review of Psychology, 37,* 351-380.

Hale, M. (1982). History of employment testing. In A. Wigdor & W. Garner (Eds.), *Ability testing: Uses, consequences, and controversies: Part II.* Washington, DC: National Academy Press.

Hammond, K. R., McClelland, G. H., & Mumpower, J. (1980). *Human judgment and decision making: Theories, methods, and procedures.* New York: Praeger.

Harper, S. C. (1980). Adding purpose to performance reviews. *Training and Development Journal, 40,* 53-55.

Harris, M. H., & Sackett, P. R. (1988). *Interpersonal affect and performance rating level: An individual differences analysis.* Presented at Annual Convention of Society for Industrial and Organizational Psychology, Dallas.

Harris, M. H., & Schaubroeck, J. (1988). A meta-analysis of self-supervisory, self-peer, and peer-supervisor ratings. *Personnel Psychology, 41,* 43-62.

Hartel, C. E. J. (1988). *The effects of cognitive availability of behavioral exemplars on performance ratings.* Unpublished master's thesis, Colorado State University.

Harvey, R. J. (1982). The future of partial correlation as a means to reduce halo in performance ratings. *Journal of Applied Psychology, 67,* 171-176.

Hastie, R. (1980). Memory for behavioral information that confirms or contradicts a personality impression. In R. Hastie et al. (Eds.), *Person memory: The cognitive basis of social perception.* Hillsdale, NJ: Erlbaum.

Hastie, R., & Kumar, P. (1979). Person memory: Personality traits as organizing principles in memory for behaviors. *Journal of Personality and Social Psychology, 37,* 25-38.

Hastie, R., & Park, B. (1986). The relationship between memory and judgment depends on whether the judgment task is memory-based or on-line. *Psychological Review, 93,* 256-268.

Haynes, M. E. (1986). Partnerships in management: Employee involvement gets results. *Personnel Journal, 65,* 46-55.

Heilbroner, .R. L. (1953). *The worldly philosophers.* New York: Simon & Schuster.

Heilman, M. E. (1980). The impact of situational factors on personnel decisions concerning women: Varying the sex composition of the applicant pool. *Organizational Behavior and Human Performance, 26,* 386-395.

Heneman, R. L. (1986). The relationship between supervisory ratings and results-oriented measures of performance: A meta-analysis. *Personnel Psychology, 39,* 811-826.

Heneman, R. L., & Wexley, K. N. (1983). The effects of delay in rating and amount of information observed on performance rating accuracy. *Academy of Management Journal, 26,* 677-686.

Heneman, R. L., & Wexley, K. N., & Moore, M. L. (1987). Performance-rating accuracy: A critical review. *Journal of Business Research, 15,* 431-448.

Heron, A. (1956). The effects of real-life motivation on questionnaire response. *Journal of Applied Psychology, 40,* 65-68.

Higgins, E. T., & King, G. (1981). Accessibility of social constructs: Information processing consequences of individual and contextual variability. In N. Cantor & J. Kihlstrom (Eds.), *Personality, cognition, and social interaction.* Hillsdale, NJ: Erlbaum.

Higgins, E. T., King, G., & Mavin, G. H. (1982). Individual construct accessibility and subjective impressions and recall. *Journal of Personality and Social Psychology, 43,* 35-47.

Higgins, E. T., & Stangor, C. (1988). A "change-of-standard" perspective on relations among context, judgment, and memory. *Journal of Personality and Social Psychology, 54,* 181-192.

Hobson, C. J., & Gibson, F. W. (1983). Policy capturing as an approach to understanding and improving performance appraisal: A review of the literature. *Academy of Management Review, 8,* 640-649.

Hogan, E. A. (1987). Effects of prior expectations on performance ratings: A longitudinal study. *Academy of Management Journal, 30,* 354-368.

Hogarth, R. M. (1980). *Judgment and choice: The psychology of decision.* Chichester, UK: Wiley.

House, R. J. (1971). A path goal theory of leader effectiveness. *Administrative Science Quarterly, 16,* 321-338.

Howard, A. (1984). I/O careers in industry. *The Industrial-Organizational Psychologist, 21,* 46-54.

Hoxworth, T. L. (1988). *The impact of feedback sign and type on perceived feedback accuracy, self-ratings, and performance.* Unpublished dissertation, Colorado State University.

Hulin, C. L. (1982). Some reflections on general performance dimensions and halo rating error. *Journal of Applied Psychology, 67,* 165-170.

Hunter, J. E., & Hunter, R. F. (1984). Validity and utility of alternate predictors of job performance. *Psychological Bulletin, 96,* 72-98.

Ilgen, D. R. (1983). Gender issues in performance appraisal: A discussion of O'Leary and Hansen. In F. Landy, S. Zedeck, and J. Cleveland (Eds.), *Performance measurement and theory.* Hillsdale, NJ: Erlbaum.

Ilgen, D. R. (1986). Laboratory research: A question of when, not if. In E. Locke (Ed.), *Generalizing from laboratory to field settings.* Lexington, MA: Lexington Books.

Ilgen, D. R., & Favero, J. L. (1985). Limits in generalization from psychological research to performance appraisal processes. *Academy of Management Review, 10,* 311-321.

Ilgen, D. R., & Feldman, J. M. (1983). Performance appraisal: A process focus. In L. Cummings & B. Straw (Eds.), *Research in organizational behavior, Vol. 5.* Greenwich, CT: JAI Press.

Ilgen, D. R., Fisher, C. D., & Taylor, S. M. (1979). Consequences of individual feedback on behavior in organization. *Journal of Applied Psychology, 64,* 347-371.

Ilgen, D. R., & Hollenback, J. H. (1977). The role of job satisfaction in absence behavior. *Organizational Behavior and Human Performance, 19,* 148-161.

Ilgen, D. R., Mitchell, T. R., & Frederickson, J. W. (1981). Poor performers: Supervisors' and subordinates' responses. *Organizational Behavior and Human Performance, 27,* 386-410.

Imada, A. S. (1982). Social interaction, observation and stereotypes as determinants of differentiation in peer ratings. *Organizational Behavior and Human Performance, 29,* 397-415.

Imada, A. S., & Hakel, M. D. (1977). The effects of nonverbal communication and rater proximity on impressions and decisions in simulated employment interviews. *Journal of Applied Psychology, 62,* 295-300.

Isen, A. M. (1984). Toward understanding the role of affect in cognition. In R. Wyer & T. Srull (Eds.), *Handbook of social cognition, Vol. 3.* Hillsdale, NJ: Erlbaum.

Isen, A. M., & Daubman, K. A. (1984). The influence of affect on categorization. *Journal of Personality and Social Psychology, 47,* 1207-1217.

Isen, A. M., Shalker, T. E., Clark, M. S., & Karp, L. (1978). Positive affect, accessibility of material in memory, and behavior: A cognitive loop? *Journal of Personality and Social Psychology, 36,* 1-12.

Jackson, J. (1965). Structural characteristics of norms. In I. Steiner & M. Fishbein (Eds.), *Current studies in social psychology.* New York: Holt, Rinehart & Winston.

Jackson, S. E., & Zedeck, S. (1982). Explaining performance variability: Contributions of goal setting, task characteristics, and evaluative contexts. *Journal of Applied Psychology, 67,* 759-768.

Jacobs, M., Jacobs, A., Feldman, D., & Cavior, N. (1973). Feedback II — The "credibility gap": Delivery of positive and negative and emotional and behavioral feedback in groups. *Journal of Consulting and Clinical Psychology, 41,* 215-223.

Jacobs, R., & Campbell, D. T. (1961). The perpetuation of an arbitrary tradition through several generations of a laboratory microculture. *Journal of Abnormal and Social Psychology, 62,* 649-658.

Jacobs, R., Kafry, D., & Zedeck, S. (1980). Expectations of behaviorally anchored rating scales. *Personnel Psychology, 33,* 595-640.

James, L. (1973). Criterion models and construct validity for criteria. *Pschological Bulletin, 80,* 75-83.

Jeffry, K. M., & Mischel, W. (1979). Effects of purpose on the organization and recall of information in person perception. *Journal of Personality, 47,* 397-419.

Jones, A. P., Tait, M., & Butler, M. C. (1983). Perceived punishment and reward values of supervisory actions. *Motivation and Emotion, 1,* 313-329.

Jones, E., Kanhouse, D., Kelley, H., Nisbett, R., Valins, S., & Weiner, B. (1972). *Attribution: Perceiving the causes of behavior.* Morristown, NJ: General Learning Press.

Jones, E., & Nisbett, R. (1971). The actor and the observer: Divergent perceptions of the causes of behavior. In E. Jones et al. (Eds.), *Attribution: Perceiving the causes of behavior.* Morristown, NJ: General Learning Press.

Kahn, R., & Katz, D. (1953). Leadership practices in relation to productivity and morale. In D. Cartwright and A. Zander (Eds.), *Group dynamics.* Evanston, IL: Row & Peterson.

Kahn, R., & Quinn, R. (1970). Role stress: A framework for analysis. In A. McLean (Ed.), *Mental health and work organizations.* Chicago: Rand-McNally.

Kahn, R., Wolf, D., Quinn, R., Snoeck, J., & Rosenthal, R. (1964). *Organizational stress: Studies in role conflict and ambiguity.* New York: Wiley.

Kahneman, D., & Tversky, A. (1979). Prospect theory: An analysis of decision under risk. *Econometrica, 47,* 263-291.

Kallejian, V., Brown, P., & Weschler, I. R. (1953). The impact of interpersonal relations on ratings of performance. *Public Personnel Review,* (Oct.), 166-170.

Kane, J. (1981). *Improving the measurement basis of performance appraisal.* Paper presented at the American Psychological Association Convention, Los Angeles.

Kane, J. S. (1986). Performance distribution assessment. In R. Berk (Ed.), *The state of art in performance assessment.* Baltimore: John Hopkins University Press.

Kane, J. S. (1987). Measure for measure in performance appraisal. *Computers in Personnel, 2,* 31-39.

Kane, J. S., & Lawler, E. E. (1978). Methods of peer assessment. *Psychological Bulletin, 85,* 555-586.

Kane, J. S., & Lawler, E. E. (1979). Performance appraisal effectiveness: Its assessment and determinants. In B. Straw (Ed.), *Research in organizational behavior, Vol. 1.* Greenwich, CT: JAI Press.

Kane, J. S., & Lawler, E. E. (1980). In defense of peer assessment: A rebuttal to Brief's critique. *Psychological Bulletin, 88,* 80-81.

Kanter, R. M. (1977). *Men and women of the organization.* New York: Basic Books.

Katz, D., & Kahn, R. (1978). *The social psychology & organizations* (2nd ed.). New York: Wiley.

Kaufman, H. (1960). *The forest ranger: A study in administrative behavior.* Baltimore: Johns Hopkins University Press.

Kavanaugh, M. J. (1971). The content issue in performance appraisal: A review. *Personnel Psychology, 24,* 653-668.

Kavanaugh, M. J., MacKinney, A. C., & Wolins, L. (1971). Issues in managerial performance: Multitrait-multimethod analysis of ratings. *Psychological Bulletin, 75,* 34-49.

Kay, E., Meyer, H., & French, J. (1965). Effects of threat in a performance interview. *Journal of Applied Psychology, 49,* 311-317.

Keeney, R. L., & Raiffa, H. (1976). *Decisions with multiple objectives: Preferences and value tradeoffs.* New York: Wiley.

Keller, R. T. (1983). Predicting absenteeism from prior absenteeism, attitudinal factors, and nonattitudinal factors. *Journal of Applied Psychology, 68,* 536-540.

Kelley, H. H. (1971). Attribution in social interaction. In E. Jones et al. (Eds.), *Attribution: Perceiving the causes of behavior.* Morristown, NJ: General Learning Press.

Kenny, D. A., & Berman, J. S. (1980). Statistical approaches to the correction of bias. *Psychological Bulletin, 88,* 288-295.

Kidd, J. S., & Christy, R. T. (1961). Supervisory procedures and work-team productivity. *Journal of Applied Psychology, 45,* 388-392.

Kim, M., & Rosenberg, S. (1980). Comparison of two structural models of implicit personality theory. *Journal of Personality and Social Psychology, 38,* 375-389.

Kimble, G. A. (1984). Psychology's two cultures. *American Psychology, 39,* 833-839.

Kingsbury, F. A. (1922). Analyzing ratings and training raters. *Journal of Personnel Research, 1,* 377-382.

Kingsbury, F. A. (1933). Psychological tests for executives. *Personnel, 9,* 121-133.

Kingstrom, P. O., & Mainstone, L. E. (1985). An investigation of rater ratee' acquaintance and rater bias. *Academy of Management, 28,* 641-653.

Kirkpatrick, D. L. (1967). Evaluation of training. In R. L. Craig & L. R. Bittel (Eds.), *Training and development handbook.* New York: McGraw-Hill.

Kleiger, W. A., & Mosel, J. N. (1953). The effect of opportunity of observe and rater status on the reliability of performance ratings. *Personnel Psychology, 6,* 57-64.

Kohn, M. L., & Schooner, C. (1978). The reciprocal effects of the substantive complexity of work and intellectual flexibility. A longitudinal assessment. *American Journal of Sociology, 84,* 24-52.

Komaki, J., Collins, R. L., & Thoene, T. (1980). Behavioral measurement in business, industry, and government. *Behavioral assessment, 2,* 103-123.

Kopelman, R. E. (1986). Objective feedback. In E. A. Locke (Ed.), *Generalizing from laboratory to field settings.* Lexington, MA: Lexington Books.

Koprowski, E. J. (1983). Cultural myths: Clues to effective management. *Organizational Dynamics, 12,* 39-51.

Kosslyn, S. M. (1980). *Image and mind.* Cambridge, MA: Harvard University Press.

Kozlowski, S. W., & Farr, J. (1988). An integrative model of updating and performance. *Human Performance, 1,* 5-29.

Kozlowski, S. W., & Hults, B. M. (1987). An exploration of climates for technical updating, and performance. *Personnel Psychology, 40,* 539-563.

Kozlowski, S. W., & Kirsch, M. (1986). *The systematic distortion hypothesis and halo error: An individual-level analysis.* Presented at Annual Convention of Society for Industrial and Organizational Psychology, Chicago.

Kozlowski, S. W., Kirsch, M. P., & Chao, G. T. (1986). Job knowledge, ratee familiarity, conceptual similarity, and halo error: An exploration. *Journal of Applied Psychology, 71,* 45-49.

Krause, M. S. (1970). Use of social situations for research purposes. *American Psychology, 25,* 748-753.

Krystofiak, F., Cardy, R., & Newman, J. (1988). Implicit personality and performance appraisal: The influence of trait inferences on evaluations of behavior. *Journal of Applied Psycholoy, 73,* 515-521.

Lacho, K. J., Stearns, G. K., & Villere, M. F. (1979). A study of employee appraisal systems of major cities in the United States. *Public Personnel Management, 8,* 111-125.

Lahey, M. A., & Saal, F. E. (1981). Evidence incompatible with a cognitive complexity theory of rating behavior. *Journal of Applied Psychology, 66,* 706-715.

Landy, F. J. (1985). *Psychology of work behavior* (3rd ed.). Homewood, IL: Dorsey.

Landy, F. J. (1987). *Psychology: The science of people.* (2nd ed.). Englewood Cliffs, NJ: Prentice-Hall.

Landy, F. J., Barnes, J., & Murphy, K. (1978). Correlates of perceived fairness and accuracy of performance appraisals. *Journal of Applied Psychology, 63,* 751-754.

Landy, F. J., Barnes-Farrell, J., & Cleveland, J. (1980). Perceived fairness and accuracy of performance appraisals: A follow-up. *Journal of Applied Psychology, 65,* 355-356.

Landy, F. J., & Farr, J. L. (1976). Police performance appraisal. *JSAS Catalog of Selected Documents in Psychology, 6,* 83. M.S. No. 1315.

Landy, F. J., & Farr, J. L. (1980). Performance rating. *Psychological Bulletin, 87,* 72-107.

Landy, F. J., & Farr, J. L. (1983). *The measurement of work performance: Methods, theory, and applications.* New York: Academic Press.

Landy, F. J., Farr, J. L. & Jacobs, R. R. (1982). Utility concepts in performance measurement. *Organizational Behavior and Human Performance, 30,* 15-40.

Landy, F. J., & Guion, R. M. (1970). Development of scales for the measurement of work motivation. *Organizational Behavior and Human Performance, 5,* 93-103.

Landy, F. J., Vance, R. J., Barnes-Farrell, J. L., & Steele, J. W. (1980). Statistical control of halo error in performance ratings. *Journal of Applied Psychology, 65,* 177-180.

Landy, F. J., Zedeck, S., & Cleveland, J. N. (1983). *Performance measurement and theory.* Hillsdale, NJ: Erlbaum.

Lane, D. M., Murphy, K. R., & Marques, T. (1982). Measuring the importance of cues in policy capturing. *Organizational Behavior and Human Performance, 30,* 231-240.

Langer, E. J., Taylor, S. E., Fiske, S. T., & Chantowitz, B. (1976). Stigma, staring and discomfort: A novel-stimulus hypothesis. *Journal of Experimental Social Psychology, 12,* 451-463.

Latham, G. (1986). Job performance and appraisal. In C. Cooper & I. Robertson (Eds.), *International review of industrial and organizational psychology.* Chichester, England: Wiley.

Latham, G. P., Fay, C. H., & Saari, L. M. (1979). The development of behavioral observation scales for appraising the performance of foremen. *Personnel Psychology, 32,* 299-311.

Latham, G. P., & Pursell, E. D. (1975). Measuring absenteeism from the opposite side of the coin. *Journal of Applied Psychology, 60,* 369-371.

Latham, G. P., & Wexley, K. N. (1977). Behavioral observation scales. *Personnel Psychology, 30,* 255-268.

Latham, G. P., Wexley, K. N., & Pursell, E. D. (1975). Training managers to minimize rating errors in the observation of behavior. *Journal of Applied Psychology, 60,* 550-555.

Lawler, E. E. (1967). The multitrait-multirate approach to measuring managerial job performance. *Journal of Applied Psychology, 51,* 369-381.

Lawler, E. E. (1971). *Pay and organizational effectiveness: A psychological view.* New York: McGraw-Hill.

Lawler, E. E. (1972). Secrecy and the need to know. In M. Dunnette, R. House, & H. Tosi (Eds.). *Readings in managerial motivation and compensation.* East Lansing: Michigan State University Press.

Lawler, E. E. (1976). Control system in organizations. In M. Dunnette (Ed.), *Handbook of industrial/organizational psychology.* Chicago: Rand-McNally.

Lawrence, B. S. (1984). Age grading: The implicit organizational timetable. *Journal of Occupational Behavior, 5,* 23-35.

Lawrence. B. S. (1987). An organizational theory of age effects. In S. Bacharach & N. DiTomaso (Eds.), *Research in the sociology of organizations, Vol. 5* (pp. 37-71). Greenwich, CT: JAI Press.

Lawrence, P. R., & Lorsch, J. W. (1969). *Organization and environment: Managing differentiation and integration.* Homewood, IL: Irwin.

Lay, C. H., & Jackson, D. N. (1969). Analysis of the generality of trait-inferential relationships. *Journal of Personality and Social Psychology, 12,* 12-21.

Lazer, R. I., & Wikstrom, W. S. (1977). *Appraising managerial performance: Current practices and future directions* (Conference Boar Rep. No. 723). New York: Conference Board.

Lee, C. (1985). Increasing performance appraisal effectiveness. Matching task types, appraisal processes, and rater training. *Academy of Management Review, 10,* 322-331.

Lerner, B. (1983). Reality, utopia, and performance appraisal: Another view. In F. Landy, S. Zedeck, & J. Cleveland (Eds.), *Performance measurement and theory.* Hillsdale, NJ: Erlbaum.

Lewin, K., Dembo, T., Festinger, L., & Sears, P. (1944). Level of aspiration. In J. McV. Hunt (Ed.), *Personality and behavioral disorders.* New York: Ronald Press.

Lichtenstein, S., Slovic, P., Fischoff, B., Layman, M., & Combs, B. (1978). Judged frequency of lethal events. *Journal of Experimental Psychology: Human Learning and Memory, 4,* 551-578.

Lincoln, J. R., & Zeitz, G. (1980). Organizational properties from aggregate data. Separating individual and structural effects. *American Sociological Review, 45,* 391-408.

Linden, R. C., & Graen, G. (1980). Generalizability of the vertical dyadic linkage model of leadership. *Academy of Management Journal, 23,* 451-465.

Liden, R. C., & Mitchell, T. R. (1983). The effects of group interdependence on supervisor performance evaluations. *Personnel Psychology, 36,* 289-300.

Linvolle, P. W., & Jones, E. J. (1980). Polarized appraisals of out-group members. *Journal of Personality and Social Psychology, 38,* 689-703.

Lissitz, R. W., & Green, S. B. (1975). Effect of the number of scale points on reliability: A Monte Carlo approach. *Journal of Applied Psychology, 60,* 10-13.

Locke, E. A. (1983). Performance appraisal under capitalism, socialism, and the mixed economy. In F. Landy, S. Zedeck, & J. Cleveland (Eds.), *Performance measurement and theory.* Hillsdale, NJ: Erlbaum.

Locke, E. A. (1986). *Generalizing from laboratory to field settings.* Lexington, MA: Lexington Books.

Locke, E. A., Shaw, K. N., Saari, L. M., & Latham, G. P. (1981). Goal setting and task performance: 1969-1980. *Psychological Bulletin, 90,* 125-152.

Long, P. (1986) *Performance appraisal revisited.* London: Institute of Personnel Management.

Longenecker, C. O., & Gioia, D. A. (1988, Winter). Neglected at the top: Executives talk about executive appraisal. *Sloan Management Review,* 41-47.

Longenecker, C. O., Sims, H. P., & Gioia, D. A. (1987). Behind the mask: The politics of employee appraisal. *Academy of Management Executive, 1,* 183-193.

Lopez, F. M. (1968). *Evaluating employee performance.* Chicago: Public Personnel Association.

Lord, C. O. (1982). Predicting behavioral consistency from an individual's perception of situational similarities. *Journal of Personality and Social Psychology, 42,* 1076-1088.

Lord, F. M., & Novick, M. R. (1968). *Statistical theories of mental test scores.* Reading, MA: Addison-Wesley.

Lord, R. G. (1985a). Accuracy in behavioral measurement: An alternative definition based on raters' cognitive schema and signal detection. *Journal of Applied Psychology, 70,* 66-71.

Lord, R. G. (1985b). An information processing approach to social perception, leadership and behavioral measurement in organizations. In B. Staw & L. Cummings (Eds.), *Research in organizational behavior, Vol. 7.* Greenwich, CT: JAI Press.

Lord, R. G., Foti, R. J., & DeVader, C. (1984). A test of leadership categorization theory: Internal structure, information processing, and leadership perceptions. *Organizational Behavior and Human Performance, 34,* 343-378.

Lorenzo, R. V. (1984). Effect of assessorship on managers' proficiency in acquiring, evaluating, and communicating information about people. *Personnel Psychology, 37,* 617-636.

Magnusson, D. (1971). An analysis of situational dimensions. *Perceptual and Motor Skills, 32,* 851-867.

Magnusson, D. (1976.) The person and the situation in an interactional model of behavior. *Scandinavian Journal of Psychology, 17,* 253-271.

Magnusson, D. (1981). Wanted: A psychology of situations. In D. Magnusson (Ed.), *Toward a psychology of situations.* Hillsdale, NJ: Erlbaum.

Magnusson, D., & Endler, N. S. (1977). *Personality at the crossroads: Current issues in interactional psychology,* Hillsdale, NJ: Erlbaum.

Mahew, B. H. (1983). Hierarchical differentiation in imperatively coordinated associations. In S. Bacharach (Ed.), *Research in the sociology of organizations, Vol. 2.* Greenwich, CT: JAI Press.

Maier, N. F., & Thurber, J. A. (1968). Accuracy of judgments of deception when an interview is watched, heard, or read. *Personnel Psychology, 21,* 23-30.

March, J. C., & March, J. G. (1978). Performance sampling in social matches. *Administrative Science Quarterly, 23,* 434-453.

March, J. G., & Simon, H. A. (1958). *Organizations.* New York: Wiley.

Martin, D. C. (1986). Performance appraisal 2: Improving the raters effectiveness. *Personnel, 63,* 28-33.

Martin, J., & Siehl, C. (1983). Organizational culture and counter culture: An uneasy symbiosis. *Organizational Dynamics, 12,* 52-64.

Martinko, M. J., & Gardner, W. L. (1985). Beyond structural observation: Methodological issues and new directions. *Academy of Management Review, 10,* 676-695.

Maslow, A. H. (1970). *Motivation and personality* (2nd ed.). New York: Harper and Row.

Massey, D. J. (1975). Narrowing the gap between intended and existing results of appraisal systems. *Personnel Journal, 54,* 522-524.

McArthur, L. (1980). What grabs you? The role of attention in impression formation causal attribution. In E. Higgins, C. Herman, & M. Zanna (Eds.), *Social cognition: The Ontario symposium on personality and social psychology.* Hillsdale, NJ: Erlbaum.

McCall, M. W., & DeVries, D. L. (1977). *Appraisal in context: Clashing with organizational realities* (Tech. Tep. No. 4). Greensboro, NC: Center for Creative Leadership.

McCall, M. W., & Lombardo, M. M. (Eds.). (1978). *Leadership: Where else can we go?* Durham, NC: Duke University Press.

McCormick, E. J. (1976). Job and task analysis. In M. Dunnette (Ed.), *Handbook of industrial and organizational psychology.* Chicago: Rand McNally.

McCormick, E. J. (1979). *Job analysis: Methods and applications.* New York: Amacon.

McCormick, E. J., Jeanneret, P. R., & Mecham, R. C. (1972). A study of job characteristics and job dimensions as based on the position analysis questionnaire (PAQ). *Journal of Applied Psychology, 56,* 247-267.

McEvoy, G. M., & Buller, P. F. (1987). User acceptance of peer appraisals in an industrial setting. *Personnel Psychology, 40,* 785-797.

McGregor, D. (1957). An uneasy look at performance appraisal. *Harvard Business Review, 35* (3), 89-94.

McGregor, D. (1960). *The human side of enterprise.* New York: McGraw-Hill.

McIntyre, R. M., Smith, D., & Hassett, C. E. (1984). Accuracy of performance ratings as affected by rater training and perceived purpose of rating. *Journal of Applied Psychology, 69,* 147-156.

McMillan, J. D., & Doyel, H. W. (1980). Performance appraisal: Match the tool to the task. *Personnel, 57,* 12-20.

Mead, G. H. (1934). *The social psychology of George Herbert Mead.* A. Strauss (Ed.). Chicago: University of Chicago Press.

Mechanic, D. (1962). Sources of power of lower participants in complex organizations. *Administrative Science Quarterly, 7,* 349-364.

Medin, E. L., & Schaffer, M. M. (1978). Context theory of classification learning. *Psychological Review, 85,* 207-238.

Meier, R. A., & Feldhusen, J. F. (1979). Another look at Dr. Fox: Effect of stated purpose of evaluation lecturers expressiveness and density of lecture content on student ratings. *Journal of Educational Psychology, 71,* 339-345.

Merton, R. K. (1957). *Social theory and social structure.* New York: Free Press.

Meyer, H. H. (1980). Self appraisal of job performance. *Personnel Psychology, 33,* 291-295.

Meyer, H. H., Kay, E., & French, J. (1965). Split roles in performance appraisale. *Harvard Business Review, 43,*123-129.

Miller, D. T., & Ross, M. (1975). Self-serving biases in the attribution of causality: Fact or fiction? *Psychological Bulletin, 82,* 213-225.

Miller, D. T., & Ross, M. (1975). Self-serving biases in the attribution of causality: Fact or fiction? *Psychological Bulletin, 82,* 213-225.

Miller, G. A., Galanter, E., & Pribram, K. H. (1960). *Plans and the structure of behavior.* New York: Holt, Rinehart & Winston.

Miner, J. B. (1971). Changes in student attitudes toward bureaucratic role prescription during the 1960's. *Administrative Science Quarterly, 16,* 351-364.

Mintzberg, H. (1980). *The nature of managerial work.* Englewood Cliffs, NJ: Prentice-Hall.

Mischel, W. (1977). The interaction of person and situation. In D. Magnusson & N. S. Endler (Eds.), *Personality at the crossroads: Current issues in interactional psychology.* Hillsdale, NJ: Erlbaum.

Mischel, W., & Peake, P. K. (1982). Beyond deja vu in the search for cross-situational consistency. *Psychological Review, 89,* 730-755.

Mitchell, T. D., Green, S. G., & Wood, R. E. (1981). An attributional model of leadership and the poor performing subordinate: Development and validation. In B. Staw and L. Cummings (Eds.), *Research in organizational behavior, Vol. 3.*Greenwich, CT: JAI Press.

Mitchell, T. R., & Liden, R. C. (1982). The effects of the social context on performance evaluations. *Organizational Behavior and Human Performance, 29,* 241-256.

Mitchell, T. R., & O'Reilly, C. A. (1983). Managing poor performance and productivity in organizations. In K. Rowland and G. Ferris (Eds.), *Research in personnel and human resources management, Vol. 1.* Greenwich, CT: JAI Press.

Mitroff, I. (1983). Archetypal social systems analysis: On the deeper structure of human systems. *Academy of Management Review, 8,* 387-397.

Mohr, L. B. (1973). The concept of organizational goal. *American Political Science Review, 67,* 470-481.

Mohrman, A. M. (1986). *Multiple purposes in appraisal events.* Presented at Society for Industrial Organizational Psychology, Chicago.

Mohrman, A. M., & Lawler, E. E. (1983). Motivation and performance appraisal behavior. In F. Landy, S. Zedeck, & J. Cleveland (Eds.), *Performance measurement and theory.* Hillsdale, NJ: Erlbaum.

Moos, R. (1973). Conceptualizations of human environments. *American Psychologist, 28,* 652-665.

Mora, N. D. (1985). *Work belief systems: An extension of Kanungo's model of job involvement.* Unpublished dissertation, New York University.

Mortimer, J. T., & Lorence, J. (1979). Work experience and occupational value socialization: A longitudinal study. *American Journal of Sociology, 84,* 1361-1385.

Motowidlo, S. J. (1986). Information processing in organizations. In K. Rowland & G. Ferris (Eds.), *Research in personnel and human resources management, Vol. 4.* Greenwich, CT: JAI Press.

Mount, M. K. (1983). Compassion of managerial and employee satisfaction with a performance appraisal system. *Personnel Psychology, 36,* 99-110.

Mount, M. K. (1984a). Psychometric properties of subordinate ratings of managerial performance. *Personnel Psychology, 37,* 687-702.

Mount, M. K. (1984b). Satisfaction with a performance appraisal system and appraisal discussion. *Journal of Occupational Behavior, 5,* 271-279.

Mowday, R. T., Porter, L. W., & Steers, R. M. (1981). *Employee-organization linkages: The psychology of commitment, absenteeism, and turnover.* New York: Academic Press.

Muchinsky, P. (1977). Employee absenteeism: A review of the literature. *Journal of Vocational Behavior, 10,* 316-340.

Mullins, C. S., & Ratliff, F. R. (1979). Criterion problems. In C. J. Mullins (Ed.), *Criterion development for job performance evaluations.* Proceedings from symposium. (AFHRL Technical Report 78-85). Brooks AFB, TX: Air Force Human Resource Laboratory.

Murphy, K. R. (1979). *Convergent and discriminant validity of subjectively weighted models and regression models of decision making processes.* Unpublished dissertation, Pennsylvania State University.

Murphy, K. R. (1982a). Assessing the discriminant validity of regression models and subjectively weighted models of judgments. *Multivariate Behavioral Research, 17,* 354-370.

Murphy, K. R. (1982b). Difficulties in the statistical control of halo. *Journal of Applied Psychology, 67,* 161-164.

Murphy, K. R. (1986). When your top choice turns you down: Effects of rejected offers on the utility of selection tests. *Psychological Bulletin, 99,* 133-138.

Murphy, K. R. (1987). *Are we doing a good job measuring the wrong thing?* Proceedings of DOD/ETS Conference on Job Performance Measurement Technologies, San Diego.

Murphy, K. R. (1988). *Do we remember behaviors or evaluations?* Presented at Annual Convention of the Academy of Management, Anaheim.

Murphy, K. R. (1989). Is the relationship between cognitive ability and job performance stable over time? *Human Performance, 2,* 183-200.

Murphy, K. R. (in press). Dimensions of job performance. In R. Dillon (Ed.), *Testing: Theoretical and applied perspectives.* New York: Praeger.

Murphy, K. R., & Balzer, W. K. (1981). *Rater errors and rating accuracy.* Presented at Annual Convention of American Psychological Association, Los Angeles.

Murphy, K. R., & Balzer, W. K. (1986). Systematic distortions in memory-based behavior ratings and performance evaluations: Consequences for rating accuracy. *Journal of Applied Psychology, 71,* 39-44.

Murphy, K. R. & Balzer, W. K. (1989). Rater errors and rating accuracy. *Journal of Applied Psychology, 74,* 619-624.

Murphy, K. R., Balzer, W. K., Kellam, K. L., & Armstrong, J. (1984). Effect of purpose of rating on accuracy in observing teacher behavior and evaluating teaching performance. *Journal of Educational Psychology, 76,* 45-54.

Murphy, K. R., Balzer, W. K., Lockhart, M., & Eisenman E. (1985). Effects of previous performance on evaluations of present performance. *Journal of Applied Psychology, 70,* 72-84.

Murphy, K. R., & Constans, J. I. (1987). Behavioral anchors as a source of bias in rating. *Journal of Applied Psychology, 72,* 523-579.

Murphy, K. R., & Constans, J. I. (1988). Psychological issues in scale format research: Behavioral anchors as a source of bias in rating. In R.Cardy, S. Peiffer, & J. Newman (Eds.), *Advances in information processing in organizations, Vol. 3.* Greenwich, CT: JAI Press.

Murphy, K. R., & Davidshofer, C. O. (1988). *Psychological testing: Principles and applications.* Englewood Cliffs, NJ: Prentice-Hall.

Murphy, K. R., Gannett, B. A., Herr, B. M., & Chen, J. A. (1986). Effects of subsequent performance on evaluations of previous performance. *Journal of Applied Psychology, 71,* 427-431.

Murphy, K. R., Garcia, M., Kerkar, S., Martin, C., & Balzer, W. K. (1982). Relationship between observational accuracy and accuracy in evaluating performance. *Journal of Applied Psychology, 67,* 320-325.

Murphy, K. R., Herr, B. M., Lockhart, M. C., & Maguire, E. (1986). Evaluating the performance of paper people. *Journal of Applied Psychology, 71,* 654-661.

Murphy, K. R., & Jako, B. (1989). Under what conditions are observed intercorrelations greater than or smaller than true intercorrelations? *Journal of Applied Psychology, 74,* 827-830.

Murphy, K. R., & Kroeker, L. P. (1988). *Dimensions of job performance.* NPRDC TN 88-39. Navy Personnel Research and Development Center, San Diego.

Murphy, K. R., Martin, C., & Garcia, M. (1982). Do behavioral observation scales measure observation? *Journal of Applied Psychology, 67,* 562-567.

Murphy, K. R., & Pardaffy, V. (1989). Bias in behaviorally anchored rating scales: Global or scale-specific? *Journal of Applied Psychology, 74,* 343-346.

Murphy, K. R., Philbin, T. A., & Adams, S. R. (1989). Effect of purpose of observation on accuracy of immediate and delayed performance ratings. *Organizational Behavior and Human Decision Processes, 43,* 336-354.

Murphy, K. R., & Reynolds, D. H. (1988a). Does true halo affect observed halo? *Journal of Applied Psychology, 73,* 235-238.

Murphy, K. R., & Reynolds, D. H. (1988b). *Student attitudes toward employee drug testing.* Unpublished manuscript, Colorado State University.

Murphy, K. R., & Saal, F. E. (in press). *Psychology in organizations: Integrating science and practice.* Boston: Allyn and Bacon.

Nagle, B. F. (1953). Criterion development. *Personnel Psychology, 6,* 271-289.

Naiper, N., & Latham, G. (1986). Outcome expectancies of people who conduct performance appraisals. *Personnel Psychology, 39,* 827-837.

Nathan, B., & Alexander, R. A. (1988). A comparison of criteria for test validation: A meta-analytic investigation. *Personnel Psychology, 41,* 517-535.

Nathan, B., & Lord, R. G. (1983). Cognitive categorization and dimensional schemata: A process approach to the study of halo in performance ratings. *Journal of Applied Psychology, 68,* 102-114.

Naylor, J. C., Pritchard, R. D., & Ilgen, D. R. (1980). *A theory of behavior in organizations.* New York: Academic Press.

Newcomb, T. (1931). A design to test the validity of a rating technique. *Journal of Educational Psychology, 22,* 279-289.

Newtson, D. (1976). Foundations of attribution: The perception of ongoing behavior. In J. Harvey, W. Ikes, and R. Kidd (Eds.), *New directions in attribution research, Vol. 1.* Hillsdale, NJ: Erlbaum.

Normann, R. (1969). Organization, mediation, and environment. Stockholm: Swedish Institute for Administrative Research, Report Mr. UPM-RN-91. Cited in W. Starbuck (1976). Organizations and their environments. In M. Dunnette (Ed.), *Handbook of industrial and organizational psychology.* Chicago: Rand-McNally.

O'Connor, E. J., Peters, L. H., Pooyang, A., Weekly, J., Frank, B., & Erenkrantz, B. (1984). Situational constraint effects on performance, affective reactions, and turnover: A field replication and extension. *Journal of Applied Psychology, 69,* 663-672.

Odiorne, G. S. (1965). *Management by objectives. A system of managerial leadership.* New York: Pitman.

Oldham, G. R., Kulik, C. T., Stepina, L. P., & Ambrose, M. L. (1986). Relations between situational factors and the comparative referents used by employees. *Academy of Management Journal, 29,* 599-608.

Olsen, L. O., & Bennett, A. C. (1975). Performance appraisal: Management technique or social process. Part I: Management technique. *Management Review, 64,* 18-23.

Olsen, L. O., & Bennett, A. C. (1976). Performance appraisal: Management technique or social process. Part II: Social process. *Management Review, 65,* 22-28.

Osgood, C. E. (1962). Studies of the generality of affective meaning systems. *American Psychologist, 17,* 10-28.

Ostroff, C., & Ilgen, D. R. (1986). *The relationship between cognitive categories of raters and rating accuracy.* Presented at Annual Meeting of Society for Industrial and Organizational Psychology, Chicago.

Paese, P. W., & Switzer, F. S. (1988). Validity generalization and hypothetical reliability distributions: A test of the Schmidt-Hunter procedure. *Journal of Applied Psychology, 73,* 267-274.

Palermo, D. S. (1983). Cognition, concepts, and an employee's theory of the world. In F. Landy, S. Zedeck, & J. Cleveland (Eds.), *Performance measurement and theory.* Hillsdale, NJ: Erlbaum.

Park, B., & Rothbart, M. (1982). Perception of out-group homogeneity and levels of social categorization: Memory for subordinate attributes of in-group members. *Journal of Personality and Social Psychology, 42,* 1051-1068.

Pascale., R., & Athos, A. (1981). *The art of Japanese management: Applications for American executives.* New York: Simon & Schuster.

Patten, T. H., Jr. (1977). *Pay: Employee compensation and incentive plans.* London: The Free Press.

Patz, A. L. (1975). Performance appraisal: Useful but still resisted. *Harvard Business Review, 53,* 74-80.

Perrow, C. (1970). The analysis of goals in a complex organization. *American Sociological Review, 26,* 855-866.

Perrow, C. (1973). The short and glorious history of organizational theory. *Organizational dynamics,* Summer, 192-202.

Pervin, L. A. (1968). Performance and satisfaction as a function of individual environment fit. *Psychological Bulletin, 69,* 56-68.

Pervin, L. A. (1981). The relation of situations to behavior. In D. Magnusson (Ed.), *Toward a psychology of situations.* Hillsdale: NJ: Erlbaum.

Pervin, L. A., & Lewis, M. (Eds.). (1978). *Perspectives in interactional psychology.* New York: Plenum.

Peters, L. H., Fisher, C. D., & O'Connor, E. J. (1982). The moderating effect of situational control of performance variance on the relationship between individual differences and performance. *Personnel Psychology, 35,* 609-621.

Peters, L. H., & O'Connor, E. J. (1980). Situational constraints and work outcomes: The influences of a frequently overlooked construct. *Academy of Management Review, 5,* 391-397.

Peters, L. H., & O'Connor, E. J. (1988). Measuring work obstacles: Procedures, issues and implications. In. F. D. Schoorman and B. Schneider (Eds.), *Facilitating work effectiveness* (pp. 105-124). Lexington, MA: Lexington Books.

Peters, L. H., O'Connor, E. J., & Eulberg, J. R. (1985). Situational constraints: Sources, consequences, and future considerations. In K. Rowland and G. Ferris (Eds.), *Research in personnel and human resource management, Vol. 3.* Greenwich, CT: JAI Press.

Peters, L. H., O'Connor, E. J., & Rudolph, C. J. (1980). The behavioral and affective consequences of performance-relevant situational variables. *Organizational Behavior and Human Performance, 25,* 79-96.

Peterson, C. R., & Beach, L. R. (1967). Man as an intuitive statistician. *Psychological Bulletin, 68,* 29-46.

Petrie, F. A. (1950). Is there something new in efficiency rating? *Personnel Administrator, 13,* 24.

Pfeffer, J. (1981). *Power in organizations.* Belmont, CA: Pitman.

Pfeffer, J., & Salancik, G. (1978). *The external control of organizations: A resource dependence perspective.* New York: Harper and Row.

Philbin, T. A. (1988). *Conceptual and behavioral factors associated with expertise.* Unpublished dissertation, Colorado State University.

Phillips, J. S., & Freedman, S. M. (1982). *Situational constraints, task characteristics, and affective task reactions*. Presented at Annual Meeting of the Academy of Management, New York.

Phillips, J. S., & Lord, R. G. (1982). Schematic information processing and perceptions of leadership in problem-solving groups. *Journal of Applied Psychology, 67,* 486–492.

Porter, L. W., Allen, R. W., & Angle, L. L. (1981). The politics of upward influence in organizations. *Research in Organizational Behavior, 3,* 109–149.

Porter, L. W., & Lawler, E. E. (1968). *Managerial attitudes and performance*. Homewood, IL: Dorsey Press.

Posner, M. I. (1978). *Chronometric explorations of the mind*. Hillsdale, NJ: Erlbaum.

Poulton, E. C. (1968). Range effects in experiments with people. *American Psychologist, 88,* 3–32.

Prince, J. B., & Lawler, E. E. (1981). *The impact of discussion salary action in the performance appraisal meeting*. (Technical Report). Los Angeles: Center for Effective Organizations, University of Southern California.

Pritchard, R. D., & Karasick, B. W. (1973). The effect of organizational climate on managerial job perceptions and job satisfaction. *Organizational Behavior and Human Performance, 9,* 126–146.

Pulakos, E. D. (1986). The development of training programs to increased accuracy in different rating tasks. *Organizational Behavior and Human Decision Processes, 38,* 76–91.

Pulakos, E. D., Schmitt, N., & Ostroff, C. (1986). A warning about the use of a standard deviation across dimensions to measure halo. *Journal of Applied Psychology, 71,* 29–32.

Quattrone, G. A., & Jones, E. E. (1980). The perception of variability within in-groups and out-groups: Implications for the law of small numbers. *Journal of Personality and Social Psychology, 38,* 141–152.

Raiffa, H. (1968). *Decision analysis: Introductory lectures on choices under uncertainty*. Reading, MA: Addison-Wesley.

Rambo, W. W., Chomiak, A. M., & Price, J. M. (1983). Consistency of performance under stable conditions of work. *Journal of Applied Psychology, 68,* 78–87.

Rand, T. M., & Wexley, K. N. (1975). A demonstration of the Byrnes similarity hypothesis in simulated employment interviews. *Psychological Reports, 36,* 535–544.

Reilly, C. E., & Balzer, W. K. (1988). *Effect of purpose on observation and evaluation of teaching performance*. Unpublished manuscript, Bowling Green State University.

Reither, F., & Staudel, T. (1985). Thinking and action. In M. Frese and J. Sabini (Eds.). *Goal directed behavior: The concept of action in psychology*. Hillsdale, NJ: Erlbaum.

Richardson, M. W. (1950). Forced choice performance reports. In M. J. Dooher and V. Marquis (Eds.). *Rating employee and supervisory performance*. New York: American Management Association.

Ritti, R. R. (1964). Control of "halo" in factor analysis of a supervisory behavior inventory. *Personnel Psychology, 17,* 305–318.

Roach, D. E., & Wherry, R. J. (1970). Performance dimensions of multi-line insurance agents. *Personnel Psychology, 23,* 239–250.

Roethlisberger, F. I., & Dickson, W. J. (1939). *Management and the worker*. Cambridge, MA: Harvard University Press.

Rommetveit, R. (1981). On meanings of situations and social control of such meaning in human communication. IN D. Magnusson (Ed.), *Toward a psychology of situations*. Hillsdale, NJ: Erlbaum.

Rosch, E. (1977). Human categorization. In N. Warren (Ed.), *Studies in cross-cultural psychology, Vol. 1*. New York: Academic Press.

Rosch, E. (1978). Principles of categorization. In E. Rosch & B. Lloyd (Eds.), *Cognition and categorization*. Hillsdale, NJ: Erlbaum.

Rosch, E., & Lloyd, B. B. (1978). *Cognition and categorization*. Hillsdale, NJ: Erlbaum.

Rosch, E., Mervis, C. G., Gray, W. D., Johnson, D. M., & Boyes-Braem, P. (1976). Basic objects in natural categories. *Cognitive Psychology, 8,* 382–439.

Rothe, H. F. (1946a). Output rates among butter wrappers: I. Work curves and their stability. *Journal of Applied Psychology, 30,* 199–211.

Rothe, H. F. (1946b). Output rates among butter wrappers: II. Frequency distributions and hypotheses regarding the "restriction of output." *Journal of Applied Psychology, 30,* 320-327.

Rothe, H. F. (1947). Output rates among machine operators: I. Distribution and their reliability. *Journal of Applied Psychology, 31,* 384-389.

Rothe, H. F. (1949). The relation of merit ratings to length of service *Personnel Psychology, 2,* 237-242.

Rothe, H. F. (1951). Output rates among chocolate dippers. *Journal of Applied Psychology, 35,* 94-97.

Rothe, H. F. (1978). Output rates among industrial employees. *Journal of Applied Psychology, 63,* 40-46.

Rothe, H. F., & Nye, C. T. (1958). Output rates among coil workers. *Journal of Applied Psychology, 42,* 182-186.

Rothe, H. F., & Nye, C. T. (1959). Output rates among machine operators: II. Consistency-related methods of pay. *Journal of Applied Psychology, 43,* 417-420.

Rothe, H. F., & Nye, C. T. (1961). Output rates among machine operators: III. A nonincentive situation in two levels of business activity. *Journal of Applied Psychology, 45,* 50-54.

Rotter, J. B. (1955). The role of the psychological situation in determining the direction of human behavior. In M. R. Jones (Ed.), *Nebraska Symposium on Motivation.* Lincoln: University of Nebraska Press.

Rotter, J. B. (1982). *The development and application of social learning theory.* New York: Praeger.

Rousseau, D. M. (1988). The construction of climate in organizational research. In C. Cooper & I. Robertson (Eds.), *International review of industrial and organizational psychology, Vol. 3.* Chichester, UK: Wiley.

Rudd, H. (1921). Is the rating of human character practicable? *Journal of Educational Psychology, 12,* 425-438.

Russell, J. S., Terborg, J. R. Jr., & Powers, M. L. (1985). Organizational performance and organizational level training and support. *Personnel Psychology, 38,* 849-863.

Russo. A. & Hartman, E. A. (1987). *Comparison of four career stage theories using data from self and significant others.* Presented at Annual Conference of the Academy of Managements, New Orleans.

Saal, F. E., Downey, R. G., & Lahey, M. A. (1980). Rating the ratings: Assessing the quality of rating data. *Psychological Bulletin, 88,* 413-428.

Saal, F. E., & Knight, P. A. (1988). *Industrial/organizational psychology: Science and practice.* Pacific Grove, CA: Brooks/Cole.

Sackett, P. R., Zedeck, S., & Fogli, L. (1988). Relations between measures of typical and maximum job performance. *Journal of Applied Psychology, 73,* 482-486.

Salvendy, G., & Seymour, W. (1973). *Prediction and development of industrial work performance.* New York: Wiley.

Sandlands, L. E., & Calder, B. J. (1987). Perceptual organization in task performance. *Organizational Behavior and Human Decision Processes, 40,* 287-306.

Schall, M. S. (1983). A communication-rules approach to organizational culture. *Administrative Science Quarterly, 28,* 557-581.

Schein, E. H. (1971). The individual, the organization, and the career: A conceptual scheme. *Journal of Applied Behavioral Science, 1,* 401-426.

Schein, E. H. (1985). *Organizational culture and leadership.* San Francisco: Jossey Bass.

Schein, E. H., & Ott, J. (1962). The legitimacy of organizational influence. *American Journal of Sociology, 67,* 682-689.

Schmidt, F. L., & Hunter, J. E. (1977). Development of a general solution to the problem of validity generalization. *Journal of Applied Psychology, 62,* 529-540.

Schmidt, F. L., & Hunter, J. E. (1981). Employment testing: Old theories and new research findings. *American Psychologist, 36,* 1128-1137.

Schmidt, F. E., Hunter, J. E., & Caplan, J. R. (1981). Validity generalization results for two jobs in the petroleum industry. *Journal of Applied Psychology, 66,* 261-273.

Schmidt, F. L., Hunter, J. E., McKenzie, R. C., & Muldrow, T. (1979). The impact of valid selection procedures on work force productivity. *Journal of Applied Psychology, 64,* 609-626.

Schmidt, F. L., Hunter, J. E., & Outerbridge, A. N. (1986). Impact of job experience and ability on job knowledge, work sample performance, and supervisory ratings of job performance. *Journal of Applied Psychology, 71,* 432-439.

Schmidt, F. L., & Kaplan, L. B. (1971). Composite versus multiple criteria: A review and resolution of the controversy. *Personnel Psychology, 24,* 419-434.

Schmitt, N., Gooding, R. Z., Noe, R. A., & Kirsch, M. (1984). Meta-analysis of validity studies published between 1964 and 1982 and the investigation of study characteristics. *Personnel Psychology, 37,* 407-422.

Schmitt, N., & Schneider, B. (1983). Current issues in personnel selection. In K. Rowland & R. Ferris (Eds.), *Research in personnel and human resources management, Vol. 1.* Greenwich, CT: JAI Press.

Schneider, B. (1975). Organizational climates: An easy. *Personnel Psychology, 28,* 447-479.

Schneider, B. (1978). Person-situation selection: A review of some ability situation interaction research. *Personnel Psychology, 31,* 281-304.

Schneider, B. (1983a). Interactional psychology and organizational behavior. In H. Cummings and B. M. Staw (Eds.), *Research in Organizational Behavior, 5,* 1-31.

Schneider, B. (1983b). Organizational effectiveness: An interactional perspective. In D. Whetten & K. S. Cameron (eds.), *Organizational efectiveness: A comparison of multiple models* (pp. 27-54). New York: Academic Press.

Schneider, B. (1985). Organizational behavior. *Annual Review of Psychology, 36,* 573-611.

Schneider, B. (1987). The people make the place. *Personnel Psychology, 40,* 437-454.

Schneider, B., & Reichers, A. E. (1983). On the etiology of climates. *Personnel Psychology, 36,* 19-40.

Schneider, C. E. (1977). Operational utility and psychometric characteristics of behavioral expectation scales. *Journal of Applied Psychology, 62,* 541-548.

Schneier, C. E., & Beatty, R. W. (1978). The influence of role prescriptions on the performance appraisal processes. *Academy of Management Journal, 21,* 129-134.

Schneier, C., Beatty, R., & Baird, L (1986). How to construct a successful performance appraisal system. *Training and Development Journal, 40,* 38-42.

Schroeder, H. M., Drive, M. J., & Streufert, S. (1967). *Human information processing:* New York: Holt, Rinehart and Winston.

Schwab, D. P., Heneman, H. G., III, & DeCotiis, T. (1975). Behaviorally anchored scales: A review of the literature. *Personnel Psychology, 28,* 549-562.

Schwab, D. P., Olian-Gottlieb, J., & Heneman, H. (1979). Between subjects expectancy theory research: A statistical review of studies predicting effort and performance. *Psychological Bulletin, 86,* 139-147.

Schwab, D. P., Rynes, S. L., & Aldag, R. J. (1987). Theories and research on job search and choice. In K. Rowland & G. Ferris (Eds.), *Research in personnel and human resource management, Vol. 5,* Greenwich, CT: JAI Press.

Scott, W. D., Clothier, R. C., & Spriegel, W. R. (1941). *Personnel Management.* New York: McGraw-Hill.

Shamir, B., & Salomon, I. (1985). Work-at-home and the quality of working life. *Academy of Management Review, 10,* 455-464.

Shannon, C., & Weaver, W. (1948). *The mathematical theory of communication.* Champaign: University of Illinois Press.

Shapira, Z., & Shirom, A. (1980). New issues in the use of behaviorally anchored rating scales: Level of analysis, the effects of incident frequency and external validation. *Journal of Applied Psychology, 65,* 517-523.

Sharon, A. (1970). Eliminating bias from student rating of college instructors. *Journal of Applied Psychology, 54,* 278-281.

Sharon, A., & Bartlett, C. (1969). Effect of instructional conditions in producing leniency on two types of rating scales. *Personnel Psychology, 22,* 252-263.

Sherif, M., & Sherif, C. W. (1964). *Reference groups: Exploration into the conformity and deviation of adolescents.* New York: Harper and Row.

Sherif, M., & Sherif, C. W. (1969). *Social psychology.* New York: Harper and Row.

Shweder, R. A. (1975). How relevant is an individual difference theory of personality? *Journal of Personality, 43,* 455-483.

Shweder, R. A., & D'Andrade, R. G. (1980). The systematic distortion hypothesis. In R. A. Shweder (Ed.), *Fallible judgment in behavioral research: New directions for methodology of social and behavioral science, Vol. 4.* San Francisco: Jossey Bass.

Silverman, S. B., & Wexley, K. N. (1984). Reactions of employees to performance appraisal interviews as a function of their participation in rating scale development. *Personnel Psychology, 37,* 703-710.

Sinclair, R. C. (1988). Mood, categorization, breadth, and performance appraisal: The effects of order of information acquisition and affective state on halo, accuracy, information retrieval, and evaluations. *Organizational Behavior and Human Decision Processes, 42,* 22-46.

Sisson, E. D. (1948). Forced-choice: The new Army rating. *Personnel Psychology, 1,* 365-381.

Sjoeberg, L. (1981). Life situations and episodes as a basis for situational influence on action. In D. Magnusson (Ed.), *Toward a psychology of situations.* Hillsdale, NJ: Erlbaum.

Sloan, S., & Johnson, A. C. (1968). New context of personnel appraisal. *Harvard Business Review, 46,* 14-16, 18, 20, 29-30, 194.

Slovic, P. (1966). Cue consistency and cue utilization in judgment. *American Journal of Psychology, 79,* 427-434.

Slovic, P., & Lichtenstein, S. (1971). Comparison of Bayesian and regression approaches to the study of information processing in judgment. *Organizational Behavior and Human Performance, 6,* 649-744.

Smith, P. C. (1976). Behaviors, results, and organizational effectiveness. In M. Dunnette (Ed.), *Handbook of industrial and organizational psychology.* Chicago: Rand-McNally.

Smith, P. C., & Kendall, L. M. (1963). Retranslation of expectations: An approach to the construction of unambiguous anchors for rating scales. *Journal of Applied Psychology, 47,* 149-155.

Sonnenfeld, J. (1982). Clarifying critical confusion in the Hawthorne hysteria. *American Psychologist, 37,* 1397-1399.

Spence, J. T. (1987). Centrifugual versus centripetal tendencies in psychology: Will the center hold? *American Psychologist, 42,* 1052-1054.

Spool, M. D. (1978). Training programs for observers of behavior: A review. *Personnel Psychology, 31,* 853-888.

Spriegel, W. R. (1962). Company practices in appraisal of managerial performance. *Personnel, 39,* 77.

Srull, T. K., & Brand, J. F. (1983). Memory for information about persons: The effect of encoding operations on subsequent retrieval. *Journal of Verbal Learning and Verbal Behavior, 22,* 219-230.

Srull, T. K., & Wyer, R. S. (1980). Category accessibility and social perception: Some implications for the study of person memory and interpersonal judgment. *Journal of Personality and Social Psychology, 38,* 841-856.

Starbuck, W. H. (1976). Organizations and their environments. In M. Dunnette (Ed.), *Handbook of industrial and organizational psychology.* Chicago: Rand-McNally.

Steel, R. P., & Mento, A. J. (1986). Impact of situational constraints on subjective and objective criteria of managerial performance. *Organizational Behavior and Human Decision Processes, 37,* 254-265.

Steel, R. P., & Ovalle, N. K. (1984). Self-appraisal based on supervisory feedback. *Personnel Psychology, 37,* 667-685.

Steers, R. M., & Rhodes, S. R. (1978). Major influences on employee attendance: A process model. *Journal of Applied Psychology, 63,* 391-407.

Stein, D., & Raine, J. (1989). Immediate and delayed primacy and recency effects in performance evaluation. *Journal of Applied Psychology, 74,* 136-142.

Sternberg, R. J., & Wagner, R. K. (1986). *Practical intelligence: Nature and origins of competence in the everyday world.* New York: Cambridge University Press.

Stokols, D. (1981). Group x place transactions: Some neglected issues in psychological research on settings. In D. Magnusson (Ed.), *Toward a psychology of situations.* Hillsdale, NJ: Erlbaum.

Stone, D. L., Gueuthal, H. G., & McIntosh, B. (1984). The effects of feedback sequence and expertise of the rater on perceived feedback accuracy. *Personnel Psychology, 37,* 487-506.

Stricker, L. J., Jacobs, P. I., & Kogan, N. (1974). Trait interrelations in implicit personality theories and questionnaire data. *Journal of Personality and Social Psychology, 30,* 198-207.

Sulsky, L. M., & Balzer, W. K. (1988). The meaning and measurement of performance rating accuracy: Some methodological concerns. *Journal of Applied Psychology, 73,* 497-506.

Szilagyi, A. D., & Wallace, M. J. (1983) *Organizational behavior and performance* (3rd ed.). Glenview, IL: Scott, Foresman.

Tagiuri, R., & Litwin, G. H. (1968). *Organizational climate: Exploration of a concept.* Cambridge, MA: Harvard University Press.

Tajfel, H. (1969). Social and cultural factors in perception. In G. Lindzey & E. Aronson (Eds.), *Handbook of social psychology* (2nd ed.) (pp. 315-394). Reading, MA: Addison Wesley.

Taylor, E., & Wherry, R. (1951). A study of leniency of two rating systems. *Personnel Psychology, 4,* 39-47.

Tayor, M. S., Fisher, C. D., & Ilgen, D. R. (1984). Individual reactions to performance feedback in organizations: A control theory perspective. In K. Rowland & G. Ferris (Eds.), *Research in personnel and human resources management, Vol. 2.* Greenwich, CT: JAI Press.

Tayor, S. E., & Fiske, S. T. (1978). Salience, attention, and attributions: Top of the head phenomena. In L. Berkowitz (Ed.), *Advances in experimental social psychology, Vol. 11.* New York: Academic Press.

Teasdale, J. D., & Fogarty, S.J. (1979). Differential effects of induced mood on retrieval of pleasant and unpleasant events from episodic memory. *Journal of Abnormal Psychology, 88,* 248-257.

Tedeschi, J. T., & Melburgh, V. (1984). Impression management and influence in the organization. In S. B. Bacharach & E. O. Lawler (Eds.), *Research in the sociology of organizations, Vol. 3.* Greenwich, CT: JAI Press.

Terborg, J. R. (1981). Interactional psychology and research on human behavior in organizations. *Academy of Management Review, 6,* 569-576.

Thibaut, J. W., & Kelly, H. H. (1959). *The social psychology of groups.* New York: Wiley.

Thibaut, J., & Walker, L. (1975). *Procedural justice: A psychological analysis.* Hillsdale, NJ: Erlbaum.

Thompson, J. D. (1967). *Organizations in action.* New York: McGraw-Hill.

Thorndike, E. L. (1920). A constant error in psychological ratings. *Journal of Applied Psychology, 4,* 25-29.

Thorndike, R. L. (1949). *Personnel selection.* New York: Wiley.

Thornton, G. C., III (1980). Psychometric properties of self-appraisals of job performance. *Personnel Psychology, 33,* 263-271.

Thornton, G. C., III, & Zorich, S. (1980). Training to improve observer accuracy. *Journal of Applied Psychology, 65,* 351-354.

Tiffin, J., & McCormick, E. J. (1958). *Industrial psychology.* Englewood Cliffs, NJ: Prentice-Hall.

Triandis, H. C. (1966). Notes on the design of organizations. In J. D. Thompson (Ed.), *Approaches to organizational design.* Pittsburgh: University of Pittsbrugh Press.

Tsui, A. S., & Barry, B. (1986). Interpersonal affect and rating errors. *Academy of Management Journal, 29,* 586-599.

Tulving, E. (1974). Recall and recognition of semantically encoded words. *Journal of Experimental Psychology, 102,* 778-787.

Tulving, E. (1983). *Essentials of episodic memory.* New York: Oxford University Press.

Tulving, E., & Thompson, D. (1973). Encoding specificity and retrieval processes in episodic memory. *Psychological Review, 80,* 352-373.

Tversky, A. (1977). Features of similarity. *Psychological Review, 84,* 327-352.

Tversky, A., & Gati, I. (1978). Studies of similarity. In E. Rosch & B. Lloyd (Eds.), *Cognition and categorization.* Hillsdale, NJ: Erlbaum.

Tversky, A., & Kahneman, D. (1974). Judgment under uncertainty: Heuristics and biases. *Science, 185,* 1124-1131.

Uniform Guidelines on Employee Selection Procedures. (1978). *Federal Register, 43,* (166), 38209-38309.

Vance, R. J., Kuhnert, K. W., Farr, J.L. (1978). Interview judgments: Using external criteria to compare behavioral and graphic scale ratings. *Organizational Behavior and Human Performance, 22,* 279-294.

Vance, R. J., MacCallum, R. C., Coovert, M. D., & Hedge, J. W. (1988). Construct validity of multiple job performance measures using conformatory factor analysis. *Journal of Applied Psychology, 73,* 74-80.

Vance, R. J., Winne, P. S., & Wright, E. S. (1983). A longitudinal examination of rater and ratee effects in performance ratings. *Personnel Psychology, 36,* 609-620.

VanMaanen, J. (1975). Police socialization. *Administrative Science Quarterly, 20,* 207-228.

VanMaanan, J. (1976). Breaking in: Socialization to work. In R. Dubin (Ed.), *Handbook of work, organization, and society.* Chicago: Rand-McNally.

VanMaanen, J., & Schein, E. H. (1979). Toward a theory of organizational socialization. In B. Staw (Ed.), *Research in organizational behavior, Vol. 1.* Greenwich, CT: JAI Press.

Vecchio, R. P., & Gobdel, B. C. (1984). The vertical dyadic linkage mode of leadership: Problems and prospects. *Organizational Behavior and Human Performance, 34,* 5-20.

Vroom, V. (1964). *Work and motivation.* New York: Wiley.

Vroom, V. (1969). Industrial social psychology. In G. Lindsey & E. Aronson (Eds.), *The handbook of social psychology* (2nd ed.). Reading, MA: Addison-Wesley.

Wachtel, P. L. (1973). Psychodynamics, behavior therapy, and the implacable experimenter: An inquiry into the consistency of personality. *Journal of Abnormal Psychology, 82,* 324-334.

Wagner, R. K. (1986). Tacit knowledge in everyday-intelligent behavior. *Journal of Personality and Social Psychology, 52,* 1236-1247.

Wainer, H. (1976). Estimating coefficients in linear models: It don't make no never mind. *Psychological Bulletin, 83,* 213-217.

Waldman, D. A., Bass, B. M., & Einstein, W. O. (1987). Leadership and outcomes of performance appraisal process. *Journal of Occupational Psychology, 60,*177-186.

Waldman, D. A., & Thornton, G. C., III (1988). A field study of rating conditions and leniency in performance appraisal. *Psychological Reports, 63,* 835-840.

Wanous, J. P. (1980). *Organizational entry: Recruitment, selection, and socialization of newcomers.* Reading, MA: Addison-Wesley.

Ward, W. D., & Jenkins, J. (1965). The display of information and the judgment of contingency. *Canadian Journal of Psychology, 19,* 231-241.

Webster, E. C. (1964). *Decision making in the employment interview.* Montreal: Industrial Relations Center, McGill University.

Webster, E. C. (1982). *The employment interview: A social judgment process.* Schomberg, Ontario: SIP Publications.

Wegner, D., & Vallecher, R. (1977). *Implicit psychology.* New York: Oxford University Press.

Weick, K. (1977). Enactment processes in organizations. In B. Staw and G. Salancik (Ed.), *New directions in organizational behavior.* Chicago: St. Claire Press.

Weiss, H. M. (1978). Social learning of work values in organizations. *Journal of Applied Psychology, 63,* 711-718.

Weiss, H. M., & Adler, S. (1984). Personality and organizational behavior. *Research in Organizational Behavior, 6,* 1-50.

Wendelken, D., & Inn, A. (1981). Nonperformance influences on performance evaluations: A laboratory phenomenon? *Journal of Applied Psychology, 66,* 752-758.

Wexley, K. N. (1987). Discussant remarks in symposium chaired by K. R. Murphy. *Cognitive Research in performance appraisal: Prospects for application.* New York: American Psychological Association.

Wexley, K. N., & Klimoski, R. (1984). Performance appraisal: An update. In K. Rowland and G. Ferris (Eds.), *Research in personnel and human resources, Vol. 2.* Greenwich, CT: JAI Press.

Wexley, K. N., & Youtz, M. A. (1985). Rater beliefs about others: Their effects on rating errors and rater accuracy. *Journal of Occupational Psychology, 58,* 265-275.

Wherry, R. J., & Bartlett, C. J. (1982). The control of bias in ratings: A theory of rating. *Personnel Psychology, 35,* 521-555.

Wherry, R. J., & Fryer, D. H. (1949). Buddy ratings: Popularity contest or leadership criteria? *Personnel Psychology, 2,* 147-159.

Whetten, D. A. (1987). Organizational growth and decline processes. *Annual Review of Sociology, 13,* 335-358.

Whetten, D. A., & Cameron, K. S. (1983). *Organizational effectiveness: A comparison of multiple models.* New York: Academic Press.

Whisler, T. L. (1958). Performance appraisal and the organizational man. *Journal of Business, 31,* 19-27.

Whisler, T. L., & Harper, S. F. (Eds.). (1962). *Performance appraisal: Research and practice.* New York: Holt, Rinehart and Winston.

Wicker, A., Kirmeyer, S., Hanson, L., & Alexander, D. (1976). Effects of manning levels on subjective experiences, performance, and verbal interactions in groups. *Organizational Behavior and Human Performance, 17,* 251-274.

Wigdor, A., & Garner, W. (1982). *Ability testing: Uses, consequences, and controversies: Part I.* Washington, DC: National Academy Press.

Wiggins, J. S. (1973). *Personality and prediction: Principles of personality measurement.* Reading, MA: Addison-Wesley.

Williams, K. J., Allinger, G. M., & Pulliam, R. (1988). *Rater affect and performance ratings: Evidence for the moderating effects of rater perceptions.* Presented at Annual Convention of Society for Industrial and Organizational Psychology, Dallas.

Williams, K. J., DeNisi, A. S., Blencoe, A. G., & Cafferty, T. P. (1985). The role of appraisal purpose: Effects of purpose on information acquisition and utilization. *Organizational Behavior and Human Performance, 35,* 314-339.

Williams, K. J., DeNisi, A. S., Meglini, B. M., & Cafferty, T. P. (1986). Initial decisions and subsequent performance ratings. *Journal of Applied Psychology, 71,* 189-195.

Williams, K. J., & Keating, C. W. (1987). *Affect and the processing of performance appraisal.* Presented at Annual Convention of Society for Industrial and Organizational Psychology, Atlanta.

Woodward, J. (1965). *Industrial organization: Theory and practice.* London: Oxford University Press.

Wright, P. (1974). The harassed decision-maker: Time pressures, distraction and use of evidence. *Journal of Applied Psychology, 59,* 555-561.

Wyer, J. C. (1988). A stochastic, psychometric valuation model for personnel selection systems. *Decision Sciences, 19,* 700-707.

Wyer, R. S. (1976). An investigation of the relations among probability estimates. *Organizational Behavior and Human Performance, 15,* 1-8.

Wyer, R. S., Jr., & Srull, T. K., (1986). Category accessibility: Some theoretical and empirical issues concerning the processing of social stimulus information. In E. T. Higgins, C. P. Herman, & M. P. Zanna (Eds.), *Social cognition: The Ontario symposium on personality and social psychology.* Hillsdale, NJ: Erlbaum.

Yammarino, F. J., Dubinsky, A. J., & Hartley, S. W. (1987). An approach for assessing individual versus group effects in performance evaluations. *Journal of Occupational Psychology, 60,* 157-167.

Yasai-Adekani, M. (1986). Structural adaptations to environments. *Academy of Management Review, 11,* 9-21.

Yoder, D., & Heneman, H. G. (1979). *ASPA Handbook of personnel and industrial relations.* Washington, DC: Bureau of Natural Affairs.

Yukl, G. A., & Latham, G. P. (1975). Consequences of reinforcement schedules and incentive magnitudes for employee performance: Problems encountered in an industrial setting. *Journal of Applied Psychology, 60,* 294-298.

Zajonc, R. B. (1980). Feeling and thinking: Preferences need no inferences. *American Psychologist, 35,* 151-175.

Zald, M. N. (1962). Power balance and stall conflict in correctional institutions. *Administrative Science Quarterly, 7,* 22-49.

Zaleznik, A., Christensen, C. R., & Roethlisberger, F. J. (1958). *The motivation, productivity, and satisfaction of workers: A production study.* Cambridge: Harvard University Press.

Zand, D. E. (1981). *Information, organization and power: Effective management in the knowledge society.* New York: McGraw-Hill.

Zavala, A. (1965). Development of the forced-choice rating scale technique. *Psychological Bulletin, 63,* 117-124.

Zedeck, S., & Cascio, W. F. (1982). Performance appraisal decisions as a function of rater training and purpose of the appraisal. *Journal of Applied Psychology, 67,* 752-758.

Zohar, D. (1980). Safety climate in industrial organizations: Theoretical and applied implications. *Journal of Applied Psychology, 65,* 96-102.

Author Index

Subject Index